Entrepreneurs

Entrepreneurs
Talent, Temperament, Technique

Bill Bolton and John Thompson

OXFORD   AUCKLAND   BOSTON   JOHANNESBURG   MELBOURNE   NEW DELHI

Butterworth-Heinemann
Linacre House, Jordan Hill, Oxford OX2 8DP
225 Wildwood Avenue, Woburn, MA 01801-2041
A division of Reed Educational and Professional Publishing Ltd

A member of the Reed Elsevier plc group

First published 2000

British Library Cataloguing in Publication Data
Bolton, W.K.
    Entrepreneurs: talent, temperament, technique
    1. Entrepreneurship   2. Entrepreneurship – Case studies
    3. Success in business   4. Business people
    I. Title   II. Thompson, J.L.
    338'.04

ISBN 0 7506 4623 3

Typeset by Florence Production Ltd, Stoodleigh, Devon
Printed and bound in Great Britain by
Biddles Ltd, Guildford and King's Lynn

Contents

About the authors

Bill Bolton

Dr Bolton is an international consultant in enterprise development and entre-preneurship. He has held a personal UNITWIN (UNESCO) chair in Innovation and Technology Transfer. Dr Bolton was the founding director of the St John's Innovation Centre in Cambridge and taught engineering at Cambridge University. He has more than twenty-five years' experience in business and industry and is currently a non-executive director of several companies. Dr Bolton is a Visiting Professor at the universities of Huddersfield and Middlesex. His other publications include *The University Handbook on Enterprise Development* (1997).

John Thompson

John Thompson is Professor of Entrepreneurship at the University of Hudders-field and a Visiting Professor in Finland and New Zealand. Prior to this post he was Head of the Department of Management at the same university and he has held management posts in retailing and the steel industry. He has written a number of books and articles on strategic management and acts as a consultant to both profit-seeking and not-for-profit organizations. He has raised funding to open a business generator for creative businesses in Huddersfield and has started a number of entrepreneurial ventures for charitable causes.

Figures

x *List of figures*

Tables

Introduction: defining the entrepreneur

We believe that entrepreneurs create and build the future and that they are to be found in every walk of life and in every group of people. This book provides a wide range of examples of entrepreneurs that give substance to that belief.

We also believe that every community group, every public organization and every private corporation has within it an entrepreneurial potential waiting to be released. There are far more entrepreneurs around than we realize but for many it is a talent that lies unrecognized, unused and undeveloped. Yet it is precisely these people that we need so desperately in today's world of change and challenge. In this book we want to show how this 'well of entrepreneurial talent' can be tapped and used for the benefit of all.

This book has many examples of successful entrepreneurs and so we want to begin with a cautionary tale of an entrepreneur who never made it.

'Cyril was the first entrepreneur I ever met. He was my brother-in-law. Cyril's enthusiasm and optimism for business were contagious. He was an exciting person to be with, always full of ideas. Cyril lived in Coventry and ran a precursor of what was to become the mail-order business, except that in the late 1950s he sold his wares on the doorstep and his clients paid by instalments that he collected every week.

Cyril started the business after the Second World War when he served in the bomb disposal squad and learnt about risk! The business prospered and enabled him to buy his own home and support his family. Things were always going well; Cyril was an optimist and a great salesman. He had a generous and outgoing nature. His customers loved him.

Financing the business was obviously a problem because I can remember how pleased he was when a friend won some money on the football pools and put it into the business. This friend came with me on the money collection round one day – for I sometimes worked for Cyril at weekends – and when a customer made her final payment he simply thanked her for her business and walked away. 'Why didn't you try and sell her something else,' I asked. This was an early warning sign that Cyril had a weak team.

Although Cyril was a brilliant salesman, he had difficulties in grasping the difference between sales and profit. Once when I returned, after completing the Saturday morning round with a bag full of money he said, 'Give the girls a fiver to go and get some fish and chips'. 'Aren't you going to check what I have collected first?' I asked, and then added, 'Don't you realize that this money is not profit. You can't just go and spend it!' Was this another warning sign? Did he understand the financial side of business?

Cyril was keen to grow his business and decided he would rent premises and set up a shop in which to display his wares and to be his base. Until then he had worked from home but now, with four children, space was becoming a problem. It was difficult to argue with Cyril about the wisdom of such a move because his optimism and confidence carried things along.

Just as the shop came on stream Cyril fell ill and was off work for about three months. Without Cyril at the helm things began to slide. When he recovered he had to try to rescue what was a dying business. He had built up large debts with his suppliers and with the extra cash flow demands of the shop he was not able to make repayments that were due.

The result was that the suppliers took legal action to recover their debts and the bailiffs moved into the family home. They stripped it of everything except a sewing machine that my sister was able to prove belonged to her. The house was also taken and Cyril, my sister and their four children were literally out on the street with nowhere to go. Cyril was declared bankrupt.

His family remained supportive throughout this catastrophe and to my surprise and delight Cyril bounced back and found a job in sales. He was so successful that he was awarded 'Salesman of the Year' for four years in succession and was finally given the silver trophy as recognition of his achievement. When one of his directors left to set up a rival company and invited Cyril to join him, he did so with enthusiasm. He enjoyed the challenge of moving from a secure job to a start-up business but he was never to launch his own business again. Cyril died in his mid-fifties after a severe asthma attack. His asthma had been getting worse over the years, no doubt triggered by the stress of his entrepreneurial activities.'

(Bill Bolton)

This true story raises many of the issues addressed in this book and our hope is that if Cyril had been able to read it things might have been different.

Was Cyril really an entrepreneur or did he just aspire to be one? Was he more a self-employed businessman than a true entrepreneur? He had many of the qualities we associate with entrepreneurs. He was a dynamic hard-working person who got things done; he was an outstanding salesman. He was always optimistic and had great plans for what he was going to do. Cyril was an achiever. He was comfortable with risk and seemed relaxed about it, as his wartime role in bomb disposal showed. Cyril enjoyed a happy married life with a family that always supported him. Despite all this he did not succeed as an entrepreneur – so what was missing?

Was it that Cyril just did not have the *talent* to be a successful entrepreneur – possessing the aspiration but lacking the innate ability? Perhaps it was something in his personality that let him down? Maybe he had the wrong *temperament*. Or was it that he never received any formal training in how to run a business so that his business skills – his *technique* – was not sufficiently well developed?

In this book we want to use the three keys of *talent, temperament* and *technique* to unlock the subject and reveal the entrepreneur, to make it more accessible and to go some way to understanding people like Cyril. We appreciate that many of our other examples are about successful entrepreneurs, but that is the nature of things, the failures simply disappear.

We also appreciate that many people are sceptical about the existence of talent, that others think temperament is too subjective a topic to be of practical use and that technique has so many books already written about it that another is not needed. If you hold any or all of these views we would ask you to suspend judgement until you have read the stories and heard the arguments.

Despite many studies and much research the entrepreneurs and their ways remain elusive. It is a case of 'you know one when you see one' and little else. Attempts to 'pick winners' never seem to work. This book seeks to address these entrepreneur issues and to provide a framework for taking our understanding forward.

We want this book to be fun to read. We hope that the stories interest and excite you but we also hope that it makes you think and reflect on the entrepreneur in a new way. Above all we hope that it will lead to more winners and less losers amongst those who start and grow their business from scratch, especially if that person is you or someone that your are helping along that road!

Entrepreneurs: a definition

> The teacher asked his English class to write a sentence that showed the meaning of the word 'unique'. One pupil wrote 'My girlfriend is unique'. The teacher's comment was 'Are you quite sure!'

Maybe you have the same reaction to any claim that entrepreneurs are unique. Yet in many ways they are. They come in many different shapes and sizes. No two entrepreneurs seem to be the same, so it is very difficult to pin down exactly *who* is an entrepreneur. Some are extroverts and some introverts, some have a family history of entrepreneurs whilst others do not, some start from poverty when others begin with wealth, some are young and some are old. This ambiguity is found in much of the research into entrepreneurs and is why it has been so difficult to build a clear picture of the entrepreneur as a person.

Entrepreneurs are certainly not like most of us. They are a minority group. From experience with engineering undergraduates at Cambridge University in the 1980s it was concluded that 10 per cent to 15 per cent of this student group were potential entrepreneurs (Bolton, 1986). More rigorous assessments, by the late Professor M. Scott of Stirling University, of the population at large came up with a similar figure. On making this comment to many audiences we have been told that this might be the potential number of entrepreneurs but the real number is more like 1 per cent. Others have said that the potential number is much higher and have quoted figures for the US of more than 40 per cent (Bygrave, 1998).

The difference between the number of potential and actual entrepreneurs is one of the central themes of this book. We believe that as with all talent, entrepreneurial talent has first to be discovered before it can be developed. Sadly, our culture and our educational system – to name but two factors – not only inhibit the flowering of entrepreneurial talent; they positively discourage it.

Whilst the *who* of an entrepreneur may be difficult to prescribe, the *what* is easier. This can be based upon what the entrepreneur does – the process – or what he or she achieves – the results.

The origin of the word 'entrepreneur' is an important indicator of the process. It derives from the French words *entre* meaning 'between' and *prendre* being the verb 'to take'. This would imply that it was another name for a merchant who acts as a go-between for parties in the trading process. However the French economist Richard Cantillan (1725), who is reputed to have first used the word, related it to those who carried the risk in the economy, so it may have been the one who took the risk between supplier and customer. The modern usage of the word in English is broader and is focused more on results, although the original idea of the risk-taker is still there.

The French verb *entreprendre* means 'to undertake', as when undertaking a venture, but it can also be used in relation to starting a new venture, and this is central to the use of the word 'entrepreneur' in English. In the French language the word *entrepreneur* means a contractor, such as a building contractor, but it is now also used in the same sense as it is in English. Hence the recently published French bimonthly magazine with the title '*Le nouvel Entrepreneur* – le magazine pour créer et développer son entreprise'.

The entrepreneur, of course, goes back much further than the word we use today, to the merchants and traders who saw a commercial opportunity and turned it into profit. The following examples taken from the ancient and the medieval world show that the 'who' and the 'what' of the entrepreneur have not changed very much.

The ancient world example of an entrepreneur is Jacob in the Bible, perhaps better known as the father of Joseph and provider of his 'coat of many colours'. Jacob is a classic example of the Arthur Daley car salesman type of entrepreneur, though he did reform later in his career. In his long-running dispute with his father-in-law, Laban, (described in Genesis 30) he negotiates a spin-off from Laban's shepherding business with such words as 'Don't give me anything' and 'My honesty will testify for me in the future'. Jacob then puts his rather innovative veterinary methods into practice with the planned outcome that 'the weak animals went to Laban and the strong ones to Jacob'. The result was that Jacob 'grew exceedingly prosperous and came to own large flocks, and maidservants and menservants, and camels and donkeys'. Jacob was a successful entrepreneur.

In her book, *Worldly Goods*, Jardine (1997) develops a new history of the Renaissance which sees the fifteenth century as not so much as an age of outstanding artistic creativity as an age of entrepreneurs that then made possible the funding of great works of art. The immense wealth created at that time 'came from individual pieces of brilliant financial wheeler-dealing conducted at precisely the right moment' by entrepreneurs like the Fuggers and the Medicis. In reviewing the work of the painter Carlo Crivelli, Jardine (1997) comments that in his religious paintings 'celebrating global mercantilism is part and parcel of what is, after all, for him a commercial project – the entrepreneurial and the spiritual rub shoulders in this early Renaissance world'.

These two examples from history are supplemented in this book by other more contemporary ones that tell the same story in different ways. So who or what is an entrepreneur?

In building up our definition we see the 'who' as a person and the 'what' as a process that is habitual and involves creativity and innovation, and results in something of value that can be recognized by others. The building process, of course, first needs an opportunity to build on.

Thus we define an entrepreneur as:

> a person who habitually creates and innovates to build something of recognized value around perceived opportunities.

'A person' can be also a group of people as it is possible to describe teams and even organizations as entrepreneurial, and we give some examples in this book. The word 'person' emphasizes that a personality rather than a system is involved.

'Habitually' is an important characteristic of entrepreneurs that distinguishes them from business owner-managers or people who build a business simply to achieve a comfortable lifestyle. True entrepreneurs just cannot stop being entrepreneurs.

> People ask me how to become an entrepreneur and I can't tell them. It's something innate. I couldn't stop even if I wanted to.
> (Bo Peabody, entrepreneur, millionaire and
> founder of Internet business, Tripod)

The word 'creates' is used to emphasize the fact that entrepreneurs start from scratch and bring into being something that was not there before. But entrepreneurs are not 'hey presto' magicians, for they build as they create and fashion their venture. They are creators first and builders second but both are involved in the process.

True entrepreneurs 'innovate' as well as create. This is how they are able to overcome obstacles that would stop most people. It is how they turn problems into opportunities. They also see their ideas through to final application – they deliver.

'To build something' describes the output. The words 'habitually creates and innovates' refer to the process. 'To build something' is the aim of that process and for successful entrepreneurs this is their achievement. The word 'something' means that they build an entity that can be identified and is not just an idea or a concept, though it may start that way.

'Of recognized value' broadens the definition from the purely commercial. The traditional view of entrepreneurs is that they create financial capital. Whilst this is an important category of entrepreneur we want to expand upon the use of the word 'entrepreneur' so that it also includes those who create social capital and aesthetic capital. For example Dr Barnardo (1845–1905) was a social entrepreneur who created the now famous Barnardo's Homes that have a recognized social 'value' that is still current today. It is interesting to note that history describes Barnardo as a philanthropist rather than as an entrepreneur. Whilst his motive may have been philanthropy, he was only able to achieve what he did because he was an entrepreneur. Andrew Lloyd Webber is an example of an aesthetic and business entrepreneur who has created financial capital as a result of first creating aesthetic capital.

'Perceived opportunities' are essential to provide direction and focus. The idea behind the opportunity may or may not be original to the entrepreneur, but spotting the opportunity to exploit the idea is a characteristic of the entrepreneur. Entrepreneurs see something others miss or only see in retrospect – the good idea seen with the benefit of hindsight.

> Among the many thousands of things that I have never been able to understand, one in particular stands out. That is the question of who was the first person who stood by a pile of sand and said . . . *You know, I bet if we took some of this and mixed it with a little potash and heated it, we could make a material that would be solid and yet transparent. We could call it glass.* Call me obtuse, but you could stand me on a beach till the end of time and it would never occur to me to try to make it into windows.
>
> (Bill Bryson, *Notes from a Small Island*)

We will return to our definition of the entrepreneur throughout this book to illustrate and expand upon its meaning.

How the book works

The book is structured in three parts.

- Part One: Entrepreneurs
- Part Two: Entrepreneurs in action
- Part Three: Entrepreneurs and enterprise

In Part One, Chapter 1 is concerned with the 'who' question. Who is an entrepreneur? It sets out the argument for our approach to the understanding of entrepreneurs and explains what we mean by talent, temperament and technique. It puts this in the context of other talent-related activities such as sport. Chapter 2 explores the strategic contribution of entrepreneurs to provide an introduction into what they actually do and achieve. The entrepreneurs we discuss in the story chapters which comprise Part Two can then be seen in a strategic context and also as demonstrations of how talent, temperament and technique can be combined and developed to produce 'élite entrepreneurs' similar to 'élite athletes' whose outstanding achievements we all recognize.

Part Two then deals in detail with the 'what' questions. What does an entrepreneur do, what actually happens in the real world and what do they achieve? It tells the stories of a wide range of entrepreneurs, from legendary entrepreneurs such as Henry Ford, Walt Disney and Bill Gates to social entrepreneurs such as Cicely Saunders, who established the first modern hospice in the UK and inspired many others to follow her lead. There is a section on 'entrepreneurs in the shadows' where, amongst others, we look at unsociable entrepreneurs such as Robert Maxwell and Al Capone, who destroy some forms of capital to create financial wealth for themselves. Because Part Two adopts a storytelling approach it is inevitably different in style from Parts One and Three.

Part Three covers the 'how' question. How do entrepreneurs do what they do? How do the systems operate? This part deals with the practical issues of finding, developing and supporting entrepreneurs. We believe that releasing the entrepreneurial talent in a community, region or nation is one of the most untapped resources of our time and Part Three explains how this can be done.

These three parts are laid out in a logical progression that we hope will appeal to the general reader. From discussing this topic with a wide number of people we recognize that some readers will want to focus on the results and will be more concerned with the 'what' questions than the 'who' and the 'how'. For these readers we recommend starting with the entrepreneur stories in Part Two before moving to the 'who' and 'how' of Parts One and Three.

Others will prefer to consider concept before application, and for these readers Parts One and Three should be read first and the examples in Part Two left to the end. It is important, if you follow this approach, that you do not get lost in the theory and ideas side of things. We want you to catch the excitement and buzz of the entrepreneur and to realize that there are entrepreneurs out there already making things happen. If you do not feel able to join them, then at the least you can encourage and support them.

We hope that this book will make you think differently about entrepreneurs. In particular we would like to redeem the understanding of the word 'entrepreneur' from its present 'fast buck at someone else's expense' image. We would like concepts of integrity and philanthropy to be part of a new entrepreneurial ethic. Our focus on talent as a given should engender a desire to want to share the fruits of that gift with others. This may sound idealistic but the two statements below, often heard from successful entrepreneurs, suggest that this is already an ethic shared if not articulated:

'I have been very lucky.'

'Life has been very kind to me and I would like to put something back.'

These statements recognize that success has been achieved by more than just the entrepreneurs' own efforts and that entrepreneurs often want to show their gratitude.

We want entrepreneurs to be both socially acceptable and academically respectable in order that the barriers of culture in society in general, and the academic world in particular, come down. We hope this book will help to make entrepreneurship a serious career option for the young graduate, with the right talents and temperament, through new courses and staff that support and enable this.

We want the role of the entrepreneur to be valued in society and in established organizations, and the unnecessary barriers that frustrate and impede the would-be entrepreneur to be replaced by mechanisms that actually facilitate their identification and development. We recognize the fact that we cannot all become entrepreneurs in the context of our definition. But many more of us could start and run successful small organizations if we set our mind to it. Those of us who work in large organizations could be more enterprising. We want to encourage this by providing greater insight into what entrepreneurs do and achieve, thereby stimulating people to come up with new ideas and opportunities, coupled with a determination to follow them through.

We do not subscribe to the macho view of entrepreneurship that the tougher the environment the better the quality of entrepreneurs that emerge. It is true they might be tougher but there will be significantly fewer of them and the number of entrepreneurs is a critical factor. What, in fact, is needed within a community or region is a sufficient number of entrepreneurs to achieve critical mass. Once this point is reached a chain reaction is set in motion. Economic growth and social development become self-sustaining and an entrepreneurial culture develops. The Renaissance, the Industrial Revolution and today's High-Technology Revolution are all examples of such entrepreneurial flowering.

> An agglomeration of spin-offs in the same neighbourhood as their parent firms is why a high-technology complex builds up in a certain region. The chain reaction of spin-offs from spin-offs is a kind of natural process, once it is begun.
>
> (Larson and Rogers, 1986)

Entrepreneurs not only bring economic growth and social development they also directly create jobs. Larson and Rogers (1986) calculate that in Silicon Valley each entrepreneur creates between 500 and 1000 jobs. By comparison each technologist represents only sixteen additional jobs. There can surely be no stronger case than this for us to take entrepreneurs much more seriously than we do and to develop ways of identifying and nurturing the entrepreneurial talent that lies dormant in our midst. After all, it is entrepreneurs who create and build the future. Our hope is that this book will help to change attitudes and move these key issues forward.

References

Bolton, W. K. (1986). Entrepreneurial opportunities for the academic. UK Science Park Association, Annual Conference.

Bygrave, B. (1998). Building an entrepreneurial economy: lessons from the United States. *Business Strategy Review*, **9** (2), 11–18

Jardine, L. (1997). *Worldly Goods*. Papermac.

Larson, J. K. and Rogers, E. M. (1986). *Silicon Valley Fever*. Unwin Counterpoint.

Part One
Entrepreneurs

1 Identifying the entrepreneur

In the Introduction to this book we defined the entrepreneur as 'a person who habitually creates and innovates to build something of recognized value around perceived opportunities'. In this chapter we set out to identify the entrepreneur. We summarize previous work and research which helps us understand both the entrepreneur as a person and the process through which he or she builds value. We then develop a new framework based on talent, temperament and technique, which we believe provides a key for dealing with the challenge of spotting the potential entrepreneur. But we begin with a short story that summarizes the way entrepreneurs behave.

On 25 February 1983 Nolan Bushnell, founder of Atari, Pizza Time Theatres and Catalyst Technologies delivered a speech at the National Engineers Week in Sunnyvale, California in the heart of Silicon Valley. He described the entrepreneur with this story:

> A guy wakes up in the morning and says 'I'm going to be an entrepreneur.' So he goes into work and he walks up to the best technologist in the company where he's working and whispers: 'Would you like to join my company? Ten o'clock, Saturday, my place. And bring some donuts.' Then he goes to the best finance guy he knows, and says, 'Bring some coffee.' Then he gets a marketing guy. And if you are the right entrepreneur, you have three or four of the best minds in the business. Ten o'clock Saturday rolls around. They say, 'Hey, what is our company going to do?' You say, 'Build left-handed widgets.' Another hour and you've got a business plan roughed out. The finance guy says he knows where he can get some money. So what have you done? You've not provided the coffee. You've not provided the donuts. You've not provided the ideas. You've been the entrepreneur. You made it all happen.
>
> (Larson and Rogers, 1986)

For Nolan Bushnell an entrepreneur is someone who knows the right people, can pick a good team, act quickly and make it all happen. There is a dynamic about the entrepreneur that is captured well in this story; he or she is a person in a hurry.

Bushnell's entrepreneur is a blend of talent, temperament and technique, which in the right proportions creates outstanding businesses.

Present understanding

In the first part of this chapter we summarize and synthesize the main conclusions about entrepreneurs and entrepreneurship by several people who have studied the subject. Largely it is an assessment of entrepreneurs from the outside. We group the findings into three sections:

- What entrepreneurs are like – the *personality* factors.
- Where entrepreneurs come from – the *environmental* factors.
- What entrepreneurs do – the *action* factors.

This summary clearly helps us understand the entrepreneurial personality and partially explains what entrepreneurs do, and why. But we do not believe these factors are sufficient to allow us to 'spot potential winners', and instead contend that a study and appreciation of talent, temperament and technique provides a stronger key for unlocking this door and offers a basis for identifying those with the potential to become entrepreneurs.

As a prelude, though, we would wish to clarify three points. First, and unlike Burns (1999) – and others who take a similarly prescriptive approach – we do not accept that 'anyone who applies four key principles can become a successful entrepreneur' and develop a successful business. Burns's four principles are belief (in one's personal ability to succeed), focused knowledge (prioritized relevant learning), a proactive approach (evaluating information deliberately and acting on the conclusions) and perseverance (working through the rough periods). These are important and relevant principles; but we do not accept that they explain entrepreneurs in the context of the definition we provided in the Introduction. Many people who might wish they could be entrepreneurs do not possess important elements of talent or temperament, without which their likelihood of success as an entrepreneur is low. It is irresponsible to raise their expectations to unrealistic levels.

Second, and linked to this first point, people who 'dabble in business' are not necessarily entrepreneurs, although on occasions some of them will start something which really takes off and grows. Here we are thinking of people who are unemployed and are persuaded to do something themselves rather than look for another job, or people with some spare time on their hands who are looking to spend it in some meaningful way or people who invent something because they enjoy playing with ideas. Nevertheless, wherever they find an activity or project in which they believe, and to which they can commit, 'dabblers' can achieve something that is useful and valuable. In addition, we exclude from our definition of entrepreneurs those people who start small businesses because they crave independence, and do not want to work for a large organization, but who are content with something that stays small and provides them with a living. We might describe them as 'lifestyle entrepreneurs' but they do not 'habitually create and innovate to build something of recognized value'.

Third, many people who do possess entrepreneurial talent and temperament prefer to stay employed in a larger organization, rather than start out on their own, particularly if they are encouraged to use their initiative and follow up their ideas. So, whilst many small businesses – which in their particular context may be very successful – are not started by entrepreneurs, and do not behave in a truly entrepreneurial way, entrepreneurs who do make a real difference can be found championing causes and initiatives in larger organizations.

What entrepreneurs are like: the personality factors

Questions about personality are not special to entrepreneurs. Why we do what we do, why we are often alike and yet are so different are questions that psychologists have been studying for some time (Butler and McManus, 1998).

In this section we apply these questions to the entrepreneur and consider:

- motivation and emotion
- the born or made debate
- behavioural characteristics
- personality attributes.

Motivation and emotion   An engineer recently told us he felt real pleasure and satisfaction when he walked around his factory and saw it working like clockwork with raw material coming in and finished product going out. Even for the mechanistic engineer this was an emotional experience. Put together by his head, it stirred his heart.

For all of us our motivation comes from the heart as well as the head (Goleman, 1996) and so it is not surprising that psychologists link motivation and emotion together. In many ways it is the motivation and emotion of entrepreneurs that gives them a special kind of drive and purpose that marks them out from the rest of us. It is how they keep going and win through when lesser people would give up.

For some this can be very close to what the psychiatrist calls 'mania'. Whybrow (1999) comments that 'when the extraordinary energy, enthusiasm and self-confidence of the condition are found harnessed with a natural talent – for leadership or the creative arts – such states can become the engines of achievement, driving accomplishments much revered in human culture'. He lists Cromwell, Napoleon, Lincoln and Churchill as leaders in this mould.

Some entrepreneurs are also driven in this way, as one sufferer recounts. 'I'll bet you that many successful businessmen, who have taken risks and almost lost their company, can describe something similar to my experiences in early mania. But they edit them out; they decide that such feelings have no relevance to anything but competition and risk, and they put them aside' (Whybrow, 1999).

Some of course are not able to put such feelings aside and suffer from what has been called 'entrepreneurial stress' (Buttner, 1992). This ranges from back problems and insomnia to more serious matters such as depression. We know of entrepreneurs who have driven past their offices rather than go into work because they could not face another day.

Other insights into motivation have been provided by McClelland (1961) who looked at the psychological and social elements that drove economic development. He saw motivation of individuals within a society as a crucial factor and linked it to three basic human needs: the need for achievement, the need for power and the need for affiliation. McClelland (1965) was particularly interested in the need for achievement because he believed that it was people with that need – the entrepreneurs – who drove economic development.

Various tests have been developed to measure these need-based drives. Roberts (1991) followed McClelland in using the Thematic Apperception Test (TAT) to assess the needs profile of technical entrepreneurs. (The TAT involves the verbal interpretation of fuzzy sketches.) Whilst McClelland (1965) concluded that entrepreneurs had a high need for achievement, Roberts found that on average technical entrepreneurs had only a 'moderate' need for achievement. However when he related his results to company performance he found that almost 80 per cent of the high-growth companies were run by entrepreneurs with a 'high' need for achievement.

Although this was an important finding it would be wrong to conclude that people with a high need for achievement would necessarily make good entrepreneurs. As sports psychologists have found, there is no clear correlation between achievement motivation and the level of performance achieved (Woods, 1998). Other factors, most notably talent, have to be there as well.

Competitiveness is one aspect of motivation that is well-recognized in sport (Martens, 1976) but has received little attention in regard to entrepreneurs. In studies of entrepreneurship competitiveness is generally set in the context of the external competitive forces on the business rather than the competitive spirit within the individual entrepreneur. Yet it is a character trait of entrepreneurs that they are people who do not like to be beaten; they want to be winners. This competitive streak is for many a main motivator. We recall an entrepreneur who competed with another entrepreneur all his life and this rivalry drove them both. When one died the other remarked that he was pleased to have him finally out of the way. There was no sadness or remorse, only triumph.

If motivational analysis is taken out of the psychological domain and entrepreneurs are simply asked why they started a business then the answers are clearer. Roberts (1991) found that for 39 per cent of a sample of seventy-two technical entrepreneurs the answer was that they sought independence, wanting to be their own boss. Thirty per cent were responding to a challenge and only 12 per cent were motivated by the possibility of wealth.

The low rating of money and wealth as a motivator with entrepreneurs is against the general perception of the entrepreneur. In reality money is a by-product of the business entrepreneurs, but it is this that people see and, so, assume it to be the main motivator.

Many of the examples given in this book support Roberts's finding for technical entrepreneurs, that the primary motivation for most entrepreneurs is independence. They want to be able to develop their own ideas in their own way without having to answer to anybody else. They want to be able to say 'I did it my way'. This is the entrepreneur's ultimate satisfaction.

The born or made debate   The concept of personality as something distinct and individual that directs a person's behaviour begs the same question we consider here for entrepreneurs. Is personality 'born' or is it 'made'? Are we a product of 'nature' or 'nurture'?

Derlega, Winstead and Jones (1991) state that: 'Personality refers to the enduring, inner characteristics of individuals that organize behaviour.' Some psychologists see these 'enduring, inner characteristics' (Hollander, 1971) as coming from an inner psychological core at the centre of our personality that is relatively permanent.

Such a model presupposes that a proportion of our personality is inborn and enduring. Hans Eysenck (1965) has suggested that we have two dimensions of personality that roughly correspond to motivation and emotion. He sees the two dimensions as related to biological differences in brain function (Butler and McManus, 1998) and on this basis has proposed that 75 per cent of our personality traits are due to genetic influence and 25 per cent due to environmental influence (Woods, 1998).

Research at the University of Minnesota on identical twins separated at birth and reared in different environments has built up a solid body of evidence that shows that many character traits are shaped by genetics. From this work it is estimated 'that the genetic contribution to "personality" is around 40 per cent' (Whybrow, 1999).

Individually our genetic inheritance leads us to seek particular opportunities and tread particular paths. Our experiences on these journeys, and whether we are encouraged or discouraged in our endeavours and experiments, affect our personality and future behaviour.

Whatever the exact ratios are it is clear that personality is now understood as having an inborn component and an environment component. In so far as the entrepreneur is a function of personality we would conclude that entrepreneurs are both born and made. We come back to this idea later in this chapter when we consider talent and temperament.

Contrary to this finding from psychology, several books on entrepreneurship state that the argument is over and that entrepreneurs are 'made' (Burns and Dewhurst, 1989; Kent, 1984). One of the standard texts on entrepreneurship now in its fourth edition (Kuratko and Hodgetts, 1998) says that it is a myth of entrepreneurship that entrepreneurs are born and not made. It states that entrepreneurship is a discipline that can be taught and mastered like any other. Whilst it may be true that the techniques of entrepreneurship can be 'taught' or more correctly 'learned', we do not believe that educators can make people into entrepreneurs. Whilst such a claim may fill the classroom we believe it to be irresponsible. We have seen too many failed entrepreneurs, who have lost the family home and whose marriage has failed, to believe otherwise. We are particularly concerned that such a standard text should recommend that those who score twenty-five out of 103 in its Entrepreneur Quotient questionnaire should be advised 'You still have a chance. Go for it'.

We do however believe that educational programmes for entrepreneurs have their place – but they must recognize their boundaries. Whether the born/made ratio is 75:25 or 40:60 the environment is still an important parameter and one which those who wish to promote entrepreneurship can do something about.

Behavioural characteristics   The behavioural characteristics of the entrepreneur have received the most attention from researchers over the years. After reviewing a number of sources, Hornaday (1982) drew up a list of forty-two characteristics including:

- perseverance and determination
- ability to take calculated risks
- need to achieve
- initiative and taking responsibility
- orientation to clear goals
- creativity
- honesty and integrity
- independence.

Although his full list was long it is rather surprising that it did not include opportunity orientation, persistent problem-solving and internal locus of control, which have been identified by others (Kao, 1991; Kuratko and Hodgetts, 1998).

The characteristics given in these lists are mainly straightforward but two require some comment. The first is to explain what is meant by 'internal locus of control'. This is a term used by psychologists (Rotter, 1966; 1971) to describe the extent to which people feel they are in control of what happens in their lives. People with an internal locus of control see themselves as being in control and believe that their own actions can dictate events, which of course is typical of the entrepreneur. Those with an external locus of control believe that their lives are controlled by external things such as luck and fate or the actions of others. Whilst entrepreneurs often acknowledge that circumstances did combine to give them a great opportunity and they were lucky, they believe that they were the ones who seized that opportunity and made it happen.

The second is to note the inclusion of honesty and integrity on the lists of Hornaday (1982), Kao (1991) and Kuratko and Hodgetts (1998). This is perhaps surprising given the image of entrepreneurs as people who take opportunities without too much thought as to the consequences for others. Some people think that there is no such thing as an honest entrepreneur and that you have to 'cut corners' and 'sail close to the wind' if you are to make it as an entrepreneur in today's competitive world. This is a view we do not share.

Of course there are dishonest people amongst entrepreneurs just as there are in all walks of life and when they are found out they receive a great deal of publicity. Robert Maxwell is an obvious case in point and is given as an example of an 'entrepreneur in the shadows' in Chapter 7. There are also particular temptations for those who acquire wealth and influence but there is no evidence that they 'fall from grace' more often than others. The main difficulty, particularly in the UK, is one of culture where we are suspicious of people who become wealthy. Like the story of the Englishman and the American waiting at a bus stop when a Rolls-Royce drives by. The Englishman comments 'I wonder who he cheated to be able to have a car like that', the American says 'Gee that's a great car, I wonder how I can get one'.

It is now generally recognized that ethical issues such as trust (Fukuyama, 1995) are important in a capitalist society and that business cannot function unless those involved can work together on a commonly accepted ethical basis. Entrepreneurs who like to move quickly and act decisively often build up a network of people they can trust rather than take the time on dotting 'i's and crossing 't's. They will shake hands on a deal and leave the 'legal boys' to sort out the details.

Social responsibility and business ethics are new and important topics in our business schools and courses on entrepreneurship also include them. The standard text referred to earlier includes a chapter on the 'Ethical and social responsibility challenges for entrepreneurs' (Kuratko and Hodgetts, 1998).

Personality attributes   Like a fingerprint, we all have our own unique personality. The question for us is whether there is a collection or cluster of personality attributes that distinguish the entrepreneur from the general public. Is there such a thing as the 'entrepreneur personality'?

Personality attributes have been studied extensively and a wide range of tests has been developed to identify and even measure them. Such testing, termed 'psychometric testing', has become commonplace and is now a standard part of the interview process with many companies, particularly when the interviewee has to be part of a team. Jones (1993) lists nineteen such tests and describes them as 'Popular recruitment and career development tests'. One of the more popular tests developed by Cattell between 1946 and 1949 defines a set of sixteen personality factors (PF) and uses a questionnaire to evaluate them.

The Myers-Briggs Type Indicator (MBTI) is another popular test and a number of books are available which describe the test and its application (Goldsmith and Wharton, 1993; Keirsey and Bates, 1984; Kummerow, Barger and Kirby, 1997).

The MBTI was devised by Isobel Briggs Myers and her mother Katharine Briggs, and is based on four dimensions of personality proposed by the psychologist Jung, namely extroversion (E)/introversion (I), sensation (S)/intuition (N), thinking (T)/feeling (F) and judging (J)/perceiving (P). Combinations of the letters from each of the four dimensions give the personality indicator, making sixteen personality types in all. Goldsmith and Wharton (1993) state that ESTP types can be good innovators, negotiators and entrepreneurs, where E means that they are extroverted rather than introverted, S that they use their senses rather than intuition, T that they think rather than feel and P that they perceive rather than judge.

Roberts (1991) used a shortened version of the MBTI on seventy-three people who attended the Massachusetts Institute of Technology (MIT) Enterprise Forum and the 128 Venture Group. About two-thirds of the sample were known to be entrepreneurs and all were interested in entrepreneurship. Roberts found that as a group they were classed as ENTPs. The difference with the assessment of Goldsmith and Wharton quoted above is only in the sensing (S)/intuition (N) dimension.

Before carrying out his research, and based on his personal experience of entrepreneurs, Roberts assessed entrepreneurs as ENTJ types. Keirsey and Bates (1984) describe ENTJs as 'the field marshal' which Roberts (1991) comments is 'perhaps an apt label for some entrepreneurs!'

Whilst this kind of personality test does not seem to point to a definable entrepreneur personality – they can be ESTPs, ENTPs or ENTJs – such tests can be useful in business start-up programmes.

From 1995 to 1997 we were involved in a programme in which new team-based businesses were set up around a business opportunity. The participants in the programme were drawn from the general public who had responded to advertisements in local newspapers. A personality and team profile was built up for each person using psychometric testing methods. The Occupational Personality Questionnaire (OPQ) developed by Saville and Holdsworth and Belbin's Team Role definitions (Jones, 1993) were used. This psychometric profile was then combined with the skill profile for each person and teams selected to give an appropriate personality and skill mix. This methodology worked well and succeeded in producing balanced and effective teams, though of course they were not necessarily entrepreneurial teams.

Where entrepreneurs come from: the environmental factors

Here we consider entrepreneurs' roots and their surrounding influences. These can be grouped under the following three headings:

- Family background.
- Education and age.
- Work experience.

Though these can be powerful environmental factors they are essentially 'static'. They mould the entrepreneur. Situation triggers, discussed in Chapter 11, are 'dynamic' environmental factors. They provide the spark that lights the flame. This can be an introduction to something or somebody, a particular experience, a change of circumstances such as redundancy and so on.

Family background   Roberts (1991) has developed the idea of 'the entrepreneurial heritage' to describe the importance of the family background for the entrepreneur. This 'heritage' includes factors such as the father's occupation, the family work ethic and religion, family size and the first-born son, growing up experiences and so on. Roberts was interested in entrepreneurs in high technology but many of his findings apply to entrepreneurs in general.

Roberts found that the strongest of these influences came from the father's career. His research showed that across several sample groups the proportion of entrepreneurs whose fathers were self-employed was between 48 per cent and 65 per cent as compared with a figure of 25 per cent that would be expected if it was by chance alone. Although Roberts was looking at technology entrepreneurs very few of the fathers were in technology. Typically they would own small retail stores, farms or small non-technical manufacturing firms. Roberts (1991) comments that 'indeed it may be that simply familiarity with a business environment, growing from 'table talk' at home, is the key to increasing the probability that an offspring will later become an entrepreneur'. In a similar vein Timmons (1986) speaks of entrepreneurial roots in which the parents provide the role model for the child.

Other researchers (Hisrich, 1990) have found similar figures for entrepreneurs in general. A study of 500 women entrepreneurs found that the majority of those in the sample had fathers who were self-employed (Hisrich and Brush, 1984).

We can thus conclude with Roberts (1991) that 'a disproportionate number of entrepreneurs are the sons of entrepreneurs', but we would also add 'daughters'.

Some have found that small families and being the first-born son are important for the emergence of entrepreneurs because in that environment they can develop a greater self-confidence (Hisrich, 1990). Research in Canada evaluated twelve personal and family variables among participants in an entrepreneurship programme and concluded that 'the characteristic most frequently associated with the entrepreneurial group was being the oldest child in the family' (Brockhaus and Horwitz, 1986).

The 'number one' son is an important consideration in some cultures, such as the Japanese, where there is a strong expectation on the first-born son (Fukuyama, 1995). This, of course, can be difficult when the son is not the entrepreneur his father was. Even in Western culture this can be a problem as the son either seeks to emulate his entrepreneur father or simply decides he would rather spend his father's money; the 'rags to riches and back again in three generations' syndrome.

Whilst these family factors can be important they are by no means deciding factors. The research in this area often assumes that those who run their own business are entrepreneurs and, as we stated earlier, we do not believe that this is the case. Charles Forte was a first-born son and his father set up and ran a successful local business in Scotland. Charles's first-born son Rocco took over the empire his father Charles had built. All three were successful businessmen but a reading of Charles Forte's biography makes it quite clear that only Charles was a true entrepreneur (Forte, 1997). He was the only one of the three who 'habitually created and innovated to build something of recognized value'.

Education and age   Entrepreneurs seem to turn the importance of education and age upside down. Kevin Threlfall did not get enough A levels to go to university but as a ten-year-old would go out with his father and learn about sales techniques. Today he has one of the larger retail businesses in the UK (T and S Stores, incorporating Supercigs, Buy-Wise and Preedy/Dillons) with sales of £500 million (Steiner, 1998).

It seems that entrepreneurs themselves do not generally rate education as having been an important factor for them. Studies of entrepreneurs appear to support this view. Comparing the educational level of entrepreneurs and managers, Brockhaus and Nord (1979) found that the managers had more than two years' extra education than the entrepreneurs. In an earlier entrepreneur sample from Michigan, Collins and Moore (1964) found that 60 per cent had not been educated beyond high school, and this in a country where higher education is open to all. In the Third World countries where educational opportunities are limited compared with the West, the charity Opportunity International that provides loans to the poor has found no shortage of entrepreneurs.

Thus we can conclude that the education of the entrepreneur does not exceed that of the average person in the community and may be lower. Our own anecdotal evidence with entrepreneur programmes for undergraduates in the UK suggests that too much education can actually deter entrepreneurs and bury their talent even deeper.

The exception to this conclusion, as one would expect, is in high technology. Roberts's (1991) work with technical entrepreneurs from MIT showed that 91 per cent had a bachelor degree or higher and 31 per cent had a doctorate. These were mainly in technical fields and, so, related to the expertise demanded by the product rather then their entrepreneurial activities. Roberts (1991) comments significantly that 'in fact relatively few of the technical entrepreneurs had ever taken business courses before company formation'.

Even this exception has its exceptions. Bill Gates spent most of his time at Harvard preparing the groundwork for what became Microsoft, that is, when he was not playing poker (Wallace and Erickson, 1993). Finally he dropped out and never graduated. Steve Jobs of Apple, and a millionaire before he was thirty, never made university. But Gates and Jobs were both into computers in their teens. Their hobby became a consuming passion and laid the foundation for two amazing companies. To them further formal education was not important. They felt they knew more about computers than the teachers did and, anyway, they had a business to get off the ground. So even in the technology world education may not be as important as academics like to think.

Age is another interesting determinant for entrepreneurs. It is true that people start businesses at all ages but the real entrepreneurs just cannot wait and often begin in their late teens or early twenties. Two-thirds of the forty-two entrepreneurs whose start-up stories were first reported in the *Sunday Times* and then summarized in a book (Steiner, 1998) set up their first business before they were twenty-five years old. In our experience with business start-up programmes around the UK we found that there were two age groups where entrepreneurs emerge. The first was between twenty-two and twenty-eight years. By this time people have had some experience and may have less family and financial commitments than in their thirties. The second was forty-five years and over when people often start a second career and, again, their family and financial responsibilities are less. We shall see in Chapter 3 how Ray Kroc was over fifty years old, and had worked for thirty years as a salesman, before he began McDonald's.

Roberts (1991) found that two-thirds of the MIT spin-off entrepreneurs (a sample of 119) were aged between twenty-eight and thirty-nine. Whilst this contradicts our view of UK entrepreneurs among the general public, it is consistent with our knowledge of the high technology entrepreneurs in and around the Cambridge area. It is therefore likely that the special nature of high technology and the support structures that have been built around MIT in the USA and Cambridge, England, make it possible and acceptable to spin-off a new enterprise despite a family and a mortgage.

In principle we do not believe that age is a determining factor for entrepreneurs except that the true entrepreneur is likely to do it sooner rather than later. We agree with Larson and Rogers (1986) who have experienced and studied the Silicon Valley story and conclude that 'anybody, even an eleven-year-old, can become an entrepreneur'.

Work experience   Several researchers have noted that entrepreneurs first gain some work experience in the line of business they later start up (Vesper, 1980). Studies have shown that as many as 90 per cent of entrepreneurs start their business in the same market and industry as they were working in (Brockhaus, 1982). The term 'apprenticeship' has been used by Timmons (1986) to describe this idea and he comments that most successful entrepreneurs 'have accumulated five to ten years experience or more of general management and industry experience prior to their first start-up'.

Entrepreneurs themselves, and those who study them, all agree that experience in the 'university of life' or 'the school of hard knocks' is what develops the entrepreneur (Collins and Moore, 1964). Some do this by starting a number of businesses over a period that do not grow and may even fail. Through this experience they learn lessons they never forget so that when the real opportunity comes along they are ready for it.

Others work for somebody else and learn that way. This has the advantage that they can learn at someone else's expense and get a feel of what makes a business successful before they have to carry the full responsibility themselves. At this point they are at their most receptive and objective. When they have their own business to run, things become rather more subjective and perceptions can get distorted.

A second advantage is that working for someone else often means that potential entrepreneurs find a role model. This can work both ways. If the role model is good then they will be inspired and much can be learnt. Role models can become mentors and often have a hand in getting the new entrepreneur started. If the role model is a bad one then the potential entrepreneur can find the experience so frustrating that he or she hops from job to job and then starts a business too early before having had enough experience.

So far, our consideration of the entrepreneur factors has been largely descriptive and, though they paint a general picture of the entrepreneur, there are many exceptions. Whilst we may be able to *describe* the 'typical entrepreneur' we do not feel that this brings us any nearer to being able to *identify potential* entrepreneurs. The fact that research has repeatedly shown that many entrepreneurs share certain background and personality characteristics, for example, does not mean we have a predictive cause-and-effect model. Others with the same characteristics do not become entrepreneurs.

The analogy of sport with entrepreneurship is relevant to this debate. The personality profile of an athlete can be defined in general terms as it can for the entrepreneur. The motivational, emotional and personality characteristics of both can be assessed, but when all this is done we are no closer to being able to identify potential winners either in sport or in entrepreneurship. Yet it is clear that there are winners and that their performances speak for themselves. We judge a successful athlete and a successful entrepreneur by their outstanding performance.

Recognizing the limitations to this nevertheless valuable research, we now move on a stage and discuss what entrepreneurs actually do, and then set this within the entrepreneur process.

What entrepreneurs do: the action factors

In this section we examine ten key action roles associated with entrepreneurs and entrepreneurship, regardless of the context:

1 Entrepreneurs are individuals who make a significant difference.
2 Entrepreneurs are creative and innovative.
3 Entrepreneurs spot and exploit opportunities.
4 Entrepreneurs find the resources required to exploit opportunities.
5 Entrepreneurs are good networkers.
6 Entrepreneurs are determined in the face of adversity.
7 Entrepreneurs manage risk.
8 Entrepreneurs have control of the business.
9 Entrepreneurs put the customer first.
10 Entrepreneurs create capital.

1 Entrepreneurs are individuals who make a significant difference

> It is individuals who have always made the difference – not only in business,
> but in enterprises generally.
> > (Sir Clive Thompson, Chief Executive, Rentokil Initial)

Entrepreneurs translate 'what is possible' into reality (Kao, 1989). Put another way,
they transform a simple, ill-defined idea into something that works (Kets de Vries,
1997). They have their own ways of dealing with opportunities, setbacks and uncertainties to 'creatively create' new products, new services, new organizations and
new ways of satisfying customers or doing business.

Entrepreneurs disturb the status quo. They make a difference because they *are*
different from most of us. They initiate change and enjoy it. For the entrepreneur
it is always 'onwards and upwards'. Barriers and problems that would stop or
hinder most of us are for them a spur and a challenge. They get involved directly
in the whole operation, they are 'hands on' people, they 'push the cart'.

The remaining nine things on our list of ten that entrepreneurs 'do' all contribute
to their ability to make a difference. Obviously not all entrepreneurs do these things
equally well but they are all present to some degree and a few of them to an
outstanding degree. It is the combination of these special strengths that enable the
entrepreneur to make a significant difference.

2 Entrepreneurs are creative and innovative

> My Golden Rule is that there are no golden rules.
> > (George Bernard Shaw, *Maxims for Revolutionists*)

> The best way to forecast the future is to invent it!
> > (George Bernard Shaw, *Man and Superman*, Act IV)

Creativity and innovation are the distinguishing marks of the entrepreneur. This
is why they disturb markets and can challenge the large established business. It is
the entrepreneur who 'thrives on chaos' as Tom Peters (1989) describes today's
business world.

Creativity is a continuous activity for the entrepreneur, always seeing new ways
of doing things with little concern for how difficult they might be or whether the
resources are available. But creativity in the entrepreneur is combined with
the ability to innovate, to take the idea and make it work in practice. This seeing

something through to the end and not being satisfied until all is accomplished is a central motivation for the entrepreneur. Indeed once the project is accomplished the entrepreneur seeks another 'mountain to climb' because for him or her creativity and innovation are habitual, something that he or she just has to keep on doing.

After forty years as an entrepreneur Armand Hammer was a wealthy man and needed a tax shelter – so he bought into Occidental Petroleum. With only dry oil wells this company was trading at a loss and had total assets of just $78 000. Thirty years later Armand Hammer had grown Occidental to rival the major oil companies of the world. His original investment of $100 000 was worth $11.5 million in a company valued at $16 billion. By then Mr Hammer was eighty-six years old (Hammer, 1988)!

3 Entrepreneurs spot and exploit opportunities

A story is told of a shoe manufacturer who, many years ago, sent two of his marketing graduates to the interior of Australia to see if they could come up with new product ideas for the undeveloped aborigine market. The first one responded: 'There's no business here; the natives don't wear shoes of any type!' The second one was more enthusiastic about the prospects: 'This is a great opportunity; the natives haven't even discovered shoes yet!'

People's perceptions about opportunities vary. How often do we only see an opportunity in retrospect? The 'good idea' was always there to be spotted, but for many of us it is a case of 'Why didn't I think of it first? It's so obvious!'

Entrepreneurs are able to see or craft opportunities that other people miss, even though the data or information that generates the idea is often there for all to see. They are able to synthesize the available information and clarify patterns that escape others. They are comfortable with ambiguity and they can bring clarity by piecing together previously unrelated messages and signals (McGrath, 1997). Not only do they see the opportunities they seem to know, as if by instinct, which of the many is actually worth pursuing.

In some cases the opportunity and need is widely recognized and talked about. We have been told that great wealth awaits the person who designs a reliable and low-product cost vending machine for French fries. The inventor might be the person who solves the problem but it is the entrepreneur who exploits that opportunity and turns it into a reality. Those gifted few who, like James Dyson reported in Chapter 3, are both inventors and entrepreneurs, have a special edge.

4 Entrepreneurs find the resources required to exploit opportunities

Charles Forte did not have the financial resources to buy the Café Royal in London but he wanted it badly. His bankers would not advance the money under any circumstances and yet he found the resources, signed the deal and reported back to his colleagues 'We haven't paid for it yet, but we've bought it'.

(Forte, 1997)

The success of the entrepreneur is rarely due to a flash of inspiration or luck; rather it is the conscientious and disciplined exploitation of resources which are already to hand or which can somehow be found. Entrepreneurs are not put off by not having the resources they need; in some ways it seems to stimulate and challenge them. They are expert at exploiting contacts and sources, 'begging, stealing and borrowing' when necessary (Stevenson, 1997). In many cases, it is not necessary that resources are 'state of the art' or the 'best available' but are simply ones that will perform satisfactorily. Entrepreneurs are pragmatists who find and put together the minimum resources required for the job.

5 Entrepreneurs are good networkers

> The close networks that characterize Silicon Valley give the region an advantage over other areas.
>
> (Larson and Rogers, 1986)

Entrepreneurs know 'where' to find resources (action factor 4) and 'how' to control a business (action factor 8) but they also know 'who' (Gibb, 1998). They are quick to build up networks of people that they know can help them. They have what has been called 'expertise orientation' (Clifton and Harding, 1986) – that is, they know when they need experts and know how to use them effectively. Rather than exploiting such people they often become friends that stay with them over the years. When Charles Forte set up his first milk bar in London he used two young property agents to find him the premises he needed. 'They were even younger than I was, but had already established a considerable business. I was truly impressed by them and they remained life-long friends' (Forte, 1997).

Entrepreneurs are good networkers. When it comes to putting a team together as Nolan Bushnell's earlier story illustrates, they know who to talk to. In Bushnell's Silicon Valley the bars and the restaurants were favourite places to 'talk shop'. The informal, no fee, no bylaws Home Brew Club in Silicon Valley had a membership of 500 or so computerphiles almost as soon as it was started. It was a networkers' delight. Larson and Rogers (1986) reached the important conclusion that 'information exchange is a dominant, distinguishing characteristic of Silicon Valley'.

6 Entrepreneurs are determined in the face of adversity

> People fall into three categories:
> Those who make things happen.
> Those who watch things happen.
> Those who are left to ask what did happen.
>
> If you think you can, you can.
> If you think you can't, you're right.
>
> (George Bernard Shaw, *Reason*)

Entrepreneurs are motivated to succeed; they possess determination and self-belief. On the one hand, this is a major reason for their success; they refuse to be beaten and persevere when 'the going gets tough'. On the other hand, this also explains why some would-be entrepreneurs fail. They have too much faith in their own ability; they believe they are infallible and can do almost anything; they refuse to accept they might be wrong; they fail to seek help when they need it.

Successful entrepreneurs are also able to deal with unexpected obstacles, the kind that cannot be predicted in a business plan. Most companies experience three or four life-threatening crises in their early years; to survive this period the true entre-preneur deals with these crises and wins through. He or she is an 'overcomer' who can resolve problems under pressure.

Entrepreneurs use their creative and innovation skills in these difficult times. Somehow they really do turn problems into opportunities. Allen Jones of AJ Restaurants comments: 'I think I am a persistent devil. When things go wrong I generally go harder. I try not to be beaten and find another way to solve the problem' (Williams, 1994).

7 Entrepreneurs manage risk

There are two times in a man's life when he should not speculate – when he cannot afford it – and when he can.

(Mark Twain)

We invariably associate entrepreneurs with risk, but here we need to use our terms carefully. Entrepreneurs certainly take risks, but risks they believe they understand and can manage. Whilst they may well take risks that other less enterprising people would avoid, relatively few fall into the category of mere *adventurers,* very high risk-takers who take chances intuitively and with little analytical rigour. These ventures will sometimes pay off handsomely, but they are also prone to fail because they are always based more on hope than judgement (Derr, 1982).

In reality, many entrepreneurs will avoid this 'bridge too far' situation and instead prefer perpetual movement and improvement, continually hoping to find and exploit manageable risks and opportunities (Churchill, 1997). Their approach to strategy is a quick but careful initial screening of an idea, using only limited analysis to evaluate the quality of the idea. Their success lies in vigilance, learning, flexi-bility and change during implementation (Bhide, 1994).

Entrepreneurs are not risk averse, they prefer to find ways of saying 'yes' rather than 'no' and then are willing to accept responsibility for their decision.

8 Entrepreneurs have control of the business

I now learnt a lesson I shall never forget. I realized that until I could find the right balance between income on the one hand, and the cost of raw materials, wages, rent, rates and other overheads on the other, the sums would not add up. In fact there and then I worked out the essential ratios which would guarantee the profits.

(Forte, 1997)

It is easy for a business to get out of control and for the directors and managers to feel that the business is running them. Entrepreneurs do not allow this to happen. They are not 'control freaks' but they pay attention to detail and develop their own key indicators of performance that they monitor carefully. The *essential ratios* that Charles Forte worked out in his twenties were the same ones he used when he bought the Lyons Hotel group and turned it into profit. 'We used our tried financial formu-lae, the ratio of sales to gross profit that we knew was obtainable' (Forte, 1997).

Some entrepreneurs keep a loose rein on the business whilst others manage it very tightly, but both know exactly the state of their business. They seem to have a knack for knowing what is important and what to keep an eye on. They *are* able to see 'the wood for the trees' but they also know which trees to watch. Thus it is that they are able to exercise strategic control over their business. Tim Waterstone of the Waterstone book chain tells us he has 'the gift of simplicity, of understanding how simple business is. I can lift out the only things that really matter' (Williams, 1994).

9 Entrepreneurs put the customer first

We always accepted that success is never based on a one-off transaction; it comes only by encouraging the customer to return again and again. It all sounds very simple; put like this, almost too simple. But it is true.

(Forte, 1997)

It is perhaps fairly obvious that entrepreneurs put the customer first and yet most of the studies of entrepreneurs do not mention this directly. Instead they speak of the need for market knowledge or observe that the best entrepreneurs are salespeople.

The market for any new enterprise is always a difficult place, with surprises just around the corner. But entrepreneurs thrive on this uncertainty and generally end up making a success of a product or of a market sector that was quite different to the one they started with. The reason they do this is that they listen to the customer, they are quick to find out why they won a sale as much as why they lost one. They are able and willing to respond to what the customer is telling them.

10 Entrepreneurs create capital

Society is always in deep debt to the entrepreneurs who sustain it and rarely consume by themselves more than the smallest share of what they give society.

(Gilder, 1986)

Creativity and innovation, resource acquisition, control of the business, networking and the other 'action' factors are all part of the entrepreneur's intellectual and emotional capital. They are the currency that the entrepreneur brings to the table and which he or she uses to generate new kinds of capital external to him or herself. These are:

● financial capital
● social capital
● aesthetic capital.

The entrepreneur is generally associated with the first of these, financial capital, but we want to extend its use to include those who create social capital and aesthetic capital. This is because we see people operating in these areas who are clearly entrepreneurs by our definition. They create and innovate to build something of recognized value, but of course we do need to use measures other than pounds sterling or dollars to define this capital.

The measures of 'people helped' and 'jobs created' are used by the charity Opportunity International, which was set up by an Australian entrepreneur David Bussau. 'From 1981 to 1993 David and his partners in the Opportunity Network made loans to 46,000 entrepreneurs and created 77,700 jobs among the poor' (Sider,

1996). Their Annual Reports use 'the number of lives transformed' as a measure of social capital generated in the year. Bussau is discussed further under 'Social and environmental entrepreneurs' in Chapter 5.

The action factors and entrepreneur process We have been considering what entrepreneurs do – their action factors. Rather than set these in the context of entrepreneurship, as one might set the actions of a craft worker within a body of knowledge termed 'expertise', we want to place them within the *entrepreneur process*. We do this using two process models.

In the first model, shown in Figure 1.1, the starting point of the process is the *motivation to make a difference* (action factor 1). As we discuss later in this section there are other motivators for the entrepreneur but this we believe to be the most important. The ability to *create and innovate* (2) is the lifeblood of the process, without this vital blood flow the process would not happen. The first step in the process is to *spot and exploit an opportunity* (3) and then as things move forward obstacles appear. We group the next four action factors around the way in which the entrepreneur deals with these obstacles. He or she *finds the required resources* (4), *uses networks extensively* (5), is *determined in the face of adversity* (6) and *manages risk (7)*. Using his or her creativity and innovation talent the entrepreneur turns the obstacles into opportunities. All these contribute to a growing enterprise that succeeds because the entrepreneur knows how to *control the business* (8) and is consistent in *putting the customer first* (9). The outcome of the entrepreneur process is the *creation of capital* (10).

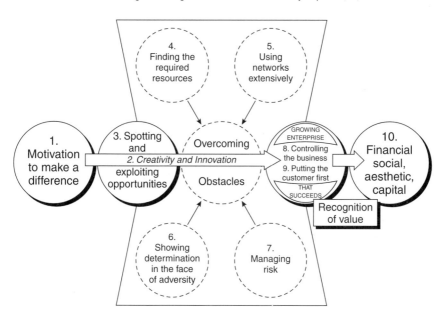

Figure 1.1 *The entrepreneur process diagram*

The second entrepreneur process model condenses the action factors into two distinct stages as indicated in Figure 1.2.

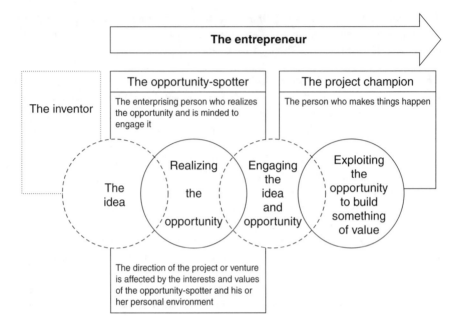

Figure 1.2   *The entrepreneur, the opportunity spotter and the project champion*

The first stage or area of activity is *spotting the opportunity*. The person who spots or realizes the potential for an idea may not be the originator of the idea; in turn, the inventor of the idea may not appreciate how it might be exploited. The opportunity-spotter sees the gap in the market. It could be an opportunity for making money, or for creating something of perceived value for the community (social entrepreneurship), or for adding to our artistic or aesthetic environment. The direction will depend upon the personal environment of the individual and the world in which he or she is looking for opportunities. Whilst business entrepreneurs will always emerge in a capitalist economy, people operating in a religious environment will find their opportunity there. This choice of environment is affected by personal values and interests – it is important in developing entrepreneurs that a person is able to work in the environment which is right and appropriate for his or her talents and interests. Whilst business entrepreneurs and some social entrepreneurs are responsive to external environmental opportunities and gaps, other social entrepreneurs and most artistic entrepreneurs are driven from within to search for ways in which they can exploit their personal gifts and talents.

The second stage is the *project championing* of the opportunity. This is the area of activity in which things are made to happen. The opportunity-spotter may well be minded to engage the idea and take it forward, and if he or she is capable of doing this effectively he or she is an entrepreneur. The entrepreneur is both an opportunity-spotter and a project champion. But he or she may not possess these implementation capabilities – in which case the individual will need a partner who is able to do this well, or must hand the idea and opportunity over to a project champion if it is successfully to come to fruition. Some people who are excellent project champions are not the people who realize the opportunity in the first place. Rather they are people who make things happen and build whatever it is that makes the real difference. They gather together the necessary resources, and they know where they can find help and support.

The true entrepreneur, as we have said, is able to combine and execute both roles successfully.

Many of us do see limited opportunities – we might even be described as ideas people – but we do not possess either the abilities or the inclination to exploit the opportunity and build something distinctive and valuable. At the same time, others are extremely capable implementers. When provided with a challenge, a task or a project, they can organize and lead a team, manage the necessary stages and bring everything to a successful conclusion. They simply need the good idea or a defined goal.

Whilst an individual's personal talents will affect whether he or she operates most comfortably as an opportunity-spotter in a business, social, religious or artistic environment, project-championing skills and abilities are similar in every area of activity. It can be difficult, or even traumatic, when opportunity-spotters are not natural project champions but remain in charge of the project and fail to engage the necessary help and support. The story is told of Sir Christopher Wren over-running his completion deadline for St Paul's Cathedral by fifteen years. For the last two of these he was required to work without pay, in danger of imprisonment for alleged incompetence!

Small-business people spot a limited opportunity for something they can do, and choose to exploit it – but essentially that is where it stops. The opportunity does not have real growth potential. They are not true project champions. Or they do not behave habitually and keep finding further new opportunities to graft on to the business.

Managers who champion change in larger organizations are often project champions acting on behalf of their organizations. Sometimes they are encouraged to come up with new ideas and see them through to fruition – as we shall see in Chapter 2. They are known as intrapreneurs, or internal entrepreneurs.

It will be appreciated that a study of the 'action' factors is vital for understanding the entrepreneur process, but again, like the personality and environmental factors, it does not help us spot those people with the potential to be a successful entrepreneur. If we are to fully reveal the entrepreneur, we need more. Consequently, we now move to develop our approach based upon the three elements of talent, temperament and technique. We explain that talent and temperament factors are partly inherited and partly the outcome of early learning experiences. What is critical is that they are fundamental in our *habitual* behaviour, the things we do most readily, without thought, without hesitation and without undue effort. We identify the talent and temperament components found in the entrepreneur and stress that we expect to find some, but not all, of these to an outstanding degree in the successful entrepreneur. With this approach, it then becomes possible to identify the potential entrepreneur and monitor his or her development over time. The role of technique in this process is to impart skills and know-how but also to develop the talent and manage the temperament to produce outstanding performance. In Chapter 11 we discuss the importance of a trigger, something that causes a potential entrepreneur to emerge, to engage an opportunity and to do something about it. Without this trigger the process will neither start nor gather momentum. Instead, the entrepreneurial talent will lie dormant and there will be one less entrepreneur to help change the world.

Talent, temperament and technique

Len Hutton was perhaps the greatest opening batsman that England has ever produced. He had a *talent* as a batsman that few possess, he was a natural. The coach who took Hutton under his wing when he was 16 years old and taught him the *technique* of batting commented that 'no instructor was ever blessed with a more voracious learner' – a sure sign of real talent. Yet Hutton rarely gave his talent free rein because of his obsession with batting technique. He was a perfectionist always striving to improve so that his natural ability was often inhibited.

Temperament was Hutton's area of greatest ambiguity. His ability to focus and concentrate was legendary. He once batted for more than thirteen hours to set a world record individual score of 364. His weakness was his caution and low risk approach. He found it difficult to cope with stress and believed that 'tension was the root cause of failure and the bane of cricket'. He knew this from bitter experience for in his first match in county cricket and his first at international level he failed to score.

(Tyson, 1987)

Len Hutton's story is an example of the interplay between *talent*, *temperament* and *technique*. It shows the importance that each has but also how they combine to produce or limit excellence as the case may be. This trinity of talent, temperament and technique is like the three-legged stool, if one leg is missing it will fall over and if they are not all in balance it will be uncomfortable and even dangerous to sit on!

In this section we want to develop this tripartite approach as it applies to entrepreneurs. Whilst we will be talking mainly about talent and temperament, it does not mean that we relegate the importance of technique. We concentrate on talent and temperament because these are the areas where a case has to be made. The importance of technique for the entrepreneur is already well accepted, perhaps too much so for it cannot stand alone. Training courses and how-to-do-it books for entrepreneurs and those wanting to start a business are readily available.

We set out our approach under the following headings, in order systematically to build our profile of the entrepreneur:

- The entrepreneur among others.
- Linking talent, temperament and technique.
- Gallup's 'life themes'.
- Gallup's 'entrepreneur perceiver' interview.

- Towards a profile of the entrepreneur.
- The well of talent.

We explain how we have extended important work carried out over a number of years by the Gallup Organization to produce the ideas and themes for this section.

The entrepreneur among others

Each of us combines talent, temperament and technique in order to do what we do. Whether we are concert pianists or chess players, entrepreneurs or leaders, these three elements and their interaction decide whether we attain excellence or even greatness. What is special about the entrepreneur is the possession of a range of talents and a temperament profile that together with a specific skill set enables an individual to create and innovate to build something of recognized value. However, there is sufficient variety within these three elements for entrepreneurs to come in 'all shapes and sizes' which is why it proves so difficult to identify potential entrepreneurs and why known entrepreneurs are all so different – as the stories in Part Two confirm.

Another reason for this difficulty is the fact that the elements that are important to the entrepreneur are also to be found in others who are not entrepreneurs by our definition. In day-to-day conversation the word 'entrepreneurial' is used to describe a particular type of behaviour. If you are an inventor or a leader then you have some very specific characteristics in common with the entrepreneur.

By way of example, Table 1.1 breaks the three elements of talent, temperament and technique into some of their constituent parts. Here we seek to illustrate that whilst the entrepreneur possesses all these characteristics to some degree the others only possess some of them. Thus the true entrepreneur, the person who behaves entrepreneurially and the inventor all have creative talent, whereas the leader typically has little or none. Indeed, where he or she has creative talent, it might well prove a major handicap. In the same way, the temperament that is high on urgency differentiates true entrepreneurs from those who only demonstrate entrepreneurial behaviour. Inventors generally take their time, whereas urgency is an important

Table 1.1 *The entrepreneur among others*

Element	The entrepreneur	'Entrepreneurial' behaviour	The inventor	The leader
Talent	Creativity	Yes	Yes	Probably not
	Opportunity-spotting	Yes	Yes	Possibly
	Courage	No	Possibly	Yes
Temperament	Urgency	No	No	Yes
	Risk-taking	Yes	No	Possibly
	Ego drive	Possibly	Possibly	Yes
Technique	Financial skills	No	No	Possibly
	Planning skills	No	No	Yes
	Personnel skills	No	No	Yes

characteristic of a leader. The techniques that the entrepreneur has to master are fairly specific to the entrepreneur, though some are shared with leaders, particularly those concerned with planning and personnel.

An entrepreneur will possess to different degrees the attributes listed. Thus the entrepreneur who succeeds in an environment which is hostile to him or her is likely to be high on the 'courage' attribute. Some years ago we visited Brazil when inflation was around 600 per cent per annum – yet we found entrepreneurs there. These were remarkable people who we might describe as 'off the scale' in both courage and risk-taking! A successful inventor–entrepreneur like James Dyson (Chapter 3) will almost certainly be outstanding in the creativity attribute. A leader–entrepreneur like Richard Branson (also Chapter 3) will possess the entrepreneur attributes plus the attribute of 'vision', which is more typically associated with leaders.

In summary, we are saying that we all have a grouping of different talents and temperaments which together with techniques that we learn, enable us to fulfil a particular role so well that some of us can be described by a generic term such as entrepreneur, inventor or leader. Our concern here is with the grouping for the entrepreneur and how the elements interact. In Part Three we will return to a comparison of the entrepreneur and the leader.

Linking talent, temperament and technique

In cricket Tyson (1987) remarks that 'skill and success flow from the inner wells of temperament and character'. In athletics Harre (1982) comments: 'The athlete must bring to bear not only physical faculties, skill and intellectual abilities, but also willpower and character, moral convictions and traits.' It is, therefore, interesting to compare the prevailing media opinion concerning the current demise of the England cricket and football teams.

In 1998 a BBC Radio commentator, reviewing why England had again lost the Ashes series against Australia, commented that man for man both teams matched each other in talent and technique. The difference lay in their temperament. Australia had a will to win that the English team could not equal. In contrast, the character and commitment of English footballers is an acknowledged strength. Many of them repeatedly 'give everything' for the full ninety minutes of a match, but still the team fails to win. Passes go astray; shots fly past the post or go straight into the goalkeeper's hands; free kicks are conceded in dangerous positions. Few supporters will ever forget the team's failure in penalty shoot-outs at the end of important World Cup and European Cup matches. 'Footballers with a high standard of technical ability and coaches with a sophisticated understanding of the technical requirements of the modern international game . . . are missing' (Harverson, 1999). In other words, the weakness this time concerns talent and technique, not temperament.

Although we generally know what we mean by talent and temperament, and we can recognize them as different things, they remain difficult to define in a precise way. Yet, there is relatively little written about talent, and what there is often uses words other than 'talent' to describe the same thing. Thus Woods (1998) uses 'innate ability' which is closest to the dictionary definition. Others use words like 'strengths' (Clifton and Nelson, 1996), 'expertise' (Ericsson and Smith, 1991) and 'exceptional abilities' (Howe, 1990a). Psychologists often seem sceptical about the idea of 'gifts and talents' and see them as unscientific labels, though some are prepared to accept that there is truth in the claim that their origins are innate (Howe, 1990b).

Our view is that talent does exist, that we all have a collection of talents but that for a whole host of reasons we all too often fail to identify and therefore develop and exploit them. Sometimes the reason is found in our temperament, but on other occasions it is a matter of opportunity. By providing loans to the poor David Bussau (Chapter 5) showed that entrepreneurial talent does show itself when given the opportunity.

Temperament is a more 'academically respectable' word than talent and a number of recent books have brought new findings about temperament to the attention of the general public. Goleman (1996) tells us that 'temperament can be defined in terms of moods that typify our emotional life. To some degree we each have such a favoured emotional range; temperament is given at birth, part of the genetic lottery'. But he says that 'temperament is not destiny and that life's experiences, particularly the emotional lessons of childhood, can have a profound effect on temperament, either amplifying or muting an innate predisposition'. Whybrow (1999) and Buckingham and Coffman (1999) describe temperament respectively in terms of an 'emotional landscape' and 'highways through the brain' that are formed as we grow up and learn from our environment and experiences, but relate back to a genetic template.

For our purposes it is important to note that there is an inborn element in temperament that is later shaped by our environment, particularly in childhood. We can always act out of character in certain situations but our temperament defines our preferred emotional response.

We also see talent as inborn but with a potential to be developed. It is like a seed that needs the right environment if it is to flower and reach its full potential. By providing the setting for the talent seed, temperament is talent's emotional internal environment.

The role of technique is to train talent and temperament so that both are enhanced and can work jointly towards the achievement of excellence. There is some evidence of techniques that develop and refine the talent or that build temperament in key areas. We once spoke with a person who had achieved international standard in his chosen sport of rifle shooting. He explained that excellence in his sport required two opposites. You needed the concentration to hold the rifle perfectly still and the relaxation to pull the trigger without snatching. After research in the laboratory that monitored impulses in his brain he found he was able to exert the mental control to be both concentrated and relaxed at the same time. This learnt technique enabled him to move up from national to international standard and represent his country in the Olympics.

Figure 1.3 presents a nature–nurture model in which the starting point is our inborn talent and temperament. The processes involved to achieve excellence in our talent area must develop the talent, manage the temperament and impart technique. These processes include both structured and unstructured learning and experiences.

If we can clarify which elements of talent, temperament and technique are most commonly associated with successful entrepreneurs, then we can begin to draw up

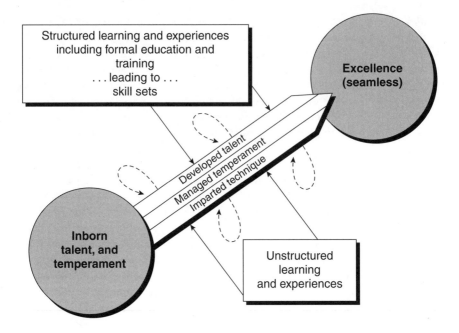

Figure 1.3   *Nature–nurture model*

an entrepreneur's profile. We have found that Gallup's analysis of life themes provides a valuable and robust framework for accomplishing this, and consequently, in the next section, we explain how Gallup has developed this work over a twenty-five-year period.

Gallup's 'life themes'

> Every person can do something better than 10,000 other people. It's OK to be you.
>
> (Jill Garrett, Managing Director, Gallup UK)

Gallup, although better known for its opinion polls, has had a strong interest in personnel selection over many years and has developed its own approach based on role and talent (Buckingham and Coffman, 1999). This side of their business was pioneered by Don Clifton, himself an entrepreneur, who was previously Professor of Educational Psychology at the University of Nebraska in the 1950s and 1960s. From his university base Clifton set up Selection Research Inc. (SRI) and became its full-time chief executive officer (CEO) in 1969. Over the next twenty years SRI developed a series of 'perceiver' interviews to identify and measure talent in many roles from professional athlete to religious leader. In 1987 SRI acquired Gallup of which Don Clifton became Chairman and his son, Jim Clifton, CEO.

Gallup use the term 'life theme' for talent which they describe as a 'person's innate behaviour, thoughts and feelings' (Garrett, 1998). Don Clifton defines it as 'a consistent and recurring pattern of thought and/or behaviour' (Clifton and Harding, 1986).

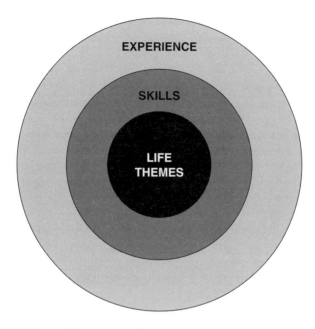

Figure 1.4 *The Gallup model*

Gallup's view that life themes come from an inner psychological core that is inborn and enduring is similar to that of Hollander (1971) reported earlier. Figure 1.4 shows the underpinning model used by Gallup, with life themes at the centre, surrounded first by skills and then by experience.

When the life themes, skills and experiences are the right ones for the job or task, then we have a person who can fulfil a given role with excellence. Gallup is very specific about the need for excellence and about what it means by *excellence*. It is not just better than average, or simply the opposite of bad, but it is 'the capacity for recurrent high levels of performance' (Garrett, 1998). Individually we are all capable of high achievement in some area of activity. If we can identify this activity, based on a person's real strengths, then we can exploit them to build satisfyingly high outcomes – but if we fail to diagnose someone's true strengths, there is an increased likelihood that they will be required to take on activities in which they are naturally weak. Not only is this deflating and stressful for the individual, it is a waste of a valuable resource.

Although in some ways Gallup's 'perceiver' interviews could be considered a variant of psychometric testing there are important differences. First, it is role rather than personality focused. Gallup works out the life themes for a particular role by using focus groups made up of people who are already performing to a high level in that role. From this input by high performers Gallup develops an appropriate questionnaire and identifies the replies their interviewer should be listening for.

Second, Gallup believes that each role has its own distinct combination of life themes. Excellence is achieved in a role by people who possess some but not all of these themes to an exceptional degree. The role of *leader*, for example, has twenty distinct life themes and a typical profile for an outstanding leader would have, perhaps, three *unsuppressible* themes, thirteen *habitual* themes and four themes *achievable with effort*. Thus Gallup looks for the presence of strengths in designated areas rather than seeks average competencies in a role. They are looking for 'Mr or Ms Something Special' rather than 'Mr or Ms Average'. It should be stressed that the twenty leader life themes can be in any mix as long as there are some that are unsuppressible. This is why leaders come in all shapes and sizes. Their personal style of leadership and the areas where they are found – from industry to the military, and from charities to exploration – are influenced by their profile of relative strengths across the twenty life themes, and by their circumstances that encourage them to follow certain paths. In exactly the same way entrepreneurs can be found in industry, in the community, in music – and even in criminal activity as we discuss in Chapter 7.

Buckingham and Coffman (1999) have summarized the work of Gallup (SRI) over the last twenty-five years. They use the word 'talent' when referring to life themes and by way of example provide a list of thirty-nine talents, which they have drawn from the study of more than 150 distinct roles. They group these talents into the following three basic categories:

1   *Striving* talents that explain the *why* of a person.
2   *Thinking* talents that explain the *how* of a person.
3   *Relating* talents that explain the *who* of a person.

Table 1.2 is a selection from their list of thirty-nine talents to show the general spread but are not representative of any specific role.

Inspection of Table 1.2 shows that there are two sets of classification possible. The first is the one used by Buckingham and Coffman with talents or life themes being either *striving, thinking* or *relating*. The second is found within their description of talents as *drives, needs* or *abilities*. Of the two we consider that our words 'talent' and 'temperament' correlate more closely with the second classification. Thus 'talent' equals *abilities* and 'temperament' divides into *needs* and *drives*, which are different sides of the same coin – the coin of 'temperament'. 'Technique' is not involved here because it is not a life theme but it does relate to the skill set that surrounds the life themes as Figure 1.4 indicates.

Figure 1.5 (page 38) shows in diagrammatic form how Gallup's abilities, needs and drives (from Table 1.2) can fit in with our terms, talent and temperament. In Buckingham and Coffman's (1999) full list of thirty-nine talents, twenty are *abilities*, fourteen are *needs* and five are *drives*. This suggests a 50:50 split between talent and temperament across the wide range of different roles to which these talents or life themes relate.

Gallup's 'entrepreneur perceiver' interview

In 1986 SRI developed an 'entrepreneur perceiver' questionnaire from a series of focus groups and interviews with successful entrepreneurs which identified twelve 'life themes' for the entrepreneur. These are set out in Table 1.3 and include some of those listed in Table 1.2 (indicated by an asterisk). The brief descriptions of each

Table 1.2 *A selection of Gallup's life themes*

Striving talents (six selected from eleven)

Achiever	A drive that is internal, constant and self-imposed
Competition	A need to gauge your success comparatively
Belief	A need to orient your life around prevailing values
Mission	A drive to put your beliefs into action
Service	A drive to be of service to others
Vision	A drive to paint value-based word pictures about the future

Thinking talents (seven selected from fourteen)

Focus	An ability to set goals and use them every day to guide actions
Responsibility	A need to assume personal accountability for your work
Performance orientation	A need to be objective and to measure performance
Strategic thinking	An ability to play out alternative scenarios in the future
Problem-solving	An ability to think things through with incomplete data
Formulation	An ability to find coherent patterns within incoherent data sets
Creativity	An ability to break existing configurations in favour of more effective/appealing ones

Relating talents (seven selected from fourteen)

Woo	A need to gain the approval of others
Multirelator	An ability to build an extensive network of acquaintances
Interpersonal	An ability to purposefully capitalize on relationships
Individualized perception	An awareness of and attentiveness to individual differences (ability)
Team	A need to build feelings of mutual support
Activator	An impatience to move others to action (drive)
Courage	An ability to use emotion to overcome resistance

Table 1.3 *The original Gallup entrepreneur themes*

Entrepreneur life themes	Summary description
1. Dedication	Consumed by a goal or purpose
2. Focus*	Discriminates and targets
3. Profit orientation	Advantage focused
4. Ego drive	Wants to make a recognized difference
5. Urgency	No time to waste, must take action now
6. Courage*	Determined in the face of adversity
7. Activator*	Wants to make it happen
8. Opportunity	Sees possibilities not problems
9. Creativity*	Buzzing with ideas
10. Expertise orientation	Knows own limits and finds experts
11. Team*	Gets the right people together
12. Individualized perception*	Sees and uses strengths in others

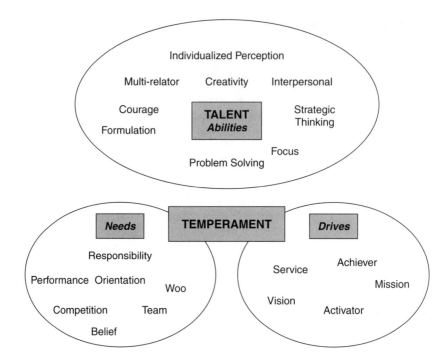

Figure 1.5 *Talent and temperament*

theme are our own based on more detailed descriptions provided to us by Don Clifton.

In practice these life themes rarely stand alone. For example *creativity* and *focus* come together in the entrepreneur so that the best ideas are identified and targeted effectively. *Courage* goes with *focus* in a similar way. *Opportunity* would not make progress without *urgency*. We see *urgency* as the extreme end of *activator* and close to mania discussed earlier. *Team* and *individual perception* work together.

As with the general Gallup approach the successful entrepreneur will possess some of these life themes to an exceptional degree but not all and they will be different for each entrepreneur, hence the diversity we find among entrepreneurs. However, some themes are more dominant or important than others. An unpublished study by Gallup of twenty entrepreneurs (Clifton and Harding, 1986) gives some indication of which they are. In the study entrepreneurs were taken through the 'entrepreneur perceiver' interview and the results evaluated statistically. When we compared the more successful entrepreneurs in the sample the themes that came out the strongest for them were *creativity, profit orientation, courage* and *focus,* and in that order.

Another way to see the inter-relation of these entrepreneur life themes is to set them within the context of the 'entrepreneurs' triangle' shown in Figure 1.6. This maps Gallup's twelve entrepreneur life themes in terms of the four broad activities involved in the entrepreneur process. These activities are:

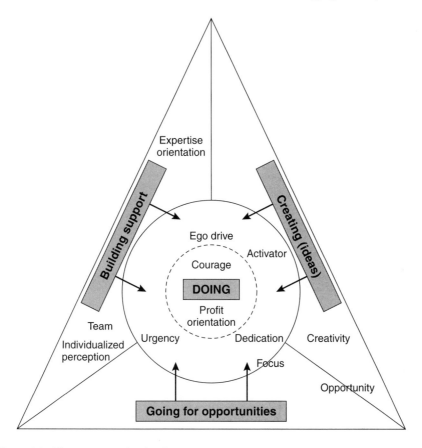

Figure 1.6   *The entrepreneur's triangle*

- Creating ideas
- Going for opprtunities   } *Opportunity-spotting*

- Building support
- Doing   } *Project-championing*

The outcome of these activities, of course, is the building of something of recognized value. It will be appreciated that 'creating ideas' and 'going for opportunities' relate to the opportunity-spotting we discussed earlier in the chapter; and that 'building support' and 'doing' corresponds to project-championing.

The entrepreneur's triangle shows that the special thing about the entrepreneur is creativity combined with the ability to identify and go for opportunities in a focused way. These two sides of the triangle are the special inputs required before any progress can be made. We see the third element of the triangle, 'building support', as important but not as something unique to the entrepreneur. When it comes to 'doing', courage and profit orientation are the distinguishing marks of the successful entrepreneur. The other 'doing' themes we see as important but not critical; they are secondary and not primary.

Towards a profile of the entrepreneur: talent, temperament and technique revisited

In this section we revisit 'talent' and 'temperament' and to a limited extent 'technique' in the light of the work reported above by Gallup and our own under-standing of the entrepreneur.

The Gallup/SRI 'entrepreneur perceiver' questionnaire has seven questions for each of the twelve themes, making eighty-four questions in all. We have assessed these questions and the preferred answers on the basis of whether they were talent-, temperament- or technique-related questions, or some combination of the three. We found that talent aspects were present in just over 30 per cent of the questions, temperament aspects in 70 per cent and technique in less than 15 per cent. If legitimate answers, rather than Gallup's preferred ones, were considered then the technique element was actually present in 45 per cent of the questions. This is because in technique-related questions we have taken both an entrepreneur answer and a business answer as legitimate.

The Gallup research was largely conducted in the 1980s, before Gallup switched its research emphasis to leadership characteristics. Our personal observations of many entrepreneurs in a variety of activities reinforce the significance of the twelve Gallup themes, but to provide a more comprehensive profile of the entrepreneur we would supplement the list. In this section we offer our opinion on those other, additional, life themes that we believe are relevant. This supplementary work should be seen as a refinement of Gallup's list; there is no contradiction in our findings.

In Table 1.4 we give our own preferred list of life themes for the entrepreneur. Notably, this adds other Gallup themes to those that they have identified for entre-preneurs, qualified with a few variations of our own.

To reduce the list in Table 1.4 to more manageable size we have grouped 'creativity', 'formulation' and 'problem-solving' under 'creativity'. Similarly 'team', 'individualized perception' and 'expertise orientation' are grouped under 'team'. 'Desire' (a need to claim significance through independence, excellence, risk and recognition) and 'urgency' are grouped under 'urgency'. Other things to note in this table are that 'opportunity' has been separated into 'opportunity-spotting' and 'opportunity-taking'. Additionally we prefer the words 'networker' to 'multirelator' and 'advantage orientation' to 'profit orientation'. We also add the new term 'resourcing' meaning 'an *ability* to identify and gather required resources'.

Figure 1.7 (page 42) presents the same information diagrammatically, adding three elements of technique to produce our life themes profile of the entrepreneur.

Our work with these themes continues, and on the basis of Figure 1.7 it would be possible to construct a new entrepreneur questionnaire which would identify the strengths of the entrepreneurs in each of the areas. When this is done then perhaps the progress of a selection of entrepreneurs could be monitored over time as the three elements develop. For example, there could be one response at the stage of identifying potential entrepreneurs, another when talent has been devel-oped and techniques learnt, and another when some experience had been gained.

To conclude this section, we return to our earlier distinction between the oppor-tunity-spotter, the project champion and the entrepreneur. Opportunity-spotters are

Table 1.4 *Profiling the entrepreneur*

Element	Entrepreneur themes	Summary themes
Talent (abilities both thinking and emotional)	Creativity ⎫	
	Formulation ⎬	Creativity
	Problem-solving ⎭	
	Courage	Courage
	Focus	Focus
	Opportunity-spotting	Opportunity-spotting
	Team ⎫	
	Individualized perception ⎬	Team
	Expertise orientation ⎭	
	Networker	Networker
	Advantage orientation	Advantage orientation
	Resourcing	Resourcing
Temperament (needs)	Competition	Competition
	Desire ⎫	
	Urgency ⎬	Urgency
	Opportunity-taking	Opportunity-taking
	Performance orientation	Performance orientation
	Responsibility	Responsibility
(drives)	Ego drive	Ego drive
	Mission	Mission
	Activator	Activator
	Dedication	Dedication

typically creative, and able to see things other people miss. They are formulators, able to find coherent patters from incoherent and often incomplete data. Project champions, on the other hand, are typically focused and strategic – they can conceptualize future scenarios before choosing a direction and broad strategy and then stick with it. They have a strong ego drive and a key talent for being able to grow something. Whilst the opportunity-spotter opens the window of opportunity, project champions are able to grasp and enact the opportunity. They can acquire and allocate resources; they are excellent networkers (something opportunity-spotters also do well); they can engineer and build winning teams. They are courageous and able to deal with hurdles and setbacks. Not unexpectedly, some of these project-championing life themes are also typically found in the leader.

Table 1.5 (page 43) takes the twenty-two life themes we used to profile the entrepreneur (Table 1.4) and re-presents them in the context of opportunity-spotting and project-championing. Some are relevant for both. The fact that more life themes can be attributed to the project champion (a ratio of 2:1 with the opportunity-spotter, in fact) reflects the reality that the really significant contribution of the true entrepreneur is that he or she builds something distinctive and valuable. But, of course, without the opportunity for making this difference, a person with some entrepreneurial talent will find him or herself championing something for somebody else.

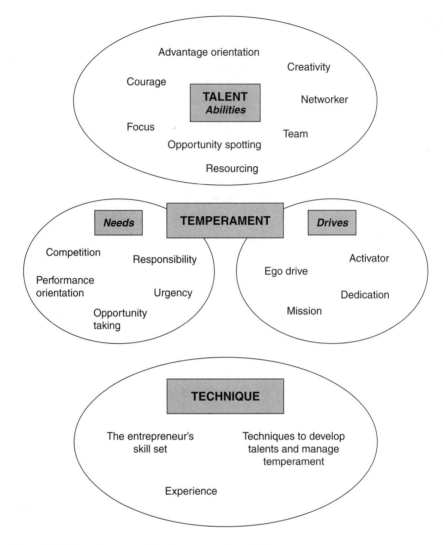

Figure 1.7   *The entrepreneur: talent, temperament and technique*

The well of talent

The time has come to broaden our notion of the spectrum of talents. The single most important contribution education can make to a child's development is to help him towards a field where his talents best suit him, where he will be satisfied and competent. We should spend less time ranking children and more time helping them to identify their natural competencies and gifts, and cultivate those.

(Howard Gardner, Harvard School of Education, in Goleman 1996)

Table 1.5 *The opportunity-spotter and the project champion: talent, temperament and technique*

	Talent	Temperament	Technique
Opportunity-spotting (being able to see and grasp the opportunity)	Creativity Formulation Opportunity-spotting	Mission	Techniques to develop talent
Project-championing (being able to grow something)	Problem-solving Courage Focus Team Expertise orientation Advantage orientation Individualized perception Resourcing	Competition Desire Urgency Opportunity-taking Performance orientation Ego drive	Techniques for managing temperament
Themes common to both	Networker	Responsibility Activator Dedication	Experience Skill set

When talent in sport has received serious attention the results have been outstanding. In the 1956 Olympics East Germany gained only seven medals, of which one was gold. Twelve years later in 1968 they achieved twenty-six medals including nine gold. Once their selection and training programme was in full swing the results were dramatic. In 1976 they won ninety medals, forty of them gold, and in 1980 126 medals of which forty-seven were gold.

The East German sports authority achieved this remarkable result by screening as many children as possible at age groups appropriate to the sport. For figure skating and gymnastics they started with children as young as four to six years. For sprinting and jumping the beginners' age was nine to twelve years. They identified talent through training. The greater the talent the quicker the learning. After the beginners' stage people moved through to advanced, final and top performance stages. They started with many and ended up with a few who then achieved excellence.

We believe that the identification and development of talent is one of the greatest challenges facing education today. If it can be done in sport we see no reason why it cannot be done with other talents. Our educational methods and our culture are the main obstacles. The examples we give in this book are clear proof of this statement. Most have become entrepreneurs in spite of the system and not because of it.

Within any group of people there is an amazing mix of talent but we fail to harness it because in the main we fail to recognize that it is there. Talent remains buried and therefore untapped in our society. Offering training to everyone, regardless of their talent and likelihood of succeeding, can be a mistake. In any field where we want to develop excellence, we have to identify those people with the 'right' talent and temperament for the task in hand, and focus our endeavours and investment on them.

Figure 1.8 shows our idea for a 'well of talent' with talents buried at different depths according to how difficult they are to get at and exploit.

We believe that *inventor* talent is the most deeply buried of all the talents in the UK although, of course, it is a talent that has great commercial value. Over the years various government schemes have tried to promote invention and innovation but to little avail. One reason for the lack of success apart from simple bureaucracy is that a *well of talent* approach has not been adopted. We were speaking recently to an inventor who suggested that if £20 million were made available across 200 inventors then we would see some remarkable results. In principle he is right because it is a talent approach to the problem.

The *follower* talent is the least buried and most easily tapped because our educational system operates that way. We educate people to work for somebody else and equip them to be employees rather than employers. They become competent followers.

Between the *follower* and the *inventor* we place *managers*, some of whom may be enterprising, *project champions*, *leaders* and *entrepreneurs*. Because we do not think in terms of talent, people become managers and leaders as they move up an organization, often unrelated to whether they have the talent to do so or not. In fact we reward talented managers by making them leaders and wonder why they perform badly. For many, the so-called Peter Principle, promotion to a level of incompetence, then applies.

Entrepreneurs are in an even worse position because there has been no reason for an organization to want them within a traditional hierarchy structure. When no one looks for them they are not found and remain buried. The move to flatter organizations and more dynamic flexible businesses means that entrepreneurs are now, finally, being talked about though even then we find we have to invent new words like intrapreneurs to describe entrepreneurs within the larger organization.

Using the analogy of drilling for oil, if we could only tap the pool of entrepreneurial talent buried amongst us then we would suddenly find an entrepreneurial pressure that we would need to cap and control. As it is we are happy that it seeps out of the ground now and then.

The first step towards tapping this entrepreneurial talent is to recognize that there is a considerable amount of it around and in Part Two we give examples of individual entrepreneurs and companies that demonstrate this. We begin Part Two with a chapter on legendary entrepreneurs. The life themes we have discussed are clearly visible in many of the stories and people described, reinforcing the value and potential of this fresh approach. We follow this with a chapter on business entrepreneurs which explains the vast range of opportunities that different, successful entrepreneurs engage and exploit; this chapter is an expansion of the points we next discuss in Chapter 2. Subsequent chapters in Part Two then consider entrepreneurs whose main contribution has been social and aesthetic capital, as distinct from financial capital creation. A brief discussion of entrepreneurs 'in the shadows', using examples of both failure and capital *destruction* precedes two chap-

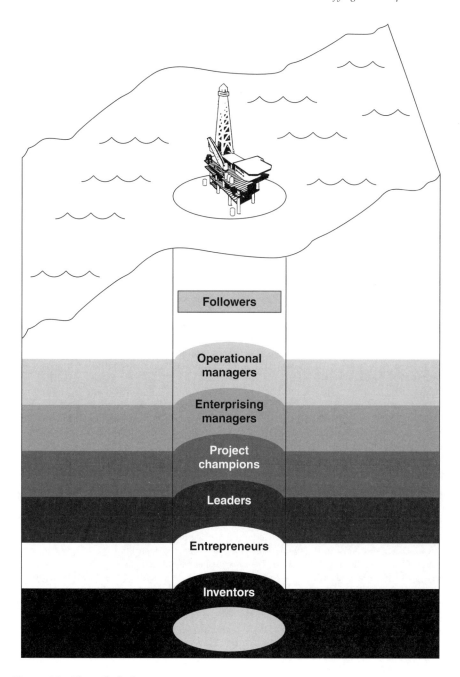

Figure 1.8 *The well of talent*

ters which look at entrepreneurs in the age of the Internet. The story of the development of Silicon Valley is followed by a chapter on the new Internet entrepreneurs.

The second step is to find ways of tapping and developing the pool of entrepreneurial talent so that it can make a difference to our economic and social well being. In Part Three we give our views as to how this might be achieved. Part Three systematically explores five themes:

1 The entrepreneur's world.
2 How the entrepreneur operates.
3 How the entrepreneur can be helped and supported.
4 How he survives and wins.
5 Techniques for the entrepreneur.

References

Bhide, A. (1994). How entrepreneurs craft strategies that work. *Harvard Business Review*, March–April.

Brockhaus, R. H. (1982). The psychology of the entrepreneur. In *Encyclopaedia of Entrepreneurship* (C. A. Kent, D. Sexton and K. Vesper, eds), Prentice Hall.

Brockhaus, R. H. and Horwitz, P. S. (1986). The psychology of the entrepreneur. In *The Art and Science of Entrepreneurship* (D. Sexton and R. W. Smilor, eds), Ballinger.

Brockhaus, R. H. and Nord, W. R. (1979). An exploration of factors affecting the entrepreneurial decision: personal characteristics vs environmental conditions. *Proceedings of the National Academy of Management*. NAC.

Buckingham, M. and Coffman, C. (1999). *First, Break All the Rules*. Simon and Schuster.

Burns, T. (1999) *Break the Curve: The Entrepreneur's Blueprint for Small Business Success*. International Thompson Business Press.

Burns, P. and Dewhurst, J. (eds) (1989). *Small Business and Entrepreneurship*. Macmillan Education.

Butler, G. and McManus, F. (1998). *Psychology*. Oxford University Press.

Buttner, E. H. (1992) Entrepreneurial stress: is it hazardous to your health? *Journal of Managerial Issues*, Summer, 223–240.

Churchill, N. C. (1997) *Breaking Down the Wall; Scaling the Ladder*. In *Mastering Enterprise* (S. Birley and D. Muzyka, eds), Financial Times/Pitman.

Clifton, D. O. and Harding, R. E. (1986). A statistical analysis of the psychometric properties of the SRI Entrepreneur Interview. *Gallup Report*, September.

Clifton, D. O. and Nelson, P. (1996). *Soar with your Strengths*. Dell Books.

Collins, O. F. and Moore, D. B. (1964). *The Enterprising Man*. Michigan State University Press.

Derlega, V. J., Winstead, B. A. and Jones, W. H. (1991). *Personality: Contemporary Theory and Research*. Nelson-Hall.

Derr, C. B. (1982) Living on adrenalin: the adventurer-entrepreneur. *Human Resource Management*, Summer.

Ericsson, K. A. and Smith, J. (eds) (1991). *Toward a General Theory of Expertise*. Cambridge University Press.

Eysenk, H. J. (1965). *Fact and Fiction in Psychology*. Penguin.

Forte, C. (1997). *Forte*. Pan Books.

Fukuyama, F. (1995). *Trust*. Hamish Hamilton.

Garrett, J. (1998). Gallup's discoveries about leaders. At work together, Spring Harvest Conference, Sheffield.

Gibb, A. (1998). In Management development for small and medium enterprises: setting out the challenge, *TEC National Council Policy Paper*, July.

Gilder, G. (1986). *The Spirit of Enterprise*. Penguin.
Goldsmith, M. and Wharton, M. (1993). *Knowing Me, Knowing You*. SPCK.
Goleman, D. (1996). *Emotional Intelligence*. Bloomsbury.
Hammer, H. (1988). *Hammer: Witness to History*. Coronet edn. Hodder and Stoughton.
Harre, D. (ed.) (1982). *Principles of Sports Training*. Sportverlag.
Harverson, P. (1999) A surfeit of character, *Financial Times*, 10 September, p. 5.
Hisrich, R. D. (1990). Entrepreneurship/intrapreneurship. *American Psychologist*, February, 209–222.
Hisrich, R. D. and Brush, C. (1984). The women entrepreneurs. *Journal of Small Business Management*, **22** (1), 31–37.
Hollander, E. P. (1971) *Principles and Methods of Social Psychology*. 2nd edn. Oxford University Press.
Hornaday, J. A. (1982) *Research about Living Entrepreneurs*. In *Encyclopaedia of Entrepreneurship* (C. A. Kent, D. L. Sexton and K. Vesper. eds), Prentice-Hall.
Howe, M. J. A. (1990a). *The Origins of Exceptional Ability*. Blackwell.
Howe, M. J. A. (ed.) (1990b). *Encouraging the Development of Exceptional Skills and Talents*. British Psychological Society.
Jones, S. (1993). *Psychological Testing for Managers*. Piatkus.
Kao, J. J. (1989). *Entrepreneurship, Creativity and Organisation*. Prentice-Hall.
Kao, J. J. (1991). *The Entrepreneur*. Prentice-Hall.
Kets de Vries, M. (1997). Creative rebels with a cause. In *Mastering Enterprise* (S. Birley and D. Muzyka, eds), Financial Times/Pitman.
Keirsey, D. and Bates, M. (1984). *Please Understand Me: Character and Temperament Types*, Prometheus Nemesis Books.
Kent, C. A. (ed.) (1984). *The Environment of Entrepreneurship*. Lexington Books.
Kummerow, J. M., Barger, N. J. and Kirby, L. K. (1997). *Work Types*. Warner Books.
Kuratko, D. F. and Hodgetts, R. M. (1998). *Entrepreneurship: A Contemporary Approach*. 4th edn. Dryden Press.
Larson, J. K. and Rogers, E. M. (1986). *Silicon Valley Fever*. Unwin Counterpoint.
Martens, R. A. (1976). Competitiveness and sport. International Congress of Physical Activity Sciences, Quebec City.
McClelland, D. C. (1961). *The Achieving Society*. Van Nostrand.
McClelland, D. C. (1965). Need for achievement and entrepreneurship: a longitudinal study. *Journal of Personality and Social Psychology*, **1**, 389–392.
McGrath, R. G. (1997). The parsimonious path to profit. In *Mastering Enterprise* (S. Birley and D. Muzyka, eds), Financial Times/Pitman.
Peters, T. (1989). *Thriving on Chaos*. Pan Books.
Roberts, E. B. (1991). *Entrepreneurs in High-Technology*. Oxford University Press.
Rotter, J. B. (1966). Generalised expectancies for internal versus external control of reinforcement. *Psychological Monographs*, **80**, 609.
Rotter, J. B. (1971) External control and internal control. *Psychology Today*, **5** (1), 37–42, 58–59.
Sider, R. (1996). *Bread of Life*. SPCK.
Steiner, R. (1998). *My First Break*. News International.
Stevenson, H. (1997). The six dimensions of entrepreneurship. In *Mastering Enterprise* (S. Birley and D. Muzyka, eds), Financial Times/Pitman.
Timmons, J. A. (1986). Growing up big: entrepreneurship and the creation of high-potential ventures. In *The Art and Science of Entrepreneurship* (D. Sexton and R. W. Smilor, eds), Ballinger.
Tyson, F. (1987). *The Test Within*. Hutchinson.
Vesper, K. H. (1980). *New Venture Strategies*. Prentice-Hall.
Wallace, J. and Erickson, J. (1993). *Hard Drive*. John Wiley.
Whybrow, P. C. (1999). *A Mood Apart*. Picador.
Williams, S. (1994). *Break-Out: Life beyond the Corporation*. Penguin.
Woods, B. (1998). *Applying Psychology in Sport*. Hodder and Stoughton.

2 Entrepreneurs and strategy

Strategy matters in entrepreneurship, but good ideas, in isolation, are inadequate – making things happen and implementing strategic ideas is a crucial element. In this chapter we look at how strategies are created, how they form, how they are implemented and how they are changed. We explore strategic positioning in relation to value-building opportunities and we consider how established organizations can promote and sustain growth through intrapreneurship, the encouragement of internal entrepreneurs. We conclude with a section on strategic weaknesses. The points raised here are then explored in greater detail in Chapter 4.

Entrepreneurs who succeed have a purpose and direction and they build value. They accomplish this with successful strategies, which we can define as 'means to ends' – ways of achieving objectives and fulfilling the purpose of the organization. Strategies are the things that businesses do, the paths they follow and the decisions they take in order to reach certain points and levels of success. The term *corporate strategy* is used for the range of activities, products and services embraced by the organization. At the beginning of an organization's life, there is likely to be only one or a very limited range of products or services, but this can expand considerably as the organization prospers. The growth can be focused around related activities or show increased diversity, although contemporary strategic wisdom would counsel against too much diversification, as diversity often fails to deliver synergistic benefits. As well as a range of complementary – synergistic – activities which all benefit from being part of the same organization, it is important that each activity is individually a strong competitor in its market or market segment. This implies it enjoys competitive advantage, an edge over its rivals, which comes from building values that customers appreciate and competitors find difficult to copy. These individual *competitive strategies* are themselves the result of a bundle or collection of functional activities and strategies, each of which relates to a particular aspect of, say, production, marketing, information or financial management. In this chapter we concentrate mainly on competitive strategy – reflected in strategic positioning – whilst recognizing that suitable and carefully timed acquisitions and divestments which change the scope and diversity of the organization can also be entrepreneurial and opportunistic.

As we have said earlier, entrepreneurs see or realize where there is an untapped opportunity, they engage it and they make things happen. There is often a visionary element to this for the idea alone is clearly inadequate and, indeed, the idea might not be original to the entrepreneur. It is what entrepreneurs do and achieve which holds the key to success. Figure 2.1 suggests that an idea becomes an opportunity when it promises an effective strategic position – which, in turn, implies a match between those factors that are critical for success with the customers in the targeted market and the knowledge, skills and competency the entrepreneur and the business can offer and provide. Figure 2.2 takes this argument further and relates it back to issues we discussed in Chapter 1. The opportunity-spotter realizes where there is a gap in the market, and has or sees an idea to fill it. The project champion grasps the opportunity and builds the business that successfully fills the market gap. The entrepreneur, of course, accomplishes both.

This success then brings its own demands. Entrepreneurs need to build a team of appropriate key support people and they need to ensure a suitable organization structure emerges – one which enables control as the business becomes more complex and the decisions that have to be made increase in magnitude. Whilst this happens the original idea and strategic position – the competitive strategy – will need constant refinement and improvement to sustain the growth and momentum, especially if competition intensifies. On occasions the relevant product or service

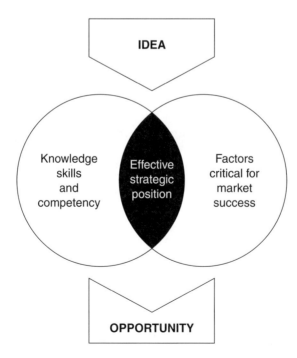

Figure 2.1 *From an idea to an opportunity*

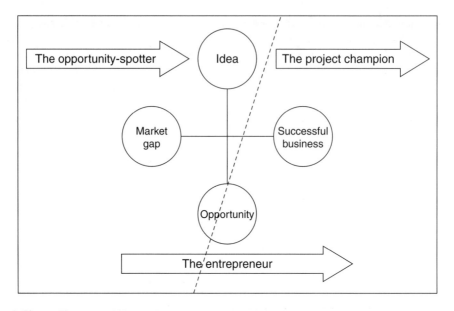

Figure 2.2   *The entrepreneur, the opportunity spotter and the project champion revisited*

may itself have to be abandoned and replaced by a new, fresh strategic idea and position. The emerging structure must not inhibit these changes; indeed it should positively encourage them.

As a summary of these points, Stevenson and Gumpert (1985) argue that entrepreneurs are opportunity driven and that they constantly seek answers to a series of key questions, namely:

- Where are the opportunities?
- How do I capitalize on them?
- What resources do I need?
- How do I gain control over them? We referred earlier to the fact that entrepreneurs use networks and contacts to 'beg, steal or borrow' suitable resources.
- What structure is best? Accepting that without this, renewal and growth is less likely to happen.

We can see these points brought together in Figure 2.3. The entrepreneur is placed in the centre of the diagram, the orchestrator of the whole process. His or her contribution is to input a vision, realize where there is an *opportunity*, engage it and stimulate action. To develop and grow effectively, the organization needs to find a *strategic position* in the market where it can offer – and be seen to be offering – something which provides value for the customer. Either the product or the service is different from everything else, and different in a meaningful way, or it offers 'better value', perhaps by being cheaper but not of inferior quality. The idea for the winning position can start with ideas from inside the organization, perhaps using new technologies to do new things, or it can be a response to issues raised by customers. Where it starts is less relevant than the need to bring together the

Path 1: Intrapreneurship/corporate entrepreneurship.
A flow of ideas from inside the organization

Path 2: Fresh ideas from an entrepreneurial strategic leadership

Figure 2.3 *The entrepreneur: seeing and activating opportunities*

customers' needs and the resources required to satisfy them. Finding this position, then, is the theme of *strategy creation*. Planning will play an important role in the process, but it may well be the actual implementation of the idea that is planned rather than the idea itself, which might have been realized more opportunistically, largely reliant on the entrepreneur's attentiveness and insight into the market. Plans should be flexible rather than rigid, as implementation is a learning process. Ideas are refined with experience. It is impossible to foresee all the issues involved in activating the idea.

As we move further with *strategy implementation*, the team- and organization-building we discussed above become increasingly significant. But, and again reinforcing points made above, strong and winning strategic positions will have finite lives, which in today's world can be relatively short ones. Successful companies attract competitors, who are themselves looking for new, profitable opportunities. Success is maintained by innovation and *strategic change*, which keeps an organization perpetually one step (or even more) ahead of its competitors. The Path 1 loop in Figure 2.3 highlights how intrapreneurship can foster new ideas and improvements in a flexible and entrepreneurial organization. Generally, here, we are implying changes to functional and competitive strategies. New ideas, of course, may well be input by the founding entrepreneur – Path 2 in the diagram. Sustained growth really needs more than one source of ideas; realistically, major changes to the overall corporate strategy will require a significant input from the strategic leader. Where there is a string of these 'giant steps', they are often linked to visionary entrepreneurs – whom we discuss below.

The key message is that opportunity → strategy → implementation is a circular loop and it must be maintained with change. The successful entrepreneur will make sure there is a constant flow of new ideas and a commitment to try out at least some of these new ideas. If an organization loses this momentum and the ideas dry up, perhaps because the developing structure promotes order and control rather than flexibility and change, the organization will, sooner or later, hit a crisis point – as we will discover later in this chapter. When this happens it is likely that a change of strategic leader will be needed before growth can be restored, always assuming it is not too late!

> Where a company comes from is less important than where it is going. As boundaries are erased, corporate birth certificates won't count for much.
>
> (Ron Sommer, when President, Sony Corporation of America)

To conclude this section the following list cross-relates Figure 2.3 with some of the ten key action points on what entrepreneurs do, which we explained in Chapter 1:

- *Strategic positioning*: spotting and exploiting opportunities; prioritizing customers' interests; creating value.
- *Strategy implementation*: finding the resources required; understanding and managing the risks involved.
- *Strategic change*: ensuring there is creativity and innovation in the business.

The visionary entrepreneur

Mintzberg, Ahlstrand and Lampel (1998) contend that for a visionary entrepreneur, strategy is a mental representation of the successful position or competitive paradigm[1] inside his or her head. It could be thought through quite carefully or it could be largely intuitive. This representation, or insight, then serves as an inspirational driving force for the organization. The vision or idea alone is inadequate; the entrepreneur must persuade others – customers, partners, employees and suppliers – to see it, share it and support it. Flexibility will always be an inherent factor; detail emerges through experience and learning.

Kets de Vries (1996) concludes that the most successful strategic leaders perform two key roles, a charismatic role and an architectural one, effectively. As a result, their strategies are owned, customers are satisfied, employees enjoy work and things can, and do, happen and change quickly. The charismatic role involves establishing and gaining support for a (winning) vision and direction, empowering employees and 'energizing' them, gaining their enthusiastic support for what has to be done. The architectural role concerns building an appropriate organization structure, together with systems for controlling and rewarding people. We can see that these arguments embrace visionary entrepreneurs and a process of intrapreneurship within the organization.

Related to this latter point, Hamel (1999) distinguishes between stewardship and entrepreneurship. Stewardship concerns the continued exploitation of opportunities spotted in the past. Costs will be managed for efficiencies; some incremental changes and improvements will be made to reinforce the strategic position in a competitive environment. On its own, however, in an increasingly dynamic environment, this may well prove inadequate. Hamel uses the metaphor of Silicon Valley[2] to contend that organizations need to bring together new ideas, talented and entrepreneurial managers, and the resources they need in order to exploit new opportunities in an entrepreneurial way. The style of these people is dictated more by aspiration than it is by analysis – hence their link to the visionary entrepreneur.

We have extended these ideas in Figure 2.4. Here we argue that an underemphasis on the visionary, charismatic role and an overemphasis on structure and procedures results in a bureaucratic organization which is risk averse, likely to miss new opportunities and eventually, as a result, becomes crisis prone. At the other extreme, an overemphasis on the visionary role at the expense of adequate structure and systems implies an opportunistic 'cowboy' who takes unnecessarily high risks and again becomes prone to crises. The term 'adventurer entrepreneurs' has been adopted by Derr (1982) to describe people who take risks that others would perceive to be high ones. 'They live on adrenalin; those who work with them live on Valium.' They are able to exercise some control over the risks they perceive to be manageable. Entrepreneurs, entrepreneurial leaders and enterprising managers all balance the two roles in order to manage both opportunities and risks effectively.

For Mintzberg, Ahlstrand and Lampel (1998), visionary entrepreneurs often, but not always, conceptualize the winning strategic position as a result of immersion in the industry. They may simply have a genuine interest; equally they may have worked in the industry for some length of time. Their secret is an ability to learn and understand, making sense of their experiences and the signals they see. Whilst some people would never be able to make sense of a pattern of strategic signals pertinent to an industry, others learn very quickly.

> There are two types of people in the world – reasonable and unreasonable.
> A reasonable man adapts himself to the world; the unreasonable man persists
> in trying to adapt the world to himself.
>
> (George Bernard Shaw)

This quotation from Shaw appears to reinforce the relative merits of two schools of thought concerning what entrepreneurs are actually doing. Schumpeter (1949)

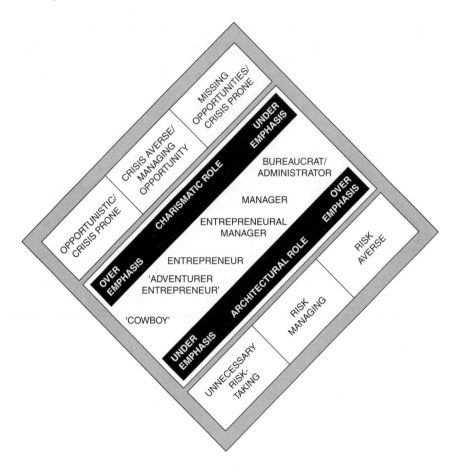

Figure 2.4 *Entrepreneurship, opportunity and risk*

believes that entrepreneurs disturb the existing market equilibrium and stability with innovation, whilst the so-called Austrian School of Economists (see, for example, Kirzner, 1973) contend that entrepreneurs actually create equilibrium and market stability by finding new, clear, positive strategic positions in a business environment characterized by chaos and turbulence. The Austrian perspective is that of the reasonable man who observes chaos and uncertainty, and looks for an opportunity gap that others have missed. Schumpeter's innovators are unreasonable; they are trying to disturb the status quo, turn things upside down, find new strategic positions and make life hard for any existing competitors. Blanchard and Waghorn (1997) claim that Ted Turner (CNN) and Steve Jobs (Apple) are unreasonable men who, like entrepreneurs in the mobile phones business, have been instrumental in changing the world we know.

Successful visionary, aspirational entrepreneurs, then, are not all the same. It is simply that when they emerge from our so-called 'well of talent' they follow different paths. In Figure 2.5, hard entrepreneurship represents the paradigm of

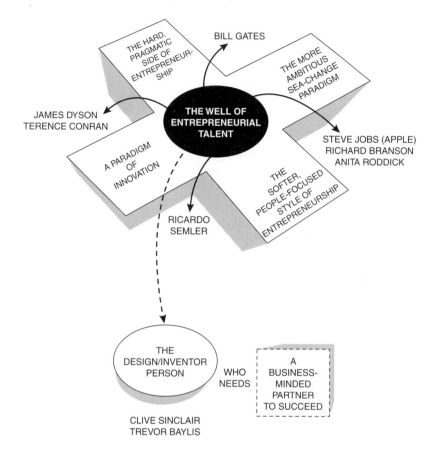

Figure 2.5 *Four dimensions of entrepreneurship*

the independent, pragmatic, opportunistic and competitive entrepreneur. These achievement-oriented people are our typical managed risk takers and natural networkers in search of a deal. Not every entrepreneur fits this pattern. Some present a softer image. They operate in a more informal manner; they are strong on communication and they sell their vision to engage and motivate others. The hard and soft approaches lead to quite different cultures, of course.

Some visionary, adventurous entrepreneurs set out to change the world. These are people with a real ability to galvanize others; they work hard, play hard and operate at the leading edge. They have to have enormous energy and generally they would be described as 'having a presence'. Again this approach is not, and need not, be ubiquitous. The fourth arm, innovation, still requires imagination, creativity, passion and a commitment to bring about change (see Lessem, 1986; 1998).

We would suggest that Bill Gates is a typical hard adventurer – Microsoft has literally changed the world of computing – whilst James Dyson is a hard innovator. Steve Jobs, Richard Branson and Anita Roddick are certainly visionaries – their products have had a major impact on our lives – but they have all adopted a softer style and approach. Ricardo Semler is a visionary as far as management style is concerned, but Semco's engineering products – they include pumps and industrial dishwashers – are hardly revolutionary. He appears to typify the soft innovator.

There is a final category. The designer-inventor who lacks the necessary business acumen or interest to build the business on his or her own. Sir Clive Sinclair and Trevor Baylis fit here. All of these entrepreneurs are discussed in Part Two.

The entrepreneur's environment

The future was predictable – though very few predicted it!
(Allen Kay, when Research Fellow, Apple Computer)

Hamel (1997) argues that a changing business (or external) environment opens up the possibility for finding new business and competitive opportunities all the time. There are opportunities for entrepreneurs and the entrepreneurially minded organization; for the others there are threats. He cites globalization, shorter product and service life cycles (linked to technology improvements and to consumer willingness to change more frequently than in the past) and faster, more sophisticated communication networks as typical sources of opportunity. He explains that there are known and visible areas of opportunity – such as gene-engineered drugs, non-branch banking and multimedia – but stresses the secret lies in finding the 'right' strategic position to exploit the opportunity. As we have already said, because of the constant environmental turbulence any strategic position must be seen as temporary and sensitive to unexpected events; innovation is needed to reinforce and defend a position of strength.

Without constant improvement, renewal and intrapreneurship there are obvious dangers in this changing environment, but alone this may well prove inadequate. The most entrepreneurial companies will, at the same time, be searching for new ways of competing. Linked to this is the difficulty for many organizations that future competitive threats are as likely to come from unknown or unexpected organizations currently outside the industry as they are from existing, known rivals. In the early 1980s it is highly likely that British Airways was particularly concerned with the possible actions over routes and fares by its main American and European rivals; it seems much more improbable that they anticipated the threat that Richard Branson and Virgin Atlantic was going to pose. British Airways may well have recognized the potential for new competitors as deregulation changed the air travel environment, but predicting the source was another matter. As we will see in Chapter 4, the outsider, Direct Line, had the same impact on the insurance industry.

Successful entrepreneurs find new products and new needs ahead of both their rivals and their customers. Market research can tap into issues that are important for customers, but it is unlikely to provide the answers. Creativity, insight and innovation stimulated within the organization is more likely to achieve this. Entrepreneurs and entrepreneurial organizations thus *create proprietary foresight from public knowledge* by synthesizing information and environmental signals and creating new patterns and opportunities.

This intellectual foresight has a number of possible sources according to Hamel and Prahalad (1994):

- It can be a personal restlessness with the existing status quo – the Schumpeter view. In Chapter 4 we point out that the serial entrepreneur Paul Sykes was, from an early age, not content with his lot.
- It can be a natural curiosity – which the education system does not manage to stifle – that leads to creativity. Sometimes the entrepreneurs concerned have a childlike innocence in the questions they ask, and the process is stimulated by a wide network of contacts.
- It may be a willingness on the part of certain individuals to speculate and manage the risk of investigation. Invention has to precede learning.
- It is sometimes a desire to change things and 'leave footprints'.
- Often there is an empathy with the industry and market concerned, coupled with
- The ability to conceptualize what does not yet exist . . . 'you can't create a future you can't imagine'.

Strategic positioning

E-V-R congruence

Figure 2.6 develops ideas in Thompson (1997) and shows strategic positioning as an overlap between the business environment and the organization's resources. In other words, the organization possesses strategic or core competencies which enable it to meet the relevant environmental key success factors effectively – an analysis which, essentially, can be traced back to a strengths, weaknesses, opportunities, threats (SWOT) analysis. This accords with Porter's (1996) view that strategic positioning, *per se*, is not a source of competitive advantage. Positions can be understood by competitors and copied. The activities that create, and sustain with change, the position are the source of any advantage. It is through activities that organizations build value. As we have said, positions must be seen as temporary. To ensure there is ongoing opportunity recognition, together with an ability and commitment to change, values is shown as a third circle, the overlap of this with the others creating an overall E-V-R congruence. It is useful to see 'values' representing the organization culture and style of management, themselves dependent upon the style and approach of the strategic leader.

Figure 2.7 recrafts this basic model and shows entrepreneurship as the key factor in balancing strategic competencies with windows of opportunity. Windows of opportunity are always opening in the environment – but, to exploit the opportunity, organizations – and entrepreneurs – must first spot them and then capture them ahead of any rivals by obtaining and deploying the necessary resources in an appropriate way. Sometimes the resources needed will already be available; on other occasions they will have to be found.

The alternative, and equally valid, resource-based approach to strategy emphasizes that organizations must be aware of their main strengths, skills and

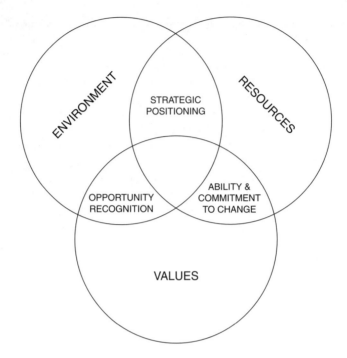

Figure 2.6   *E-V-R congruence*

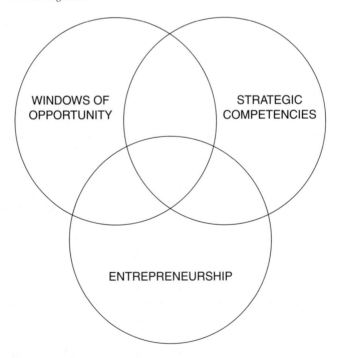

Figure 2.7   *Entrepreneurship and E-V-R congruence*

competencies, and be constantly vigilant for new opportunities for deploying and exploiting them. Prahalad and Hamel (1990) define core competencies as those distinctive skills which yield competitive advantage because they provide access to important market areas or segments, make a significant contribution to the perceived customer benefits of the product or service and, particularly, prove difficult for competitors to imitate.

These two approaches should be seen as complementary and used together.

Figure 2.8 brings in our earlier points about strategic change. Single-loop learning around an existing strategic position and competitive paradigm should result in continuous improvement through innovation and greater operating efficiencies. Parallel to this, more visionary double-loop learning is required to find those new positions which represent real change and movement away from existing ways of competing. The sources of information and the thinking processes are different for single and double-loop learning; and some managers and employees will be much more comfortable with one than with the other.

Competitive divergence

Porter (1996; 1997) concludes that strategy is 'about doing things differently from your rivals'. It involves trade-offs and, in particular, critical decisions about what not to do and where not to compete. In this respect, Porter highlights the key need

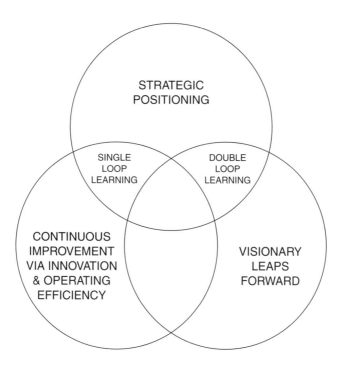

Figure 2.8 *Entrepreneurship and strategic change*

for strategic focus. However, he points out that in many industries there is more evidence of competitor *convergence* than there is of difference and *divergence*. Divergers – and entrepreneurs – create and build value where it can make a difference; they do not concentrate and focus on things that are only of limited significance to their customers. These rule-breakers look to tread new ground rather than copy what everyone else is already doing. They are creative innovators. They are likely to gain only limited benefit from those consultants who import ideas they have seen work elsewhere. In addition, they carefully select which customers and market niches actually matter to them and focus on these. Together these issues and choices represent strategic positioning decisions.

Porter nominates the company Enterprise as a successful, different, divergent competitor in the car rental industry. The main names we would recognize and recall are Avis, Hertz, Budget, National and Alamo. They all compete with each other for business. Their prices do vary, and different customers have different perceptions of their service, typically based on their experiences with the cars and, in particular, with their staff. Around the world, much of their business comes from people on the move and their desks can usually be found in airport terminals. Enterprise is family run; it is more profitable than either Avis or Hertz – although smaller – and it avoids airport locations. Instead Enterprise has targeted customers whose cars are off the road for whatever reason. Perhaps they are being serviced or repaired; perhaps they have been involved in an accident. They access many of their customers through car dealers and insurance companies. They are willing to deliver cars to the customer (although clearly this does not make them unique) and they seem able to keep their cars longer – thus reducing their costs and allowing them to pass on these savings in competitive prices.

Strategic differences and divergence come from organizational activities and their unique bundling – which constitutes the way things are done in an organization. We can see this as 'values' in the E-V-R congruence model above. It is an implementation issue. In Chapter 6 we explain the long-term, consistent success of Southwest Air in America, suggesting that whilst all Southwest's rivals know what the strategy is, it is the implementation, and the synergistic bundle of activities which support this, that make the difference.

Simon (1996) reinforces this point by separating three main levels of competitive difference and advantage. The first, and lowest, level is technology and products. Patents can help, but often these can be overcome and good ideas copied. The second level is the organization itself, with its *operating* processes and systems. Although more difficult, these are again visible to some degree, and can be copied. People comprise the third and highest level. The processes they utilize, individually and collectively, to deliver service are the hidden resource that provides the most potent competitive weapon.

Porter distinguishes between three positioning approaches:

1 Begin with the (different) product or service, built around important, core strategic competencies, and offer the same product or service to anyone who might be interested.

    Bic pens are widely available. They are sold through a wide range of retail outlets; they are used by many organizations, such as hotel groups, for promotional items and low-cost give-aways.

Southwest Air provides a no-frills, short-haul, point-to-point service between medium-size cities and secondary airports in large cities. Different groups of business and leisure traveller find Southwest's service and prices attractive.

2 Target a specific segment of the market and provide a range of products to meet a range of needs for the relevant target customers.

> Ikea shall offer a wide range of home furnishing items of good design and function at prices so low that a majority of people can afford to buy them.
>
> (Ikea mission statement)

Ikea's *main* target customers are young or first-time homeowners who are looking for modern styles at affordable prices. To satisfy this need Ikea have chosen to focus on certain strategies and ignore or sacrifice others – their carefully chosen trade-offs. There is only a limited choice of each product line (many competitors offer wider ranges); the majority of products are exclusive to Ikea and other brands are not available; expensive materials and style is traded off against affordable prices; customers self-select rather than find help from sales assistants; and every store carries a large inventory, allowing for customers to buy on the spot – whilst many rivals carry only display items and rely on warehouse deliveries to people's homes.

3 Focus on a single product or service for a tightly defined niche. The small, footwear business which switched to focus on the fetish market – which we discuss in Chapter 4 (page 99) – illustrates this approach.

Developing new strategies and positions

To deal effectively with the challenges of the future, and reinforcing points we have made earlier, Hamel (1994) argues that the organization must go through three distinct but overlapping stages if it is survive in a dynamic environment and capitalize on Path 1 growth opportunities. First, it must conceive a future position by competing for intellectual leadership in its chosen industry. To accomplish this it must understand the relevant technology, the market and the regulatory environment – and, in particular, any discontinuities that are likely to have an impact. Second, it must gestate the strategy by acquiring the resources and competencies necessary to be a strong player and to be able to deal with the identified discontinuities. These resources will embrace technology and people and may be acquired with carefully selected alliance partners. Few companies possess all the competencies they will need. Nike, for example, developed competencies in product design and supplier-sourcing and secured important endorsements from international sports stars. They realized that manufacturing was not an essential requirement if they worked with the right partners and suppliers. The resources must then be deployed to compete for position and market share. The third stage is to actually implement the strategy and deliver the promise.

Thompson (1997) offers the following criteria for evaluating proposed new strategies:

- *Appropriateness*: is it a potentially winning strategic position?
- *Feasibility*: can it be implemented? Are the necessary resources available or obtainable?
- *Desirability*: is there a belief in it and a will to follow it through?

Building the organization

Entrepreneurs possess a number of leadership characteristics; they set direction and they inspire others. But their strong leadership should not throttle flexibility and learning by a resistance to trusting other managers and involving them in key decisions. The most successful entrepreneurs realize they cannot do everything on their own and they build a team to whom they can delegate important decisions and contributions. Whilst some of these people will, by necessity, be specialists, professionals and technocrats, Horovitz (1997) stresses the importance of also recruiting or developing entrepreneurial managers to ensure the flow of innovation and change and to prevent entropy. He argues that one of the reasons Club Méditerranée lost momentum in the 1990s was the result of a failure to accomplish this backfilling effectively. Quinn (1980) also emphasizes the importance of innovation and ongoing learning by this team because all the issues and difficulties that will have to be faced cannot be foreseen.

> The aim in a global business is to get the best ideas from everywhere. *[In General Electric]* each team puts up its best ideas and processes constantly. That raises the bar. Our culture is designed around making a hero out of those who translate ideas from one place to another, who get help from somebody else. They get an award, they get praised and promoted.
>
> (Jack Welch, Chief Executive, General Electric)

Horovitz (1997) contends organizations should look for the problems before they even arise, by questioning what the (possibly very successful) organization is doing wrong. At times it is important to abandon products, services and strategies that have served the organization well in the past – they are not the future. Kanter (1989) goes further still by arguing that the whole organization holds the key to competitive advantage. She suggests that there are five criteria that are found in successful, entrepreneurial organizations. They are:

1 *Focused* on essential core competencies and long-term values.
2 *Flexible* – searching for new opportunities and new internal and external synergies with the belief that ever-increasing returns and results can be obtained from the same resources if they are developed properly and innovatively.
3 *Friendly* – recognizing the power of alliances in the search for new competencies.
4 *Fast* and able to act at the right time to get ahead and stay ahead of competitors.
5 *Fun* – creative and with a culture which features some irreverence in the search for ways to be different; people feel free to express themselves.

In an earlier book, Kanter (1983) warned about the potential for stifling innovation by:

- blocking ideas from lower down the organization, on the grounds that only senior or very experienced managers are in a position to spot new opportunities. On the contrary, she argues, younger people with fresh minds are in an excellent position to question and challenge the status quo
- building too many levels in the hierarchy so that decision-making is slowed almost to a point of non-existence
- withholding praise from people who do offer good, innovative ideas, and instilling a culture of insecurity so that people feel too terrified to even question authority, policies or procedures
- being unwilling to innovate until someone else has tried out the idea – a fear of leading change.

In Chapters 3 and 4 we consider the success stories of Wal-Mart, Asda and Richer Sounds, all of which have benefited substantially from involving employees widely in new strategy creation.

Whilst robust questioning and assumption-testing of new ideas is crucial, it is particularly important to remember that many people fear change, partly because of uncertainty about its impact on them personally. As a result, some people will seek to resist valuable change initiatives, and may even attempt to mount an active and orchestrated opposition. They are, in fact, enterprising and entrepreneurial, but they channel their energy in an unhelpful way. Their tactics may be aimed at preventing an idea ever taking off; equally they may wait until it has taken root and is gaining some support and momentum. Managing change effectively, therefore, requires continuous effort and sometimes patience – reinforcing the significant contribution made by the project champion.

The process of intrapreneurship

Bridge, O'Neill and Cromie (1998) highlight the importance of recruiting, spotting and using people with entrepreneurial talent who are motivated to use their abilities and initiative and do something on their own, but who may not want to start their own business. These internal entrepreneurs have been called *intrapreneurs* by Pinchot (1985) and they are instrumental in effective Path 2 growth. 'Intrapreneurship', then, is the term given to the establishment and fostering of entrepreneurial activity in large organizations which results in incremental improvements to existing products and services and occasionally to brand new products. We can see an illustration of this with the example of 3M and Post-it notes (explained in Chapter 4) but it is an extreme. The innovation is more likely to be a minor, but significant, improvement to a product or service or process – anything that makes a valuable difference.

Intrapreneurs, typically, are strategically aware, ideas-driven, creative, flexible, innovative, good networkers, individualistic but also able to work well in a team, persistent and courageous. If frustrated by a lack of freedom they will underachieve or possibly leave. But they are volunteers; intrapreneurship is not right for everyone.

According to Pinchot (1985), the key lies in engaging people's efforts and energy for championing, capturing and exploiting new ideas and strategic changes. This must stretch beyond the most senior managers in the organization – who do not have a monopoly on good ideas. On the contrary, the potentially most valuable and lucrative ideas are likely to come from those people who are closest to the latest developments in technology or to customers. Suggestion schemes are linked in, but on their own do not constitute intrapreneurship. The ideas need to be taken forward, and they can only be developed if the potential intrapreneurs are able to obtain the necessary internal resources – and, moreover, they are willing to do something. This in turn requires encouragement and appropriate rewards for success. People must feel involved in the process and comfortable they are being supported. Intrapreneurship cannot work where people feel 'frozen out' or 'dumped on'. Churchill (1997) summarizes the philosophy as skills following opportunities. People in entrepreneurial businesses see the opportunities and set about acquiring the necessary resources. The whole process of change then becomes gradual and evolutionary. The momentum for change and improvement is never lost and the organization is less likely to be exposed and weakened by its competitors, resulting in it having to cross a 'bridge too far'.

Maitland (1999) has described how Bass developed new pub brands. In the early 1990s Bass's traditional customers (older people, and more working class than middle class) were deserting pubs; young people became the new target. '[Bass] needed a radical "break-out" strategy of new product development and concept innovation.' Bass spotted the new It's A Scream format, conceived by entrepreneur David Lee and popular with students. Lee was a builder in Farnham who had been given a pub in lieu of an unpaid debt and had transformed it. Bass bought the pub and the concept, and recruited Lee as a consultant with a profit-share and a fixed fee for every new It's A Scream pub which opens. The All Bar One theme pubs, an up-market, well-lit, city-centre chain with large windows which attracts young female drinkers on their own, reflects a similar story. At the same time, other initiatives have been developed from ideas put forward by existing managers, who have been offered secondment to champion their project ideas. Bass recognized the importance of visible support and encouragement from the top so this became an engineered and not a random process. Bass also ensured that adequate financial resources were available. In other words, they brought together ideas, talented intrapreneurs and the resources they needed.

To summarize these points, Hurst (1995) likens entrepreneurial strategists to gardeners. They prune. They clear out. They plant – by recruiting other entrepreneurial managers. They feed – by encouraging and rewarding managers for being creative and innovative. They simply nurture and manage the organization as they would a garden. Paradoxically, many good ideas begin in the same way that weeds emerge in a garden – randomly. They then need spotting and looking after – the equivalent of transfer to a hothouse?

The intrapreneurial organization

Fradette and Michaud (1998) describe four main elements to an organization that succeeds with intrapreneurship. First, the strategic and structural environment is 'right'. The purpose and direction implies a realistic vision and it is widely understood and shared. Formal systems and controls do not stifle innovation and people are free to make limited changes. Inhibitive internal 'chimneys' are pulled down so people can collaborate and share ideas readily. Second, an appropriate workforce has been built. Enterprising people – with entrepreneurial talent and temperament – have been recruited. They have been trained in key skills and there is an appropriate reward system. The organization's main heroes and heroines are the entrepreneurial ones. Third, the workforce is backed by the necessary support systems. Teamworking is commonplace, people collaborate and network naturally, information is shared and learning is fostered. After all, several people in the organization may be thinking along the same lines at the same time about future possibilities. Fourth, successes are visibly rewarded and mistakes are not sanctioned so harshly that people are dissuaded from further initiatives.

An intrapreneurial organization will often feature a relatively flat structure with few layers in the hierarchy – too many layers tend to slow down decision-making. The culture and atmosphere will be one of collaboration and trust. The style of management will be more coaching than instructional, and mentoring will be in evidence. Ideally it will be an exciting place to work. The entrepreneur's enthusiasm will have spread to others.

Terazano (1999), however, reminds us that effective intrapreneurship is not that easily achieved, and that many organizations set off down the road but fail to reap the anticipated rewards. Balancing control (to ensure current activities and strategies are implemented efficiently) with flexibility (to foster and embrace changes to the same strategies) can imply different cultures, which are difficult to achieve without tension and conflict. Another difficulty frequently lies with finding the appropriate reward and remuneration systems to ensure fairness. It is a brave organization that only awards bonuses to the visibly entrepreneurial people. Managers in established companies often find it difficult to handle setbacks and disappointments when initiatives fail. But there always has to be the risk of failure – albeit temporary – when experimenting with new and unproven ideas. Whilst intrapreneurs often have the security of large company employment, such that the penalty for failure is to some extent protected, the rewards for real success are unlikely to equal those of the true entrepreneur. Nevertheless 'increased competition in global markets and the pressure for innovation is forcing Britain's large companies to look for methods to stimulate ideas for new products'.

Corporate strategic change

Companies typically grow around a range of related products and services, at times extending the range or replacing models, and seeking new market opportunities. If growth ambitions start to exceed the growth potential from these somewhat limited strategies, they may look at more ambitious alternatives. Investing in their supply chain (by, say, acquiring a supplier or a distributor) is one possibility, but this invariably requires the subsequent development of new competencies. Acquiring a direct competitor or a related business is another possibility; here the organization is seeking to build on its core competencies, normally in marketing or technology. The highest risk alternative is diversification into some unrelated activity. Ideally, with any acquisition or merger some skills or resources will be transferable between the businesses to generate savings and benefits – which we usually term 'synergy'. But synergy is sometimes easier to promise than to achieve. Porter (1987) has identified three tests for a successful acquisition – and the more entrepreneurial businesses will score well against these:

- The new industry should offer profit potential in excess of the cost of capital (debt or equity) involved.
- The entry cost (acquisition price) should not compromise the future profit stream.
- Both companies should be able to benefit from the merger. There should be true synergy from transferring skills or sharing resources.

Where a company fails against these tests, it is a reflection of a lack of entrepreneurialism in the strategic change. Most strategies, however, can be made to work if the implementation is handled well.

Reinforcing earlier points, some entrepreneurial businesses are very creative and opportunistic in their search for alliance partners to open up new market opportunities. In every case the challenge lies in fusing together two distinct cultures; where this fails to happen E-V-R congruence can be lost.

When the growth decisions are misjudged – either the decisions taken are not appropriate and feasible or good opportunities are missed – the organization's performance can deteriorate and force disinvestment. This may simply require cutting back and retrenchment; it may, alternatively, require a sale of parts of the business to enable a renewed focus on core competencies. Organizations that fail to take the initiative and tackle the need for change with new, entrepreneurial ideas and ventures may be forced into this style if they are to survive – but it may turn out to be too late. Turnaround issues are discussed in the next section on strategic weaknesses.

Strategic weaknesses

We have already mentioned two important strategic pressures that can leave the unprepared organization weakened. First, competitive and other environmental pressures and, second, focusing too much on controls at the expense of flexibility.

Hurst (1995) has shown how management and control becomes increasingly necessary as organizations grow and become more complex, but that this development contains the seeds of potential failure. We can see in Figure 2.9 that organizations often start life with an entrepreneurial vision but that the significance of this vision soon gives way to learning and emergence as the entrepreneur and the organization learns to cope with the pressures of a dynamic and competitive environment. This flexibility maintains the momentum and the organization grows and prospers. To ensure the organization is managed efficiently, planning and control systems run by specialist professional managers become increasingly prominent – but this often reduces the flexibility which has proved so valuable. If the flexibility is lost, if the organization fails to address what it is doing wrong whilst

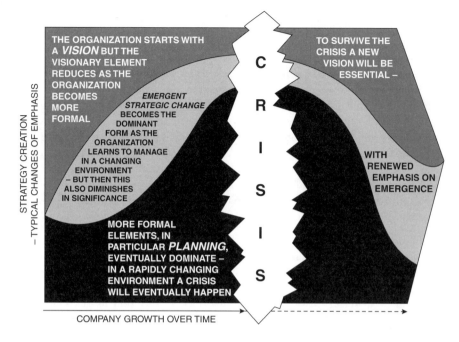

STRATEGY CREATION
– TYPICAL CHANGES OF EMPHASIS

THE ORGANIZATION STARTS WITH A *VISION* BUT THE VISIONARY ELEMENT REDUCES AS THE ORGANIZATION BECOMES MORE FORMAL

EMERGENT STRATEGIC CHANGE BECOMES THE DOMINANT FORM AS THE ORGANIZATION LEARNS TO MANAGE IN A CHANGING ENVIRONMENT – BUT THEN THIS ALSO DIMINISHES IN SIGNIFICANCE

MORE FORMAL ELEMENTS, IN PARTICULAR *PLANNING*, EVENTUALLY DOMINATE – IN A RAPIDLY CHANGING ENVIRONMENT A CRISIS WILL EVENTUALLY HAPPEN

CRISIS

TO SURVIVE THE CRISIS A NEW VISION WILL BE ESSENTIAL –

WITH RENEWED EMPHASIS ON EMERGENCE

COMPANY GROWTH OVER TIME

Figure 2.9 *Strategic change*

it is still succeeding, some of the momentum for Path 2 innovation is lost. Unless the entrepreneur and the organization foresees the impending problem and finds a major Path 1 initiative, a crisis is likely to happen. If the organization is to survive the crisis it will need a new Path 1 opportunity – together with a renewed reliance on innovation and learning.

Businesses hit these crisis points when they run short of money, usually because they have failed to remain competitive and to attract sufficient resource contributions from customers and other important resource suppliers. Sometimes turnaround is possible, frequently accompanied by a change of strategic leader to input the new vision and inspiration. On other occasions the intervention is too late, and the organization either collapses or is taken over as a means of providing the necessary new leadership and resourcing.

Businesses in trouble, then, may be realistically non-recoverable, recoverable but only to a level of survival or capable of genuine renewal. The immediate need is to stop any financial haemorrhaging before new opportunities are sought and pursued. The first step does not need someone with entrepreneurial talent and temperament – it is largely based on technique, backed by a willingness to take tough decisions – but the second stage does.

Hurst further argues that on occasions it can be valuable to actually engineer an internal crisis and upset in order to drive through major changes in an organization that has lost its dynamism and become too change resistant. A controlled crisis is better than one resulting from external events, as it can be used for positive change rather than constitute a more desperate reaction.

Another way of presenting these arguments is the following four-stage model of organizational progression and development:

1   The first stage is a *creative* one, when new ideas are put forward.
2   That stage is followed by *reflection and nurturing* as the idea is crafted into a winning opportunity. We have already said that the person who has the original idea may not be the person who takes it forward in the most opportune way.
3   Stage 3 is an *action* stage as the entrepreneur and the organization develop the business from the opportunity. As the business takes off, and more and more products are sold, some element of order becomes vital if the organization is to control events, manage its cash flow and deliver on time.
4   This stage is one of *management* and administration, with clear policies and procedures which deliver smooth running and efficiencies. This can become a dangerous stage if stasis sets in and new, creative ideas are not forthcoming.

Clearly each stage has a downside. A constant stream of new ideas may not constitute entrepreneurial opportunities. Too much deliberation may inhibit action. An overemphasis on 'doing' and competitiveness may mean inadequate attention is given to structural necessities. And finally, as we saw in Figure 2.4, too much bureaucracy can mean missed opportunities. The organization begins to need a fresh input of creative ideas. Every one of us is different and our affinity and fit with each of these stages varies; some of us are not able to switch styles. Whilst the most successful and habitual entrepreneurs ensure there is a constant flow of activity between these stages and the potential downsides do not materialize, others need to recognize their relative strengths and weaknesses and recruit other people carefully to ensure there is a balance of skills and constant progression. Moreover, the positive organization we are implying here will be in a better position to exploit and retain its most talented intrapreneurial managers.

Baden-Fuller and Stopford (1992) have proposed another four-stage model to explain the effective turnaround of an organization in difficulty. First, the senior management is galvanized into action by the poor results and the obvious need to act. The team element here is critical; individual lone voices will be inadequate if they are baulked by resistant colleagues opposed to the next step. Stage two demands that the crisis situation is simplified – by divesting loss-making activities in order to protect the organization's core and preserve valuable resources. If there is a will, this stage is easy – at least at one level. The cutting back should not be indiscriminate; it should leave a new base upon which a fresh future can be built. It is all too easy to downsize and strip out important core competencies that weaken the organization irredeemably. If the remaining core is strong, stage three, building new capabilities, can follow. This implies new strategic positions, which, if defensible and exploitable, are the basis for stage four where new core competencies are leveraged to create further new and synergistic opportunities.

Business failures

Richardson, Nwankwo and Richardson (1994) identify a number of business failure situations, and these are summarized in Table 2.1 and described below. In the

Table 2.1 *Business failures*

Reason for failure	Early stages	Later stages
Poor strategic positioning	No real differentiation	Strategic drift
Lack of innovation	Failure to see a niche can become a tomb	Inability or unwillingness to change in a bureaucratic structure
Other errors . . .	Inability to take advice or build a strong team of managers	Overambitious growth, sometimes by ill-judged acquisitions and sometimes linked to a failure to understand why they are successful
. . . and flaws	The entrepreneur takes too much money out of the business to support a personal lifestyle – leading to inadequate investment	Inability of the entrepreneur to delegate

commentary, reference is made to the entrepreneurial life themes we introduced in Chapter 1.

Poor strategic positioning can occur at various stages in the life of an organization. Early on it can reflect an organization which might try very hard but is never really different in a meaningful way, or a business started by an inventor who is not an entrepreneur. At a later stage it implies an organization which has been subject to strategic drift – an organization which enjoyed E-V-R congruence at an earlier stage, but which has allowed its resources and values to drift away from a changing environment such that it is too reliant on past successes and is relatively unprepared for the future. One example might be ICI, once a leading world player in the chemical industry, but which eventually had to split into two parts, a bulk chemicals business and the more successful Zeneca, which concentrates on pharmaceuticals and speciality chemicals.

Villiers (1989) uses the metaphor of the boiling frog to explain this state. If a frog is dropped into a pan of boiling water, it will quickly feel discomfort and jump out. If, however, the same frog is placed in cold water it will not feel the same discomfort. When heat is introduced very gradually the frog remains comfortable and soporific, quite unaware of the developing threat as the water slowly reaches boiling point.

In organizational terms, the problem issues build up gradually and are not dealt with properly. When difficulties arise, there is a tendency to look for a 'quick fix' resolution rather than, as entrepreneurs arguably do, look for a more lasting solution which deals with the real issue and reduces the likelihood of recurrence in a fresh guise.

The second reason for failure is a lack of innovation. A small business often begins by targeting a niche and succeeds by offering something different. Without innovation this niche can become a tomb. For larger organizations the crisis scenario discussed above can become a reality if planning and rigidity takes over from flexibility and emergent change. There are several reasons for this:

- complacency – the entrepreneur loses the important urgency which once characterized the business
- a lack of current awareness and strategic thinking
- inflexibility and a reluctance to abandon the past
- a focus on growth rather than profitability such that issues of size draw attention away from more important performance indicators – true entrepreneurs understand profit
- inadequate investment to build new core competencies.

Leadership errors are often coincident with high ambition. Richardson, Nwankwo and Richardson (1994) develop the frog analogy and suggest this is reminiscent of a drowned frog, one which tries too hard to be 'king of the pond' but lacks the necessary resources. In a small company environment this is the entrepreneur who 'knows it all' and either fails to look for advice, fails to take good advice or fails to build a strong team of support managers to help build the business. Important skills and *techniques* are missing. This entrepreneur fails to appreciate the strengths and potential contributions of others and believes him or herself – wrongly – to be infallible. Ironically this is sometimes the price of success. If a new business takes off very quickly and is instantly successful, the entrepreneur can be deluded into feelings of personal brilliance; but the success may be as much dependent on luck as judgement and the *unconscious competency* must be understood by honest reflection and questioning.

In a similar vein, large and successful companies sometimes fail to diagnose just why they are successful, so they can build on very solid foundations. They again rely on assumptions, which tempt their strategic leaders to make poor strategic decisions, such as ill-judged acquisitions that fail to deliver the hoped for synergies and benefits.

Leadership flaws reflect the wrong motivation and the bullfrog, the 'show-off' for whom status and power is more important than achievement. The person concerned enjoys being the 'centre of attention' and basking in personal glory from any success the business enjoys. Whilst he or she may well be the main reason behind the success, the future of the business will inevitably require additional inputs.

Some would-be entrepreneurs begin businesses with the main aim of supporting a particular lifestyle. Any early profits are invested in large cars and new houses rather than the business. This approach is even more indictable when the people spend money before the business has even earned it.

The large company parallel is the strategic leader who fails to delegate and build an appropriate organization structure. Although it enjoyed several years of growth, success and prosperity, the mining and trading conglomerate, Lonrho, was unable to survive the entrepreneur behind the success, Tiny Rowland. For all the years he led Lonrho, Rowland maintained a tight hold on all key corporate strategic decisions, allowable because he remained the major shareholder. Rowland's buccaneering style was loved by Lonrho's smaller shareholders, which enabled him to survive adverse criticism from both the larger institutional shareholders and the regulatory authorities – but eventually his own succession plan brought in a new entrepreneur who split the business into parts to realize its hidden value.

Behind these leadership failings are an overreliance on a single person and a consequent failure to involve others in important decisions, which itself can reflect a flawed ego drive. The typical outcome is poor financial controls and inadequate measures of performance.

Signals of weak entrepreneurial leadership

We now conclude this chapter with a list of warning signals that draw together many of the points made earlier and signify failing entrepreneurship. They have been largely derived from Heller (1998) and Oates (1990).

1 *The existence of (too many) Would-be's.* Something critical is missing. Possibly the interested people have a will to do something but lack a good idea; some key entrepreneurial competence or *talent* is missing – the person(s) concerned is unlikely to make it as an entrepreneur; there is a lack of true commitment to the idea/opportunity/venture – *temperament* is too weak.
2 *The single dimension paradox.* The start-up stage progresses well but there is a lack of ability or opportunity to grow the business beyond the initial stages. The idea might only be viable in the short term; there may be inadequate funding; the entrepreneur may be unwilling to let go at the critical time; the initiative could simply run out of steam. The paradox is that the clear focus and individual drive that gets the initiative moving in the first place can be what brings it down – through a lack of necessary flexibility.
3 *The business is a so-called halfway house.* In other words it is a franchise or co-operative (or something conceptually similar) and critically dependent upon the continued support and engagement of others who may be outside the business.
4 *The business is impoverished.* Specifically it fails to achieve a winning strategic position – it is not sufficiently different. Funding is difficult or mismanaged and the business is undercapitalized. Insufficient attention is given to getting the quality right to 'delight' customers. The team is not developed in the appropriate way – such that key skills are missing. The business cannot cope when succession becomes an issue.
5 *The business is blinkered.* There is too much self-belief – perhaps driven by an orientation to production rather than customers – the 'we know best' syndrome. The entrepreneur is unwilling to accept outside views and advice.
6 *The business is technology-shy.* There is a tension here – the business needs capital and technology, but it all costs money. The key questions are just when do you invest and how much do you spend?
7 *The business has become smothered.* Specifically, it has become overly bureaucratic – either because of government or even European legislation or rules and regulations, or because it has become bigger and more structured and has lost its creative spark.
8 *The business is (now) run by a crisis manager* – a manager who relies too much on an ability to deal (or not deal!) with setbacks and crises as they arise, often implying the wrong trade-off between reaction and proaction.

9   *The business has started making (too many) mistakes.* Possibly it has become too
     ambitious – say with misjudged diversification or acquisition. Maybe it has
     ignored warning signs such as a cash shortage. Maybe it is simply too greedy.

This concludes the first part of this book on entrepreneurs and provides a theoretical underpinning against which we can usefully explore the various stories and
cases which comprise Part Two. In Chapter 3 we see the Gallup life themes illustrated in the stories of a selection of legendary entrepreneurs. This is followed by
a chapter on business entrepreneurs which encapsulates the themes of opportunity
and change that we have discussed in this chapter.

Notes

1. We are using the word 'paradigm' here as it is commonly used in strategy literature to
   explain a view or perspective of a strong and advantageous competitive position. There
   is a case to be made that the word 'paradigm' should be reserved for a more significant
   and higher-order context, and this argument will be debated later in the book (Chapter
   10).
2. We discuss Silicon Valley in depth in Chapter 8.

References

Baden-Fuller, C. and Stopford, J. (1992). *Rejuvenating the Mature Business: The Competitive
    Challenge*. Routledge.
Blanchard, K. and Waghorn, T. (1997). *Mission Possible*. McGraw-Hill.
Bridge, S., O'Neill, K. and Cromie, S. (1998). *Understanding Enterprise, Entrepreneurship and
    Small Business*. Macmillan.
Churchill, N. C. (1997) *Breaking Down the Wall, Scaling the Ladder*. In *Mastering Enterprise*
    (S. Birley and D. Muzyka, eds), Financial Times/Pitman.
Derr, C. B. (1982). Living on adrenalin – the adventurer entrepreneur. *Human Resource
    Management*, Summer.
Fradette, M. and Michaud, S. (1998). *The Power of Corporate Kinetics: Create the Self-Adapting,
    Self-Renewing, Instant Action Enterprise*. Simon and Schuster.
Hamel, G. (1994) Address to the Competing for the Future conference, *The Economist*, London,
    July.
Hamel, G. (1997). Address to the Strategic Planning Society conference, London, November.
Hamel, G. (1999). Bringing Silicon Valley inside. *Harvard Business Review*, September–October.
Hamel, G. and Prahalad, C. K. (1994). *Competing for the Future*. Harvard Business School Press.
Heller, R. (1998). *Goldfinger: How Entrepreneurs Get Rich by Starting Small*. HarperCollins.
Horovitz, J. (1997). *Growth Without Losing the Entrepreneurial Spirit*. In *Mastering Enterprise*
    (S. Birley and D. Muzyka, eds), Financial Times/Pitman.
Hurst, D. K. (1995). *Crisis and Renewal: Meeting the Challenge of Organizational Change*. Harvard
    Business School Press.
Kanter, R. M. (1983). *The Change Masters: Innovation and Entrepreneurship in the American
    Corporation*. Simon and Schuster.
Kanter, R. M. (1989). *When Giants Learn to Dance*. Simon and Schuster.
Kets de Vries, M. (1996). Leaders who make a difference. *European Management Journal*, **14** (5),
    October.
Kirzner, I. M. (1973). *Competition and Entrepreneurship*. Cambridge University Press.

Lessem, R. (1986). *Enterprising Development*. Gower.

Lessem, R. (1998). *Managing Development through Cultural Diversity*. Routledge.

Maitland, A. (1999). Strategy for creativity. *Financial Times*, 11 November.

Mintzberg, H., Ahlstrand, B. and Lampel, J. (1998). *Strategy Safari*. Prentice-Hall.

Oates, D. (1990). *The Complete Entrepreneur*. Mercury.

Pinchot, G. III (1985). *Intrapreneuring*. Harper and Row.

Porter, M. E. (1987). From competitive advantage to corporate strategy. *Harvard Business Review*, May–June.

Porter, M. E. (1996). What is strategy? *Harvard Business Review*, November–December.

Porter, M. E. (1997). Dare to be different. Interview for the *Financial Times*, 19 June.

Prahalad, C. K. and Hamel, G. (1990). The core competence of the corporation. *Harvard Business Review*, May–June.

Quinn, J. B. (1980). *Strategies for Change: Logical Incrementalism*. Irwin.

Richardson, B., Nwankwo, S. and Richardson, S. (1994). Understanding the causes of business failure crises. *Management Decision*, **32** (4).

Schumpeter, J. (1949). *The Theory of Economic Development*. Harvard University Press.

Simon, H. (1996). *Hidden Champions*. Harvard Business School Press.

Stevenson, H. H. and Gumpert, D. E. (1985). The heart of entrepreneurship. *Harvard Business Review*, March–April.

Terazano, E. (1999). Fresh impetus from the need to innovate. *Financial Times*, 25 June.

Thompson, J. L. (1997). *Strategic Management: Awareness and Change*. 3rd edn. International Thomson Business Press.

Villiers, C. (1989). The boiled frog syndrome. *Management Today*, March.

Part Two
Entrepreneurs in action

3 Legendary entrepreneurs

What can we see if we study a selection of legendary names from the world of enterprise? We can sometimes see evidence of true vision and always the ability to see the potential of a real opportunity. Driven by an inner need to succeed and to make a difference in some way, the truly successful entrepreneurs focus on their opportunities and pursue them with great dedication and courage in the face of opposition and setbacks. Invariably we see the creative development of a business that looks after its customers and employees, one which grows by learning and finding new opportunities. We might say that they are 'off the scale' in terms of opportunity and people. Having wealthy parents and the benefit of a university education seems never to have been a prerequisite for entrepreneurial success – but the ability to learn from the 'university of life' is a critical factor.

One hundred and fifty years ago the UK prospered from the Industrial Revolution. The inventors and entrepreneurs who had contributed to this economic growth and global prosperity were popular heroes. Richard Arkwright (founder of the cotton mills), Richard Hargreaves (pioneer of the modern woollen industry), Thomas Chippendale (furniture) and Josiah Wedgwood (pottery) are still remembered for their differentiated, high-quality products. Samuel Cunard (shipping), George Stephenson (inventor of the first truly successful railway locomotive) and Isambard Brunel (pioneer of the Great Western Railway) left us a transport infrastructure. Rowland Hill made sure we have a postal service. Alongside some of these great achievements of the nineteenth century, social entrepreneurs also made an impact. Thomas Barnardo opened homes for homeless children, William Booth founded the Salvation Army, Elizabeth Fry pioneered prison reform, Florence Nightingale invented modern nursing and Robert Owen inspired trade unions and the Co-operative movement.

They were all visionary entrepreneurs who had made a difference, albeit in quite distinct ways. Many of them were leaders in their field as well as entrepreneurs and, to coin a popular phrase, 'we will remember them'. Some of them accumulated huge personal fortunes (an outcome we invariably associate with entrepreneurship) but others remained relatively poor.

But where are the great heroes and heroines today? And will we remember them in centuries to come? Successive UK governments appear to recognize that prosperous economies need a constant flow of new businesses with high growth potential and to offer some encouragement. Successful entrepreneurs can still be found in several walks of life, but is it an issue that we often fail properly to appreciate the ones who do succeed? People are still 'changing history' but arguably we have become less willing to celebrate their achievements. In contrast, and driven by the media, society certainly accords hero status to popular musicians and sports personalities, who invariably do build financial fortunes very quickly. Although countries other than the UK persist with these priorities, failing to appreciate entrepreneurs is not ubiquitous around the world. The 'geeks' and 'nerds' of Silicon Valley are American cult heroes and, essentially, they are business entrepreneurs. Greater visibility is one essential factor in understanding the contributions of the leading entrepreneurs, and this is now happening. Confirming this movement, serial entrepreneur Luke Johnson, who made his fortune with pizza parlours and dental laboratories, has commented recently that 'you can now go to a dinner party in Britain and be unashamed to say that you run a shop'.

Before looking at contemporary entrepreneurs in business and other sectors, this chapter first reflects upon the contribution of a number of business people who have been accorded legendary status. Whilst most of them are associated with products, services and brands we still buy regularly, we begin with Carnegie and Edison. Carnegie did not invent steel, but he built the American foundries that supplied materials to the railway and construction industries. Thomas Edison did not invent electricity, but he used it to provide products that improved people's lives. Similar and later, Henry Ford did not invent the motorcar but he was the first to make it affordable for less affluent consumers. The business he bequeathed to his descendants remains a powerful and dominant force in the industry. These entrepreneurs all saw a real opportunity to do something that would make a difference – and, by harnessing the contribution of other people, actually made that difference.

Andrew Carnegie

Carnegie was a focused risk-taker who saw and seized opportunities. An insatiable learner all his life, he believed 'the true road to pre-eminent success in any line is to make yourself master in that line'. Dedicated to pursuit, he claimed that 'whatever I engage in I must push inordinately'. He made things happen (he detested speculators – 'parasites feeding upon values but creating none'), he managed detail well and he was a team-builder dedicated to bringing out the best in other people. He is probably remembered more for his philanthropic legacies of some $300 million to charities, arts, libraries and education – partially reflecting his strong ego drive – than for his industrial achievements, though these were hugely significant. Few visitors to New York would appreciate he built the magnificent Brooklyn Bridge.

Carnegie was a Scot, born in 1835; his father and grandfather were weavers. An astute opportunist from an early age, he bred rabbits and called them after his friends if they would help scavenge the rabbit food. Helping his father with his accounts, he learnt the principles of business at an early age. His family emigrated to America when he was thirteen and he was immediately sent out to work, where an uncle found him a job as a telegraph boy, delivering messages. Andrew taught himself to translate Morse code by ear, becoming the third person in the country able to do this. His skill proved useful for the developing railroad network, which Carnegie joined. Through the railroads he met several prominent businessmen, and acted on tips and information he picked up. He became a serial entrepreneur, starting when he saw an opportunity to be a supplier to the growing railroad network with Pullman railcars, so passengers could rest and sleep on long journeys. When oil was discovered in Pennsylvania, where he lived, he became an early investor in oilfield development. He then began to construct iron bridges for the railroads, to replace the less robust wooden ones – and, hearing of the new Bessemer steel-making process in the UK, he graduated into steel for manufacturing the rolling stock and the lines themselves. He was the founder of the American steel industry.

Whilst it is alleged he had flashes of inspiration and acted on them, he was at the same time a leading proponent of cost accounting. His father's teaching had ensured he was numerate and he believed in accounting for costs at every stage of production. It is generally acknowledged that his true genius was the way he was able to work with others for a common vision – an entrepreneur who was also a strong and charismatic leader. He believed 'you must capture the heart of the original and extremely able man before his brain can do its best'.

Thomas Edison

Edison was a more reflective thinker who nurtured opportunities, many of which he stumbled on. Creative and innovative, he accumulated over 1000 patents, the most ever granted to one individual. 'All progress, all success springs from thinking.' He was persistent and courageous, overcoming numerous hurdles and setbacks – 'genius is one percent inspiration and ninety-nine percent perspiration' – but his efforts and inventions were always focused firmly on commercial opportunities.

Edison was born in Ohio in 1847 and by the age of twelve he was selling news-papers on railway trains; three years later he was publishing his own weekly news-sheet from a freight wagon. He was taught telegraphy by a local station-master as a reward for saving his son's life and, like Carnegie, telegraphy provided Edison with an opportunity he would not squander. Inquisitive by nature, he developed a number of technical enhancements, in particular devices for automating transmission and reception and for multiplexing, which enabled simultaneous multiple transmissions on a single telegraph line. Saving his earnings, he opened a laboratory and soon improved on the telephone, invented earlier by Alexander Graham Bell. Later Edison's laboratory – an 'invention factory' – would pioneer the cylinder phonograph (1877), the first incandescent light bulb (1879), the kineto-scope (the earliest rapid-motion projector of individual images, upon which the movie industry developed) and alkaline storage batteries. Income from the sale of some of his patents helped fund the laboratory. Edison also built power stations for transmitting the electricity needed for his lights.

Like Carnegie, Edison was committed to building a strong team of helpers, a network whose contributions were influential in ideas generation and development. Some of his work was greeted with great scepticism, as the *Scientific American* (June 1879) confirms:

> Six months ago popular attention was strongly drawn to the development of the electric light, and a panic prevailed among the holders of gas stock. That flurry has blown over. The electric light has not fulfilled its promises, and Mr. Edison's assertion that his latest lamp is a complete success falls on indifferent ears. The world is not so eager for the change as it appeared, and on all sides the disposition is to await developments patiently.

Edison was essentially a technologist who made quantum improvements to what was known already, rather than discovering anything really new – with perhaps the exception of the electric light. For this Edison discovered the potential of the flow of electrons from a heated filament, but it was not an instant breakthrough. After some 10 000 failed attempts he refused to give up, and commented: 'I haven't failed . . . I've simply found 10 000 ways it doesn't work!' Focused on commercial opportunities, he believed there was an enormous potential for exploiting electricity to help improve the lives of ordinary people, and persisted. Fundamentally an inventor, Edison was a true entrepreneur because he understood the opportunities for exploiting his inventions, and followed them through to successful application. When we look at James Dyson later in this chapter we will see similar issues coming through.

Isambard Kingdom Brunel

James Dyson has claimed Brunel was 'unable to think small – nothing was a barrier to him'. He was the visionary engineer who built the Great Western Railway and the Clifton Suspension Bridge. A pioneer of steamships, his idea for a screw propeller was nevertheless greeted with criticism and great scepticism. Brunel's family was wealthy, and he enjoyed the best technical education available in Europe. When his French father was commissioned to build a tunnel under the Thames, Brunel was able to gain early practical experience – employed by his father as an engineer. Whilst much of his work had enormous influence on the progress of other engineers and builders, Brunel was commercially unsuccessful and when he died in 1859 (aged fifty-three) he left his widow impoverished. Fellow engineers accused him of pursuing novelty for the sake of novelty – he endeavoured to develop beyond the levels of current competency – and then stole many of his ideas! Brunel was certainly an engineer and risk-taker, but was he an entrepreneur? He certainly saw several opportunities and followed them through. His Great Western Railway from London to Bristol has always been regarded as one of Britain's most significant infrastructure projects, but the vitally important railways were never enormously profitable. His *Great Eastern*, at its launch the largest ship ever built, was a commercial failure. In the end, consumers have been the main beneficiaries – he did not accumulate financial capital and wealth, but he did contribute enormous social and aesthetic capital. Moreover, his contributions helped other entrepreneurs make money. In Brunel's case one might ask: 'Who best deserves the laurels – he who achieves worldly success and contemporary acclaim by a safe route or he who risks failure for posterity to follow?'

Brunel was regarded as a perfectionist – the best was never good enough – who was a poor delegator. He chose a broad gauge for the Great Western Railway, believing it to be so superior others would follow. But (and here we can draw parallels between Sony's preference for the technically superior Betamax video which lost out to the perfectly satisfactory and cheaper VHS format pioneered by JVC) other railway companies developed with the lower-cost narrower gauge. George Stephenson was his main rival and the two acted as a spur for each other – but their rivalry remained friendly and they willingly helped each other. Stephenson, for example, laid his rails on stone block sleepers, which were unsuitable for the speed Brunel wanted. It was the creative and innovative Brunel who pioneered hollow (not solid steel) rails on longitudinal timber sleepers.

Henry Ford

'I will build a motor car for the multitude, so low in price that the man of moderate means may own one.' Henry Ford was a visionary dedicated to the pursuit of his vision. Possessor of a very strong ego drive he was nevertheless a businessman with a conscience. He activated his vision by exploiting production-line techniques but paid his workers above the average going rate, increasing wages when his profits grew. He adopted a five-day working week and employed handicapped people for jobs they could handle satisfactorily. Ironically his failure to appreciate that customers might prefer other colours than black is also legendary!

Ford's father was an immigrant Irish farmer and he was born in Michigan in 1863. Brought up on a farm the young Henry was a 'tinkerer' and he soon proved to be a natural at repairing farm machinery. Presented with a watch at the age of eleven he proceeded to take it apart and then started making his own – which he sold for $1 each. At the age of twelve he was absorbed when he saw that an agricultural steam engine mounted on a wagon could cause the wagon to move forward without a horse pulling it. He had experienced his trigger. With hindsight we can see that his life's work was then dedicated to the production of a motorized replacement for the ubiquitous horse and cart, and a tractor to do the work of the horses on the farm. His experimenting continued after he left the family farm and started working in a steam-engine workshop at the age of sixteen – a job he soon left in order to work for Thomas Edison. Ford became manager of one of Edison's power-generating plants. Edison was aware that Ford was using and refining the gasoline-driven internal combustion engine invented by Daimler and Benz in Germany to produce early motor cars, and he encouraged him in this endeavour. The two men never lost touch and Edison's laboratory has been reconstructed for Ford's world-famous Greenfield Village Museum. Henry built three cars in his own workshop in his spare time and then moved on to racing cars before branching out as a manufacturer.

In 1907 Ford drew up plans for the largest automobile factory in the world, intending to build just one car in it, the Model T. He intended to use the production line, which he had seen used for less complex products such as sewing machines, bicycles and guns. Ford's unique contribution was to go for minute division of labour and a methodological arrangement of the machine tools. In this ability to transfer ideas he resembles James Dyson as we shall see later. Interestingly this ability to transfer was crucial in the Second World War. In 1941 the Consolidated Aircraft Company was failing to achieve its production target of fifty B-24 Liberator bombers every month. This four-engined aeroplane had 500 000 separate parts in its assembly. Ford was asked to help and within a year his engineers had built a mile-long factory which could complete planes at a rate of more than one every hour.

For all his successes, Henry Ford made mistakes. He was an autocrat who failed to build a strong team of managers, which inevitably hindered his progress. He did not replace the Model T as quickly as he should have done, and thus lost new opportunities. He first thought that all his production should be concentrated in one huge plant, before realizing that separate and dedicated plants were more efficient.

Bill Gates

Henry Ford was fascinated by cars and believed others would be the same once they could afford them. Bill Gates had a similar vision for transforming the lives of ordinary people, foreseeing 'a single operating system for every personal computer around the world' to complement Steve Jobs's (Apple) vision of 'a personal computer on every desk in every home and office around the world'. Dedicated pursuit of this focused vision through Microsoft has made him the world's richest person. Like Ford he had a strong ego drive; and like Edison, but unlike Carnegie and Ford, Gates was born to wealthy parents. Again like Edison, he was only concerned with tight control mechanisms once his business had grown, he was energetic and worked 'ridiculously long hours', and he has inspired criticism.

There are several reasons behind Gates's phenomenal success. Among them are his ability to absorb information quickly and his technical expertise – he can actually write computer code. He understands consumers and is uncannily aware of market needs. He has an 'eye for the main chance' coupled with an ability and will to make things happen. Moreover he is an aggressive defender of his corner, which in the end may work against him with the American Anti-Trust Authorities.

Born in 1955 in Seattle, Gates quickly became interested in science fiction and, unusually, went to a school which had a computer that students could use. A 'nerd' from an early age it has been said Gates 'preferred playing with computers to playing with other children'. He nevertheless teamed up with his friend, Paul Allen, and together they 'begged, borrowed and bootlegged' time on the school computer, undertaking small software commissions. Gates and Allen went to Harvard together, where Gates proved to be an unpopular student because of his high self-opinion. Surreptitiously using Harvard's computer laboratories they began a small business on the campus. Gates later left Harvard to start Microsoft – never completing this formal part of his education. Allen was his formal partner in the venture, but Gates always held a majority control. Bill Gates's visionary contribution was the realization that operating systems and software (rather than the computer hardware) held the key to growth and industry domination.

Gates took risks in the early days but, assisted by some good luck, his gambles largely paid off. When the first commercial microcomputer (the Altair) needed a customized version of the Basic programming language, Gates accepted the challenge. His package was later licensed to Apple, Commodore and IBM, the companies that developed the personal computer market. When IBM decided seriously to attack the personal computer market Gates was commissioned to develop the operating system. Innovatively improving an existing off-the-shelf package and renaming it Microsoft Disk Operating System (MS DOS) Gates was now 'on his way'. Since then Windows has become the ubiquitous first-choice operating system for most personal computer (PC) manufacturers. By-and-large his success has depended on his ability to create 'standard products', the benchmark against which others are judged.

Gates hires the best and brightest people and he has made many of them millionaires. He prefers a college-style working environment with a culture dedicated to learning, sharing and overcoming hurdles. Gates personally thrives on combat and confrontation. His colleagues have to be able to stand up to him – but it does generate creative energy. However, he is also seen as enormously charismatic, and employees desperately want to please him. In his younger days he was branded a risk-taker; stories are told of his love of fast cars and his tendency to leave late for meetings in order to provide him with an excuse for driving fast.

Walt Disney

The talent we will always associate with Walt Disney is creativity. He was also very clearly opportunistic, focused, dedicated, courageous (overcoming several setbacks) and visionary. Although it was Walt's drive and charisma that built Disney, the corporation has survived his death and continued to grow and prosper, testimony to a robust organizational legacy. He left a strong team of people and a culture that has enabled Disney continuously to improve its existing activities and, at the same time, build in new directions.

Walt Disney was born in 1901 and raised on a small farm. Chasing work, his father moved the family to Kansas City, where he obtained a newspaper distribution franchise. He forced Walt to work for him without pay at the age of nine, but the canny Walt quickly realized he could earn pocket money (to buy the sweets he was forbidden at home) if he found his own customers without telling his father. His 'university of life' education continued when he went to France in 1917 (lying about his age) to help the Red Cross. He started doctoring German steel helmets recovered from the battlefields to make it appear as if the soldier had been shot in the head. He found a ready market for his souvenirs.

The artistic Walt dreamed of being a newspaper cartoonist, but could not find employment. Joining forces with another talented artist, Walt formed a small advertising business and persuaded the publisher of a low-price throwaway paper that sales would improve with illustrated advertising. The business succeeded, but when he was offered a job as a cartoonist with a film company Walt unhesitatingly sold his share of the business to his partner. After developing the necessary skills Walt left to form his own cartoon production company, persuading local citizens to invest in shares. The cartoons may have proved popular but the business was not profitable. After it collapsed in 1923 Walt left for Hollywood, where his elder brother, Roy, was working.

Partnered by Roy, Walt started again, adding sound and colour to his cartoons. Eventually his Mickey Mouse creation reached the cinemas, and this success persuaded Walt to gamble everything on a version of *Snow White and the Seven Dwarfs*. When he made this in 1937 it cost ten times the normal amount for a feature film – a huge risk. It succeeded, to be followed by *Pinocchio*, *Bambi* and *Fantasia* – all produced over budget! As he had before, and showing poor technique, Disney failed to control his costs and was forced to sell stock to stay in business. Like Richard Branson, as we shall see later in the chapter, he did not enjoy being accountable to external shareholders, but he persevered. Quite simply, Walt Disney was an extraordinary storyteller who understood his market. Adopting Mark Twain's philosophy of his own books, Disney was never a classic film-maker. If classic films are like wine, Disney's films are like water. But everyone drinks water!

The creative Disney worked in three separate areas. His most creative work was accomplished in a colourful open-space area, with illustrations on every wall. Planning and organizing was relegated to a formal office, whilst a third, darkened room with comfortable furniture was reserved for discussions and opportunities for colleagues to question his ideas and thinking in a more intense atmosphere.

Disney diversified into non-cartoon family films and then Walt had the idea for a theme park. He could see a new opportunity for exploiting his characters – he had always been able to tell stories and he now wanted to provide a live stage for his characters. But would he be able to convince others with his vision? His brother Roy was sceptical and persuaded investors not to back the project. Undeterred Walt struck a deal with ABC Television. For $5 million ABC could use Mickey Mouse. Walt had the money for Disneyland, which eventually opened in Anaheim, south of Los Angeles, in 1955. A winner from day one, the theme park was contributing 30 per cent of the corporation's revenue in its first year of operations.

Disney died in 1966 but the growth and success has continued. Magic Kingdom opened in 1971, followed later by Epcot (1982) and Disney-MGM Studios (1989) – all in Florida – and EuroDisney in 1992. The Disney Corporation bought ABC Television in 1995, thereby merging its content with a key distributor. Through its Touchstone Pictures Disney also produces restricted-audience films. Character licensing and astute marketing of videos of the cartoon feature films are major revenue generators. Headed for the last fifteen years by Michael Eisner, Disney has proved it understands service and how it is delivered through people – a competency it shares with McDonald's, Wal-Mart and Virgin, as we shall see.

Sam Walton and Wal-Mart

If Walt Disney was a truly great entertainer, Sam Walton was a truly great retailer. His Wal-Mart stores provide huge ranges and choices of household goods. Prices are kept low through scale economies and a first-class supply chain network. Despite their size, the stores seem friendly and Walton employed people simply to answer customer queries and show them where particular goods are shelved. Again a visionary, he was focused and dedicated. He worked long hours and 'talked retailing outside work'. Strong on the people and team elements and willing to take measured risks, Walton sought to learn from other organizations. In this respect he was opportunistic, but reflective. He never claimed to be an original thinker and he networked widely to find his new ideas.

Born in 1918 (in Missouri) and raised in relative poverty, Walton started earning money from selling newspapers when he was very young. As a footballer he showed he was highly competitive, a trait which again proved valuable when he started his career in retailing. After he graduated in 1940 he began selling shirts in a J. C. Penney store. Because of a minor heart murmur he was not drafted for the war effort and instead worked in a gunpowder factory. Afterwards, and in partnership with his brother, he took on the franchise for a Ben Franklin five-and-dime store in Arkansas. The two brothers bought additional outlets, abandoned counters in favour of self-service, established central buying and promotion, and quickly became the most successful Ben Franklin franchisees in America. In 1962, the same year that K-Mart began opening discount stores in larger cities, Walton began with discount stores in small towns. Both had seen the concept pioneered elsewhere. Walton's principle was simple – mark everything up by 30 per cent, regardless of the purchase cost. This proved to be a winning formula. He toured, observed, absorbed and learned to develop his 'buy it low, stack it high, sell it cheap' strategy. Walton's first Wal-Mart store opened in Arkansas in 1962; turnover now exceeds the figures for McDonald's, Coca-Cola and Disney combined! With 3600 stores in the USA alone, and with annual sales of $85 billion, Wal-Mart is the world's largest retailer. It is exceeded only by the Indian National Railways, the Russian Army and the British National Health Service in terms of numbers employed. Yet the wealthy Sam Walton is alleged to have driven himself around in a pick-up truck and to have been a mean tipper!

Growth was gradual in the early years, but there were thirty Wal-Mart stores by 1970. Once Walton opened his own distribution warehouse (another idea he copied) growth would explode. In addition, Wal-Mart was the first major retailer to share sales data electronically with its leading suppliers. 'We got big by replacing inventory with information.' Wal-Mart has always been careful to contain the risk by 'not investing more capital than is justified by results'. But Sam Walton was always willing to try out new ideas, quickly abandoning those that did not work. He successfully combined emergent strategy with his vision to create a potent organization and formula.

Walton's very strong ego drive was manifested in three guiding principles: respect for individual employees, service to customers ('exceed their expectations') and striving for excellence. An intuitive and inspirational retailer, Walton was also a cheer-leading orator and inspirer. He preached that 'extraordinary results can come from empowering ordinary people'. His showman style was also reflected in glitzy store openings. He created a 'culture that in many ways represents a religion – in the devotion it inspires amongst its associates and in the Jesuit-like demands it makes on its executives'. Following the lead of the John Lewis Partnership in the UK, Walton called his employees 'associates' and personally spent much of his time in stores exchanging ideas with them. Profits were shared with employees. 'Ownership means people watch costs and push sales.' Like Andrew Carnegie, Walton provided support for many good causes, but largely anonymously. Recognizing his own weaknesses, Walton recruited an analytical businessman, David Glass, to be his number two. Glass commented once that Walton 'wasn't organized – I saw one store he was running with water melons piled outside in temperatures of 115 degrees'. Glass has continued as Chief Executive since Walton's death.

Founded by individual entrepreneurs, Disney Corporation and Wal-Mart have become entrepreneurial businesses; their growth and prosperity has continued after the death of the founder. Wal-Mart is now expanding selectively into other countries and, in 1999, acquired Asda in the UK.

Before concluding this chapter with a review of two contemporary but quite different legendary entrepreneurs, Richard Branson and James Dyson, we next look at three other entrepreneurial organizations: McDonald's, Sony and Coca-Cola. Whilst McDonald's was the inspiration of a single entrepreneur, Ray Kroc, Sony was founded by two entrepreneurial partners. Coca-Cola has benefited from a series of entrepreneurial inputs. All three have become hugely powerful and influential brands, which have touched the lives of millions of people around the world.

Ray Kroc and McDonald's

Ray Kroc has been described by *Time Magazine* as 'one of the most influential builders of the twentieth century'. Few children refuse a McDonald's burger – and its golden arches logo symbolizes American enterprise. Kroc was a truly opportunistic and focused entrepreneur who built an organizational network of dedicated franchisees. Yet his entrepreneurial contribution began late in life and the McDonald's chain of hamburger restaurants was certainly not his own invention. Instead he saw – really he stumbled on – an opportunity where others missed the true potential for an idea. Once he had seen the opportunity he rigorously applied business acumen and techniques to focus on providing value for his customers. By standardizing his product and restaurants he was able to guarantee high and consistent quality at relatively low cost. Kroc was also wise enough to use the expertise his franchisees were developing.

In 1955, at the age of fifty-two, Ray Kroc completed thirty years as a salesman, mainly selling milkshake machines to various types of restaurant across America, including hamburger joints. His customers included the McDonald brothers who, having moved from New Hampshire to Hollywood and failed to make any headway in the movie business, had opened a small drive-through restaurant in San Bernadino, California. They offered a limited menu, paper plates and plastic cups –

and guaranteed the food in sixty seconds. When their success drove them to buy eight milkshake machines, instead of the two their small size would logically suggest, Ray Kroc's interest was alerted and he set off to see the restaurant. Kroc's vision was for a national chain that could benefit from organization and business techniques. He bought out the McDonald brothers and set about building a global empire. After he officially retired from running the business, and until his death in 1984, Ray Kroc stayed on as President and visited two or three different restaurants every week. He saw himself as the 'company's conscience', checking standards against his QSCV vision – *q*uality food, fast and friendly *s*ervice, *c*lean restaurants and *v*alue for money.

McDonald's has always been a focused business, never straying from fast-food. For many years its products were the same everywhere they were served, but local variations have developed. Branches opened in hospitals, military bases, airport terminals, zoos and roadside service areas as well as in towns and cities. Success depends on a strong supply chain, careful control over production and employee engagement. Many employees are young part-timers but they must still enthusi-astically deliver a high-quality service. Like Disney, McDonald's was an early pioneer of its own corporate university for training its staff.

It would be a mistake to underestimate the contribution of Ray Kroc's franchise and supplier 'partners', who have always been encouraged to contribute their ideas and expertise. The Big Mac, introduced nationally in the USA in 1968, was the idea of an entrepreneurial Pittsburgh franchisee who had seen a similar product in a rival hamburger restaurant, and who was allowed to trial the product in his own restaurant. Its success allowed McDonald's to strengthen its appeal to adults. The launch of Egg McMuffins a few years later was a response to a perceived oppor-tunity – earlier opening times and a breakfast menu. It took McDonald's four years to develop the product to a satisfactory standard, using a new cooking utensil invented by a Santa Barbara franchisee. When Chicken McNuggets were launched in 1982, it was the first time these small boneless pieces of chicken had been mass-produced. The difficult development of the product was carried out in conjunction with a supplier and there was immediate competitive advantage. The product could not be copied readily. From being essentially a hamburger chain, McDonald's quickly became Number 2 to Kentucky Fried Chicken for fast-food chicken meals.

By the mid-1990s there were 20 000 McDonald's restaurants around the world, the company held 40 per cent of the US market for its products, and yet its burgers were not coming out as superior to Wendy's and Burger King in taste tests. After a period of criticism and disappointing results McDonald's has fought back coura-geously. With franchisees paying half the costs, new computerized kitchen equipment has been systematically installed in its (now) 25 000 restaurants, allowing 'fast cooking to order'. Ready-to-serve meals no longer have to stand for a few minutes on heated trays. In addition, McDonald's has begun to experiment with new low-risk opportunities for its competencies in supply chain management, fran-chising, promotion and merchandising by acquiring new restaurant chains. Included are a group of eighteen Mexican restaurants in Colorado, 143 pizza outlets in Ohio and a chain of twenty-three Aroma coffee shops in London. Ray Kroc has been dead for over fifteen years but his legacy lives on in a brand name that is recog-nized and revered around the world.

Sony

Sony truly deserves its reputation as a creative, innovative business. A pioneer of new consumer electronics, it has been instrumental in the development of several important products and, unusual for a Japanese organization, it has been described as 'a young, maverick company' by the *Financial Times*. Sony was only started after the Second World War. Its two complementary founding partners, Masaru Ibuka (a passionate inventor) and Akio Morita (a business-minded member of a leading brewing family), wanted to build consumer products. 'We started with the basic concept that we had to do something no other company has done before.' Driven by inventions, Sony, like Thomas Edison, has rarely lost sight of its customers and their needs. Elements of opportunism and risk, and a mixture of good and poor judgement, characterize its growth.

After its first new product, a rice cooker, was a failure, Sony's breakthrough came with tape recorders. Ibuka had seen the large American reel-to-reel machines used by the Occupying Forces and envisioned a small consumer version. True resourcefulness was required to overcome a shortage of plastic for the recording tapes – importing plastics was prohibited. Instead Sony created a smooth calendered paper which could be coated with magnetic powder. Ibuka then visited America and saw a potential for transistors that the American inventors were missing. He licensed the patent and went on to create the first portable radios. In reducing these to pocket size, Sony began to develop a ground-breaking competency in miniaturization. Televisions – Sony pioneered its Trinitron system for better picture quality – and video recorders followed. Here Sony took a risk that proved to be a misjudgement, backing its own higher-quality Betamax system and initially ignoring the cheaper but perfectly satisfactory VHS system pioneered by its rival, JVC.

In 1979 Sony's legendary status was secured with the Walkman, an idea of Akio Morita which 'changed the lifestyle of a generation'. There was nothing new about the technology involved in these miniature personal listening devices – Morita saw an opportunity for a cassette player which allowed people to listen to music anywhere through personal headphones without disturbing anyone else. Unlike other cassette players, recording was not possible, and more recently new radio and compact disc (CD) versions have been spawned. Really the opportunity had existed for a while, and the product was feasible – it needed an entrepreneur to spot the gap in the market. Sony has followed later with pioneering contributions to the popularity and success of compact discs, camcorders, computers and floppy discs. Its computer game, Playstation, is again a market leader.

A different form of risk and entrepreneurship was evident when Sony chose to acquire CBS Records and Columbia Pictures and link its own expertise in electronics hardware with American competency in software and entertainment. This brave move forced structural and cultural changes; and even after twenty years of mixed successes the 'jury remains out' concerning whether this was an appropriate move for a Japanese company, even though many Americans are reputed to believe Sony is actually American.

Coca-Cola

Coca-Cola is the world's premier soft drink; the company's global market share for carbonated soft drinks exceeds 50 per cent. It has been said the company sees its main competitor as water, as this is the one drink that people consume in greater quantities! The company's success cannot be attributed to one person, but rather to a series of individual entrepreneurs, all of whom saw different but important opportunities.

The original syrup for Coca-Cola was invented in 1886 by an Atlanta pharmacist, John Pemberton. Records do not clarify how carbonated water came to be added to his medicinal syrup to produce the 'delicious and refreshing drink' that soda fountains sold for 5 cents a glass. It is known, however, that the brand name was suggested by Pemberton's partner and book-keeper, Frank Robinson. Pemberton never realized the potential for his invention and readily sold more and more shares in his business until, in 1888, all rights to the product were owned by businessman, Asa Candler. Pemberton had earned some $2300 for his product.

Candler understood merchandising, and this was to provide the foundations for the real early growth – he gave away free-drink coupons, advertised the product and introduced Coca-Cola souvenirs. More recent advertising slogans such as 'It's the real thing', 'Things go better with Coke', 'Coke adds life' and 'Always Coca-Cola' are testimony to Candler's legacy. By 1895 there were production plants and sales into every state in America. The second important entrepreneur was a soda fountain owner in Vicksburg, Mississippi – Joseph Biedenhorn. Impressed by customer reaction, Biedenhorn installed a bottling machine and started taking bottled Coca-Cola out to plantations and lumber camps. But really this was the extent of his ambition and his idea was copied by two Chattanooga businessmen, Benjamin Thomas and Joseph Whitehead, who in 1899 secured exclusive rights to bottle and sell Coca-Cola in most American states. Candler was willing to 'almost give the rights away' because he was not convinced that bottling was the answer. A wide variety of different stoppers were being used, none of which was ideal. The solution lay with the crimped cap, which, although invented, was slow to gain wide acceptance because of the need for huge investments in new machinery and new bottles. Thomas and Whitehead timed their move perfectly. These partners set up a network of franchised local bottlers, and thus established a pattern ubiquitous in soft drinks distribution to this day. 'They gave birth to one of the most innovative, dynamic franchising systems in the world.' The distinctively shaped contour bottle first appeared in 1916, a design the company ultimately patented in 1960.

A new era began when the Candler family sold Coca-Cola to another businessman, Ernest Woodruff, for $25 million in 1919. Ernest's son, Robert, took over the business in 1923. Under his innovatory leadership came the six-bottle pack, exports of the syrup to other countries (1926), metal-top open coolers for selling ice-cold Coca-Cola in retail stores (1929) and automatic fountain dispensers (1933). In 1941, with sugar rationed and the Americans at war, Woodruff instructed his managers to 'see that every man in uniform gets a bottle of Coca-Cola for 5 cents, wherever he is and whatever it costs the company'. This led to the opening of new bottling plants wherever troops were stationed and eventually to the new intent – 'always have Coke within an arm's reach of desire'. Both Woodruff and General (later President) Eisenhower realized the power of the Coca-Cola brand – more than anything else it symbolized America and reminded the troops of just what they were fighting for. Woodruff continued the earlier emphasis on marketing such that Coke calendars, desk blotters, napkins and the like became ubiquitous. He also insisted that the secret formula for the concentrate was known only to two people at any one time, and that they never flew together. In itself, this was never really an important issue, but the mystique it conveyed proved invaluable.

Distribution has always been the key to success. The company has always retained control over the syrup, but has not seen it essential to own the bottling plants, as long as the supply arrangements were robust. There is little logic in transporting the canned or bottled product over great distances – its main constituent is water! There are special Coca-Cola aisles in Wal-Mart stores and exclusive supply arrangements for certain products with McDonald's.

Coca-Cola was first canned in 1964, and plastic bottles came on the scene in 1969. Different sizes and packs have followed, as have related new products – Fanta, Tab (sugar-free Coke), Fresca, Diet Coke and Minute Maid (fruit juices, and a business that Coca-Cola acquired). None the less there have been strategic misjudgements, which arguably reflect the dangers in losing focus on what a business is really about. The 1982 acquisition of Columbia Pictures culminated in its sale to Sony when the hoped for synergistic benefits did not accrue; and the decision in 1985 to change the flavour with New Coke was quickly reversed when customer reaction was hostile. Ironically, Robert Woodruff, who had maintained an active involvement with the company after his retirement and until his death in 1984 (at the age of ninety-four), had always been steadfast in his refusal to countenance a change to the formula. It was not that he believed the taste was incapable of improvement, but because of the symbolism of the original. He always realized that Coca-Cola has never been just a soft drink.

Richard Branson and Virgin

Richard Branson is unquestionably a legend in his own lifetime. His name and presence are associated closely with all the Virgin activities and businesses, and he has demonstrated a unique ability to exploit a brand name and apply it to a range of diversified products and services. He *is* Virgin – so, will he leave a lasting business legacy like Ray Kroc has done? Could this company outlive its founder? Or would Virgin be split up into its many constituent businesses without Branson to lead it?

Branson is creative, opportunistic and dedicated to those activities he engages in. Possessed of a strong ego drive, he is an excellent self-publicist. Popular with customers and employees, he has created a hugely successful people-driven business. His determination to succeed and his willingness to take risks are manifest in his transatlantic powerboating and round-the-world ballooning exploits. Although he has said that he 'wouldn't do this if I didn't think I'd survive', the *Financial Times* has commented that 'all those associated with Mr Branson have to accept that he is an adventurer . . . he takes risks few of us would contemplate'. He has chosen to enter and compete in industries dominated by large and powerful corporations. Having challenged British Airways for example, Coca-Cola has been a more recent target. Significantly, and not unexpectedly, his name comes up frequently when other business people are asked to name the person they most admire.

Now fifty years old, Branson has been running businesses for over thirty years. He began *Student* magazine when he was a sixteen-year-old public schoolboy, selling advertising from a public phone booth. Ever opportunistic, he incorporated a mail-order record business, buying the records from wholesalers once he himself had a firm order and cash in advance. Thwarted by a two-month postal strike, Branson decided to enter retailing. Realizing the importance of location, he started looking for something along Oxford Street in London. Spotting an unused first floor above a shoe shop, he persuaded the owner to let him use it rent-free until a paying tenant came along, on the grounds that if he was successful he would generate extra business for the shoe shop! He had a queue stretching 100 yards when it opened and never looked back – characteristically he had turned a threat into an opportunity. The London record shop was followed by record production – Branson signed and released Mike Oldfield's *Tubular Bells* after Oldfield had been turned down by all the leading record companies. Branson was always an astute and visionary businessman, carefully recruiting people with the necessary expertise to manage the detail of his various enterprises. His main skill has been in networking, finding opportunities and securing the resources necessary for their exploitation. In this he has had to show courage and flexibility.

Virgin Atlantic Airways was started after an American businessman suggested the idea of an all business-class transatlantic airline. Branson rejected this particular strategy but was hooked on the idea. Initially he minimized the risk by leasing everything, and he was able to compete with the larger airlines by offering a perceived higher level of service at attractive prices. Over many years he has successfully marketed a range of products and services by systematically applying the Virgin brand name. The products and services may have been diversified – holidays, consumer products such as Virgin Vodka and Virgin Cola, cinemas, a radio station, financial services and Virgin Railways are examples – but the customer-focused brand image has remained constant.

Virgin was floated in 1986 but later reprivatized; Branson had been uncomfortable with the accountability expectations of institutional shareholders. Since then he has used joint ventures, minority partners and divestments (such as the sales of his music business and record shops) to raise money for new ventures and changes of direction. In 1999 Branson sold a 49 per cent stake in the airline to Singapore Airlines, partly to strengthen its competitiveness, but also to raise money for investment in further new ventures. Describing itself as a 'branded venture capital company' Virgin had already created over 200 businesses and Branson decided to target electronic commerce and the Internet, believing a vast range of products and services can be sold this way under the Virgin umbrella.

Branson's business philosophy is built around quality products and services, value for money, innovation and an element of fun. 'I never let accountants get in the way of business. You only live once and you might as well have a fun time while you're living.' By focusing on customers and service he has frequently been able to add value where larger competitors have developed a degree of complacency. 'The challenge of learning and trying to do something better than in the past is irresistible.' Branson always realized that this would be impossible without the appropriate people and he created an organization with a devolved and informal culture. Business ideas can – and do – come from anywhere in Virgin. Employees with ideas that Branson likes will be given encouragement and development capital. Once a venture reaches a certain size it is freed to operate as an independent business within the Virgin Group – and the intrapreneur retains an equity stake. Branson runs Virgin from a large house in London's Holland Park, having outgrown the canal narrowboat he used for many years. There has never been a traditional head office infrastructure.

James Dyson

Dyson is another entrepreneur who challenged the industry giants, in his case with a revolutionary vacuum cleaner. His dual cyclone cleaner now has a UK market share in excess of 50 per cent and international sales are booming. A Hoover spokesman has said on the BBC's *Money Programme*: 'I regret Hoover as a company did not take the product technology of Dyson ... it would have been lain on a shelf and not been used.' Dyson has been compared by Professor Christopher Frayling, Rector of the Royal College of Art, with 'the great Victorian ironmasters ... a one-man attempt to revive British manufacturing industry through design'. Dyson is creative, innovative, totally focused on customers and driven by a desire to improve everyday products. His dedication and ego drive is reflected in the following comment: 'the only way to make a genuine breakthrough is to pursue a vision with a single-minded determination in the face of criticism' – and this is exactly what he has done. Clearly a risk-taker, he invested all his resources in his venture. In the end his rise to fame and fortune came quickly, but the preceding years had been painful and protracted, and characterized by courage and persistence. They reflect the adage that 'instant success takes time'.

James Dyson's schoolmaster father died when James was just nine years old. The public school to which he was then sent 'made him a fighter'. At school he excelled in running, practising by running cross countries on his own; and it was on these runs that he began to appreciate the magnificence of the railway bridges constructed by Brunel in the last century – an experience which helped form his personal vision. An early leap in the dark came when he volunteered to play bassoon in the school orchestra, without ever having seen a bassoon! Naturally artistic, he won a painting competition sponsored by the *Eagle* comic when he was ten years old. Art became a passion and he later went on to complete a degree in interior design – Dyson may be an inventor, but he has no formal engineering background.

Dyson's first successful product and business was a flat-bottomed boat, the Sea Truck. At this time he learnt how a spherical plastic ball could be moulded, an idea he turned to good use in the wild garden of his new home. His wheelbarrow was inadequate as the wheels sank into the ground, so he substituted the wheel with a light plastic ball and thus invented the Ballbarrow. Backed by his brother-in-law on a 50:50 basis, Dyson invested in his new idea. Made of colourful, light plastic the barrow was offered to garden centres and the building trade, both of whom were less than enthusiastic. With a switch to direct mail via newspaper advertisements, the business took off. A new sales manager was appointed but his renewed attempt to sell the barrow through more traditional retail channels was again a failure. The financial penalty was the need for external investors, who later persuaded Dyson's brother-in-law to sell the business. A second painful experience came when the sales manager took the idea and design to America, where Dyson later failed with a legal action against him.

Dyson's idea for a dual cyclone household cleaner came in 1979, when he was thirty-one years old. Again it was a case of a need creating an opportunity. He was converting his old house and becoming frustrated that his vacuum cleaner would not clear all the dust he was creating. Particles were clogging the pores of the dust bags and reducing the suction capability of the cleaner. Needing something to collect paint particles from his plastic-spraying operation for the Ballbarrows, Dyson had developed a smaller version of the large industrial cyclone machines, which separate particles from air by using centrifugal forces in spinning cylinders. He believed this technology could be adapted for home vacuum cleaners, removing the need for bags, but his partners in the Ballbarrow business failed to share his enthusiasm. Out of work when the business was sold, his previous employer, Jeremy Fry (for whom he had developed the Sea Truck) loaned him £25 000. Dyson matched this by selling his vegetable garden for £18 000 and taking out an additional £7000 overdraft on his house. Working from home, risking everything and drawing just £10 000 a year to keep himself, his wife and three children, he pursued his idea. Over the years he produced 5000 different prototypes.

When he ultimately approached the established manufacturers his idea was, perhaps predictably, rejected. Replacement dust bags are an important source of additional revenue. A series of discussions with potential partners who might license his idea brought mixed results. Fresh legal actions in America for patent infringement – 'with hindsight I didn't patent enough features' – were only partially offset by a deal with Apex of Japan. Dyson designed the G-Force upright cleaner which Apex manufactured and sold to a niche in the Japanese market for the equivalent of £1200 per machine, from which Dyson received just £20. At least there was now an income stream, but this had taken seven years to achieve. Finally in 1991 Lloyds Bank provided finance for the design and manufacture of a machine in the UK. Several venture capitalists and the Welsh Development Agency had turned him down. Dyson was determined to give his latest version the looks of National Aeronautics and Space Administration (NASA) technology, but further setbacks were still to occur. Dyson was let down by the plastic moulder and assembler he contracted with, and was eventually forced to set up his own plant. Early sales through mail-order catalogues were followed by deals with John Lewis stores and eventually (in 1995) with Comet and Currys. In this year a cylinder version joined the upright. Dyson continues to improve the designs to extend his patent protection. By 1999 his personal wealth was estimated to be £500 million.

Dyson has always seen himself as more of an inventor than a businessman. He runs two separate businesses, both in Malmesbury, Wiltshire – he keeps Dyson Manufacturing and Dyson Research (design and patenting) apart. The dress code for employees is perpetually informal and communications are predominantly face to face. Memos are banned and even e-mails are discouraged. Every employee is encouraged to be creative and contribute ideas. Most new employees are young – 'not contaminated by other employers' – and they all begin by assembling their own vacuum cleaner, which they can then buy for £20. There are over sixty designers, who work on improvements to the dual cyclone cleaners as well as new product ideas. In early 2000 Dyson launched a robot version of the dual cyclone cleaner, which is battery-powered, self-propelled and able to manoeuvre itself around furniture. It retails at about £2500, which may limit it to a select segment of the market. Dyson is also reported to be working on a super-fast washing machine with short wash cycles and an ability to spin clothes almost dry – another challenge to the manufacturers of both washing machines and tumble dryers. This time, however, Dyson has his own resources to launch the product! Moreover Dyson controls 100 per cent of the shares in the business. He has learnt some painful lessons but is now enjoying the rewards of his dogged determination.

In this chapter we have looked at a number of legendary individuals and businesses to illustrate the key points introduced in Chapter 1. Entrepreneurs have the ability to see a potential opportunity and obtain the resources required to exploit it. Sometimes things happen quickly; sometimes it takes longer. The most robust and entrepreneurial businesses sustain their growth with renewed innovation – but rarely do they lose sight of the essential values upon which the business has been built. Understanding – and satisfying – the needs and expectations of customers and the development of committed employees are both essential. Our truly successful entrepreneurs have this ability to focus on key issues and remain dedicated to the business, creatively overcoming the inevitable setbacks and hurdles. Sometimes they are visionary, but not always. They are, however, all possessed by a desire to achieve. We take these points further in the next chapter by showing how entrepreneurs and entrepreneurship can be found in all types of business and business activity.

4 Business entrepreneurs

Entrepreneurship is about opportunity. Successful entrepreneurs spot opportunities, often where others fail to see the same idea at the same time, although the same information is available to them. But this is merely the beginning of a process. The good idea has to be made to happen. The project has to be championed. Customers have to be found and consumers satisfied. Service has to be delivered. Changes, modifications and improvements will be required to sustain a competitive advantage. To achieve all this, an organization and a strong team of people has to be developed. In this chapter we look at the successful execution of this process in the context of a wide range of different business ideas and opportunities.

Entrepreneurship has been defined by Murray Low, Dean of the Columbia Business School in America as 'identifying, valuing and capturing opportunity'. It follows, therefore, that entrepreneurs recognize opportunities – they may or may not actually invent the ideas personally – and then exploit these opportunities by creating and building successful operations or organizations. It was commented at the beginning of Chapter 3 that the truly successful entrepreneurs are 'off the scale' in terms of opportunity and people. Some of their activities and behaviours are the result of training (which enhances their technique), but talent and temperament are critical. In fact, it has been suggested that 'if Thomas Edison had gone to Business School, we would all be reading by larger candles!'

Reinforcing points made in Chapter 2, strategy matters in entrepreneurship. Businesses cannot grow and prosper without an underlying 'good idea' which creates and adds value for customers and consumers, positions the company distinctively in terms of its competitors and represents a valuable competitive edge. This added value and difference generates the all-important profit. But the idea alone is inadequate. It must be implemented successfully, and then the advantage must be sustained with flexibility, innovation and change. For this to happen, the support and contribution of people is essential to create a virtuous circle. Committed and motivated employees deliver satisfaction to customers; with loyal and satisfied customers, companies are able to grow and prosper. To complete the circle, employees have to be rewarded accordingly to maintain their contribution.

Buckingham and Coffman (1999) delineate four levels of customer expectation. The first level is accuracy – making sure the details are correct – and the second level is availability – making things convenient for the customer. These are relatively easily met and largely taken for granted by the market. Without them continued business is unlikely. The most successful organizations achieve at levels three and four – forming working partnerships with their customers and providing them with advice that can help them with other decisions they have to make. These key implementation issues come down to people. The most successful entrepreneurs are able to look outside the organization and clarify a winning direction and strategic position, and also create and nurture an internal structure and team which delivers the four levels of expectation. To be truly effective, this relies on the contribution and style of individual managers. If employees have good bosses, they stay, they commit and they produce. This requires that employees have appropriate targets for achievement, they are placed where they can exploit their strengths, they are supported and they are rewarded.

In this chapter we look at several examples of successful entrepreneurs in various types of business situation and consistently see evidence of these achievements and of the virtuous circle. In addition, we see *habitual entrepreneurship* in action, where entrepreneurs create and maintain a momentum and do not stand still. The majority of successful entrepreneurs find new opportunities to add different values in their existing businesses, changing flexibly to sustain competitive advantage. Others retire from one business and start another, but largely staying focused at any one time. A minority of successful entrepreneurs will be active in more than one activity at the same time.

These arguments are confirmed by Charan and Colvin's (1999) research, which shows the average survival rate for chief executives in large US corporations is under five years. The problem is generally not one of shortcomings in the strategy or vision but, rather, the inability to implement. Good strategic ideas soon become public property. The secret of success lies in the way the idea is implemented and changed for sustained advantage. 'Southwest Airlines [discussed in Chapter 6] is the only US airline that has been consistently profitable over its lifetime [twenty-eight years]. Everyone knows its strategy, yet no rival has successfully copied its execution.' We can see evidence of a number of entrepreneurial themes in those strategic leaders who are most successful. They are dedicated to and focused on the strategy; they are able to activate and make things happen; they are profits and results driven; and they work hard to develop individuals and teams. 'Not putting the right people in the right jobs' is the key reason for chief executive failure.

This chapter shows how entrepreneurial business opportunities can be found 'everywhere'. Some are genuinely new; others are innovatory improvements on a theme. Some are limited-growth ideas; others can be used to build global businesses. They only succeed if they are different in some meaningful way and executed effectively. There is, then, an infinite set of possibilities for people with the talent and temperament to become successful entrepreneurs to choose from. But, as we have said, spotting the idea and the opportunity is only the start. The cases and examples reported in this chapter also provide insights and a number of valuable lessons in implementation.

We explore a range of different opportunities – niche market opportunities, the creation of new markets, transposing good ideas, opportunities through privatization and management buy-outs. We look at individual and team entrepreneurs, at ones who focus on a single business and others who start several in a series, and at issues of family inheritance. We explore entrepreneurship in large organizations, in the form of both intrapreneurship and turnaround strategy; and we look at examples of successful entrepreneurs who operate on the fringe of other businesses. The chapter concludes with an illustration of how an academic background and experience can provide an ideal opportunity for people with the talent to be a successful entrepreneur. We include stories of entrepreneurs who have built something substantial from scratch, entrepreneurial managers who have built something innovative inside a larger organization and entrepreneurs who have *re*built an organization in trouble. They have all found new opportunities for creating and building new values.

This is a long chapter and to make it easier for the reader we have divided it into two discrete sections. The two parts can be read together or separately. In the first section, 'Opportunity entrepreneurs', we identify a range of successful business people about whom one might easily say, 'Why didn't I think of that?' The second section builds on this and describes a number of business opportunities that are available for people with the requisite talent and temperament.

Opportunity entrepreneurs

Niche market opportunities

David Bruce   In the late 1990s Allied Domecq had been opening forty new Firkin pubs every year, and expanding into Europe, before it sold the chain to Punch Taverns. Allied had bought the name and concept in 1991, but the first Firkin pub had been opened in 1979 when David Bruce, with a background in the brewing industry, realized there was an opportunity for a pub which brewed its own real ale on site. Bruce bought the lease on an existing pub which was about to close down at the Elephant and Castle in South London. Renaming it the Goose and Firkin, he remodelled it as an old-fashioned drinking house – with bare floorboards. Some beer was bought in, but most was brewed in the cellar. His own brews were all strong and distinctive – and with unusual names such as Bruce's Dog Bolter and Bruce's Earth Stopper. The pub was an instant success, and in 1980 he opened a second one. By 1987 he had eleven pubs in Greater London, all with Firkin in the name and nine with on-site brewing. His tongue-in-cheek promotions became increasingly outrageous. The Flounder and Firkin was 'a plaice worth whiteing home about' and you could 'spectre good pint when you ghost to the Phantom and Firkin' – for a pint of Bruce's Spook!

The structure was not developed in line with the growth, however, and the entrepreneur was stretched. David Bruce recruited a microbiologist and an accountant, and he put a manager into every pub – but he remained personally responsible for ensuring his vision and concept were delivered consistently. He believed in the personal touch. In 1988 he decided to sell his chain to Midsummer Leisure, netting a personal sum of £1 million. He then established a charitable trust to provide canal holidays for disabled people, but returned to brewing in 1990. This time he kept his organization smaller, focusing on just two pubs. They were both named the Hedgehog and Hogshead – one in Hove, Sussex, and the other in Southampton. The concept was the same one as his original Firkin pubs, none of which now brew on site.

He later moved to other ventures before entering a joint venture with W. H. Brakspear in September 1999. Brakspear has brewed in Henley-on-Thames since 1779. One of Bruce's other ideas had been the Bertie Belcher brand, 'pubs that brew the beer you'll want to repeat'. The name for the new venture is Honeypot Inns; David Bruce is chief executive. Brakspear has put seven managed pubs into the venture (six more will be added every year) and they will be retained as independent pubs which reflect the character of the building and their local communities. They will be a loose chain, linked by a common brand-name but they will all be individual. The new additions will be unusual sites rather than typical high streets.

Brakspear believe Bruce has 'tremendous skills for identifying opportunities for the development of retail operations that catch the imagination of consumers'. He is certainly a master of the weak pun. Bruce asserts that 'creating the right ambience is an innate skill – not something I can explain'. He fully intends to move on again when the venture is properly up and running: 'I put my all into these ventures for up to five years and then I have to do something else.' He is a serial entrepreneur.

Flying Flowers   Flying Flowers provides an ideal example of an opportunity waiting to be seen. It was set up in Jersey in the early 1980s when the owners of a loss-making nursery needed to create a new future for their business. The idea – mail-order boxed flowers throughout the year – has proved so successful, it has outgrown the growing capacity of the nursery. People who order Flying Flowers certainly still receive flowers *from* Jersey, but they may well have been grown as far away as Colombia and bought in. Demand for the flowers is cyclical, with massive peaks at Christmas and for Mother's Day. The company's main activity is now box-making, which it carries out all-year-round, holding stocks in readiness. One critical key success factor lies in harnessing information technology to maintain a database and handle both the promotional and ordering activities. These skills have been further exploited with a number of acquisitions. Flying Flowers has bought other businesses, including Gardening Direct (bedding plants), Stanley Gibbons (publisher and stamp supplier) and another supplier of first-day stamp covers.

Air Miles   Another example of a niche opportunity waiting to be seen is Air Miles, founded in 1988 by Keith Mills, who had a background in advertising. Air Miles provided an opportunity for airlines and hotels to sell their spare capacity in new markets when supermarket and other customers were given the opportunity to collect air miles (which they could later exchange for air tickets and leisure breaks) as a form of promotional discount. The success of Air Miles has spawned a whole range of variants, including the loyalty programmes run by the airlines and hotel chains themselves and the Profiles points (exchangeable for goods as well as leisure services) earned by Barclaycard holders.

Steve Pateman A final and more bizarre niche opportunity was found by Steve Pateman, the owner and manager of a family shoemaking business in Northamptonshire. His business, like many other British companies in this industry, had become uncompetitive against cheaper imports – so he adapted his machines and began to manufacture boots and kinky leather goods for the fetish market. To boost sales – and after shaving his legs – Pateman turns up personally at erotica shows to demonstrate his products. Local people think 'he is from another planet' but he has been described differently by Sir John Harvey-Jones: 'that man is an absolute hero . . . people laugh, but he was going to fight for his business and his people, no matter what. You have to produce something that is different. You can no longer compete just by being better at what you do'.

Opening up new markets

Occasionally a new, innovatory, entrepreneurial idea changes the nature and the rules of competition in an industry. When this happens it is by no means certain that the idea comes from an existing competitor – the idea may well provide an opportunity and a springboard for a new competitor to break in and steal market share from existing players.

Direct Line Direct Line, launched in 1985, had this impact on the established insurance industry. The idea belonged to Peter Wood, who secured financial backing (£20 million) from the Royal Bank of Scotland. Wood's background was in information technology. Direct Line used information technology (IT) to sell motor insurance direct to customers, without the need for expensive offices and brokers. The savings in overheads and commissions can be passed on to customers in the form of lower prices. Wood thus 'shook an industry that was not used to revolutionaries', and forced many existing businesses to follow his lead and change their ways of operating. Wood made sure he had a strong, albeit small, team of insurance actuaries and IT experts to run Direct Line, and within a year he had secured 1 per cent of a huge market. Within ten years, this share had grown to 10 per cent. At the end of the 1990s Direct Line is the UK's market leader for motor insurance and seventh for homes and contents. It has three million customers and Peter Wood has sold his share of the business to the Royal Bank of Scotland. Peter Wood challenged and changed an established industry; the next two illustrations show how a new market can be opened up and how emerging technologies can provide new opportunities for the astute entrepreneur.

Mrs. Fields Cookies The business which opened up a new market and spawned competition is Mrs. Fields Cookies, which has again relied extensively upon information technology for its growth and success. The company began in 1977 in Palo

Alto, California, when a young wife, the then twenty-years-old Debbi Fields, was determined to do something on her own. When she opened her first outlet selling home-made chocolate chip cookies, her sceptical husband, Randy, an economist, bet her that her first-day sales would not reach $50. When he seemed to be on to a winner, Debbi filled a tray with free samples and went out into the street. Her initiative worked and first-day sales amounted to $75. The business has continued to grow ever since. There are now over 1000 outlets in nine countries, selling a range of high-quality, premium price, fresh cookies, all made on the premises. The head office is in Utah, there are 5000 employees worldwide and annual sales exceed $300 million. The outlets are often strategically located in shopping malls and airports to tempt impulse buyers who fancy a snack. Quite often people buy just one single cookie, although many do buy a batch.

The idea was a simple one, and the business has stayed strictly focused. Debbi Fields was 'a simple person with a fire in her oven, tremendous values and a great idea'. There are smaller rival chains, and many specialist chocolate and fudge stores adopt similar principles. Mrs. Fields has prospered with a centralized information technology system that provides an hourly baking schedule for every outlet. This system allows sales staff to concentrate on customer service and it adjusts the schedule in line with the local sales pattern at every unit. In addition it flags when sales are dropping below critical target levels and when it is appropriate to go out with trays of free samples. The success of this system is attributed largely to Randy, who joined the business when it began to really take-off.

Car Phone Warehouse   With the Car Phone Warehouse Charles Dunstone saw his opportunity in the rapidly growing new market for mobile phones. Dunstone had been a sales manager with the electronics company NEC, and he used £6000 of his savings to open his first store. In just ten years the business has grown to 450 stores, including the 270 Tandy computer stores that Dunstone has bought. Sales exceeded £350 million in 1999 – and Dunstone still owns half the business. Car Phone Warehouse is Britain's leading mobile phone retailer. Dunstone has sustained his position and lead by finding new ways to add value in a rapidly changing market. He was an early national advertiser, using Capital FM radio to target specific customer groups. His theme is based on reassurance and expert, objective advice to help people select a phone and payment system that is right for them. The market is complex and potentially confusing with a huge array of choices – and, for many potential customers, a lack of knowledge about the alternatives on offer.

Enterprise magazine carries out an annual survey in the UK to identify the top 100 entrepreneurs, determined by personal wealth created, annual sales growth over a period and the number of jobs created. In 1998 the overall winner was James Dyson, who was discussed in Chapter 2. Interestingly 14 per cent of the top 100 entrepreneurs in the analysis were retailers, including Charles Dunstone, and high-lighting how this service business continuously offers fresh opportunities for adding new values. Mobile phone services contributed another 6 per cent of the hundred, and those based on the similarly rapidly emerging computing and software industries another 18 per cent.

Federal Express   Federal Express (FedEx) provides an excellent example of an organization and an entrepreneur that opened up an unrealized market opportunity and began a new industry. 'The greatest business opportunities arise when you spot things your customer didn't have a clue they needed until you offered it to them.' Again the idea is simple. It is to provide a speedy and reliable national and international 'overnight' courier service for letters and parcels based upon air cargo. 'We invented the concept of overnight delivery, creating a whole new market where previously there was none.' FedEx is, however, unusual in a number of ways. Before it could even begin, FedEx needed a nationwide (North American) distribution system with a fleet of planes and trucks.

The business was the idea of Fred Smith, whose father was also an entrepreneur who had founded and built a successful bus company. When Fred was a student at Yale in the 1960s he wrote a paper outlining his idea for a freight-only airline which delivered and collected parcels to and from a series of hubs. Traditionally parcels were shipped on scheduled passenger airlines as normal mail, whilst Smith proposed flying at night when the skies were relatively quiet. His paper was graded as a C. After graduating, Smith served as a pilot in Vietnam before he bought a controlling interest in Arkansas Aviation Sales, a company which carried out modifications and overhauls. Determined to implement his idea for a courier service he invested a $10 million family inheritance and raised a further $72 million from various sources based on a number of independent but positive feasibility studies.

FedEx took to the skies in 1973, offering a service in and out of twenty-five US East Coast cities with fourteen jet aircraft. The demand was there, as he had forecast. Unfortunately the rise in the Organization of Petroleum-Exporting Countries (OPEC) oil price made FedEx uneconomical almost as soon as it started. Two years of losses and family squabbles – Smith was accused of 'squandering the family fortune' – were followed by profits and Smith's belief and persistence were rewarded.

FedEx is successful because it delivers on time and speedily, and because it has a sophisticated tracking system for when something does go astray. There are now 600 FedEx aircraft flying one million miles every two days. The central hub is in Memphis but the flights are international. Three million packages from 200 countries are handled every night. FedEx's courier vans cover another two million miles every day collecting and delivering these parcels. To ensure FedEx can maintain its service it flies empty aircraft every night, which track close to the pick-up airports and which are brought into service if they are needed.

New opportunities based upon existing ideas

Kwik Fit   The phenomenally successful Kwik Fit outlets in the UK were transplanted from the USA, but again the potential for the idea had to be seen and exploited. Tom Farmer (now Sir Tom Farmer) was born in 1940, the seventh child of a shipping agent who lived in a two-bedroomed house in Leith, Edinburgh. Slightly built – Farmer is just over five feet tall – Tom grew up a Roman Catholic in a largely Protestant city. At the age of fifteen he began working for a tyre replacement business. Eight years later he borrowed £200 from his bank to start his own tyre business. He painted his shop with bright blue and yellow paint – selected simply because he could get these colours free – and began selling tyres at discount prices. He acquired the tyres on a sale-or-return basis. When new, tighter tyre regulations gave a boost to the tyre replacement market, Farmer quickly expanded to four shops. Before he was thirty years old he had sold up and retired with his family to California (where one of his sisters lived) with £450 000 in his pocket.

By 1971 he was bored and in need of a fresh challenge. He had seen the localized success of fast-change tyre and exhaust shops in America, and returned to Scotland with the idea. He claims the name 'Kwik Fit' came to him in a dream. He re-employed a number of his old friends and loyal employees and again adopted the distinctive blue and yellow colours. There are now 1900 outlets, 10 000 employees and eight million customers a year. Kwik Fit has diversified into insurance to exploit its name and image; and Tom Farmer sold his business to Ford for £1 billion in 1999. He is still active in the business; he has not retired.

Tom Farmer was always a dedicated workaholic with a strong sense of community. He was focused and dedicated and keen to look after his people. Kwik Fit has always been perceived to offer a high level of integrity in an industry often thought to involve dubious commercial practices. 'All sound businesses are built on good Christian ethics – don't steal, don't exploit your customers or your people, always use your profits for the benefit of your people and the community.'

Starbucks   In under fifteen years Starbucks grew from a single store on the Seattle waterfront to a chain of over 1600 across America, spawning competitors in the USA and elsewhere. As part of its drive to expand internationally, Starbucks bought its smaller UK rival, The Seattle Coffee Company, in 1998. Starbucks succeeded because it found the right way to blend sales of top-grade fresh coffee beans with sales of cups of coffee to drink. Coffee bars have existed for a very long time, but rarely have they featured the strong and distinctive aroma found in stores that sell fresh coffee. The individual drinks are relatively expensive, but they are individualized and made to order. There is a wide range of piping hot and iced cold variants to choose from. Although coffee to drink is very much the leading product, fresh coffee beans and a range of related products, such as cakes, biscuits, mugs and coffee-makers are also on offer. Customers include shoppers and working people from local stores and offices at lunchtime and teatime on their way home – people who take time to relax and converse over their coffee – as well as people who pop out from work to their nearest outlet when they have a short break because the coffee is perceived superior to the instant they might otherwise have to drink. Outlets can also be found at airport terminals and in those bookstores where people go to browse and relax. Essentially, Starbucks 'sells an emotional experience' and not just a commodity product. It thus adds value.

The success is down to Howard Schulz, who grew up the son of a blue-collar worker in Brooklyn. Schulz became a salesman, and when he was working for a house-ware products company he visited Seattle and was introduced to the Starbucks Coffee Company, a business that sold imported coffee beans. He joined the business in 1982 with the title of Marketing Director. Enthused by the espresso bars he found on a business trip to Italy, and convinced a similar concept could be developed for America, he attempted to sell the idea to his bosses. The family declined to go along with him and he left to start up on his own. He managed to raise enough money to open one outlet – within two years he was in a position to buy out Starbucks.

Schulz claims that his mission has always been to 'educate consumers everywhere about fine coffee'. Customers who visit Starbucks must feel relaxed and enjoy 'a sense of wonder and romance in the midst of their harried lives'. People will pay 'arguably outrageous prices' for their coffee whilst ever it is seen as an indulgence. If this is to be achieved, staff attitudes and behaviours are critical. Service, therefore, is everything. Schulz has created Starbucks as 'living proof that a company can lead with its heart and nurture its soul and still make money'. Employees are seen as partners. Including part-timers, they all enjoy free health insurance, stock options (known as bean stock), training programmes and wages above the industry average. Although many are young and fit, students who will not stay long enough to earn stock options and who will not need health care, they feel valued and consequently deliver the desired service. We have already seen these 'virtuous circle' themes in some of the organizations included in Chapter 3 and we will see them repeated in other successful organizations featured in this chapter. They matter. In addition, all unsold beans over eight days old are given away free to local food banks. Nevertheless the company has also been criticized for exploiting cheap labour in coffee-growing countries.

Richer Sounds   Like coffee bars, electrical goods retailers are not new. The dominant names are Comet and Currys, but Richer Sounds is different – and very successful. Richer is more focused than its main rivals, specializing in hi-fi, especially separate units. According to the *Guinness Book of Records*, Richer achieves the highest sales per square foot of any retailer in the world. Sales per employee are also high. Stock is piled high to the ceilings in relatively small stores in typically low-rent locations. All the main brands can be found; the latest models feature alongside discontinued ones, these at very competitive prices. 'We just aren't that ambitious [to justify diversifying] . . . we feel that by staying with what we know best we can concentrate our effort and resources in one field and hopefully do it well'.

Julian Richer was born in 1959; his parents both worked for Marks & Spencer. He was just nineteen when he opened his first shop at London Bridge – 'seventy thousand commuters passed the shop every day'. He now owns thirty stores in twenty-five towns and cities. Apart from Christmas, Richer will not open on Sundays. His employees are known as colleagues and they are empowered to work 'The Richer Way'. He claims his suggestion scheme has generated the highest number of suggestions per employee of any scheme anywhere in the world – the best ideas are rewarded with trips on the Orient Express. The most successful employees (in terms of sales) can win free use of a holiday home; the most successful shops earn the free use of a Bentley or Jaguar for a month. Every employee is allowed £5 per month 'to go to the pub and brainstorm'. Julian Richer has advised Asda (featured later in this chapter) on suggestion schemes, and past Asda Chairman, Archie Norman, has said: 'Julian has gone to great lengths to create a system that works without him, but, to a great extent, his business is his personality.'

Richer has established a parallel consulting arm – with eight consultants who offer 'The Richer Way as a philosophy for delighting customers'. Consultancy is provided free to charities and good causes. Richer has also established a foundation to help selected good causes, and he also owns a number of other small businesses. These include the Fox Talbot chain of photography stores, a retail recruitment agency, a property portfolio, a men's clothes shop in Bristol and an award-winning restaurant in Islington. He has, however, 'one business and a number of hobbies'.

Harry Ramsden's   Another example of an outstanding success in a very competitive market is Harry Ramsden's. Fish and chip shops are ubiquitous. Sometimes they include seating areas, but mostly they are local takeaways. Harry Ramsden was the entrepreneur who began a fish and chip restaurant business that has become an international chain. He introduced a particular style for his restaurants, but this ambience and the menu could be copied by anyone. His publicity-driven image and concentration on high quality and service have, however, provided the edge.

Harry began like most other fish and chip proprietors with a small frier, in downtown Bradford. He was forced to move out into the country when his wife was taken ill with tuberculosis in 1928. Aged forty-two, Harry borrowed £150 and opened a small cabin outside Leeds on the main road to the Yorkshire Dales and the Lake District. Largely reliant on a passing trade at the beginning he created an opportunity by offering high-quality food. His reputation for quality spread and people began to make special trips from Bradford and Leeds simply to buy his takeaway fish and chips. His success encouraged him to build the 'largest fish and chip emporium in the world' – which opened in 1931 on the same site. The restaurant was smart and stylish, 'more reminiscent of London's West End than Yorkshire', but his success continued with the same high quality at affordable prices. The business continued to succeed and prosper. Takeaway food was available as well as the seated restaurant; an accompanying shop sold memorabilia. When the restaurant was twenty-one years old in 1952, Harry offered meals at 1912 prices – for one day only. Encouraged by massive publicity and supported by a band and a fair, Harry sold 10 000 meals in a single day. In the world of Yorkshire fish and chips he was now a legend.

Harry Ramsden died in 1963. By then he had sold the business to his previous manager, who sold it again in 1965, to Associated Fisheries. By never losing sight of Harry's vision and competitive edge, the concept has been extended to a range of restaurants and shops throughout the UK, including Heathrow Airport, and to other countries, including sites in Hong Kong, Dublin, Singapore and Jeddah. The business was sold again in 1999, this time to media and hotel group, Granada.

The next cases in this chapter look at other effective entrepreneurial teams, where people find good, appropriate partners with complementary strengths which allow them to focus on their own personal strengths and not worry unduly about overcoming their weaknesses.

Team entrepreneurs

Derwent Valley Foods   Roger McKechnie, an ex-marketing director for Tudor Crisps (owned by US giant General Mills), was the founding partner of Derwent Valley Foods in 1982. He was driven by a desire to be independent and attracted to Consett, once a prosperous steel town in his native north-east where his wife is a general practitioner – and an unlikely location for a new food business – by generous investment grants. He was joined by an old university friend who had been working in international advertising – and the two began to look for a product idea and new opportunity.

They chose to focus on packeted corn-based snacks and chose the brand-name Phileas Fogg. They imported their ideas from America, where the adult premium snack market was already well established. They started with tortilla chips and progressed to California corn grits and Shanghai nuts. Joined by two other experienced managers – and acquaintances – with a food background, the team secured financial backing and persevered against initial market scepticism. Eventually they secured the distribution agreements they needed, and demand was so strong they were soon overtrading and, as a result, experiencing cash flow problems. Moreover, the wastage rates were high. Lacking experience with the particular problems of small, growing businesses, the team had to learn quickly and adapt – but with innovative new products, Derwent Valley was able to sustain a 33 per cent share of a market they pioneered once competition from major manufacturers was provoked. Their approach was always creative and tongue-in-cheek advertising exploited the Consett origins. The workforce was keen to succeed as the vast majority had been rescued from unemployment. The business was bought by United Biscuits for £24 million in 1993; the founding partners all stayed on.

Roger McKechnie has been described as 'disorganized but determined, erratic and single-minded . . . able to organize and inspire a team'. He says of himself: 'I tend to be an ideas' generator. My strengths are in the strategy and the numbers – and I can get people to be creative. My weakness is I'm disorganized . . . but I'm not a bad delegator and I can delegate problems a lot!'

His founding partner was 'a questioner and deep thinker' and the two other members of the team were 'a pusher who gets things done' and a 'creative overcomer'.

Ben and Jerry's Ice Cream   Another idiosyncratic entrepreneurial business in the same industry is Ben and Jerry's Ice Cream. There are a number of parallels, but some real differences. Ben Cohen was a college dropout who had become a potter. His friend from his schooldays was Jerry Greenfield, a laboratory assistant who had failed to make it into medical school. They had become 'seventies hippies with few real job prospects'. They again decided to do something themselves and 'looked for something they might succeed at'. They 'liked food, so food it was!' They could not afford the machinery for making bagels, but ice cream was affordable. In 1977 they opened an ice cream parlour in Burlington, Vermont, where there were 'lots of students and no real competition'. They fostered a relaxed, hippy atmosphere and employed a blues pianist. Their ice cream was different, with large and unusual chunks.

They were instantly successful in their first summer – but sales fell off in the autumn and winter. They realized they would have to find outlets outside Vermont if they were to survive. Ben went on the road. Always dressed casually, he would arrive somewhere around 4.00 a.m. and then sleep in his car until a potential distributor opened. He was able to 'charm the distributors' and the business began to grow. Ben and Jerry's success provoked a response from the dominant market leader, Häagen Dazs, owned by Pillsbury. Their market share was 70 per cent of the luxury ice cream market. Häagen Dazs threatened to withdraw their product from any distributors who also handled Ben and Jerry's. The two partners employed a lawyer and threatened legal action, but their real weapon was a publicity campaign targeted at Pillsbury itself, and its famous 'dough boy' logo. 'What's the Dough Boy afraid of?' they asked. Their gimmicks generated massive publicity and they received an out-of-court settlement. More significantly the publicity created new demand for luxury ice cream, and the company began to grow faster than had ever been envisaged. A threat had been turned into a massive opportunity. Soon Ben and Jerry's had a segment market share of 39 per cent, just 4 per cent behind Häagen Dazs. The company has expanded internationally with mixed success. They have enjoyed only limited success in the UK 'because there was only limited marketing support'.

Perhaps not unexpectedly, given their background, Ben and Jerry have created a values-driven business; some of their ice creams have been linked to causes and interests they support and promote. Rainforest Crunch ice cream features nuts from Brazil; the key ingredients for Chocolate Fudge Brownie are produced by an inner city bakery in Yonkers, New York; and they favour Vermont's dairy farming industry. When the business needed equity capital to support its growth, local Vermont residents were given priority treatment. Ben and Jerry argue they are committed to their employees who 'bring their hearts and souls as well as their bodies and minds to work' but acknowledge their internal opinion surveys show a degree of dissatisfaction with the amount of profits (7.5 per cent) given away every year to good causes.

The two realists with an unusual but definite ego drive have now dropped out of day-to-day management: 'the company needed a greater breadth of management than we had' . . . and remain 'two casual, portly, middle-aged hippies'.

In early 2000 the business was sold to the global conglomerate Unilever.

Nantucket Nectars   Nantucket Nectars is another unusual business started by two friends. When Tom First and Tom Scott graduated from Brown University in Rhode Island they decided they wanted to live on Nantucket Island, off the New England coast, and find some way of earning a living. In the summer of 1989 they started a small business for servicing the yachts belonging to visitors to the island. This was always going to be seasonal. They travelled around the harbour in a distinctive red boat, delivering newspapers, muffins, coffee, laundry and any other supplies for which there was a demand. They also washed boats, emptied sewage and shampooed dogs. This seemed to lead naturally to them later opening the Nantucket Allserve general store – which still exists. They used the following promotional slogan in the early days: 'Ain't nothing those boys won't do.'

Once the summer was over, demand for their services fell as the yachts disappeared. They decided to experiment with fruit juices, mixed in a household blender.

They first sought to replicate a peach-based nectar they had sampled in Spain. During the following summer they sold their bottled juices from their red boat. They always produced distinctive flavours from the best quality ingredients. By investing their joint savings they were able to hire a bottler to produce 1400 cases. Overall though, the business merely struggled on for a couple of years – until one wealthy yacht owner offered them a $500 000 loan to develop the business. They seized the opportunity. Nantucket Nectars then expanded quickly to cover a number of states on the American East Coast. Initially they did their own bottling, but this is now subcontracted.

'If I were on the outside looking in, I'd say Nantucket Nectars was an overnight success. Being on the inside, it's been a long, long time. We almost went out of business a thousand times' (Tom Scott).

The company now employs 100 people and sells in over thirty American states and a number of selected export markets. Values are a key element, the partners remain determined to 'create the best quality product in the juice market', and yet the company remains enigmatic. The bottle labels state: 'We're juice guys. We don't wear ties to work'; folksy radio commercials are utilized extensively; but the new head office is in an old Men's Club near Harvard University. It is furnished with antiques and managers have private offices instead of the open-plan arrangement that is increasingly popular in many informal organizations. First and Scott typically take their dogs into work. Each week every head office manager focuses on talking personally with one of their sales people in the field, staff who would otherwise have little contact with head office.

The founders claim the company has always been run on gut instinct and trial and error. Few people have any formal business qualifications. In 1997 Nantucket Nectars was awarded a contract to provide juice for Starbucks, and later that year Ocean Spray – leading manufacturer of cranberry juices and other products – acquired a 50 per cent stake. The companies believed they could make extensive savings on supplies if they joined forces. First and Scott will continue to run the business they founded.

BayGen Radio   A completely different example of team entrepreneurship can be found with the BayGen Radio, which was the idea of the English inventor, Trevor Baylis, in the early 1990s. Unlike other portable radios, this one does not use batteries; instead it is powered by clockwork. Baylis developed the idea for the Third World, where batteries are prohibitively expensive, after watching a television documentary on Africa that suggested the spread of Aids was affected by the lack of effective communications. He experimented until he had a spring that could power a small generator by releasing energy at a constant rate. Typically springs release energy at a reducing rate. Baylis failed with his early attempts to gain backing and financial support to develop the idea further. However, his prototype was shown on BBC Television's *Tomorrow's World*, where it was seen by Christopher Staines, then director of mergers and acquisitions with a leading accountancy practice. Staines was gripped with the potential, worked all night on a business plan and faxed it to Baylis the next day. Within forty-eight hours Staines had secured the worldwide development rights and, after raising financial support from the Overseas

Development Agency, he took the idea to South Africa, where he had family connections. The idea was endorsed by President Nelson Mandela, seed capital was duly raised and a new factory with a capacity to build 20 000 radios a month was ready in September 1995. Refinements to the original generator produced forty minutes' listening time from twenty seconds' winding. Many of the employees are disabled, and the first customers included the Red Cross and the United Nations Children's Fund (UNICEF) who then sell them into Third World countries at reduced prices. Trevor Baylis was – and remains – essentially an inventor who provided the idea and the technology; Christopher Staines is the entrepreneur who saw the opportunity for the idea, championed the project and exploited it to great effect.

The stories told so far in this chapter concentrate on entrepreneurs who have started and remained focused on a particular business. A minority of entrepreneurs start something and then make an exit once the venture is prospering – then start again with something new and sometimes completely different. Either through lack of interest, or by knowing where their real skills lie, these entrepreneurs are creative, innovative and opportunistic but less concerned with maintenance and nurturing.

Paul Sykes: serial entrepreneur

Paul Sykes was born in Barnsley in 1944, the elder son of a Yorkshire coal miner. He left school at fifteen and worked initially as a tyre fitter. His success as an opportunity-spotting serial entrepreneur is testimony to the value of the 'university of life'. Asked whether he regretted leaving school at the age of fifteen, Sykes has responded: 'Yes I do. I wanted to leave at eleven; the extra four years cost me a lot of money!'

Paul quickly tired of working for other people and started out on his own at the age of eighteen. He began cutting up buses for scrap, something he had already been doing part-time for a friend at weekends. He had just £170 to invest, which he used to buy his first bus and a second-hand pick-up truck; and he made sure he could return to his job as a tyre fitter if the venture failed. An ability to manage the downside risk is one of the secrets of his success. Spotting potential opportunities for adding value in the Far East, he began reconditioning bus engines for export, mainly to Hong Kong, where many were used to power junks. Some of the second-hand buses were also supplied to Asia in kit form, whilst others were refurbished for lease in the UK. These business interests grew and prospered such that, by the early 1970s, Sykes was buying some 3500 buses a year from the National Bus Company, approximately half the number it was scrapping and replacing. But eventually the number of buses available for recycling declined and at the same time Japanese competitors began to move into his markets. Typically intuitive, Paul concluded he should come out of bus recycling and he made a swift exit, selling some interests to his younger brother and a cousin. Already a multimillionaire he turned his eyes to coaches and property. His coach distribution and leasing company was later sold for £20 million.

Paul Sykes now changed direction, opting to invest £30 million of his personal wealth in property development, his initial achievement being the UK's first out-of-town cinema complex in Salford Quays. He soon became convinced that the trend for out-of-town developments in America would spread to the UK; and his prediction was correct. An early entry into London's Docklands was, however, followed by a quick exit – he was sceptical about the adequacy of the support infrastructure and worried about escalating rents for the freeholds. He saw a downside risk. This was followed by a realization – arguably a vision – that derelict land in Sheffield's Don Valley (vacated as steel firm after steel firm closed down) could be used to create wealth and jobs. The outcome was the Meadowhall shopping centre, begun in 1986, and whose success has spawned a raft of further developments, including sports stadiums, the Sheffield Arena (entertainment venue) and a new airport. Planning permission from an initially doubtful local authority was a major and time-consuming hurdle, but it was eventually granted. Sykes' persistence had been rewarded. As the embryo idea developed and borrowings of over £350 million became necessary, Sykes formed a partnership with fellow property developer, Eddie Healey, whose holding company took over management of the shopping centre. Sykes retained a 40 per cent shareholding in Meadowhall, which was valued at £1.2 billion when it was sold in 1999. At this time Sykes's wealth was estimated to exceed £400 million. Again showing prescience and skills in timing his exit, Paul Sykes has not been seriously affected by the recent rises and falls in property values, and Meadowhall was his last *major* development.

A true opportunity-spotter, Paul later turned to information technology and helped form Planet Online, which grew to become Britain's largest commercial Internet provider (for business to business transactions), employing 350 people and with a base in Leeds. He had been introduced to the man with the idea at a football match. Peter Wilkinson already ran a computer business and understood the technology. Sykes was able to appreciate where the real opportunity lay, realizing that Britain 'needs information highways more than it needs tarmac highways'. The transport system is heavily congested and information technology has the potential to streamline the distribution of both goods and services. At the same time, if organizations can outsource information management, they can focus their efforts on the heart of the business. Having committed himself within forty-eight hours of the first meeting with his new partner, Paul sold his majority shareholding in 1998 to create a fund – or war chest – which he would dedicate to his campaign to keep Britain out of the single European currency in order 'to protect our sovereignty and democracy'. With this campaign he has found a cause to which he is willing to dedicate considerable time, energy and resources – mirroring many of the social entrepreneurs we feature in Chapter 5. His Internet investment of £10 million had earned him a profit of £37 million in just three years. At the moment Europe is his leading interest and passion, but he retains a limited portfolio of business and property interests.

Paul Sykes has always been energetic, tenacious and was 'not content with his lot' when he was young. Leaving school at the earliest opportunity, and with no formal qualifications, he was committed to working hard – characteristics he inherited from his mother. Throughout his business life he has exhibited vision, opportunism and timing; he has been careful to manage any downside risk and has 'earned a profit every month for thirty-eight years'. He has used his wide network of contacts for mutual benefit and he has been willing to form suitable partnerships. His experiences have taught him that successful businesses must be kept simple. 'Success depends on value-for-money products and services which address customers' needs – and a stream of future potential customers if growth is to continue.'

Business opportunities

The privatization opportunity

The privatization of a number of businesses by the Thatcher and subsequent governments provided opportunities for several entrepreneurs in the UK, including Richard Branson with Virgin Rail. The greatest success story is undoubtedly Stagecoach, which also provides an illustration of effective team entreprenership and entrepreneurial growth through acquisition.

Stagecoach   Founders Brian Souter (aged forty-four in 1999) and his sister Ann Gloag (twelve years older than her brother) were the children of a Perth bus driver. They are now the richest people in Scotland. Souter is a deal-maker, who had earlier worked as a bus conductor to finance his university education. Gloag provides the underpinning management; she was previously a nurse. After graduating Brian Souter worked as an accountant. 'I had a terrible time [finding a job] because a lot of the people I got interviewed by are terrible snobs. I didn't go to the right school, didn't live in the right street and my father wasn't in the right occupation.' Possessing a strong ego drive, this early struggle made Souter determined to succeed.

The first (1980) Thatcher Transport Act deregulated express and excursion coach services. Seeing an opportunity in an industry they understood, Brian Souter and Ann Gloag began a Dundee to London 'Stage Coach' overnight service. Their level of service was absolutely basic and they succeeded by undercutting everyone else. They found a niche and exploited it. They had used their father's redundancy money (after forty years' driving a bus) to purchase two second-hand coaches. Further growth was possible when a rich Canadian uncle invested an additional £25 000. By 1981 Stagecoach was offering several express services. The 1985 Transport Act heralded the deregulation of local bus services and this was the springboard for the real expansion.

Bidders could only bid for a maximum of three designated franchises in England (1987) and later (1991) two in Scotland. Stagecoach won three in England – Hampshire, Cumberland and United Counties (Bedfordshire, Cambridgeshire and Northamptonshire) but later acquired East Midlands, Ribble (Lancashire) and Southdown (Hampshire, West Sussex and Portsmouth). By 1989 they were spread all over the country, and duly expanded into Scotland in 1991. All the buses are instantly recognizable with their distinctive red, blue and orange colours. Stagecoach carefully recruited experienced senior managers from other bus companies to create a strong management team. But they operate with a lean structure and relatively flat hierarchy. Expansion has continued with the acquisition of bus operations in Hong Kong, Malawi, Kenya, Canada and New Zealand and a rail franchise – South

West Trains – in 1992. In 1998 Stagecoach became a minority shareholder in Virgin Rail.

There has been controversy as Stagecoach has more than once been referred to the Monopolies and Mergers Commission for the way it has competed in certain areas, pricing aggressively and allegedly driving weaker competitors out of business. Whilst it has always remained focused on transport and a clear industry leader, Stagecoach has been flexible and very responsive when new opportunities have come along. Souter has suggested that 'tunnel vision is a great disaster for businesses and often inventors are the worst people to admit that their inventions aren't working'.

Buy-in, buy-out opportunities

Privatization provided the entrepreneurs, Brian Souter and Ann Gloag, with the opportunity to build a business from scratch. Buy-outs (where the existing management team acquire a business from its present owners) and buy-ins (where a new, external, management team buys an existing business) are turnaround opportunities for entrepreneurial managers. These entrepreneurs create new value with a business that has typically been underachieving, which often arises when the business concerned has a poor strategic fit inside its existing parent organization. The results are often quite startling. Some famous brand-names have been bought-out – including Hornby Hobbies (electric trains and Scalextric) and Parker pens.

Premier Brands   Premier Brands was created when Paul Judge bought the food and confectionery arm of Cadbury Schweppes, which included Cadbury's drinking chocolate, biscuits and cakes, Typhoo tea and the Chivers and Hartleys products. When the successful new business was floated soon after the buy-out, the multi-millionaire Judge retired and helped establish a new Management Centre at Cambridge University.

Holliday Dyes   In 1985 Michael Peagram, an experienced manager in the chemicals industry – and an MBA graduate – identified Holliday Dyes in Huddersfield as a potential management buy-in opportunity. The company, a specialist dye manufacturer, was underperforming and in financial difficulties. Although the owner of this family business knew he had succession problems, he refused to sell, but he did offer Peagram 25 per cent of the equity and the position of Managing Director, which he accepted. Within a year turnover had increased from £8 million to almost £11 million; a pre-tax loss of £1.4 million had been transformed into an operating profit of £700 000. In February 1987 Peagram bought the business with support from County Capital Development (really the NatWest Investment Bank) and the Hong Kong and Shanghai Bank.

By 1992 sales had grown to £100 million and pre-tax profits to almost £14 million. It was floated in 1993 with a value of £140 million. Five related acquisitions followed, all designed to provide a large share of focused niche markets where it was possible to avoid direct competition from the major chemical companies. Peagram was acknowledged to have developed an expertise in running businesses efficiently and imaginatively – he concentrated on higher-margin products, invested in marketing and exploited his strong sales network. The business was eventually sold to Yule Catto in 1997, for £240 million. Michael Peagram's personal stake in this was £40 million.

David Brown   Another Huddersfield-based company, David Brown, had enjoyed 130 years of family ownership when it became a management buy-in in 1990. Once a diversified and very entrepreneurial engineering business that manufactured tractors, supplied the aircraft and shipbuilding industries with a range of specialist products and owned Aston Martin, the company was now focused on gears, transmissions and pumps. The present owner, David Brown, was eighty-seven years old and resident in France.

Two managers with a background in engineering raised the finances to buy the business for £46 million. Chris Cook, a qualified engineer, had managed a successful turnaround for the diversified engineering conglomerate, FKI, with a 'combination of management focus, employee motivation and customer orientation'. He was considered to be 'tough'. His partner Chris Brown (no family connection to David Brown) was a lawyer and an MBA and seen as 'more thoughtful'.

The new team pruned the existing management, gave 'stretch targets' to the workforce, focused on quality, ensured they met delivery promises and began to develop new businesses and new customers. Similar to Hollidays, a subsequent flotation (this time with a £90 million valuation) was followed by acquisitions and a 1998 sale to Textron of the USA for £195 million.

Both of these examples show how the intervention of entrepreneurs can transform sleepy companies in mature industries by adding new values and introducing a new style of management. David Brown, like Stagecoach, has benefited from the presence of two complementary partners working together effectively. Individually we all have particular strengths and weaknesses. Ideally we will utilize and exploit our strengths and not be required to focus on areas where we are less capable. As we also saw earlier in the chapter, recognition of the implications of this can lead to the formation of, and synergistic pay-off from, effective partnerships and teams.

Succession issues

We again saw earlier how Harry Ramsden's prospered after Harry sold the business. Sometimes there is an orderly succession from one owner to another and from one generation of a family business to the next. But this has to be a managed process if entrepreneurship is to be maintained, for on other occasions the business struggles once the founder leaves. The stories that follow look at these issues and include the unusual case of an entrepreneurial founder leaving, only to return later to rescue the business.

Laura Ashley   Laura Ashley has enjoyed very mixed fortunes since the death of Laura Ashley herself. Laura and Bernard Ashley (her husband) started printing tea towels and scarves to their own designs in 1953. They began in their London flat, basing all their designs on 'traditional English country values'. The successful partners moved to a factory in Wales in 1960 – Laura was Welsh – producing their first dresses in 1966. The first Laura Ashley shop opened in London two years later. There was soon a vertical supply chain of design, fabric printing, clothing manufacture and retailing. Unlike her contemporary, Mary Quant, who opted to focus on design and license the production of all her designs, Laura Ashley diversified. The business was increasingly successful, recruiting and training its own designers. Home furnishings were then added to the range. When Laura Ashley died in 1985, after an accidental fall, there were over 200 shops.

After her death Bernard recruited new senior managers and the business diversified further into leather goods, knitwear manufacture, outdoor clothing, perfume and home furnishings in America. There was continuing investment into new manufacturing capabilities. Within five years there were financial difficulties. The company had apparently lost direction and the focus it had. Whilst the brand has always been strong and powerful, profit margins became too low. A series of new chief executives – there have, in fact, been seven, some British, some American, since Laura Ashley's death – have attempted to 'simplify, focus and enact'. A Malaysian group now owns 40 per cent of the business, manufacturing in America has ceased, and the company remains in some difficulty.

Apple   Entrepreneur Steve Jobs joined forces with a computer 'nerd', Stephen Wozniak, to start Apple in 1976, a company which has made a major and profound contribution to the personal computer industry. Begun in a garage, this creative and innovative company was a world leader by the end of the 1970s. By 1983, and with just a number of variants of a single model, Apple was turning over $1 billion a year. Wozniak had, however, left to find a new challenge and the Apple structure and management systems had not developed sufficiently. Steve Jobs persuaded John Sculley, then Chief Executive of PepsiCo, to come and help him run Apple, freeing himself up to concentrate on developing Apple's new product, the Macintosh. 'Do you want to spend the rest of your life selling sugared water, or do you want a chance to change the world?' was allegedly the challenge from Jobs that had the most influence on Sculley's decision.

At this time Jobs' attention and interest was focused entirely on the new product. He had been allowed access to the Palo Alto Research Centre owned and run by Xerox; and it was there he saw the first graphic user interface on a computer screen. 'I knew this was the future!' he claimed afterwards, although Xerox itself chose not to develop along these lines. Whilst the Macintosh was a pioneer of the mouse-driven screen display, and remains to this day a high added-value, premium-price, product and the first choice of designers, Microsoft's Windows software grew to dominate the mass market. By focusing on the top end of the market, Apple provided Bill Gates with his opportunity – and his success was clearly damaging to Apple as time went on.

Jobs, by this time, had clashed with the Apple board of directors and left to 'pursue other interests', enjoying mixed fortunes in the following years. A software business had some success; his new film animation company, Pixar, worked with Disney to produce the lucrative *Toy Story* film.

Struggling to compete with Microsoft's market dominance, Sculley then left. He was replaced initially by Michael Spindler and later by Gil Amelio, but Apple remained fragile. In 1997 Jobs returned as interim Chief Executive, insisting he would not take the job permanently; Wozniak was retained as a consultant. With a new Macintosh as its lead product and with an investment of $150 million from Microsoft, Apple is making a comeback under the leadership of Steve Jobs. We discuss Apple further in Chapter 8.

Corporate entrepreneurship

So far we have concentrated on entrepreneurs who have built something substantial from scratch; we now move on to look at entrepreneurs who work inside existing corporations, including those who successfully turn around companies in difficulty. The umbrella term for these people is 'corporate entrepreneurs', and three distinct types can be identified. One is where an existing business introduces new strategies that lead to transformational changes in its industry. When Ted Turner launched CNN, it heralded the start of twenty-four hour news broadcasting, which in turn has had a major impact upon the way the world is briefed on key events as they unravel. Another is the transformation or renewal of existing and under-performing organizations with hidden values, which happened when Archie Norman turned around Asda. We also look at the entrepreneurial style of Jack Welch, who has ensured the diversified American conglomerate, General Electric, has prospered when many similar organizations have become increasingly focused. The third type is the creation of new businesses within existing organizations, where we look briefly at the 3M approach. When corporate entrepreneurs are successful, it is because they appreciate how to add value, create differences and thereby improve the competitive position of their business. They create a new opportunity.

Ted Turner   Ted Turner is a risk-taker and an acquisitive entrepreneur. He is 'off-the-scale' as an opportunist, 'living life on the edge', but he has shown an unusual approach to delegation and people. He was one of the first people to see the oppor-tunities cable television would bring.

Turner was born in 1938; his parents were wealthy and he was always competitive. He chose to focus on competitive sailing when he found he was not outstanding at more popular sports. His dedication later paid off when he won the 1977 America's Cup race and the 1979 Fastnet race in the Solent, the year several competitors died in the severe weather conditions. Turner had earlier inherited a $1 million billboard advertising business when his father committed suicide, and he used this as a base to acquire more advertising and radio businesses. Aggressively seeking growth, he was willing to accept large debt commitments and once claimed: 'I've won more awards than anybody my age; I've probably also got more debt than anyone else in the world.' He first moved into television when he bought a station in 1969 and used it to estab-lish the first national network by beaming signals via satellite to other cable stations. This proved valuable for covering the 1981 assassination attempt on President Reagan and the 1986 space shuttle disaster. His Cable News Network (CNN) twenty-four hour news station really 'came of age' during the 1990 Gulf War.

Turner's uncanny success in starting high-risk ventures is not accidental. He is a workaholic who always retained personal control over key decisions. He employed five senior managers but 'would not let the five go out and have a beer together, let alone run the company'. In 1986 he failed to take over CBS in a costly and acrimonious battle, but he fought back by acquiring MGM Studios, with its extensive film library, which he used to establish network cable movie channels. He did acquire CBS some years later, before selling out his business empire to Time Warner – retaining a personal stake of 10 per cent in the world's largest entertainment company. Reflecting his interest in sport, he has retained ownership of the Atlanta Braves (the 1995 World Series baseball champions) and the Atlanta Hawks basketball team. With an estimated net worth of $2 billion, he has established the second largest foundation in America, to support needy causes.

Reflecting a strong ego drive and his attitude to risk, he once said:

> basically I am in business because it gives me a good feeling about myself. You learn a lot about your capabilities by putting yourself on the line. Running a successful business is not only a financial risk, it is an emotional risk as well. I get a lot of satisfaction from having dared it – and done it – and been successful.

Two of the cases which follow next, General Electric and 3M, provide a valuable illustration of a relative American strength and corresponding British weakness highlighted recently by Sir John Harvey-Jones (Ashworth, 1999). Sir John claims the UK:

> has a very unforgiving [business] environment . . . we have a low expectation of people, so far too many people can survive just by not making a really big screw-up. In America, they don't even consider you're a businessman unless you've screwed something up, because, by definition, you're not pushing the frontiers . . . almost everything in this country is an endeavour to avoid making a mistake, and if you avoid making a mistake you are never in front . . . I don't long to employ masses of people who screw everything up, but if a guy makes a mistake because he's really stretching for the stars, that's different.

General Electric   The diversified conglomerate General Electric (GE) is one of the most successful, admired and powerful companies in the world. It is also innovative and entrepreneurial. GE manufactures aircraft engines, defence electronics and household consumer goods, provides financial services and owns NBC Television in the USA. Until 1994 GE owned the Kidder Peabody Investment Bank, but now invests in a wide range of other businesses through its GE Capital subsidiary. Jack Welch has been the CEO since 1981 and he has pursued a strategy of focusing on market segments where the company can be Number One or Number Two and ambitiously emphasizing high-growth industries.

The company is decentralized and employees are encouraged to speak out and pursue ideas. External contacts and sources are constantly monitored for new ideas, leads and opportunities. 'At Head Office we don't go very deep into much of anything, but we have a smell of everything. Our job is capital allocation – intellectual and financial. Smell, feel, touch, listen, then allocate' (Welch). In 1995 NBC was anxious to win the television rights for the Sydney Olympic Games in 2000. Pre-empting its competitors, NBC bid jointly for these games and the next Winter Olympics in Salt Lake City and presented the International Olympic Committee (IOC) with a take-it-or-leave-it deal before any bids had even been invited. When Welch was asked to support the proposal – and the huge sums involved – he took just thirty minutes to give his agreement. Within a week the deal had been struck. The IOC commented afterwards that 'the reaction of NBC's rivals was one of disappointment but reluctant admiration for the initiative that NBC took'.

General Electric's structure is decentralized and systems such as regular briefings and meetings for senior managers at GE's corporate training centre seek to ensure best practices are shared. Managers move from one division to another to gain promotion and there are cross-business teams always working on new ideas 'in an organization without boundaries' – but the turnover of divisional heads is low. 'Put the right people in the right jobs . . . leave them . . . and things get better not worse' (Welch). Welch is proud of his ability to 'spot people early on, follow them, grow them and stretch them . . . we spend all our time on people!' Rewards are carefully varied between businesses, to reflect the different levels of risk.

The Anglo-Norwegian consultancy, The Performance Group, concluded in a 1999 report that GE's success has been built on 'continual "breakthroughs" in every area . . . from product development to corporate culture, from sales and marketing to labour relations'. This report concludes that 'a company that avoids upheaval and change is not long for this world' (The Performance Group, 1999). In this context Archie Norman argues that a 'failing organization is almost invariably an organization that ceases to innovate and to experiment because innovation and experimentation are risky'.

Asda   Archie Norman is, in fact, the entrepreneurial strategic leader who 'made a difference' at Asda by pioneering change and instilling a new culture. Asda is the UK's third largest supermarket group, behind Tesco and Sainsbury. Its growth and success came in the 1960s when it began to open out-of-town supermarkets – large stores for that time, but relatively small in today's terms – largely in the north of England, where the company has always been strongest. The Head Office is still in Leeds, but the company has now developed nationally. In the 1980s, Asda began to diversify, first into furniture retailing and then into carpets. This was followed by the acquisition of kitchen supplier MFI in 1985; two years later MFI became a management buy-out when the promised synergies proved illusory. Shortly after this, Asda bought sixty stores from Gateway and struck a deal with George Davies (the entrepreneur behind the growth and temporary fall of Next) which gave Asda the exclusive rights on a range of George-branded clothing. By the early 1990s Asda was, however, trading at a loss. Analysts concluded the company lacked a strong corporate identity and it had become a reactive follower in its main industry.

A new chairman was appointed in 1991 and he recruited Archie Norman to be the new Chief Executive. At this time Norman was thirty-seven years old. Originally a McKinsey consultant – where he had worked with William Hague – he was then Group Finance Director with retail group, Kingfisher. When Norman became non-executive Chairman in 1997 – after being elected a Conservative MP for Tunbridge

Wells – Asda had regained its popularity and profitability. Together with his deputy – and now successor – Allan Leighton, Norman had transformed the company. Although Norman 'took best practice from elsewhere and Asda-ized it', it was always believed that he used Wal-Mart as his model, and so perhaps it was no surprise when Wal-Mart acquired Asda in 1999. David Glass, Chief Executive of Wal-Mart commented of Asda: 'I have not seen such passion for a company amongst its employees – except at Wal-Mart.'

What exactly had Norman done? Furniture and carpets had been divested at the earliest opportunity. The business had been split into two distinct parts: the (large) supermarkets – Asda owns some of the largest food stores in the UK – where the non-food ranges were strengthened; and smaller, local, Dales stores with a limited range of grocery products. The whole business was refocused on 'ordinary working people who demand value' – advertising used the slogan 'That's Asda price!' to reinforce an average saving of some 5 per cent against Tesco and Sainsbury prices.

High productivity and high levels of service have been derived from a committed and involved staff who have seen many changes in their working lives. People are known as 'colleagues'; and Julian Richer has advised the company on its suggestion scheme. The scheme, 'Tell Archie!', has generated 45 000 suggestions in five years, and Norman has read them all. Incentives are linked into the scheme, and employees can also benefit from share options and training at the Asda Academy. Since 1995, Colleague Circles have also provided an effective forum for staff involvement in customer service innovation. At Head Office there are no reserved car parking spaces and everyone works in large open-plan offices. Staff are encouraged to wear Asda baseball caps when they do not want to be disturbed by their colleagues. In relative terms, store management has grown at the expense of head office staffing.

3M   The Minnesota Mining and Manufacturing Company (3M) is based in St Paul, Minnesota, and has developed a leading reputation for being innovative and creative. The story of 3M's Post-it notes is really 'the stuff of legends'. The internal entrepreneur in this case was an employee called Arthur Fry, who had become annoyed that pieces of paper he placed inside his church hymn book as markers kept falling out when he was singing. Fry was a 3M chemical engineer who knew of an invention by a scientist colleague called Spencer Silver. Silver had developed a new glue which possessed only a very low sticking power, and for this reason was being perceived as a failure. Fry saw the new glue as the answer to his problem – when he applied it to his paper markers, they stayed put but they were easily removed. Realizing that many others also shared the same problem, Fry sought approval to commercialize his idea – but initially he met with scepticism. The idea took hold when he passed samples around to secretaries within 3M and other organizations. The rest, as they say, is history!

Over the years the company has developed over 60 000 new products, including everything that bears the Scotch brand-name, including clear sticky-tape and video cassettes. 3M also manufactures heart-lung machines. Employees are actively encouraged to work on developing new ideas and products. They can legitimately spend 15 per cent of their working time on new projects that they initiate and they can apply for internal company development grants of up to $50 000. When ideas are taken forward they also have the option of championing the new business in its later development stages. There is an understood tolerance of both opt-out and failure, but employee bonuses depend on new product development. A supportive management accounting system is used to advise on the cost implications of bringing new ideas to market, assessing the impact on existing businesses and establishing realistic targets and milestones. This enables effective prioritization.

Opportunities on the fringe of business

The very existence of businesses provides opportunities for other businesses – and not just those that are direct suppliers and distributors.

Warren Buffett   We look first at Warren Buffett, an entrepreneur who has built a hugely successful business empire and become a multibillionaire by careful investment in other companies. Buffett began by acquiring Berkshire Hathaway in 1965, when it was focused on insurance. Shares then worth $18 each are now valued at $70 000. The annual return on equity is consistently between 20 and 30 per cent.

His strategy was to invest long term in carefully selected businesses. He is not a speculator, nor does he seek to acquire and control a business. Instead he is interested in 'good companies with good managers' and seeks to buy shares at favourable, low, market prices and then 'hold them for life'. He 'bets on managers who love their business and not the money' and he never buys without tracking a company and carrying out extensive research to determine its true value. He prefers low-risk investments: 'I don't jump over seven-foot bars ... I look around for one-foot bars I can step over.' Consequently Buffett has invested in insurance, candy stores, newspapers and the Dairy Queen fast-food outlets, amongst many others – as well as buying a large stake in Coca-Cola.

Buffett follows a number of key principles when choosing where to invest. He looks for strong brands and he avoids products which 'don't travel well'. Food, for example, does not provide the foundation for a strong global business as tastes vary so much between countries. What works in one may not be successful in another. He is also extremely careful with high-technology businesses. Reflecting this philosophy, his Managing Director has commented: 'If I taught a strategy course, I would set the following examination question, "Evaluate the following Internet company . . .." and anyone who gave an answer would be failed!' Buffett counsels against investing in something 'you don't understand . . . always look in detail at the product, its competition and its earning power'. Then . . . 'never rely on stock market valuations . . . look for the real value . . .look carefully at Annual Reports for openness, honesty and cover-ups'.

Like many other successful people, Buffett has underpinning values, ones which closely embrace certain key entrepreneurial characteristics: 'My principle is to leave enough money for your children that they can do anything they want, but not enough they can do nothing.'

Donna Sammons Carpenter   Donna Sammons Carpenter is quite different, but also very successful on a more modest scale. Her company, Wordworks, provides ghost writers for many well-known management authors – but not including the writers of this book! Tom Peters is probably the most successful author she works with, and her name can be found in the acknowledgement section of a number of his books. It is the author who takes the risk when commissioning Carpenter. There is a negotiated fee for the work, and if significant sales of the subsequent book are not achieved, the author may well be out of pocket. However, the chances of success are clearly improved with a contribution from a strong and experienced writing team. Moreover, a successful management book can be 'a calling card to high earnings from speaking engagements'!

Mark McCormack   Mark McCormack has written a number of popular management books, but his success has come from the International Management Group that he established. McCormack has been described as 'the most powerful man in sport'; he saw an opportunity for bringing together big business and sports personalities. Originally a lawyer and recreational golfer, he acted for Arnold Palmer in a legal capacity. He was then offered the opportunity to widen his portfolio, which he seized, and followed up with representation for other leading sports personalities, including golfer Tiger Woods, tennis stars Pete Sampras and André Agassi, skiers and Formula One racing driver Michael Schumacher. Opera stars José Carreras and Kiri Te Kanawa, together with several top models, can be added to the list. McCormack specializes in merchandising deals, licensing the star's name and negotiating television appearances.

Opportunities, then, are everywhere; the secret lies in seeing them and being in a position to exploit them. The background and experience a person has must affect the type of opportunity he or she sees – McCormack's practice as a lawyer brought him into contact with Arnold Palmer. Of course, the people in question must have the talent and temperament to be entrepreneurs if they are to engage and exploit the opportunity successfully.

Academic spin-off companies

Our final stories in this chapter feature academic entrepreneurs who have been able to exploit their specialist knowledge and expertise in conjunction with their entrepreneurial talent to create and build successful technology businesses.

Filtronic   David Rhodes, at the time a lecturer at the University of Leeds and in his thirties, established Filtronic as a campus spin-off company in 1977. Rhodes had a research background in microwave engineering and he had worked at universities in both the USA and UK. His intention was to develop a series of electronic and mechanical devices for separating and processing microwaves and which had a commercial potential. In the early days Filtronic secured a contract from the US military to develop products which would jam enemy radar. The company also worked on the Stealth Bomber project. Filtronic's products could identify aircraft by their radar signatures and communicate with space probes. Real growth, however, came in the late 1980s and early 1990s when Rhodes was able to capitalize on the fast-growing market for mobile phones. Filtronic could supply products which separate signals to and from mobile phones – increasingly useful as the radio wave space available to the various system providers becomes ever more congested.

Late in the 1990s, Filtronic employed 2500 people in the UK, USA and Australia. Annual sales exceed £220 million, with 20 per cent of the revenues being generated in the UK and 50 per cent in America. David Rhodes remains Chairman and Chief Executive of the company he started, and he retains a 10 per cent shareholding in the business. In addition he still lectures part time for the University of Leeds; students on an MSc programme in Microwave Engineering have several of their lectures at Filtronic, whose headquarters are just a few miles away.

PowderJect   PowderJect was formed in 1993 by Brian Belhouse, now over sixty years old and a commercially astute Oxford University scientist. Quite simply, Belhouse was able to secure financial backing for a discovery he had made in the university's laboratories. He had invented a painless way of injecting drugs – without using needles – by firing them in powdered form at supersonic speed into the body. Instead of following the more typical route of publishing the research in an academic journal, Belhouse set up a campus spin-off company. The university was granted 5.6 per cent of the equity for surrendering any rights it might have over the intellectual capital. The majority of the capital invested in the business at that time came from business angels and venture capitalists. PowderJect was floated on the Stock Exchange in June 1997, when it was capitalized at £109 million. After PowderJect formed a strategic alliance with Glaxo Wellcome in March 1998, the value of the company began to soar and in summer 1998 was valued at £285 million. Two further vaccine licences, making four in all, were sold to Glaxo in 1999, together with options for a further four. No PowderJect vaccines have yet reached the market, but trials are reported to be progressing well. The financial investment from Glaxo helps finance the expensive development costs, a critical feature of these high-risk biotechnology products.

This chapter has provided an insight into the wide and varied range of opportunities used by business entrepreneurs to build organizations and create financial capital, and has also highlighted how many of them have actually translated the idea into a successful business. The idea alone is inadequate; it must be engaged, captured and exploited. Successful ideas and opportunities imply added value and differences that are attractive to potential customers, who then reward the entrepreneur with their custom. The successful business needs structure, organization and, above all, supportive, committed people – who actually create the value. We have seen how many of the entrepreneurs featured in this chapter have understood the strategic importance of their people and ensured their competencies and endeavours have been harnessed effectively to create the virtuous circle of growth we mentioned at the beginning of the chapter.

The next two chapters feature examples of entrepreneurs who have used and exploited their talents to prioritize the creation of social and aesthetic capital. In some cases, but not all, profit-seeking businesses are involved – but in these examples, whilst the profit is an important element, it is not the key focus for the business.

References

Ashworth, J. (1999). Looking for trouble? Interview with Sir John Harvey-Jones, GNER (Great North Eastern Railways). *Travel Magazine*, July.

Buckingham, M. and Coffman, C. (1999). *First, Break All the Rules*. Simon and Schuster.

Charan, R. and Colvin, G. (1999). Why CEO's fail. *Fortune*, 21 June.

The Performance Group (1999). *Breakthrough Performance through People: Report*. The Performance Group.

5 Social and environmental entrepreneurs

In the last chapter we discussed a wide range of business entrepreneurs who have built financial wealth and capital. In this chapter, and subsequent chapters, we go on to discuss other forms of capital – namely social, environmental and aesthetic capital – and present examples of people who have made a difference by focusing on these. We intend to show that these people are also entrepreneurs. They possess the life theme profile of an entrepreneur; they identify and engage an important opportunity; they gather the necessary resources; they start and develop an initiative; and they have an important impact on our lives.

In the Introduction to this book we defined entrepreneurs and stressed that they build value and capital. In Chapters 3 and 4 we have discussed a number of legendary and business entrepreneurs who, in the main, have created and accumulated significant wealth and financial capital. They have achieved this by building successful businesses that have made money for their owners by providing value for their customers, and in the process also rewarding their employees and other stakeholders. In this chapter and Chapter 6 we move on and look at entrepreneurs who, rather than focusing on financial wealth and capital, have instead been principally motivated by a desire to build social and aesthetic – or artistic – capital and, in some cases, to preserve environmental capital.

Fukuyama (1995) has defined *social capital* as 'the ability of people to work together for common purposes in groups and organizations'. Leadbeater (1997) has refined this to suggest the building of something of real value to local communities or society. The realization that these 'builders' use one form of social capital – relationships, networks, trust and co-operation – to gain access to physical and financial capital which is then redeployed to build something of value for the community, appears to reconcile the two variations. This social entrepreneurship typically, and importantly, addresses unmet social needs that a nation's welfare system does not, cannot or will not meet. It seems inevitable that there will always be a gap between a society's welfare needs and the ability of the State to provide help and support. In some countries the gap is wider than it is in other parts of the world. Social capital of this type (like aesthetic capital, which we discuss later) is more intangible

than financial capital. Consequently, we believe that the critical test or effectiveness measure for these initiatives is the extent to which they would be missed if
they were lost. Until they happen, there is simply a gap and an unmet need, the
significance of which is dependent upon individual perceptions. Once the gap has
been filled, or at least partially filled, the significance of the need becomes more
widely apparent. Where social entrepreneurship involves the use of underutilized
community resources, such as derelict buildings, these often provide a visible and
identifiable artefact to which people can relate.

Social entrepreneurship is frequently attractive to people who feel committed to
a cause, as we shall see in a number of the examples we feature in this chapter.
Many people are willing to donate money to causes they support, but when an
individual with entrepreneurial talent or life themes feels a true commitment to a
particular cause or need we are likely to see social entrepreneurship as, in effect,
the need seems to find the person who will engage it and make something happen.
A number of people – often people with entrepreneurial life themes – have been
driven to significantly high levels of achievement by their commitment to a cause.
Whilst the sector attracts a considerable number of unpaid, volunteer helpers,
without doubt the most successful ventures invariably feature an identifiable champion, someone who will possess the life theme profile of an entrepreneur, but who
chooses to use his or her talents to build social rather than financial capital.

We have seen in earlier chapters how entrepreneurship comprises an (often opportunistic) idea and the ensuing actions which bring about desirable outcomes.
Particularly relevant for social entrepreneurship is Sykes's (1999) delineation of
three key contributions to the growth of organizations: *envisioning* a future state in
an uncertain environment, *enacting* the vision by giving it direction and purpose
and acquiring the necessary resources, and *enabling* it to happen by harnessing the
support of other key people. Entrepreneurship, as a process, clearly embraces all
three. The entrepreneur – the person – will invariably perform the enacting role
and at least initiate the enabling role, but he or she may not always be the envi-
sioner. The vision could be 'bought-in' from somewhere else, replicating a good
idea that others have proved can work. The growth of the modern hospice movement and the systematic restoration of steam railways throughout the UK provide
excellent examples of this.

Leadbeater and Goss (1998) differentiate social entrepreneurship from civic entrepreneurship, where, for example, a local authority, either by itself or by joining
forces with the private sector, sponsors innovative new products and services. An
example of an alliance would be where a local authority employee spots a need, a
gap and an opportunity, and then engineers the appointment of an entrepreneurial
person to establish the activity that can fulfil the need and close the gap. Schools
which take greater responsibility for their own resourcing – with the active support
of parents, school governors and the education authority – would be described as
entrepreneurial, and their heads as civic entrepreneurs.

Aesthetic or artistic capital brightens or enriches peoples' lives. There is an element
of the feel-good factor involved. People enjoy and gain a variety of benefits from
an imaginative urban landscape and architecture, for example. People choose
designer clothes to help fashion an image for themselves, which in turn can yield

material benefits as well as the feel-good factor. People are stimulated by certain films, pieces of music and examples of art and design. The relevant architects, directors, designers, musicians and artists who have this effect on our lives are quite often entrepreneurs. In addition to making an aesthetic difference, they often build very successful and lucrative businesses and become personally wealthy. In order to achieve this notoriety, of course, they have to market their talents. Some aesthetic entrepreneurs, such as architects, may be driven by causes, but the majority of them possess artistic and creative talent, and they are driven by a desire to exploit their talent. Entrepreneur life themes help them identify and exploit opportunities for realizing their creative potential.

Social and aesthetic capital concerns people and their impact on their environment or the world in which they live. When we discuss *environmental capital* in this chapter, we are really looking at the relatively small number of entrepreneurs who are primarily concerned with *sustaining* important global resources, rather than *building* capital, as most entrepreneurs do. Their commitment to an environmental cause constitutes a primary motivation for their business or project. However, it is perfectly feasible, and important, for other (business) entrepreneurs to seek to build financial wealth and capital without destroying greenbelt countryside, rainforests, or other natural geological or ecological resources. In Chapter 4, for example, we saw how Ben and Jerry's has drawn attention to a number of environmental concerns with its sourcing policies and with its choice of names for some of its ice creams. It is important that entrepreneurs see sustainability as an opportunity rather than a cost. For some businesses, such as mining and tourism, the issue is a particularly significant one.

Figure 5.1 shows how these various capitals can be complementary and how certain businesses and organizations are set up deliberately to build more than one type of capital. Beginning to move around the main figure (a) anti-clockwise, James Dyson (Chapter 3) is highlighted as a business entrepreneur – although he was only able to achieve his success and wealth by appreciating and exploiting the importance of product design. Trevor Baylis, with his clockwork radio for the Third World (Chapter 4), built financial and social wealth simultaneously. Dame Cicely Saunders, founder of the modern hospice movement, is a social entrepreneur. Restored steam railways build social capital, as well as providing aesthetic pleasure for many enthusiasts, but they do not become growth-oriented businesses. Featured in the inset (b), Anita Roddick, with The Body Shop, has built a successful and profitable business that has drawn attention to environmental and social causes. We look at these last three examples in this chapter.

Artistic and aesthetic capital is really the subject of Chapter 6, and this is where we discuss the wealthy American artist, Thomas Kincade – 'the world's most collected painter' – and architect Frank Gehry (again shown in the (b) inset in Figure 5.1 because of his positive impact on the environment). We also debate whether Mozart and Michelangelo were entrepreneurs. At the end of Chapter 6 we consider Sir Ernest Hall, the millionaire businessman, who converted a semi-derelict mill in Halifax into the Dean Clough complex (featured in the centre of the main diagram) and who has demonstrated how it is possible to build financial, social and aesthetic capital simultaneously.

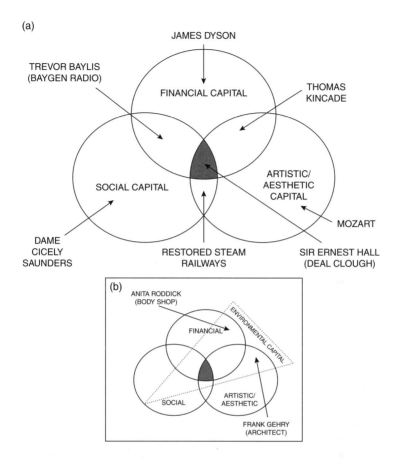

Figure 5.1 *Financial, social and artistic capital*

It will be apparent that we are arguing that financial capital is essential for building social and aesthetic capital and preserving environmental capital, and that businesses and organizations ideally will act positively in all four areas. We have to realize, however, that the accumulation of one form of capital can be at the expense of one or more of the other forms. The relative weight and importance which should be attributed to each will always remain an issue of perception and judgement, but there is a notional dividing line and those businesses which cross it are behaving in a societally unacceptable manner. Businesses, and entrepreneurs, who focus on financial capital without fair regard to social, aesthetic and environmental issues are, in effect, destroying other forms of capital to build financial wealth. Sometimes this happens with deliberate strategies and policies; at other times it is the result of oversight or ignorance rather than malicious intent. In Chapter 7 we look at this shadow side of entrepreneurship.

We begin this chapter with three legendary social entrepreneurs, before discussing a series of quite different contemporary examples. A number of the entrepreneurs we include have religious connections, and consequently we also include a short section of specifically religious entrepreneurs. The chapter continues with two businesses for which social considerations are really a way of life and then concludes with a section on environmental entrepreneurs.

Legendary social entrepreneurs

Florence Nightingale

Florence Nightingale was born in 1820, the daughter of well-off and well-connected parents. Her parents and society had expectations for the way she would grow up and spend her adult life – but Florence was determined to be different. As a child she was 'exceptionally intelligent', and at the age of seventeen she began to believe she was called to the service of God in some way or another. However, the next five years of her life comprised foreign travel. She returned to England in 1842 to find a country in the grip of an economic depression, where poverty, starvation and disease were manifest and widespread. She upset her family and friends by opting out of the social life she was expected to enjoy, turning down offers of marriage and, ultimately, deciding that that her vocation lay in hospital work and in helping sick people. In the 1840s 'the only qualification required for nursing the sick was to be a woman'. Nursing was not perceived to be a worthy occupation for Florence. No skills or training were required, the women nurses were 'frequently drunk and an occasional prostitute with the male patients'. Her parents were horrified and opposed her choice. Nevertheless, Florence was determined and persistent. Whilst caring for sick members of her family and their friends, she started studying both medicine and administration.

In 1851 she was able to visit Kaiserwerth, a dedicated training centre for nurses in Germany; and in 1853 she finally persuaded her parents to support her application for the honorary post of Superintendent at the Institute for the Care of Sick Gentlewomen in Distressed Circumstances. She used this opportunity to transform nursing practices. One year later she helped nurse cholera patients at the Middlesex Hospital during a major epidemic. Florence's vision for a new form of nursing care to support doctors was becoming clearer. She became determined to make nursing a respectable profession for women who were skilled, trained and professional. She believed this would provide a foundation for higher standards of hygiene in hospitals; at this time hygiene was inadequate except for the hospitals where nuns provided nursing care. But, of course, the nuns were again not trained in any formalized way.

Drawing on family connections she obtained permission to form a team of nurses who would travel out to the Crimea and care for the war casualties. In first obtaining the permission, and then when she was out there, she exploited the fact that this was the first overseas war where journalists were providing newspapers back home with regular reports on progress and conditions. Finding it difficult to recruit the volunteers she wanted, Florence ended up with twenty-four nuns in a group of thirty-eight women; and at Scutari she found a field hospital 'where a soldier was more likely to die than if he were fighting on the battlefield'. She was, however, resented by senior army staff and had to overcome a series of obstacles. Tackling issues of diet, supplies, sewers and drainage, and the actual physical handling of the casualties, she was still able to demonstrate a real difference in just six months. Through her persistence, she succeeded in transforming the perception people had of nurses and nursing care. Suddenly Florence Nightingale had become a national heroine!

After the Crimean War she initially withdrew from public life and devoted herself to taking her campaign to senior politicians and the Royal Family. Afterwards she was again active in the establishment of new civilian hospitals and training schools for civilian nurses. In essence, her work and inspiration provided the foundation for the modern nursing profession. The entrepreneur life themes of dedication, focus, activating, courage, opportunity and expertise orientation are clear in this short commentary on her life.

William Booth

William Booth was a contemporary of Florence Nightingale. Born the son of a Nottingham builder in 1829, he moved to London after the death of his father and found work as a pawnbroker's assistant. He had already been converted to Christianity and he became a revivalist Methodist preacher, arguing that church ministers should pursue a strong social role as well as their pastoral one. He was later to practise what he preached! Not atypically, he saw women as 'the weaker sex', but married a strong, self-willed woman, Catherine Mumford, in 1855. Outraging many Christians, Catherine began preaching herself in 1860. Soon supported by an originally sceptical husband she was 'outstanding and inspirational'.

As a preacher in Nottingham, Booth attracted socially deprived converts to Christianity at his open-air meetings, but those who were particularly dirty and smelly were not always welcomed in chapel by other Methodists. In 1865, and working together, William and Catherine opened a Christian mission in Whitechapel, in the squalid East End of London, to help feed and house the poor. Their trigger had been the poverty and social deprivation they had witnessed. At this time they had seven of their eight children; and their eldest son, Bramwell, soon joined them in the mission work, as did Booth's second key assistant, George Scott Railton, a Christian businessman from Middlesbrough, who had read of the mission and come to London specifically to work alongside Booth. William Booth had now built a strong central team. When the mission was reorganized along military command lines in 1878, with the preachers called officers and William Booth the General, the Salvation Army was formed. Influenced by Catherine, the Salvation Army gave equal preaching and welfare responsibilities to women. The services were informal and 'joyous music' played a significant role. Again not unexpectedly, there was hostility from the established Church of England. Army members were imprisoned for open-air preaching and Booth was declared the 'Antichrist' for his support of women preachers. But the Salvation Army prospered – more and more people joined and opened Citadels up and down the country. Booth started his own newspaper, *The War Cry*, and wrote a book about social conditions in England, offering his personal suggestions for overcoming poverty.

Booth's entrepreneurial characteristics were clearly demonstrated when he became determined to improve the working conditions for women at the local East End Bryant and May match factory. Pay was low, but more significantly the women's health was being damaged by Bryant and May's preference for using yellow phosphorus for the match heads. Toxic fumes caused skin discoloration, followed by discharging pores and ultimately death from necrosis of the bone. Other European countries had begun to use harmless red phosphorus as an alternative, but the campaigning Booth was told this would prove uneconomical. Consequently, in 1891, the Salvation Army opened its own match factory in competition. Workers were paid double the Bryant and May rate, but using red phosphorus. Booth was soon producing and selling 6 million boxes a year. Members of Parliament and journalists were encouraged to visit the 'model factory' and 'compare the conditions with other sweat shops'. In 1901 Bryant and May also switched to red phosphorus. An invitation to attend the coronation of King Edward VII in 1902 confirmed that William Booth's contribution had been recognized.

The Salvation Army became established abroad – Booth himself travelled widely throughout the UK, America and Australia. He died in 1912, at the age of eighty-three, twenty years after his wife. Railton died very shortly afterwards and consequently Bramwell Booth succeeded his father as General. The growth and significance of the Salvation Army has clearly continued.

Dame Cicely Saunders

Dame Cicely Saunders is the founder of the modern hospice movement. Founding the St Christopher's Hospice in Sydenham in 1967, she established new methods in pain and symptom control, and inspired others to raise funds, find premises and open over 200 new hospices all over the country. At the time she was forty-nine years old. The dream had taken several years of effort and persistence, and in some ways reflects the dedicated pursuit of a dream that we saw evidenced in James Dyson.

Again Cicely's parents were well off and she had begun studying at Oxford when she left to train as a nurse at the beginning of the Second World War. She served at St Thomas' Hospital in London. Hampered by a back condition, she had to abandon nursing as soon as the war was over, and she returned to Oxford to complete her degree in philosophy, politics and economics. At this time she converted to Christianity. Her next move was to train and become a hospital almoner, the equivalent of a modern hospital social worker. At work she became friendly with David Tasma, a Polish Jew who had escaped from the Nazis. Tasma was dying, but it was their short friendship that helped her 'realize and appreciate the needs of the dying patient'. His death spurred her to help as an evening volunteer at St Luke's Hospital in Bayswater where 'effective pain control, not practised in other hospitals' was used on terminally ill patients. Simply, pain-killing drugs were being administered at regular, controlled intervals before pain levels could rebuild. Now determined to improve the quality of care for the dying, Cicely Saunders was persuaded to retrain as a doctor. Her non-scientific background was a hurdle, but she persisted and succeeded. Totally focused, she qualified in 1957 and then obtained a research fellowship to study pain in the terminally ill. Combining her medical qualification with her experience at St Luke's she was able to trial new pain controls for cancer patients at St Joseph's Hospice, which was run by Irish nuns in Hackney.

Later she had a vision for 'The Scheme', a 100-bed home for terminally ill patients, where spiritual care would be combined with the best methods of medical care available. She also saw it as a training base for doctors and other qualified carers. She worked out that she would need £200 000 to build 'The Scheme' and documented her plans in detail. In 1961 she circulated it widely and dedicated herself to bringing 'The Scheme' to fruition. She obtained her site in 1963 and the hospice opened four years after that. During this six-year period she 'pushed ahead with faith' and 'eleventh-hour' donations became quite normal. In many respects the vision was fulfilled. The 100-bed size was always too optimistic, but the true measure of her contribution is the influence she has subsequently had on others. It remains interesting, though, that whilst 'everybody' recognizes the name Florence Nightingale and many would be able to associate William Booth with the Salvation Army, outside medical circles, few would appreciate the contribution of Cicely Saunders to the hospice movement they support financially. In aggregate terms hospices have become the most successful charity fund-raising organization in the UK in the 1990s.

In the next section on contemporary social entrepreneurs, many of the names will be 'unknowns' to the majority of readers. This is partly due to the fact that some of the initiatives are small and localized but it is also affected by the reality that social entrepreneurship does not receive the publicity that successful businesses do.

Contemporary social entrepreneurs

Elliott Tepper

Elliott Tepper is an American missionary who lives in Spain. He has an MBA but has chosen to channel his not inconsiderable energies into helping alcoholics and drug addicts. He started Betel, a not-for-profit Christian rehabilitation centre, in the early 1990s. At any one time Betel now houses over 500 young addicts, both men and women, in homes in ten Spanish cities, in Birmingham in the UK and in Brooklyn, New York. Half of the people on Betel's programme are HIV positive. Most of the single-sex houses or 'communities' – a number of which have been obtained by initially squatting and then 'doing up' – are run by volunteer ex-addicts.

In return for a place to live and an opportunity to break their addiction, the residents have to turn their backs on alcohol, cigarettes and drugs, and must work, mainly with their hands. Within the houses the rules are strict, and any resident who breaks the rules is likely to be thrown out without undue haste and ceremony. Betel provides cleaners, plumbers, painters and bricklayers as well as running charity shops which sell used clothes and household items they have been given. Most of their food is donated by local supermarkets – it is typically food which is close to its sell-by or use-by date and which otherwise would be wasted. Betel's goal is self-sufficiency but it does receive financial donations from city councils and the Red Cross and looks for free materials its workers can use.

Five thousand people have passed through in seven years. Half have stayed for at least six months. Tepper believes people need to stay for at least a year if they are to beat their addiction; and of the 5000 some 17 per cent have left fully cured. Of those who accept the Christian faith, the success rate seems to be as high as 90 per cent. The ratio of men to women has been 4:1. Three per cent have been aged under twenty, 54 per cent between twenty and thirty, leaving 43 per cent over thirty years old. Currently the annual revenue – donations plus income earned by the resident workers – is equivalent to £3 million.

It is interesting to see how Elliott Tepper's early experiences brought out his inherited entrepreneurial talents. His father was president of an electronics firm in New York and a partner in two other businesses. 'A man of vision, he tried to do the impossible and I inherited that from him'. At the age of fourteen Elliott's world began to unravel when his parents divorced and his father lost his fortune. His college education began at Lehigh University and was paid for by a wrestling schol-arship he won – he was the New York State champion. This was followed by a Cambridge (UK) MA in Economics and an MBA at Harvard. 'In my last year at Harvard I joined a commune and took part in all-night discussions about politics and philosophy. That was when I started taking hallucinogenic drugs, hashish and marijuana.' This was followed by a life-changing experience that encouraged Tepper to become active in his local church once he returned home after Harvard. He subsequently attended Bible College in America and worked as a missionary in Mexico before going to Spain.

In Elliott Tepper we can see that an obvious need is being addressed by someone with a vision who is able to gather together the financial, people and other resources required to operationalize the vision. On this occasion, and not unusually, that person is a Christian minister. At the heart of the initiative are buildings, without which the venture would be impossible. Like the partial reliance on charity shops, all these issues are commonly found in social entrepreneurship. Three other factors, however, make Betel distinctive and unusual – and different from many charities. First, in order to benefit from the rehabilitation programme, people have to do something; the support they receive is not a free gift. Second, part of Betel's income comes from the beneficiaries actually working and earning. Third, and like the modern hospice movement, the original idea has been grown into a major initiative that has broken out of a single community identity.

The next three examples illustrate social entrepreneurship in the UK in the 1990s. They are each important and significant in their own way – their non-existence would leave a gap – but we see three quite different levels of impact.

Andrew Mawson

Andrew Mawson is a Yorkshire-born United Reform Church minister who was moved to London's East End in 1984. His church in Bromley-by-Bow had a leaking roof, poor heating, a damaged piano and just a small congregation of mostly elderly people. Radical change seemed the only obvious way forward! The new Bromley-by-Bow Centre reflects a complete transformation inspired by Mawson and imple-mented by the community it serves. The church itself was redesigned to generate more open, flexible space and offered to the local community for appropriate daily use on weekdays. In the early days one local woman used it to build a boat! Local artists soon realized it could provide useful studio facilities. Word of mouth brought in a dance school, a nursery and a café. A disability group offered to landscape the gardens. In effect, the building became a community centre in the week and a church on Sundays – with a growing and active congregation.

On the back of these developments Mawson has helped raise money from the Royal and Sun Alliance and the NatWest Bank to fund projects for combating youth crime in the area and for supporting local young entrepreneurs. In addition, there is now an adjacent health centre for the local community. The area still has high unemployment and deprivation, but the community can boast a centre of excel-lence and achievement. Mawson has always set deliberately high targets to spur extra effort. One of his main contributions has been to build a central team – that has imparted a mission and values – and then to involve and encourage enter-prising members of the community. Involving artistic people from the beginning has ensured consistent creativity and there has always been an emphasis on building value for local customers.

Andrew Mawson recently has been instrumental in establishing The Community Action Foundation with a remit to identify examples of effective social entrepre-neurship and help sponsor new developments.

Margaret Handforth

The Castleford Community Learning Centre in West Yorkshire provides an excel-lent example of the need drawing in the entrepreneur. Margaret Handforth, miner's wife, ex-secretary and mother of three sons, had demonstrated her latent talent by founding a local playgroup but had never thought of herself as an entrepreneur before the 1984 miners' strike. Forming a small group, she set up a soup kitchen to help people survive the traumas of the time. Invited to speak to students at local universities in exchange for a collection, the women set foot on university campuses for the first time in their lives. They began to realize that education can broaden horizons and Margaret Handforth had a vision of a better life through self-improve-ment. She had 'no idea how to do it, just a determination to start something off'. Although the venture has grown remarkably, most of the founding team have no current involvement. Margaret has recruited a new team to help her.

The Castleford Women's Centre started gradually in humble premises they were able to restore with the help of a small grant. Support and counselling was supple-mented with tea dances and craft classes, 'really anything that would bring people in'. Additional contacts led to additional grants, and the venture took off. It was really 'growth out of necessity' – the need had found the right person to fill the gap. Known locally as the University of Life, the Women's Centre has moved into new premises with a new name. A wide raft of courses up to degree level, and validated by local colleges and universities, is now available, usually at low or no cost to women in this economically deprived area. It has succeeded because it has always been flexible, opportunistic and close to its customers. 'I daren't go out for a sandwich at lunchtime as people [I would meet] would keep stopping and talking to me ... I'd be out for two hours' (Margaret Handforth). There are clear growth plans for the development of a residential college in a nearby old mansion, and a leisure and diving centre on the site of a flooded quarry.

Genya Johnson

A few miles down the road, in Rotherham, the Get Sorted Crew also makes an important social contribution, but on a smaller and more limited scale. Genya Johnson is a full-time special needs teacher whose Russian father had moved to England after the Second World War and opened a chain of small shops. She has inherited his entrepreneurial talent, but chooses to use it for helping others in her spare time.

Get Sorted occupies the upper floors of what was a motorcycle shop and provides soundproof rehearsal rooms for teenage bands. This is supplemented by access to recording facilities, organizing gigs for the bands in order to raise funds and a management agency for those bands good enough to secure independent bookings. Genya Johnson first appreciated the gap and the opportunity when she was recruited by the local police force to help with a drugs awareness campaign. She helped the first band by allowing them to practise in her own home, before setting out to find appropriate premises. She has relied more on free handouts (such as spare tins of paint) and volunteers' time than she has on financial assistance. Nevertheless she was personally awarded a small, recurring grant to reimburse her for her time as a form of youth leader. She gives the money to a younger helper – an ex-band member – so he can work full time for Get Sorted. She herself takes no reward for her part-time commitment, which amounts to every evening and weekends! Over 100 bands and 500 young people, from a range of social backgrounds, and some from several miles away, have made use of the facilities, for which they have to pay a token rental. Friends of the musicians also use the centre and help with promotional material and renovation work. In one important respect, Get Sorted is a social centre that keeps young people off the streets and often out of trouble. Unless Genya discovers a future chart-topping band, though, Get Sorted Crew is always likely to be constrained by time and money limitations.

Charlotte Da Vita

Trade Plus Aid began more by chance than design in 1991. Charlotte Da Vita, then aged twenty-five, was in Ghana when drought ruined thousands of farms. Wanting to help in some way, she had an idea. She suggested to local tribal chiefs that she would spend her £800 savings on seed for them if they would make her 800 pendant-size carvings. The deal was struck. Back in London, and calling on her friends to help her out, she began selling the pendants at Portobello Market, plucking a price of £6.99 each out of thin air. Somewhat to her surprise, the carvings sold quickly and easily. The risk she took had paid off, and she was encouraged to want to do more. She envisioned a seed bank from which local farmers could borrow seed without any payment until they harvest their crops. To progress her idea, she negotiated an alliance with an established mail-order business in Japan – and pendant sales were strong once the infrastructure and supply chain was in place. Her seed bank was started in 1995. The venture grew rapidly with a comprehensive Japanese mail-order catalogue, which included jewellery, clothing and toiletries from various countries in Africa and South America. Unfortunately the 1995 earthquake at Kobe, in Japan, destroyed the warehouse that Da Vita's partner owned; the mail-order company was in trouble and the Japanese market disappeared overnight. Exhibiting the courage life theme, she managed to survive and rescue the business by spending hours and days searching out new mail-order buyers in America and Germany – but they would only buy her supplies at cost.

Many of the Third World village supply groups she helped establish are now trading independently; they no longer need her help. 'A good year is seeing my groups become self-sufficient, not increasing my turnover.' The ever-creative Trade Plus Aid, however, continues to experiment with new initiatives. Da Vita has been able to raise £92 000 from business people around the world, who believe in what she does, to establish a 140-employee factory in China for producing hand-enamelled teapots. She sells these at the Victoria and Albert Museum and various up-market department stores. Underestimating demand has forced her to resort to air-freighting and the operation breaks even rather than makes a profit. A second Chinese factory is planned when the cash flow permits, and a similar venture produces wind chimes in South Africa. In the UK, Trade Plus Aid relies more on volunteer helpers than it does on paid employees and Da Vita herself takes only a limited salary from the operation. She was awarded an MBE in 1998.

Charlotte Da Vita is a natural entrepreneur who could have benefited from sharper techniques and business knowledge – had she been able to find the time and opportunity to acquire them.

David Bussau: the business entrepreneur who invests in the poor

David Bussau is different from the social entrepreneurs we have considered so far. Bussau became a millionaire from a series of business interests and then focused his not inconsiderable talents on helping poor people around the world. Many millionaires do give generously and set up foundations to help create social, and sometimes aesthetic, capital – but Bussau set out to help people help themselves. In this respect he has a similar ethos to Charlotte Da Vita.

David Bussau spent the first sixteen years of his life (1940–56) in an orphanage in New Zealand and the next nineteen years making his fortune as an entrepreneurial businessman. When he left the orphanage with 'no family, no close friends and no money' he managed to start a hot-dog stand. Within six months he had six other people leasing stands from him. With his profits David bought (and later sold) a small bakery and then a biscuit factory and a pancake restaurant. He never had any formal business education; he was simply able to grow businesses!

In his mid-twenties, after marrying, he sold up and moved to Australia. His wife was ill at the time, and they believed that for her condition the medical facilities in Australia were superior to those in New Zealand. He got a job in construction. Perhaps inevitably he was soon to become a partner in the business he joined –

before he bought the business outright and used it as a base to set up a whole series of construction firms. He was a millionaire before he was thirty-five. 'It was clear that I was an entrepreneur and that whatever business I chose to take on, I was going to make a success of it.'

On Christmas Day in 1974 Darwin (in the Northern Territory) was devastated by a cyclone. A committed Christian, Bussau set off with twenty of his employees to help – short term – with rescue and rebuilding activities. This experience changed his philosophy of life. A year later, David sold a number of his businesses, leaving managers in charge of the others, and moved with his wife and family to Darwin to continue helping with the rebuilding programme. In 1976 the whole family moved on to Bali, to help there in the aftermath of an earthquake. Here he organized the construction of a dam, a bridge, a clinic and an irrigation system. He earned nothing from this – in reality he invested in the projects. Travelling around Bali he sensed potential entrepreneurs who were being held back by a lack of money at afford-able rates of interest. He started making small, short-term loans to very poor people. Some would buy tools that they would use to boost their family income. Others would buy basic ingredients and bake them into saleable products.

He returned to Australia, but was persuaded to return to Bali in 1980. With the help of others he set up a church-based revolving credit scheme to provide short-term loans. Local banks were not interested in loaning small amounts, such as the $50 (Australian dollars) which was all that new, small businesses required to start up, because their processing costs made the rates of interest prohibitive. Bussau's idea was for small loans, paid back very quickly so the money can be re-lent to others. A first loan could, of course, be followed by subsequent, and usually larger, loans as the businesses began to grow. The interest charged covered the operating costs and nothing more. Project officials also provided advice to the small busi-nesses whilst ever they had a loan. Ten years later – under the umbrella organization, Opportunity International – there were forty-seven similar agencies in nineteen other countries around the world. Some 50 000 small entrepreneurs had been provided with the limited financial support they needed to either get started or grow their business. Although Christianity is at the heart of the programme, two-thirds of the loans have been made to non-Christians. In recent years Bussau has concentrated on persuading other Christian business leaders in developing coun-tries to 'use the gifts and skills God has given them to help the poor'.

Norma Redfearn: civic entrepreneur

Norma Redfearn became the head teacher of West Walker primary school in Newcastle in 1986. The school was in a state of near collapse; the local area, once wealthy from shipbuilding, had a predominance of unemployed single mothers; three-quarters of the children qualified for free school meals. Forty per cent of the available places in the school were not taken up. Norma Redfearn realized she would have to engage the interest and support of the local parents if she was to turn the school around; she succeeded and was able to use West Walker as a cata-lyst for community renewal. Now, truancy rates are low and educational achievement encouraging. The empty spaces have been taken up with the creation of an adult day centre, such that parents and children can study side by side in the same building. A cafeteria provides subsidized breakfasts as well as lunches. In addition, through their involvement at the school, local parents have banded together to form a housing association which has built seventy houses opposite the school. Local authority architects, parents and children have together rebuilt a play area that stays open outside school hours. Community social workers have an office base in the school. Simply, the education is happening because the school has become involved in family lives. In some respects it plays a similar (albeit different) role to that of the Bromley-by-Bow Centre – namely, it provides a focus where people can come together and help themselves. Norma Redfearn, like Andrew Mawson, has succeeded because she has been able to use her talents to engage the interest and support of others and bring them together to work as a team. The life themes of opportunity, activation, creativity, dedication, courage and expertise orientation continue to manifest themselves in these various examples.

Nord Anglia

One reason why schools such as West Walker underachieve is a lack of enterprise. As public attention is increasingly drawn to this issue, the government is losing confidence in some local education authorities and turning towards the private sector. On occasions there is a willingness to appoint a specialist outside organization that will come in and turn around a school in difficulties as an alternative to finding an entrepreneurial head. One such organization, Nord Anglia, has been described as a 'pathfinder organization which has taken advantage of business opportunities in education when they have become available'. Specifically Nord Anglia has been constantly alert and responsive to new windows of opportunity.

The business was founded in 1972 and floated on the Stock Exchange exactly twenty-five years later. Annual turnover now exceeds £40 million. Kevin McNeany – 'I am naturally an entrepreneur' – had worked as a lecturer in the further education sector for thirteen years when he set up a business for teaching English as a foreign language to overseas students. Soon afterwards he saw an opportunity to run a private school and took it. The opportunity to break into the public sector did not come until the 1990s, but he was ready. Nord Anglia was an early participant when school inspections were privatized; more recently it has formed an alliance with the universities of Manchester and Liverpool to provide training for the National Professional Qualification for Headship. When John Major's government introduced nursery school vouchers, Nord Anglia built new nursery and day-care centres. McNeany has also opened schools in several countries overseas, again spotting and responding to opportunities. He believes that in the future new opportunities will arise in the university sector. Buckingham is currently the only private university with recognized degree-awarding powers – 'and that's a charity'. McNeany and Nord Anglia intend to be ready.

Religious entrepreneurs

The earlier story of businessman David Bussau is an excellent example of someone following the Christian preaching of John Wesley: 'make as much as you can; save as much as you can; give away as much as you can'. We have also seen religious themes coming through in several of the other stories we have included. William Booth founded the Salvation Army; Andrew Mawson is a vicar and Elliott Tepper a missionary; Florence Nightingale and Cicely Saunders both believed they had been called by God. In this section we develop the religious connection further and look at another church minister who has been able to use his position to raise substantial amounts of money which have then been redeployed to help others through socially entrepreneurial ventures. Whilst Andrew Mawson relies on corporate donations and Elliott Tepper's clients have to work, television evangelists in America have learned how to use the power of the media to capture the hearts and minds of a large congregation and to generate huge donations. Occasionally there has been evidence of corruption. What we see in evidence here is entrepreneurship that addresses two opportunities simultaneously and brings them together in a powerful and synergistic initiative. The first opportunity is creative fund-raising – social entrepreneurs can only spend what they can raise! The second opportunity concerns identifying appropriate causes for redirecting the funds to create demonstrable benefits for the more needy. The social capital and the need it addresses can, on the one hand, constitute a cause that provides a focus for the fund-raising. At the same time they constitute the measures which justify the effectiveness of the venture.

Pat Robertson

Pat Robertson was the founder of the American Christian Broadcasting Network (CBN) in 1960. The first Christian television network, it grew to become one of the world's largest television ministries – and the heart of a major business empire. It is still popular as a family channel with a strong religious heart, and its daily flagship programme attracts an audience of 1.5 million viewers in America alone. There are countless more in the ninety other countries where it is broadcast. Christian Broadcasting Network incorporates an extensive call centre; viewers can ring up at any time to either make donations or seek advice on any problems they have. A parallel family entertainment channel set up by Robertson was sold to Rupert Murdoch in 1997 for $1.9 billion. The stations were established on land in Virginia Beach, which Roberston owns, and where he has developed other activities and businesses. He created the private Regent University (of which he remains Chancellor) where entrepreneurship is included as a key feature programme; and his other business interests include diamond-mining, chemicals and banking. In 1978 Robertson also founded a non-profit organization, Operation Blessing, for providing humanitarian aid in the form of food, clothing, medicine and financial support to disadvantaged people and disaster victims. In twenty years $500 million was raised via CBN and dispersed through Operation Blessing.

Pat Robertson was born in 1930 in Lexington, Virginia. His father was, at different times, a member of both the House of Representatives and the Senate. His direct ancestors include a signatory of the Declaration of Independence and two American presidents. After military service in Korea, Pat Robertson qualified as a lawyer before choosing to study theology. A Southern Baptist minister from 1961 to 1987, he eventually resigned from the ministry to seek the Republication nomination for the presidency. A series of successful books has contributed to his considerable wealth.

Despite his ancestry, religious calling and clear success as a social entrepreneur, Robertson is a controversial man. In March 1999 it was announced that the Bank of Scotland was teaming up with him to establish a joint venture organization which would provide telephone-banking services (in which the Bank of Scotland has expertise) for the millions of Americans who watch CBN. Direct telephone banking has yet to develop in the USA to the extent it has in the UK. This, therefore, appeared to be an excellent and ideal opportunity for the two partners, who would bring distinct but complementary skills to the venture. Deposits and savings accounts were to be followed by credit cards and loans. By June the deal was off. Over many years Robertson has earned a reputation for strong right-wing views; he has been forthright about his hostility towards 'homosexuals, feminists, liberals, Muslims and Hindus'. When, in May 1999, he described Scotland as 'a dark land that panders to homosexuals and which has lost its morals', many Royal Bank customers were incensed. Bank executives felt they had to withdraw 'to save further embarrassment', even thought they would have to pay compensation to buy out Robertson's share in the joint venture. In February 1999, Robertson had also become a non-executive director of the troubled Laura Ashley, invited by his business colleague and friend, the Malaysian businessman who is the largest shareholder in the company. Gay Rights and other protest groups immediately started to campaign for his dismissal.

Way-of-life entrepreneurs

We are adopting the term 'way-of-life entrepreneurs' for those business owners who have chosen to run their organizations in a different, people-centred way. These entrepreneurs go much further than the strategies and policies adopted by people like Julian Richer and Archie Norman, who we discussed in Chapter 4. Significantly they have shown how a business can be driven by social concerns without sacrificing profitability. Yet many people remain sceptical and true way-of-life entrepreneurs remain a small, but nevertheless significant, minority. Neither Ernest Bader nor Ricardo Semler would be regarded as the 'arbiter of normality'.

Scott Bader

Scott Bader is a private industrial chemical company with a radically different approach to both ownership and management. It was started as a private company in 1923 by Ernest Bader to be the sole agent in the UK for a Swiss manufacturer of celluloid. At this time celluloid was being moulded into colourful knife handles, combs and cases as well as table tennis balls. It is of course the base product for film. Part of Bader's early success came down to the popularity of the small plastic windmills children used to play with at the seaside! Other products in the paint industry were later imported from Germany and America, but the depression of the 1930s squeezed these merchanting activities. Bader moved into manufacturing, concentrating on paint pigment pastes, a specialist niche within the chemical industry. 'He had a strong, entrepreneurial ability to select leading product lines ... industry buyers kept close to Bader to see what he would come up with next.'

In 1940, at the beginning of the blitz, the company was moved from its central London offices and dockland factory to the old Wollaston Hall in Northamptonshire. The hall itself provided office accommodation, the stables became laboratories and a new factory was built on the 44-acre site. Manufacturing could be extended on the new site, but the company has always remained relatively small, reaching a maximum of around 450 employees in the UK, a number that has declined and risen with trade recessions and strategic changes.

A production plant was opened in Amiens, France, in 1966; in 1972 Scott Bader acquired a manufacturer of glass reinforced plastic products, for which it supplied the raw materials, and a major distributor in 1978. Other acquisitions have followed, and in 1997 Scott Bader owned three plants in France, seven distribution centres in the UK, and distribution centres in Ireland, Sweden, the Czech Republic, South Africa and the Middle East, as well as its main site in Northamptonshire. The company has always been profitable in a very competitive industry. Again, in 1997, total group turnover amounted to £100 million (with £5.3 million operating profits) from 650 employees. The figures for the UK are £60 million turnover, £4.4 million profits and 365 employees.

However Scott Bader is not a typical company in terms of philosophy and governance. It is innovative with its style of management, seeking to achieve E-V-R congruence – see Chapter 2 – with a distinctive emphasis on values. Whilst it is, in effect, a values-driven business, it must still satisfy its customers with differentiated products and controlled costs. Ernest Bader, a Quaker since 1944, believed that 'men should employ capital rather than capital employ men', and as a result he established the Scott Bader Commonwealth in 1951 as a charitable trust. This belief, which he was willing to act on, became his cause. Bader and his family gave 90 per cent of the company shares to the Commonwealth, holding back the remaining 10 per cent (which carried over half the voting shares) until 1963, when they too were transferred. All employees who have completed a probationary period with the company can apply for membership of the Commonwealth and thus share in the ownership of the company, although shares are never individually theirs to trade.

The Commonwealth has a board of management with members elected from company employees and its prime functions are concerned with social guidance, support of charitable causes, and encouraging similar forms of common ownership elsewhere. Scott Bader has a proper management structure with a board of directors, similar to that of other companies other than that there is the equivalent of four employee directors.

The Community Council with elected members from all parts of the company can investigate and discuss any matters referred to it by any individual or group and can recommend a course of action to the company board. In the past members of the Community Council have been actively involved in the selection of a new managing director for the company. In addition there is a board of trustees, two directors, two from the Community Council and three external to the company, to deal with such things as constitutional changes.

No group has overall authority, so ultimately they have to move together as one body even though they may push and pull against each other in representing particular interests.

The principles of the Commonwealth include:

- Opportunities for personal growth and development.
- Releasing the best in all employees.
- Recognizing and sharing talents.
- To render the best possible service as a corporate body to one's fellow men.
- To produce goods beneficial to the community.
- Management by consent and not coercion.

People are allowed to serve on boards only for limited periods of time and are not allowed to stand for re-election, so individual power bases cannot be developed. Newly elected members have often had to be trained for their new roles. Things have not gone completely smoothly, however. Whilst many employees have participated, some have chosen not to. It has been claimed that the company has at times lost dynamism because there has been too much concern with the quality of working life.

One significant change happened when Scott Bader bought a Unilever subsidiary, Synthetic Resins (Speke, Liverpool) in 1982. Although some Scott Bader employees are members of trade unions, the unions are not active within the company. But Synthetic Resins was different. It was conventionally managed and traditionally unionized. Despite efforts to integrate the companies and introduce common ownership at Synthetic Resins Scott Bader failed to persuade the Liverpool workers to accept the new culture. Synthetic Resins was closed in 1985 and the essential parts of the business were transferred to Northamptonshire. After this experience, any possible acquisition has had to offer the potential for participation in both work (delegated responsibility) and governance.

Ernest Bader himself died in 1982 at the age of ninety-one. His son, Godric, acted as Chairman from 1969 to 1989, when he became Life President. He continues to encourage other organizations to adopt aspects of common ownership.

Ricardo Semler

Ricardo Semler was just twenty-one years old when he took over as chief executive of his family's business, Semco. This Brazilian company manufactures pumps, food mixers, meat slicing equipment and dishwashers. Brazil is, of course, a country characterized by high inflation and a massive relative wealth gap between the rich and the poor. His father believed that if he handed over the reigns when Ricardo was still young, 'he could make his mistakes whilst he was still around to fix them!' His father had run the business along traditional and autocratic lines; Ricardo was to change everything – and the company has thrived and prospered.

Although he has an MBA from Harvard, Ricardo Semler's stated business philosophy is 'follow your intuition'. He inherited a company where 'people did not want to come to work and managers watched everything and everybody constantly, trusting nobody' and transformed it into one which is 'ultimately democratic and based on freedom, respect, trust and commitment'. Things did not happen instantaneously; many new approaches and experimental methods were tried and abandoned. However, in a ten-year period from the mid-1980s Semco achieved 900 per cent growth.

There is no reception area, no secretaries and no offices. Managers walk around constantly to provide help and assistance when it is requested; the workers organize their own flexible working time arrangements. Employees work in small clusters, and they can also rearrange their working space and environment as they wish. Semco has come to believe that clusters of no more than ten are required if this approach is to work effectively. Twelve layers of a management and supervisory hierarchy have been reduced to three. The appointment of any manager has to be approved by the workforce, and managers are subjected to regular assessment by their subordinates and shopfloor employees. People talk openly and 'when someone says they'll do something, they do it'. Consequently managers also feel they can spend time away from the plant – with customers and suppliers.

Profit-sharing is by consultation and negotiation – 23 per cent of after-tax profits is available for the workforce – and all employees are trained to ensure they can read the company accounts. There is no longer a formal chief executive post for Ricardo, who is now President. Instead there is an informal board of six associates (the most senior managers) who elect a nominal chief executive for a six-month period. Ricardo sometimes attends their meetings – as an adviser.

Ricardo has recently taken his ideas further, encouraging employees to consider starting up satellite supply companies and subcontracting for Semco. Those who have opted for this entrepreneurial route have been allowed to take Semco machines with them, leasing them on favourable terms. One advantage for Semco is the fact that it is no longer responsible for the maintenance and safety of the equipment. In addition, there is an opportunity for the machinery to be used more effectively as the satellite companies are free to work for other organizations; their efficiency gains can be passed through in the form of lower prices. If the venture fails, Semco takes back the equipment and the men. It is a relatively low and managed risk for all concerned.

Ricardo Semler has not been a man who has hidden his achievements! He has written the story of his role at Semco with the title *Maverick*. Like Julian Richer, he helps other companies as a consultant and he has become a recognized member of the management guru circuit around the world. He has also campaigned against corruption in Brazil, and he has exposed government officials who have been demanding bribes for domestic planning permission. As a result, he has generated hostility from certain prominent people in his country.

'Successful companies will be the ones that put quality of life first. Do this and the rest – quality of product, productivity of workers, profits for all – will follow.' Ricardo Semler, like Ernest Bader, is an entrepreneur because he has pursued a vision, courageously persevered against resistance and challenges, and made things happen.

Environmental entrepreneurs

In this last section we look first at two small businesses which provide 'green' energy, both of them started by entrepreneurs who are dedicated to the preservation of the natural environment. This is their cause, and for them it is far more important than the building of financial wealth. We then consider restored steam railways, which have preserved an important element of our industrial heritage whilst providing significant social (leisure) capital for many people and earning financial wealth for several small towns and villages along the routes. The use of the Keighley and Worth Valley Railway for the film *The Railway Children*, and the location of the television programme *Heartbeat* in Goathland, a key station on the North Yorkshire Moors Railway, are both testimony to their contribution to economic wealth creation. Restored steam railways typically demonstrate enterprising behaviour from a group of enthusiasts, who together fulfil the envisioning, enacting and enabling roles we discussed at the beginning of the chapter. The section concludes with the story of Anita Roddick and her very successful Body Shop.

Dale Vince

In 1996 Dale Vince, together with two friends and £10 000, set up The Renewable Energy Company, 'Europe's largest, dedicated supplier of green electricity'. Within a year turnover exceeded £4 million, with £400 000 pre-tax profits. The energy was generated initially from landfill gas (methane) but more recently supplies have been obtained from purpose-built wind farms, specifically clusters of windmills. The early success with methane generated the cash to invest in the new windmills. One opportunity was exploited to allow another opportunity to be seized. In the long term the company must be able to keep its prices in line with those of the major, established suppliers who use gas, oil and coal – and not lay itself open to criticism for building wind farms which are considered by some to be eyesores in the countryside.

Jeremy Leggett

Jeremy Leggett was an environmental campaigner in charge of Greenpeace's global warming campaign before he became an entrepreneur. Convinced of the potential of solar energy he installed solar panels on the roof of his home in Richmond, Surrey. The panels generated 68 per cent more energy than the household needed; and over their life the panels 'should prevent more than 30 tonnes of greenhouse gas emissions'. Leggett set up his business, Solar Century, in March 1999 to promote solar energy and distribute panels manufactured by a range of alternative suppliers. Architects are seen as a key target audience, but early orders have been received from individual homeowners. At the moment the panels remain expensive, but if a mass market is generated Leggett believes the price can be brought down to a competitive level.

Steam railways

For some people, steam railways merely conjure up an image of 'train spotters in anoraks', whilst for others they are a cause to which they will devote considerable time and energy. Most of the people who work on the restored railways are unpaid volunteers. The commercial and catering staff are generally paid employees, but the drivers, conductors and engineers are enthusiastic hobbyists. A ratio of 80:20 unpaid:paid would be typical. Their hobby provides enormous enjoyment for both themselves and the passengers. Youngsters are able to experience the transport system that opened up the country, although in reality most of the routes are small branch lines. In turn, the passengers provide the cash flow necessary to sustain and develop the business. The cause is often helped by favourable media coverage. There is something of an irony in the fact that the branch lines, having abandoned steam in favour of diesel locomotives, were closed in the 1960s because they were no longer economically viable – passengers had deserted them, only to return for leisure trips once steam locomotives were restored.

The Romney, Hythe and Dymchurch Railway   Typically, restoring a derelict railway line and the rolling stock will require a champion who can gather together a committed team of people, organize the preservation work and generate any cash required to start the venture off. Once part of the line is open it can begin to generate a revenue flow which helps pay for further restoration. By contrast, The Romney, Hythe and Dymchurch Railway (RHDR) was originally built by a wealthy enthusiast as a commercial venture, but it has been able to survive for over seventy years with similar volunteer support. The RHDR runs for just 14 miles along the Sussex coast from the port of Hythe to Dungeness, where there is a lighthouse, a few cottages and a power station. Opened in 1927, it has always been a privately owned narrow gauge railway. It was the dream of two wealthy enthusiasts. They were both racing car drivers, but the final achievement was the work of Captain J. E. 'Jack' Harvey. His colleague had been killed competing in the Italian Grand Prix.

   In its early years, the railway was famous and attracted numerous visitors. During the 1930s eleven locomotives, all one-third the size of a normal locomotive, but identical in looks and design, were at work on the railway. Harvey's original hopes for freight traffic never materialized. During the Second World War the army took over this 'front-line' coastal railway and used it for moving supplies and soldiers. It was reopened to the public in 1946 and enjoyed continuous popularity and commercial success until the 1960s – when the popularity of European package holidays caused a decline in summer holidaymakers. When Jack Harvey died in 1963, the railway went into decline. In 1972, on the verge of closure, it was rescued by a group of enthusiasts.

The Flying Scotsman   A related example of individual entrepreneurship concerns engine number 4472, The Flying Scotsman, 'the most famous and admired locomotive in the world'. Tony Marchington, Chief Executive of the Oxford Molecular Group, spotted an opportunity and recently bought the distinctive apple-green engine. First built in 1923, The Flying Scotsman had accumulated some 2 million miles of commercial service when it was withdrawn in 1963. Marchington spent £1 million to rebuild it completely. Flying Scotsman Railways now offers regular premium-price, long-distance trips on normal Railtrack lines, generally at week-ends. Enthusiasts ensure the services are all full, but again this story is more about passion and dedication to a personal cause than it is about economics and the generation of financial wealth.

Body Shop

Body Shop, which sources and retails (mainly through franchises) natural lotions and cosmetics, has been a highly successful business with a price to earnings ratio that stayed well above the retail sector average throughout the 1980s, before declining as a result of expansion and acquisition. Until 1999, mainly through a series of acquisitions, Body Shop also manufactured at least half of the products it sold.

Body Shop was started in England in 1976 by Anita Roddick and her husband, Gordon who used their savings of £12 000 to open the first shop, partially to help provide an income for Anita and her two daughters. Shortly after the business was started, Gordon took a sabbatical leave to fulfil a lifelong dream and rode a horse from Buenos Aires to New York. Stores have subsequently been opened in over forty countries – there are now over 1200 stores – and Body Shop was floated on the UK Stock Exchange in 1984. Renowned for its environmental and ethical stance and strategies, Body Shop has made an impact around the world. 'If you think you are too small to have an impact, try going to bed with a mosquito' (Anita Roddick).

Anita's motivation for starting her business was always influenced by her personal commitment to the environment and to education and social change. Simply, her talent for business was channelled into a cause. The business and its financial success have been a vehicle to achieve other, more important, objectives. 'Profits are perceived as boring, but business as exciting.' Body Shop's declared 'Reason for being' 'dedicated the business to the pursuit of social and environmental change'. Anita Roddick was concerned to do something that was 'economically sustainable, meeting the needs of the present without compromising the future'. Her ideas were the outcome of her world travels. She had visited many Third World countries, 'living native', and had seen how women used natural products efficaciously and effectively. She noticed how women in Tahiti rubbed their bodies with cocoa butter to produce soft, satin-like skin despite a hot climate. She realized women in Morocco used mud to give their hair a silky sheen. She also saw Mexicans successfully treat burns with aloes, the slimy juice from cactus leaves. From these observations and experiences she conceptualized – and realized – her opportunity. She would use natural products from around the world to produce a range of new products. People in Third World villages were asked to supply her with the natural ingredients she needed – another form of 'trade not aid'.

Body Shop has always aroused enthusiasm, commitment and loyalty amongst those involved with it. 'The company must never let itself become anything other than a human enterprise.' Much of this has developed from the ethical beliefs and values of Anita Roddick, which have become manifested in a variety of distinctive policies. Gordon Roddick was the one responsible for the operational aspects of the business. Body Shop is very strong on environmental issues, offering only biodegradable products and refillable containers. Posters in the shops have been used to campaign, amongst other things, to save whales and to stop the burning of rain forests. Packaging is plain, yet the shops are characterized by strong and distinctive aromas. The packages, together with posters and shelf cards, provide comprehensive information about the products and their origins and ingredients. This has created a competitive advantage which rivals have at times found difficult to replicate. The logo and packaging were redesigned in 1995.

The sales staff are knowledgeable, but they are not forceful and do not sell aggressively, generally offering advice only if it is requested. Marketing themes concern 'health rather than glamour, and reality rather than instant rejuvenation'. Body Shop chose to avoid advertising for many years in fact, preferring in-store information to attempts at persuasion. More recently, and especially in the USA, informative advertising has been used. In 1995 in the UK, Body Shop introduced an in-store radio station, transmitted by satellite. Body Shop states that all ingredients used in its products are either natural or have been used by humans for years. There is no testing on animals. However, there have been accusations to the contrary, and Body Shop was forced into litigation (which it won) in 1992. The business has always been controversial in some circles and attracted hostility. 'When the first shop opened morticians were horrified at the name: the Body Shop!'

Employees are provided with regular newsletters, videos and training packages. Anita Roddick contributes regularly to the newsletters, which concentrate on Body Shop campaigns. Employees and franchisees can attend the Body Shop training centre in London free of charge. All the courses are product centred and informative – they do not focus on selling, marketing or how to make more money. Employees are given time off, and franchisees encouraged to take time off, during working hours, to do voluntary work for the community.

Body Shop was initially able to effectively integrate manufacturing and retailing, and was efficient and operationally strong. Fresh supplies typically were delivered to its stores with a twenty-four hour lead time. These strategies, policies and beliefs generated substantial growth and profits in the 1980s. In the year ended 28 February 1991 turnover exceeded £100 million with trading profits of some £22 million. When these results were announced the UK share price exceeded 350 pence. Between 1984 and 1991, against the Financial Times All Share index of 100, Body Shop shares rose from an index figure of 100 to 5500. However, by mid-1995 the share price had fallen to 150 pence. Profits had fallen; new professional senior managers had been brought in to add strength. One dilemma concerned whether the culture and quirky management style was still wholly appropriate as Body Shop became a much bigger multinational business. Global scale brings global competition. 'As the business grew it lost some of its entrepreneurial spirit.'

In addition, Body Shop had attracted more and more competition. Leading UK retailers such as Boots, Marks & Spencer and Sainsbury's introduced natural products in their own label ranges; a further threat was posed by the US Bath and Body Works, whose early trial stores were a joint venture with Next. Bath and Body

Works is renowned as a fast-moving organization, quick to innovate new ideas – and aggressive at advertising and promotion. Amongst its responses in the UK, Body Shop began trials of a party plan operation. The Bath and Body Works chain was also growing faster than Body Shop in the USA, and that prompted the Roddicks to expand rapidly, opening new stores very quickly. The costs had a dramatic impact on profitability. UK retailers are generally perceived to be less slick than their US competitors at managing rapid change; Body Shop was no exception. In 1994 Body Shop also began to face criticism concerning the reality behind its ethical stance; a full publication of its social audit – then being commissioned – was promised.

In October 1995 Body Shop announced its intention to reprivatize the company by buying back shares at a price of 200 pence. The objective was to escape the constraints of the City institutions, which Anita Roddick had earlier called 'the pinstriped dinosaurs'. The shares would then be placed in a charitable trust, which would be able to make donations to humanitarian and environmental causes. The plan was abandoned in March 1996 because of its loan implications; Body Shop would have had to borrow heavily to finance the plan, arguably leaving it too exposed. In 1998, with shares trading at under 100 pence, Anita joined Gordon as a co-chairman and a new chief executive was recruited from outside the company. The loss-making US stores were separated out and a joint venture business was established; a non-executive director injected $1 million in exchange for 49 per cent of the US business. Nevertheless profits did grow steadily throughout the 1990s, reaching almost £40 million in 1998. In 1999 Body Shop withdrew from manufacturing and established a strong supply network instead 'enabling it to return to its roots as a fast-moving entrepreneur'. The shares have made something of a recovery.

Body Shop is an idiosyncratic and unusual business; Anita Roddick, like Richard Branson, is an entrepreneur who has made a very individual contribution. She has shown how financial and social capital can be created in harmony – at the same time helping, rather than destroying, the environment or having no impact on it. It has not been easy and has required courage in the face of criticism, hostility and setback.

This chapter has been about entrepreneurs who have elected to focus on social and environmental wealth and capital rather than on financial wealth. The stories have been about people with entrepreneurial talent and temperament who have chosen to use their abilities to pursue causes that have been important to them – and for many others. Society has benefited substantially from their efforts and contributions. It would be quite normal not to think of many of the people we have featured in this chapter as entrepreneurs – simply because their initiatives have not been motivated primarily by financial wealth creation – but they are entrepreneurs. They possess the life themes of an entrepreneur. They have been able to spot, engage and exploit an opportunity for doing good and helping others. They have been able to recruit the support and commitment of others in their endeavours. They have built important capital and made an impact. The difference in most cases is that they have been driven by their commitment to a cause and it is this commitment that has drawn their energy in a particular direction. In the next chapter we consider another group of people who possess entrepreneur life themes but who are particularly talented in art, design or music, and are driven to find opportunities to pursue and express their creativity. In this way, they have a significant influence on the lives of others.

References

Fukuyama, F. (1995). *Trust: The Social Virtues and the Creation of Prosperity*. Hamish Hamilton.
Leadbeater, C. (1997). *The Rise of the Social Entrepreneur*. Demos.
Leadbeater, C. and Goss, S. (1998). *Civic Entrepreneurship*. Demos.
Sykes, N. (1999). Is the organisation encoded with a 'DNA' which determines its development? Unpublished paper presented at The Visioneers conference, Putteridge Bury Management Centre, April.

6 Artistic and aesthetic entrepreneurs

Some financially very successful businesses are built around the creation of artistic or aesthetic capital. Fashion design and musical entertainment are two obvious examples. Arguably the entrepreneurs behind them would prefer to be remembered for their creative contributions rather than for their business acumen. In this chapter we look at examples of these and other artistic entrepreneurs. Some gifted artists and musicians have always been able to generate wealth through the development and exploitation of their natural, creative talents, and we explore the presence of entrepreneurial life themes in the way they create and chase opportunities. We also look at examples of organizations whose success owes something to an ability to inject fun, a key theme of creativity, into what they do and achieve.

In this chapter we look at entrepreneurs whose main wealth contribution is artistic or aesthetic – the merit and value of which is linked to people's perceptions and which consequently needs to be assessed qualitatively rather than wholly quantitatively. Some would argue that the main legacy of a generation to successive generations lies with the architecture, art and music it bequeaths. At the same time, people do pay premium prices for designer clothes and quality food in good restaurants, for seats at concerts, and to buy recorded music and works of art. Here a quantitative value is being attributed and, as a result, certain designers, artists, restaurateurs and musicians become very wealthy – although monetary wealth is rarely their main motivation. Britain, of course, is often thought to excel in creative industries such as advertising, architecture, design and fashion, computer software, books, entertainment and media. We have already seen how important social entrepreneurs are for building community-based capital; here we see how many aspects of our 'general well-being' are dependent upon artistic and aesthetic entrepreneurs.

The true entrepreneurs in this field are generally 'off the scale' with their creative talent; and the most outstanding are sometimes described as eminent or 'truly great'. After all, a good proportion of the population can read music or play an instrument – but how many can write or perform inspirationally and produce a work that people want to hear over and over again? Similarly, most of us can mix colours and use a paintbrush, but rarely do our efforts genuinely 'move' other people.

Highlighting the parallels between the outstanding business people we normally associate with entrepreneurship and eminent people in all walks of life, Ludwig (1995) argues that true greatness requires a special ability, gift or talent but that not everyone who is gifted becomes eminent. They must be identified and trained to exploit their gift. Rachmaninov, for example, played music by ear at the age of seven, as did Bix Beiderbecke. Judy Garland was performing at the age of two. How many of the business entrepreneurs we have described started with some entrepreneurial venture at a very young age? Parental support, together with access to necessary resources, is essential, despite the fact that the talent is typically accompanied by an equally critical willingness to challenge existing norms and paradigms. Raymond Blanc told the first chef he worked for that his food was too salty. His reward – a flying pan which broke his nose and jaw! Those destined for greatness possess a need to accomplish something distinctive (the Gallup ego drive) and a determination to achieve, often despite hostile criticism. Sigmund Freud similarly believed that their driving force is a desire for fame and public recognition.

Truly great people do enjoy a prolonged appreciation and reputation which stretches beyond their death – as do our legendary social and business entrepreneurs. Some, of course, are only appreciated properly after they are dead. They produce original, imaginative and innovatory work – often, but not always, sustained for many years – which influences others. Although blessed with a natural talent, this still demands intense effort and persistence – reflecting the right temperament. Whilst it cannot ever be easy to bring into existence something of high perceived value that has never before existed, the most creative people do not necessarily see what they do as difficult. They do what they do, either because they enjoy doing it or because they are unable to stop themselves. They are driven. In addition, great artists and composers have not always enjoyed the very best formal training that was available. Instead they have shown a tremendous ability to develop their own talent, inspired by the work of other eminent people. It is an interesting parallel that although an increasing number of large corporation chief executives are MBA graduates, the MBA degree remains relatively uncommon amongst the most successful business entrepreneurs. We have already stressed that with certain exceptions, such as new Internet businesses, formal education to degree level or beyond is not a prerequisite for entrepreneurial success.

In this chapter we first consider a number of designers who have built successful businesses, and business entrepreneurs who have seen the potential in creative ideas. We follow these with examples of entrepreneurship in architecture and in the hotel industry, before exploring the key topics of art and music. We tackle the question: were artists like Michelangelo and musicians like Mozart actually the artistic and aesthetic entrepreneurs of their time? They focused on the most appropriate opportunities that were available to them for exploiting their talent, building significant artistic capital and leaving a priceless legacy for the world to enjoy. We then look at several entrepreneurs in different sectors of the entertainment industry before concluding the chapter with one entrepreneur whose business success has been built around an element of fun and, finally, two examples of entrepreneurs who have successfully blended social, artistic and environmental capital together, at the same time as they have generated financial wealth.

Jensen (1999) re-emphasizes the importance of these entrepreneurs who contribute to 'the dream society, based on emotion', as distinct from 'the information society, based on rational thinking'. He believes the emphasis will shift from the latter to the former as future consumers will be affected increasingly by the stories which the image and branding of products and services project. Jensen argues, for example, that the success of expensive outdoor clothing and shoes is affected by a desire for adventure by some people, and he shows how the intellectual capital lies in the design and image and not manufacturing capability. In some industries, arguably including music and cars, retro-designs provide 'peace of mind from an idealized past'; and, as we saw in the previous chapter, businesses linked to causes often succeed because they impact upon our convictions.

By way of further reinforcement, the entrepreneurial Disney Corporation (Chapter 3) has committed investment for a 'purpose-built creative and new media campus' in southern California. The campus will house Disney's expanding Internet activities and its 'imagineering division', which is charged with dreaming up new ideas for shows, videos and theme parks. Facilities will be provided for other like-minded businesses in a development that attempts to mirror the explosive growth of Silicon Valley further to the north, growth fuelled by the close proximity of several related and competing businesses in the same industry.

Designer entrepreneurs

Terence Conran

Terence Conran is a habitual, serial entrepreneur, albeit that design has been a key element of all his businesses and activities. He is a rich and successful business entrepreneur – but he will be remembered more for his creative design talents than for his business acumen. Conran is an innovator who has applied his entrepreneurial talents to furniture-making, designing, retailing , publishing and restaurant management.

Born in Surrey in 1931, his background and upbringing were middle class. Interested in crafts from an early age, he set up a workshop at home. As a young boy he spent some considerable time at a local pottery and at school he specialized in chemistry, engineering and art. Encouraged by a friend, he then went to college and studied textile design, where he became intrigued by the possibilities of screen-printing. In partnership with an architect, he also started making furniture to his own designs, mainly for his friends.

His first paid employment, in 1949, was as a librarian at a design centre – but he left to join forces with his architect friend, and together they produced designs for the 1951 Festival of Britain. They continued with their furniture, which they were able to have displayed in selected London department store windows, and they were commissioned to produce textile designs for Myers Beds. In addition, his architect partner was specifying Conran furniture for the offices, hotels and hospitals that he designed. Realizing that he was 'terribly inept at the business side', Conran began to address marketing and selling issues, employing someone to sell and to produce a brochure for him. The growth of his business was helped by cash injections as he bought, renovated and sold premises, systematically improving his base.

To help raise additional money to buy new machinery, he joined forces with another friend, a psychiatrist, to open a café-cum-soup kitchen in 1953. This developed into a chain of four before they sold it in 1954. By the mid-1950s he had set up a textiles conversion business, buying cloth or having it woven and then selling it on. He was also designing exhibition stands and accepting shop-fitting contracts. Aided by a grant, he then moved his business activities – and his eighty staff – out of London, to Thetford. In 1956 he established Conran Design as a consultancy and architects practice – the practice still exists, and is one of the largest of its type in Europe, but Conran himself withdrew in 1992 after a majority shareholding was acquired by a French competitor. Terence Conran immediately began a new design consultancy partnership.

In 1962, and in a brand-new factory, he began to manufacture domestic furniture, which he sold through eighty retailers in the UK. When he visited these outlets he was typically 'appalled by the display and presentation' and decided to open his own shop. In 1964 the Habitat concept was born, first in London and then in Manchester, selling Conran furniture together with kitchen utensils, lighting and floor coverings and targeting various ages and socioeconomic groups. His strategy was to fill the shops with stock, rather than force people to order and wait. The theme was complementary designer products, many of them bought in – but from a single-eye perspective – presented in a colourful environment. Before the 1960s were over the Habitat chain had expanded considerably and Conran had acquired Ryman's office furniture. The merger was not a success and Ryman's was sold to Burton. In 1973 he opened the more exclusive Conran Shop in London, selling high-quality, superior design furniture and household goods which were being rejected for Habitat on the grounds of price.

Habitat was floated on the Stock Exchange in 1981; a year later Mothercare was acquired. Conran knew the Mothercare founder, Selim Zhilka, and was aware the business 'was in need of a new direction – it had slipped downmarket with lack-lustre merchandise'. Finance was available from a Dutch bank that believed the conceptual ethos of Habitat was readily transferable to other retail concepts. Subsequently Heals (furniture retailer, 1983), Richard shops (clothing, 1984) and Blazer (also clothing, 1987) were acquired. When Habitat was merged with British Home Stores in 1986 the retail consortium was renamed Storehouse and Conran became Chairman and Chief Executive. However, he resigned his chief executive post in 1989 and the chairmanship in 1990, buying back the Conran Shop and using it as a base for a small chain of exclusive stores in the world's leading cities.

In parallel to his retailing activities, Conran had published his first book, *The House Book*, in 1974. In effect this was a published version of his in-house training manual for designers. Others followed before he joined forces in 1983 with Octopus Books to produce a range of lifestyle publications. At the same time, and being 'a keen cook and gastronome, Conran had begun to transform the experience of eating out in London'. After the sale of his share in the Soup Kitchens chain (1954) he began opening a series of specialist restaurants, mostly in London. His main projects include Quaglino's (originally fashionable in the 1930s and renovated to serve over 1000 people a day), Mezzo (the largest restaurant in Europe, serving 700 people at any one time) and Bluebird, a complex incorporating a restaurant where the food is cooked in a wood-fired oven, a flower market, a fresh food market, a private dining club and an exclusive furniture shop. There are now over a dozen exclusive Conran restaurants in London, and others in Paris, New York and Stockholm.

In this story we can see clear evidence of several entrepreneur life themes. Terence Conran is creative and innovative; he is dedicated to design; he has a strong ego drive and is clearly an activator; he is profit driven and able to build the teams necessary to drive his various ventures forward. Significantly he chose to draw back from the large corporation leader position.

Mary Quant

Mary Quant was a contemporary of Terence Conran and a 'trailblazer behind the swinging sixties scene in London', but she chose to use her design talents in a different way. Her story is one of focusing on what one can do best, understanding customers and team entrepreneurship – working with partners who can provide other skills and abilities, ones which are either natural weaknesses or which would only be achievable with considerable effort.

Mary Quant's first business was a boutique in London's Kings Road in 1955; her second outlet in Knightsbridge (1957) was designed by Terence Conran. Mary Quant was initially in partnership with her husband, Alexander Plunket-Green, who she had met at art school. The two were later joined by fellow entrepreneur Archie McNair, who had opened the first coffee bar in London and who had premises over the road from Mary's Bazaar boutique in the Kings Road. Initially Bazaar incorporated a small workroom; Mary Quant employed machinists and bought her fabrics mainly from Harrods. McNair was convinced that design and not manufacturing was the platform for growth, and this was the model they followed. Stock was manufactured under licence by other independent companies to Mary's designs. When Quant miniskirts were worn in America by the Beatles' girlfriends in 1964, a new fashion was born and the business simply took off. This key invention opened the door to her success and prosperity. The creative and innovative design skills were systematically transferred to other products. Dresses and coats were followed by swimwear and tights (1963), bold cosmetics (1966), household furnishings and domestic textiles (in conjunction with Du Pont and ICI, 1968), bedclothes and curtains (with Carrington Viyella, 1972), sunglasses (with Polaroid, 1977), Axminster carpets (1978), shoes (1982) and, finally, stationery with WH Smith. In 1971 Mary Quant formed a joint venture in Japan; and there is still a Quant shop in Manhattan, selling cosmetics, leather goods, T-shirts and jewellery.

Paul Smith

The story of the contemporary fashion designer Paul Smith illustrates a number of the same points, but here we have someone who needed substantial courage, to overcome the obstacles and hurdles he faced. It is the story of a person who, once he had an idea, sought opportunities and proved he had project-championing qualities. Again, though, we must ask the question: will he be remembered more as a businessman or a designer?

When he left school Paul Smith had no qualifications of any consequence and no plans for his future. His father was able to find him a job as a 'gofer' in a clothing warehouse in Nottingham. His interest was immediately engaged, and by the time he was twenty (in 1966) he was managing Nottingham's first boutique for a friend. Smith had helped his friend find a site, paint the shop and choose the stock – but all the time he was now dreaming of his own business. His problem – he had no money. He had, however, got to know Douglas Hill, a local tailor, and kept telling him: 'I can be a success.' Hill provided Paul Smith with his next opportunity: he offered him the use of the back room of his shop. In 1970 Paul had his own business. The room was only 12 feet square, but Smith transformed it into a small shop with its own entrance, opening it only on Fridays and Saturdays at first. He sold expensive, stylish clothes, some of which he bought from known designers and others he designed himself and had manufactured locally. He did receive both help and encouragement from his girlfriend, a graduate in fashion design – they are still together thirty years later. After three months Hill increased his rent from nothing to 50 pence a week! On the other days Paul Smith started to study fashion design himself. Inside four years, the business had developed into a full shop unit that he was able to open six days a week. His reputation for unusual designs had spread, and customers were coming to Nottingham from Leeds and Manchester to buy clothes that otherwise were only available in London.

Borrowing £3000 from Douglas Hill, supplemented by a loan from his father, Paul Smith next moved to London to focus on designing clothes – from his bedsit. He still had to work part time for the International Wool Secretariat and for an Italian shirt manufacturer. His early customers were buyers from Bloomingdale's in New York City and from Seibu in Japan. Cannily negotiating a reduced and deferred rent agreement for an empty unit in Covent Garden, Smith opened his first London shop in 1979. Within one year he was employing fifteen assistants, such was his popularity. He quickly expanded into the unit next door and set up in Japan where 'he is now a cult figure' with some 200 licensed outlets. His 'retail empire' has since expanded to eight London stores, together with others in Manchester, New York, Paris, Hong Kong, Singapore, Taiwan and Manila – and, of course, Nottingham. Annual turnover of the fully self-financed business exceeds £175 million. His fabrics are mainly Italian, French and British, and most of his products are manufactured in the UK. There are now eight clothing collections, supplemented by watches, shoes, spectacles, toiletries and bags. His style is 'simple and practical, characterized by wit and humour . . . his clothes provide excitement in offbeat fabrics and colours'.

Despite the size and spread of the business, Smith remains the chief designer and also takes responsibility for all wholesaling and retailing activities. This is rare for a designer who has risen to this level of success. Smith comments: 'I have never gone down obvious routes . . . the key [to my success] has been in exploring alternative routes that no one else has thought of'. His story reflects focus, dedication, persistence and courage. He has built an important network of contacts and helpers – including his girlfriend – and in the early days he 'begged and borrowed' the resources he needed to start and expand.

Creative entrepreneurs

This section contains six stories. We begin with the entrepreneurs behind two large, successful and well-known holiday businesses; they both created opportunities by appreciating what customers expect from their vacations – and made sure they provided it. The section continues with two examples of businesses which have succeeded by creating and merchandising children's characters, followed by an unusual hotelier and a leading architect. The common element is real creativity.

Gilbert Tregano

Entrepreneur Gilbert Tregano developed Club Méditerranée (Club Med) to be 'an organized melange of hedonism and back to nature'. Club Med was originally founded in France in 1950 by Gérard Blitz as a non-profit camping organization – Trigano supplied the tents. He saw the real opportunity, and under him Club Med grew unchallenged in its niche for over thirty years, pioneering the all-inclusive holiday and featuring 'beautiful people playing all sorts of sports, white sand beaches, azure sky and sea, Polynesian thatched huts, free and flowing wine at meals, simple yet superb food' (*The Economist*, 12 July 1986).

By the mid-1980s, however, occupancy rates had fallen, and profits declined and then stagnated. While the underlying concept was still sound, people's tastes were changing – and Trigano had 'taken his eye off the ball'. Holidaymakers increasingly sought higher-quality facilities than the straw huts provided. Many Americans wanted televisions and telephones – yet 'it was the absence of these which had helped make Club Med unique'. Building on the original concept and strategy Club Med now developed new products in order to better satisfy selected audiences around the world. In addition to the traditional villages, where in some cases straw huts were replaced by bungalows, there were now both cheaper, half-board holidays available in newly acquired hotels and villages, and more expensive properties with superior facilities. This latter development was pioneered at Opio, near Cannes, which opened in 1989. Opio was built with expensive rooms with facilities and, unusually, was open twelve months of the year. The international conference trade was being targeted. Attempts were also made to attract more American visitors, but there was always some scepticism. Americans are more puritanical in their tastes and expectations, and 'Club Med's sexy image' had not proved as successful in the USA.

In 1993 Gilbert, then aged seventy-two, partially retired and was succeeded by his son, Serge, who also stepped down in 1997, after they had both failed to properly turn the organization around. Profits had in fact turned to losses, and the need for stronger management had been acknowledged. Smart cards replaced beads; a cruise ship was sold, along with the budget villages; the other villages were systematically improved – and prices reduced. Phillippe Bourguignon, recruited from EuroDisney began to restore Club Med's lost fortunes.

Ted Arison

Club Med was successful in the beginning because Trigano saw and exploited an opportunity. A failure to change quickly enough, coupled with management and succession issues, proved costly. In contrast, the growth of Carnival Cruises, which also offers fun and entertainment, continues unhindered. When Ted Arison, owner of a small family shipyard in Israel, relocated to America in the early 1950s, he was virtually penniless. Some twenty years later, and after working for a period as a cruise holiday executive, he bought the *Empress of Canada*, which had run aground off Miami. Similar to Ray Kroc of McDonald's, Ted Arison was well into middle age before he began to exploit the entrepreneurial talent he possessed. From a single ship he built the Carnival Cruise Group, the largest cruise holiday organization in the world, controlling some 40 per cent of the market. He understood his customers, and met the needs of the different segments in an emerging industry with a number of distinct brand offerings, most of which he acquired. In the 1990s cruising became the fastest growing sector of the holiday industry. Carnival itself has an image of 'Las Vegas on the water' – it is about casual, contemporary fun for the mass market, and it appeals to younger holidaymakers who are looking for both relaxation and entertainment at competitive prices. With his Carnival ships Arison sought to 'take the stuffiness out of cruising and abandon its élitist image'. The group, however, also owns the more up-market Holland America Line, which attracts generally older passengers, the exclusive Cunard ships, including the *QE2*, and the even more luxurious Seabourn line. In partnership with Airtours of the UK – in which it is a significant shareholder – Carnival also owns the Italian Costa Cruises. Ted Arison himself died in 1999 – a seventy-year-old billionaire – but Carnival has been run for a number of years by his equally entrepreneurial son, Mickey.

In his later years Ted Arison showed his serial tendencies by returning to Israel and opening an investment business and buying shareholdings in several of Israel's largest businesses. In 1997 he acquired control of Bank Hapoalim, Israel's largest bank. 'He was eager to use his skills to help Israel transform its traditionally socialist economy into a free market.' Throughout his life Ted Arison lived modestly; his Israeli businesses are now run by his daughter, Shari.

Britt Allcroft

There can be few better loved children's characters than Thomas the Tank Engine, created originally by the Reverend W. Awdry in his spare time. As well as this series of illustrated books for children, Awdry also wrote serious, adult books on steam railways. Thanks to an entrepreneur who saw the real opportunity – and was determined to pursue her ideas when even Awdry himself was sceptical – Thomas's popularity continues through television, advertising and licensing deals.

The entrepreneur, Britt Allcroft, a producer of television programmes, had been to the same school at the same time as Anita Roddick. She had always had a passion for storytelling. In her younger days she had written several short stories, but had never been published. Instead she had found her way into television; and in 1978 she was making a film about the British passion for steam engines. Awdry was invited to appear in the film; he agreed, but inclement weather held up the project for several days. Awdry and Allcroft spend two days talking to each other. Although others had tried unsuccessfully to animate Awdry's characters – essentially a fleet of steam engines with distinctive faces and personalities – Britt Allcroft became determined to succeed where others had failed. Together with her business partner, who at the time was her husband, she approached venture capitalists, but the general reaction was that the time for Thomas had passed. Eventually a bank loan from Barclays – supplemented by a second mortgage – allowed her to agree a licensing deal with publisher Reed Elsevier, who owned the master rights to the character and make her first film – which was broadcast on network television in 1984. Supported by a range of toys and clothing, the film was an instant success.

Her business grew rapidly. More films were completed, with ex-Beatle Ringo Starr doing the narrating, the books were all reissued and character merchandising mushroomed. The films found an audience in forty-three countries, including America – where, for political correctness, the Fat Controller was renamed Sir Topham Hat. When Britt Allcroft's company went public in 1996, it was valued at £31 million. In 1998 she posted a profit of £3 million, roughly 10 per cent of this coming from the films and 90 per cent from merchandising. Eighteen hundred different items – books, videos, toys, clothes, bags, party supplies, bakewear, computer games, puzzles, models and carpets – were being manufactured by 400 sub-licensees. Thomas himself had become the seventh most valuable toy brand in America.

In 1997 Britt Allcroft had acquired the worldwide rights to another past-glory character, Captain Pugwash, for £1.5 million and had set about resurrecting a programme that had first appeared on television in 1957 and disappeared in 1975. In the following year she bought all the rights to Thomas from Reed Elsevier (for £13.5 million) and no longer has to pay an annual licence fee. In 1999 Britt Allcroft formed an alliance with the two venture capital businesses which own the rights to Sooty, a hugely popular puppet character since its creation by Harry Corbett in 1952. Allcroft will merchandise the characters around the world and receive a management fee. She sums up her courage, focus, dedication and determination with the following comment: 'You need courage when people tell you you are off your head ... Thomas is much more than just a steam train having adventures – it is a way of life for me.'

Anne Wood

Related, but quite different, are the *Teletubbies* – the first ever children's television programmes to be targeted directly at two- and three-year-olds. The opportunity lay in the reality that children watch television from a very early age – yet nobody was really thinking of them as viewers. Ironically, and despite the obvious success, nobody tracks how many people actually watch the programmes – UK audience research ignores anyone under four years of age! *Teletubbies* programmes are popular and successful because they creatively combine fun and entertainment with the serious tasks of nourishing young children's thinking skills, teaching them to listen, helping arouse their curiosity and developing their imagination. They are made for the BBC by Ragdoll Productions, founded in 1984 by Anne Wood, a 'reluctant entrepreneur'.

A mother of two, and originally a teacher, Anne Wood was working on children's programmes for TVam – for whom she created the infamous Roland Rat – when she was sacked. She was then in her forties and spent two years failing to find another job. 'Financial necessity forced me to set up my own production company.' In fifteen years Anne Wood has accumulated a personal fortune of £55 million and established a £20 million per year business. *Teletubbies* is popular around the world, and merchandising naturally accompanies the programmes. In the new Millennium Dome, the four characters are being described as 'one of Britain's greatest industrial achievements'.

This is the story of a creative person who saw an opportunity – or gap in the market – that others were simply failing to realize was there and found a way of filling the gap. Anne Wood attributes her success to her ability to 'find my way back to how it felt to be a three-year-old and perceive the world from that standpoint'. She thus has the ability to be close to her customers.

Having looked at two entrepreneurs who have succeeded by entertaining their customers, we now look at two who have been able to target our various senses and, in that way, build aesthetic value. We return to the entertainment theme later in the chapter.

Ian Schrager

Ian Schrager is a hotelier who, unusually, believes that all the hotels in his chain must be different and designed specifically for their individual location. Schrager is a New Yorker based in New York and he has become the 'King of boutique hotels' in the last fifteen years. He owns properties in key tourist and business centres such as New York, Miami, Los Angeles and San Francisco – and he keeps adding new ones which he buys and rebrands. When he bought his first hotel in 1984 he was attracted to an industry 'characterized by an extraordinary level of sameness'. Turned into a commodity business, he believed hotels were ignoring real opportunities for building new values and being different. All his hotels are expensive, select and sophisticated. Few expenses are spared with the furnishings, fabrics and facilities in order to provide an exclusive feel. However,

> the design is just one part of the formula – it's the way the whole thing gets put together that touches you in some visceral way [in the heart] ... when you go to see a good movie or a good play, or read a good book, or go to a good sporting event, it lifts your spirits and brings a smile to your face. It's the same thing we are after.

With this vision, Schrager sums up the ethos of artistic and aesthetic capital.

Hotels are not Schrager's first entrepreneurial venture. In the 1970s, together with his late partner, Steve Russell, he ran a leading Manhattan discotheque – until they were both convicted of tax evasion and sentenced to thirteen months' imprisonment. Typical of many entrepreneurs who are 'brought down by the system', he started all over again and built something more substantial. Not surprisingly, some of the leading hotel chains have followed Schrager's lead and entered this growing and lucrative niche segment. Interestingly his strategy and positioning has been successful at exactly the same time that lower price 'formula hotels' like Travel Inns and Travelodges have also grown in popularity.

Frank Gehry

Continuing with a theme of buildings, the new Guggenheim Museum was opened in 1997 in Bilbao in northern Spain. Described as 'one of the century's greatest buildings' – it blends titanium and stone in a 'collision of forms' – it has attracted two million visitors in two years. 'It has transformed a city once known mainly for industrial decline and Basque terrorism into a cultural landmark.' Arguably its American architect, Frank Gehry, is an entrepreneur – for he 'habitually creates and innovates to build something of recognized value'. Now seventy years old, and sometimes seen as a controversial and artistic architect, Gehry has always experimented. 'He takes chances, he pushes boundaries beyond previous limits. There are times when he misses the mark and times when he alters everyone else's vision.' His imitators 'are legion'. Interestingly the Guggenheim success won Gehry the commission for a new management school along similar lines at Case Western Reserve University in Cleveland, Ohio. The university hopes that 'creative architecture will inspire the imagination of business students'.

Artistic entrepreneurs

Thomas Kincade

Little known outside his native America, Thomas Kincade – 'the painter of light' – is America's most collected living artist. Kincade paints a mixture of old buildings and landscapes and blends summer daylight scenes with winter snows and evening darkness. He gives his work a historical perspective by using old cars and horse-drawn carts. His paintings can sometimes be bought as originals, but most sales are limited editions and lithographic copies. They are mainly available from several specialist Thomas Kincade Galleries, and they have been made affordable for the less wealthy enthusiast as well as the wealthy collector. His work is also available in the form of Christmas and gift cards, cookie tins, calendars, books and mugs. The Thomas Kincade Collectors' Society is carefully engineered to encourage people to own more than one painting or print. In other words, Kincade is a popular artist who has turned himself into a very lucrative business by successfully exploiting the marketing opportunities that have not been available to earlier painters. A deeply religious family man, Kincade 'credits God for both the ability and the inspiration to create his paintings'.

Thomas Mangelsen

The Kincade strategy is certainly not unique to him. It has also been adopted by Thomas Mangelsen, one of the world's most talented nature photographers. Trained in wildlife biology, Mangelsen began filming wildlife in northern North America over twenty years ago, spending time in both the winter and summer in Alaska, Yukon and the Hudson Bay Area. His initial subject was birds, but he later chose to specialize in polar bears. His first published collection, *Images of Nature*, was very successful; and when he followed up with *Polar Dance* (a unique collection of polar bear images) in 1996 he had accumulated over 85 000 pictures of bears and other arctic wildlife. His work has been exhibited in galleries and museums, and he has accepted commissions from various magazines, including *National Geographic*. Like Kincade, Mangelsen has turned himself into a prosperous business. He has opened a number of Images of Nature Galleries which sell his photographs as framed and unframed, limited and unlimited editions – in various sizes from gift card to large wall size. Selected images are also available as CD-ROMs.

Kincade and Mangelsen are clearly artistic entrepreneurs because they have successfully linked art and business. We look next at one leading contemporary artist and four legendary painters from the Middle Ages to see if we can trace entrepreneur life themes in the ways they have exploited their talents and blended imagination with superior technical skills.

David Hockney

Yorkshire-born David Hockney is Britain's most successful living artist. 'He is one of the only British artists this [twentieth] century to have become internationally renowned in the same way as pop and film stars.' He is a millionaire. In true entrepreneurial fashion he too has found lucrative commercial opportunities for exploiting his talent – but he is different in both style and strategy from Thomas Kincade. Born in Bradford, Hockney was encouraged to exploit his natural talents by his parents, 'from whom he inherited energy and imagination'. His father was seen by some as eccentric; he was certainly idiosyncratic and enterprising. He notably once sold a billiards table by placing a newspaper advertisement and using the telephone number of a nearby public call box. He sat outside the box for hours waiting for a potential buyer.

Although some artists only become truly famous after their deaths, Hockney was well known by the time he was 25. He had been noticed for work he submitted to the 1962 Young Contemporaries Exhibition and his paintings began to sell in London. Appreciating the value of publicity and notoriety, he immediately bleached his hair and took to wearing gold lamé jackets and large spectacles. Magazine articles made him into a celebrity figure. He was soon to move to Los Angeles where he has lived for over thirty years. However, the largest collection of his work is in a gallery in Saltaire, near Bradford, the town built in the last century by philanthropic mill owner, Titus Salt, as the 'perfect industrial community' with houses, schools and hospitals built specifically for the mill workers. Hockney's early work featured people, sometimes in portrait form, more often in simple domestic settings

– but for many years he has diverted his attention to experiments with other art forms. He has produced photo-collages by mounting several dozen small – and related – photographs to create a large image, and also experimented with fax and photocopier machines to produce a different finished image. He has earned a substantial income from designing opera stage sets, and he has generally produced the posters for promoting his own exhibitions

David Hockey is wealthy and famous because he has proved himself able to exploit a number of artistic, marketing and commercial opportunities that have been available to him and thus manage both his prolific output and his natural talent. In this way he has successfully blended the project champion role with that of the opportunity-spotter. The commercial opportunities available in the twentieth and twenty-first centuries are, of course, markedly different from those that were available to artists and painters in previous centuries. Although we do not naturally think of great artists as entrepreneurs, the ability of some of them to exploit the far more limited opportunities that were available – in order that they might utilize and exploit their natural gifts and talents – is testimony to the fact that they did possess a number of critically important entrepreneur life themes. Typically they would have to look for commissions and patrons, which demanded networking skills. The legacy of the great artists is their work, which has endured and sells for huge sums of money, even if they themselves failed to accumulate significant wealth when they were alive – although some of them did become wealthy. Their creations, simply, help us to see things differently. Particularly relevant in this context are many Renaissance artists who symbolically interpreted important religious themes and gave them meaning. In reality, many of them had to overcome a wide range of obstacles, especially the envy and hostility of their rivals, in order to pursue and complete their work – indicating the presence of both ego drive, dedication and courage. Parental position and connections mattered far more than they do today, of course. To succeed, they had to have 'know-how and know-who' and know where they could obtain patronage and resources.

Michelangelo Buonarotti

Michelangelo Buonarotti was 'a genius who few have challenged since'. He succeeded as a sculptor, an artist, an architect and a poet, and he became a legend in his own lifetime. 'He raised the status of artists by his achievements.' He was born in Italy in 1475 and lived until 1564, a long and productive life. By the age of thirteen he was apprenticed to a master sculptor, where he came under the influence and patronage of the Medici's. The Medici family had earned enormous financial wealth from trading, which they used to acquire power, to influence and support the papal monarchy and other regional dukes and to 'commission great art as an expression of their wealth and status in the world . . . the whole economy revolved around them'. Michelangelo's *Statue of David* was commissioned in 1501 by the new Republic of Florence. The marble block he used had been reserved for this purpose since 1462. The work took three years and established him as a great sculptor. In 1508 Pope Julius II brought him to Rome to paint the ceiling of the Sistine Chapel. He accepted the commission, but, bravely and very unusually, questioned the Pope's design. In the end the imagery was Michelangelo's and it was quite different from that which Julius II had planned. It took Michelangelo four years of intense, dedicated, focused effort, for throughout he worked largely unaided by anyone. It was a truly momentous and creative achievement and reflected enormous self-belief and ego drive. After 1513 the new Medici Pope, Leo X, sent Michelangelo back to Florence where he mainly worked as an architect and sculptor. In the next decade, he built the Medici Chapel in San Lorenzo and the Laurentian Library. Eventually he was to return to Rome as chief architect for St Peter's.

Leonardo da Vinci

Whilst we can readily see both the opportunity-spotter and project champion in Michelangelo, the same cannot be said of his famous contemporary, Leonardo da Vinci, who was 'not noted for completing all his ideas'. Some great artists are more entrepreneurial than others. Leonardo, born in 1452, was the illegitimate son of a lawyer, and through his family he, too, was able to gain the patronage of the Medicis. Commissioned by the Duke of Milan (in 1497) he painted *The Last Supper*; the *Mona Lisa* followed in 1500 after Milan had fallen to the French. Eventually he would remove to France 'to investigate the nature of the world around him'. He believed an artist should be a 'contemplative and creative thinker, similar to a saint or philosopher'. He was certainly a man of ideas and very innovative; he was interested in aerodynamics and flying, hydraulics and canal-building, astronomy and human anatomy. At one stage in his life he was employed as a military engineer. He left a legacy of nineteen notebooks and 3500 pages of sketches and notes on various topics.

Included was da Vinci's conceptual diagram for the modern helicopter.

El Greco

Another Renaissance painter was the religious artist, El Greco, who was born in Crete in 1541 and who, after some time in Italy, settled in Spain. 'Arrogant and uncompromising, proudly aware of his own merits and originality amongst an army of imitators, El Greco gave offence more than once . . . he made disobliging comments on [the paintings of] Michelangelo.' Using contacts he had made in Rome, El Greco was commissioned to paint for the cathedral in Toledo, and from this base he set out to secure royal patronage. However, King Philip II simply did not like the result of the work he commissioned and, although it was paid for, the painting was not hung. A resourceful El Greco turned instead to the wealthy people of Toledo. His son became his main collaborator and 'his last contracts always provided for assistance with the work'. Typically he would start a work and then others would complete it. There were many stories of his impropriety in his use of assistants, enterprising though it was.

El Greco was a great and talented artist – he also 'let it be known that there was nothing in the world superior to his paintings' – but he illustrated the 'shadow side' of entrepreneurship. He earned a great deal of money, but 'spent extensively and excessively on maintaining his household'. He died in 1614 with many unpaid debts and he left 200 paintings which had all been commissioned and started but which needed completing.

Diego Velázquez

Diego Velázquez was entrepreneurial in yet another way. Born of nobility in Seville in 1599, he has been described as 'one of the greatest painters of all time'. Through family contacts he was accepted at Court and was the established royal painter for thirty-seven of his sixty-one years. Moreover he persuaded King Philip IV to make him chief buyer of paintings. For this he was paid a retainer and a travel allowance – he was thus able to spend time in Italy and elsewhere and observe at close hand the style and approach of his renowned contemporaries. He was an early benchmarker. He became a rich man in his lifetime, although he was not personally prolific. After his death – and the protection of the Royal Family – he was 'pursued by envy'.

Wilfred Cass

It is, of course, possible to generate financial capital from art without being naturally talented oneself. Having earlier built and sold a successful electronics business, Wilfred Cass became a successful company doctor and corporate entrepreneur. Moss Bros is one of the companies he successfully turned around. After he retired he decided to establish a private sculpture park and gallery in the grounds of his home in Surrey. He and his wife were both interested in contemporary sculpture and they already owned a number of pieces. They saw that large sculptures do not enjoy the same gallery selling opportunities that are available to small pieces and to paintings – they had identified a gap. Being naturally careful planners, they looked at other (mainly display) parks around the world before designing their own. There are now twenty acres of woodland and parkland devoted to the exhibits – typically forty pieces at any one time – and the Casses commission, display and sell work. They take a sales commission to cover overheads and they charge visitors an entrance fee – but the park is fundamentally a charitable foundation. Many of the annual 40 000 visitors are from overseas. Sculptors have clearly benefited from this new opportunity – and the Casses have enjoyed themselves. However, Wilfred is now in his mid-seventies and concerned with succession issues. His son has moved to America. Wilfred is, after all, 'a businessman through and through . . . you can feel that drive for profit crackling inside him'.

Music entrepreneurs

Lord Andrew Lloyd Webber

Lord Andrew Lloyd Webber is easily Britain's most successful modern composer – in a world where popular music lyrics are increasingly being viewed as the contemporary equivalent of the poetry of old. He has composed the music for a series of hugely successful stage musicals, including *Joseph and the Amazing Technicolour Dreamcoat*, *Jesus Christ Superstar*, *Cats*, *Evita*, *Starlight Express* and *Phantom of the Opera*. He has also written a more classical Requiem. He is the only composer to have ever had three musicals running simultaneously in both London and New York. Millions of people around the world have seen his shows and listened to his music, which has been recorded by the world's leading performers. He has built both aesthetic and financial capital by providing people with entertainment and enjoyment.

He was born in 1948 and has been described as 'small, dark, intense and nerdish'. Like his brother, the cellist Julian Lloyd Webber, he has been a natural musician all his life. He was seventeen when he started looking for a 'with-it writer of lyrics' to work as his partner, and he was contacted by Tim Rice. A friendship of opposites developed – Rice was older and more outgoing. The two experimented with a number of projects before writing *Joseph* for a local boys' school concert in 1968. The performance was noticed, and its success was instant. The two young partners were soon being talked about. Although many see *Jesus Christ Superstar* (1971) as their best work, their real fame came later in 1976 with *Evita*. Before this, a musical based on the fictional character, Jeeves (recently reworked by Lloyd Webber) was less successful. By the late 1970s there were tensions between Rice and Lloyd Webber and they chose to go their separate ways and find new partners. Tim Rice eventually switched to film scores, with which he has had a number of hits. Lloyd Webber has since worked with a number of other lyricists, most notably Don Black and Charles Hart, who individually and as a pair have written the words for *Phantom* (Hart), *Song and Dance* (Black) and *Aspects of Love* (in partnership). He has demonstrated expertise in finding strong, suitable partners, but although his most recent projects have been successful, his earlier musicals have generally enjoyed greater popularity.

Lloyd Webber set up a public company, The Really Useful Group, as an umbrella organization for his various activities. The company has staged his shows and other shows, and is also involved in music and book publishing, CD, television and video production. It also owns theatres. Similar to Richard Branson, Lloyd Webber later bought back the company from its various shareholders, and then sold a 30 per cent stake to PolyGram. In 1999 he regained total control again by acquiring this 30 per cent stake from Seagram, who in turn had acquired PolyGram.

Andrew Lloyd Webber is a very wealthy modern composer. He has produced some extremely popular musicals and overcome a number of disappointments, systematically teaming up with a series of talented partners. He understands contemporary taste for musical theatre and, showing great creativity and innovation, he has found and exploited a series of opportunities. It is not difficult to accept that he is an entrepreneur. But was 'the greatest composer who ever lived' – Wolfgang Mozart – also an entrepreneur? Certainly the same commercial and marketing opportunities were not available to him! Neither was the technology and computer software that is now available to help modern composers. Arguably Mozart had a number of entrepreneur qualities, such as focus, dedication, activation, determination, creativity and innovation – but, try as he did, he was never able completely to overcome the obstacles he faced. A kind and gentle man, he was never spoilt by his genius – but, instead of being rewarded in his lifetime for his outstanding ability, he was affected by the envy of his rivals.

Mozart

Mozart was born in 1756 in Salzburg. His father was a violin teacher and a musician at the Court of the Prince-Archbishop. He was a genius – 'music came to Wolfgang Mozart as natural as did breathing' – and as a result he was denied a normal childhood. He was playing the harpsichord by ear at the age of three; he was taught musical theory and composition by his father, who was determined to exploit his talent. His father was loving but tyrannical, and a major influence for a number of years. At the age of six – a child prodigy – he was playing the concert platforms in the leading European cities – his own compositions as well as the work of others.

In his early teens he was given the post of Concert Master for the Archbishop of Salzburg – 'for a pittance of a salary'. He was never offered a permanent position in a leading European Court, the opportunity his father dreamed of securing for him. Already jealous rivals were preventing his music being played in Vienna. He was criticized and dismissed by several contemporary musicians in Rome and Paris on the grounds of his age and immaturity. Though his concert performances and his music continued to receive audience acclaim, at this time artistic success was no guarantee of financial wealth. He eventually settled in Vienna after he married, but events continued to work against him. He was an active freemason and seen by some to be frequenting the wrong social circles; he championed social causes, which also cost him friends amongst the aristocracy. But he continued to receive commissions from counts, merchants, aristocrats and opera-goers – and the music flowed. 'No other composer has been able to equal his range and variety of output.' When Austria went to war with Turkey in 1788, many aristocrats left Vienna and a number of financial opportunities left with them.

Ironically other contemporaries, who did not provoke the same envy and jealousy, were more successful – Haydn in particular. Haydn and Mozart, however, were firm friends and Haydn actively promoted Mozart's work. Mozart's greatest compositions came in his later years – he died in 1791 at the age of thirty-five. Some have speculated that he was poisoned, but this has never been proved. Between 1786 and 1790 he wrote four outstanding operas – *The Marriage of Figaro*, *Don Giovanni*, *The Magic Flute* and *Cosi fan tutte*. They were enormously popular when they were performed. At this time he was also writing his best-known symphonies and a series of concertos for solo instruments. 'He pushed every instrument to its limit.' Yet, and only in part because he liked to live comfortably, Mozart found himself having to beg for financial help from his friends. Freelance musicians without Court appointments did not become rich, however successful and acclaimed their work. He died a pauper, still composing his Requiem, and mouthing the words to his sister-in-law from his death bed. The Requiem had been commissioned anonymously by a wealthy count, who later claimed he had composed the work himself.

With Mozart, then, we have an entrepreneurial paradox. In the context of his music, he was both a genius and an entrepreneur. He pushed out the boundaries and was creative at a level others will only ever dream of attaining. His work remains popular and unrivalled. Various polls in 1999 confirmed that both experts and listeners consider him to have been the greatest composer who has ever lived. Although recognized by some in his life, his genius attracted enemies who were able to deny him key opportunities. If financial reward were of great significance to him, partly as a measure of his success, he would surely have been personally disappointed and seen by others as an underachiever. Had he not had a number of entrepreneur life themes, though, he may never have left the legacy he did.

Entertainment entrepreneurs

It is interesting to debate whether composers such as Andrew Lloyd Webber should be termed entrepreneurs because they are able to exploit their natural talents – but there can be no question that those people who successfully produce and stage the musical shows are entrepreneurs. They see an opportunity for the work in question and they champion the project.

Sir Cameron Mackintosh

Sir Cameron Mackintosh is 'King of the stage' and one of the most important influences in British and American theatre. In 1998 his production company achieved a trading profit of £20 million on a turnover of £38 million. Taken to the theatre at the age of eight, he decided there and then that he wanted to produce musicals – he had experienced his trigger, and as he grew older he dedicated himself to making it happen. Working his way through provincial theatres, he finally made it to London's West End with a production of *Anything Goes* when he was twenty-two. It lasted two weeks, but he persisted and returned. In the 1970s his major achievements were with innovative new productions of *Oliver!*, *My Fair Lady* and *Oklahoma*. He was even more successful with ones he helped create from scratch in the 1980s. In 1981 he collaborated with Andrew Lloyd Webber to stage *Cats*, and he followed this with *Phantom of the Opera* and then *Les Misérables*. Again we can see evidence of focus, dedication, activation, creativity, opportunity, profit orientation and team-building – all key entrepreneur life themes. Singer Michael Ball has commented that he has an instinctive appreciation of what audiences like, that he can spot talented performers and know exactly which role they are suited for.

Lord Lew Grade

Lord Lew Grade was known as 'Mr Showbusiness' for his contribution to films, television and the theatre. One of his great achievements was an ability to understand the 'preferences of the man in the street'. He understood his customers. Originally a dancer, but never a star, he became a theatrical agent before joining commercial television in its infancy. 'The stars', he once said, 'keep 90 per cent of my money'– he was profit-oriented.

He was one of three brothers who were born in Odessa – he in 1906 – before the family moved to England. His brothers were also successful entrepreneurs; it was in the blood. He was nearly thirty – and dancing – when he was offered the opportunity to join a theatrical agency. He seized the chance. Eight years later, and in partnership with one of his brothers, he had his own agency. The brothers became close friends with Val Parnell, then the manager of the London Palladium, and as a result they were always able to secure high-profile bookings for their star clients, who included Bob Hope. Sensing an opportunity, Parnell and Grade joined forces and became involved in the creation of Associated Television (ATV, later Central Television) in 1955. They remortgaged their houses, but succeeded in winning one of the first commercial television franchises. Their initial strategy was popular game shows and imported American action programmes – as well as the legendary *Saturday Night at the London Palladium*. Recruiting a strong creative team, they introduced popular series such as *The Persuaders, Danger Man* and *Robin Hood*. By the late 1960s Lew Grade was selling more programmes overseas than all the other independent television companies and the BBC put together.

'Had Lord Grade retired in 1971 – when he was 65 – he would be remembered as Britain's most successful showbusiness entrepreneur.' Instead he had other mountains he wished to climb. He was a habitual entrepreneur. He turned to film-making, and although he had some successes, he will always be remembered for one of the greatest and most expensive flops – *Raise The Titanic*. One banker commented that 'it would have been cheaper to lower the Atlantic'. The 1990s success of James Cameron's *Titanic* makes this story seem even more ironic.

The Lord Grade story is an excellent reminder that people can learn from their experiences and from their mistakes, and improve their mastery as a project champion – but seeing and exploiting winning new opportunity after winning new opportunity in an industry dictated by taste and fashion is inherently difficult.

Bob Geldof

Some entrepreneurial ventures, of course, are one-off projects. The Live Aid concert at Wembley Stadium in 1985 was just that; although others have since borrowed the idea from Bob Geldof. An Irish singer with the Boomtown Rats, and possessing a questionable reputation, Geldof would not have been seen as a natural entrepreneur – but he saw an opportunity to use pop music as a vehicle to raise money to help famine-stricken countries in Africa. His trigger had been a television news documentary. He channelled his energy into making it happen, using his network of contacts. Fellow stars appeared without charging a fee. The media were quickly engaged in helping publicize the innovative project which caught the imagination of the public. Seventy thousand people paid to attend the concert itself, and 1.4 billion viewers saw it on television in 170 different countries. £70 million was raised and spent.

Harvey Goldsmith

One of Bob Geldof's team for Live Aid was the impresario, Harvey Goldsmith, who project managed the actual concert event. Goldsmith's rise to fame and fortune had begun as a student at Brighton Polytechnic, where he booked bands for student dances to help pay his way. During the 1960s, 1970s and 1980s he promoted the UK tours of several leading American artists and became the 'biggest impresario of the age'. He later diversified into classical music and brought Pavarotti to Hyde Park. Concert promotion is, however, a low-margin business – the stars themselves pocket most of the proceeds – and so there is little room for error. Mistakes may not be forgiven. In 1999 Harvey Goldsmith's business went into receivership – 'he had tried to change with the times but had not quite managed it'. The 'straw that broke the camel's back' was his Total Eclipse Festival in Cornwall, which like the eclipse itself, failed to attract the anticipated audience.

George Lucas

If people were reluctant to brave the West Country traffic jams to get a view of the total eclipse of the sun, they were certainly not reticent about the fourth Star Wars movie. They had, after all, been waiting sixteen years. The success of the Star Wars phenomenon is down to creator, writer, film director and entrepreneur, George Lucas.

Lucas was born in California in 1944, and grew up a typical teenager of that time. He was hooked on adventure television and spent time cruising in his car. He drifted. His 'perspective on life changed' when he was involved in a freak car accident in 1962. He survived because his seat belt snapped. This experience made him determined to do something with his life – he had experienced his trigger. He chose to study film at the University of Southern California, where he won a major award for a short film. In turn this won him a scholarship with Warner Brothers, and through this he met Francis Coppola. The two decided to make a movie together; it was named *THX-1138* and was an extended version of Lucas's award-winning short film. The film was popular with audiences but not critics and the two separated. Whilst Coppola began his Godfather trilogy, Lucas set about raising money to make *American Graffiti*, which starred Harrison Ford. Premiered in 1973 it was another financial success and it provided him with the funds to launch his Star Wars project, which had been inspired by *Flash Gordon*. In the next few years, and together with Harrison Ford, he made three Star Wars films and, in collaboration with Steven Spielberg, three Indiana Jones films and 'rewrote box office records'. Although the Star Wars films were released by Twentieth Century Fox, Lucas has always retained the rights and ownership of merchandising licences. He also controls the distribution of the films. Lucas is, quite clearly, both an opportunity-spotter and a project champion.

We complete this section with two more individual entrepreneurs who have found winning personal opportunities in the fickle and complex world of entertainment – but who are both controversial characters.

Michael Flatley

Michael Flatley has been christened 'Lord of the Dance' and cynics have said he will only appear at the biggest venues because the others are 'too small to accommodate his ego'. Flatley counters that he is merely self-confident. He was an Irish dancer in America when he was recruited to choreograph Riverdance to fill the interval at the Eurovision Song Contest in Dublin in 1994. A window of opportunity had been opened for him. The short sequence was hugely popular and quickly spawned a full-length production. After successful performances in Dublin and London, Flatley increased his personal demands for future appearances, but negotiations with the promoters broke down. Flatley was sacked and his understudy took over at short notice; the popularity of Riverdance – The Show was largely unaffected.

Believing in his own ability, and determined to exploit the still-open window of opportunity, Flatley immediately set about devising a new Irish dance show, which he intended should be more ambitious than Riverdance. He recruited a strong management, musical and choreographic team – and contacted promoter Harvey Goldsmith. He was investing his reputation as well as his savings – he had to succeed. The team worked intensely and all hours to create the new show, which Flatley called Lord of the Dance. Publicity was easy, as the media were anxious to compare the relative merits of the two competing shows. The new show was another instant success, capitalizing on the new-found popularity of traditional Irish music and dance. Shortly after it opened, Flatley did not appear personally in a number of the shows because of torn leg muscles. Once his understudy began to receive standing ovations for every performance, Flatley fought hard to regain his fitness! Lord of the Dance has been successful; at the same time Riverdance – The Show has filled theatres and sold successfully in video format.

In Michael Flatley we can see a focused and determined entrepreneur in action. We see clear evidence of the ego drive, opportunity, urgency, activating, creativity, expertise orientation and team-building life themes. Time will tell if he is habitual and can repeat the success.

Chris Evans

The current owner of Virgin Radio, Chris Evans, is another determined individualist who has been described as 'utterly single-minded'. Brought up on a council estate in Warrington, Evans organized a squad of delivery boys for his local newsagent and an unofficial school tuck shop. He was devastated when his father died of cancer when he was fourteen years old. His ego drive and attitude are summarized in the following comment: 'I believe absolutely in one man having one vision for the way something should be done.' Following a spell as a Tarzanogram in Manchester, he secured minor opportunities on local radio stations before eventually becoming a regular morning disc jockey on BBC Radio One. Invariably controversial, he walked out when he was refused a four mornings contract – he wanted Fridays off so he would have more time to prepare for his Friday evening television show on Channel Four.

Recognizing his public popularity and attraction to the media, Richard Branson offered him the prime morning slot on Virgin Radio, where he quickly increased the number of listeners from 1.8 to 2.6 million – helped in part by the publicity generated by his move. Once he realized Branson was willing to sell Virgin Radio, and in true entrepreneurial fashion, he used his show to appeal for financial support to buy it. Allegedly an act of impulse, Evans is normally perceived to be someone who knows exactly what he is doing. He did succeed in persuading Branson to sell the station to him rather than to Capital Radio – and he was able to raise £85 million to secure the acquisition. Branson retained a 20 per cent stake in Evans's personal holding company, Ginger Media, which was sold to the Scottish Media Group for £225 million in early 2000.

Without question Evans possesses many strong entrepreneur life themes – he also has characteristics which work against him. 'People don't like Evans because he's about changing everything ... [yet] his greatest gift is that he wants to do everything differently, and better, all the time.' He is a driven man and an innovator, 'never satisfied with himself or other people's performances'. He has always been seen as a control freak; and he is prone to use his media access to air personal views and grievances. He was fined by the Radio Authority for giving out private mobile phone numbers on the air and he recently commented that 'half the BBC's staff are on drugs'. Recently he was thwarted in a bid to buy and take over a daily newspaper, the *Star*, when the vendor pulled out. It was intimated that Branson was less than happy, fearing that a link between Virgin Radio and a perceived downmarket tabloid newspaper might tarnish his own personal image.

Fun entrepreneurs

We have chosen the term 'fun entrepreneurs' to single out those entrepreneurs who use an element of fun and irreverence, either to create and build an innovative organization or to generate notoriety in an essentially serious industry – and here we focus on the latter group.

Herb Kelleher

Herb Kelleher began Southwest Air in 1971 with a simple intention – 'fly people safely, cheaply and conveniently between Dallas, Houston and San Antonio', three key cities in Texas. Kelleher set out to compete against coach and car travel rather than the other airlines. In nearly thirty years as a low-price, no-frills airline, Southwest has prospered and grown to become the fifth largest carrier in the USA. It serves over fifty cities in twenty-seven states and has some 2500 flights every day. His strategy, competitive advantage and success is based on a number of factors:

- frequent and reliable departures
- relatively short journeys by American standards, now averaging 450 miles but with the average having increased as the airline has grown in size and destinations

- where relevant, the choice of smaller airports nearer to city centres in preference to international airports which are further away from the centre
- very low prices
- automated ticketing and direct bookings (without travel agents), and now using the Internet extensively
- limited frills, with no seat assignments, no videos and just one class of seating
- fast gate turnarounds, to maximize the time the planes are in the air
- a standardized fleet of Boeing 737s, to simplify maintenance.

Southwest is now America's only significant short-distance, point-to-point carrier. Others have certainly tried to compete, but have been unable to make the equivalent impact. It has won the US Department of Transport's coveted Triple Crown award of best on-time record, best baggage handling and fewest customer complaints on several occasions. Every new route and destination is immediately popular and, as a result, Southwest has been consistently profitable for over twenty-five years, a unique record for an airline anywhere in the world.

Kelleher was a champion college athlete and a successful Texas lawyer before he started the airline when he was forty years old. The idea for Southwest came from a client (and co-founder of the business) who spotted the gap in the market.

Kelleher is a renowned 'people person'. Through profit-sharing schemes, employees own over 10 per cent of the company's stock, and he has made 'working in the airline industry an adventure'. Southwest is dynamic and responsive; employees accept empowerment and are motivated to work hard and deliver high levels of service consistently. Rules and regulations are minimized to allow staff the freedom to deal with issues as they arise. 'Ask employees what's important to them. Ask customers what's important to them. Then do it. It's that simple' (Kelleher). The frequent flyer programme, unusually, rewards passengers for the number of individual flights, not the miles flown.

But it is never that simple! Southwest is also renowned as 'one of the zaniest companies in history'. From the very beginning, Kelleher encouraged flight attendants to crack jokes during in-flight emergency briefings, but at the same time operate with very high safety standards. He was determined passengers would enjoy their flights. Some of the planes are decorated externally to reinforce the fun image. Three of them, promoting major sponsor Sea World, are flying killer whales; one is painted with the Texas flag; another is christened Arizona One, a spoof of Air Force One. Flight attendants have been known to hide in the overhead lockers as passengers come on board, startling them as they open up the lockers. Kelleher himself often appears in fancy dress for certain flights and special occasions. A special prize for the passenger with the biggest hole in his sock would be quite typical.

Consequently, a sense of humour has become a key element in the recruitment process. During their training, employees are given a book with sections on jokes, games and songs – but they are all encouraged to develop an individual style. 'At Southwest we don't want clones – everyone is expected to colour outside the lines.' Kelleher is dedicated and focused and in possession of a strong ego drive. He is creative and innovative and he understands the contribution people can make. He has always had the courage to be different. When introduced to an idea he appreciated the opportunity and activated it. Truly profit-oriented, he has been extremely successful in a dynamic and cruel industry, where many competing airlines have failed.

Blending financial, social and aesthetic capital

This final section documents the story of two remarkable men who, in very different ways and circumstances, have shown how financial, social and aesthetic capital can be blended – and have a positive impact on the wider environment.

Sir Ernest Hall

Sir Ernest Hall was not born to wealth. One of thirteen children, his parents were mill workers in Bolton. But he became wealthy through business, and he has then used this financial wealth to create social and artistic capital in the form of Dean Clough Mills in Halifax. He is another serial entrepreneur, who has achieved in different fields at various stages in his life. 'To be a successful entrepreneur, one needs a vision of greatness for one's work. If we dream extravagantly, we will be motivated to forge a reality beyond the straitjacket of practicalities.'

His first passion was music, developed when he heard classical music played on a gramophone at his primary school. He was eight years old at the time, and he then set off on a quest to listen to more and more music. He also persuaded his parents to buy a piano, which he practised playing with great enthusiasm. In 1946 he became a student at the Royal Manchester College of Music; his parents were sceptical and suggested the only way he would ever make money would be as a player in a dance band – playing music he hated! Although successful, the astute Ernest was aware of fellow students with more natural talent, and he looked to develop a career outside music. He found a job with a small textile mill in Yorkshire. From a starting belief that 'commerce was ugly' – but necessary – he found industry to be 'satisfying and exciting ... designing fabrics and running a business was a creative process, similar to composing music or writing poetry'. By the early 1960s he was running his own textile business, a management buy-out. Over the next twenty years the business prospered and he became a wealthy man.

His awareness of the declining fortunes of many northern communities – fuelled by industrial decline – intensified during these years, and he became determined to do something meaningful to help arrest the decline. Because many people and communities had lost their confidence and any belief that the area could once again be great, his task was daunting. Undeterred, he used his wealth and connections to acquire Dean Clough Mills, an integrated complex of sixteen nineteenth-century mills in Halifax. The mills had been built by the Crossley family and had grown to be one of the largest carpet factories in the world. The business was closed in 1982. He dreamed of a restored complex where 'commercial success could be used to support a wide range of activities in arts and education'. He was seeing an opportunity – and, significantly, a cause – where most others saw an insoluble problem – and he possessed the determination and project championing skills to make it happen. By 1994 he had created his dream, with over 100 companies operating alongside professional painters, sculptors and printmakers. The number of companies has since doubled, and over 3500 jobs have been created. Some of the companies have always been small start-ups, but Halifax plc also occupies office space. In addition there are six galleries showing contemporary art together with the prestigious Slade School of Art, a theatre and a theatre company; in addition, Dean Clough is the home base of the Northern Ballet Concert Orchestra and the Northern Brass Band Federation.

This momentous achievement was not enough to satisfy the entrepreneurial Sir Ernest – now in his sixties, he resurrected his musical ambitions. He played the piano for classical recitals and recorded the music of both Bartok and Chopin. At the same time, and encouraged by his second wife, a renowned equestrienne, he started riding horses. He has since become a champion dressage rider. Possessor of a strong ego drive, and a conviction that wherever people believe in themselves and their potential, they can achieve, he has used his considerable entrepreneurial talent to build financial, social and artistic capital – and shown how they can all work together harmoniously. The local environment has benefited, as a once derelict mill complex is now a thriving community.

William Randolph Hearst

Hearst Castle, near San Simeon in California, is actually a stunning and wholly idiosyncratic building designed on Spanish-Moorish lines and built part way up a 1600-foot mountain overlooking the Pacific ocean. The architect, Julia Morgan, had to build an underground reservoir to provide a water supply before construction could even begin. The original owner, William Randolph Hearst, was a successful entrepreneur and newspaper magnate, who had been born to wealth. He had been given his first newspaper by his father when he was twenty-four years old. He had used this base to build a business empire and had served as a United States Congressman. He was flying aeroplanes only seven years after the Wright Brothers' first flight and he was the producer of over 100 silent films in Hollywood. He built his castle with two main motives. First, he was an insatiable collector of art and antiques and sufficiently wealthy to indulge himself throughout Europe. His possessions (Hearst accumulated a multimillion dollar collection of antiques and works of arts) needed a home. The castle has 115 rooms, the size of some of them being determined by the antiques they were to house. Antique ceilings, wall tapestries, choir stalls and medieval dining tables required rooms of particular dimensions. Second, Hearst liked to entertain the rich and famous, especially movie stars from Hollywood, and needed a suitable estate with accommodation (there are a number of guest houses in the grounds), swimming pools (there is one outdoor and one indoor) and tennis courts. Begun in 1919, used extensively in the 1920s and 1930s, yet still incomplete when Hearst died in 1951, the castle thus represents a mixture of artistic and social capital. Since his death his descendants have transformed the estate into a hugely popular tourist attraction. Visitors can only enter the grounds on organized tours; and there are four different daytime tours that operate at regular intervals every day and evening tours during the winter months. Clearly the castle now generates substantial financial capital.

In this chapter we have told the story of a wide range of artistic and aesthetic entrepreneurs, many of whom have had very marked effects on our lives – and in quite different ways. Some of them have created great works of music and art which have 'stood [and will stand] the test of time' whilst others have used creative design to build significant businesses. We have seen how entrepreneurs are present in the world of entertainment, using their entrepreneur life themes to build financial wealth around enjoyment and pleasure. We have also seen how financial, social and aesthetic capital can all come together in a synergistic and mutually beneficial way. At the same time we have seen how some entrepreneurs also possess certain life themes which mean there is a shadow side to their activities and personality. With the ones featured in this chapter, this element has merely qualified their achievements; in the next chapter we consider those entrepreneurs whose darker side brings more damaging results. We see how capital can be destroyed as well as built.

References

Jensen, R. (1999). *The Dream Society*. McGraw-Hill.
Ludwig, A. M. (1995). *The Price of Greatness: Resolving the Creativity and Madness Controversy*. Guildford Press.

7 Entrepreneurs in the shadows

In this chapter we switch emphasis from the positive to the potentially negative side of entrepreneurship. Inevitably, amongst the most notorious stories of famous entrepreneurs, we find a limited percentage who have either failed or who have destroyed capital which was important to others. Some reflect errors of strategic judgement while others reflect overambition – promises that were realistically always too good to be true. Some of these stories, of course, are of criminal behaviour. Some of the entrepreneurs we feature were always in the shadows; others ended up there for a variety of reasons. There is an important message underpinning this chapter – the more we relax the controls on entrepreneurs, in order to encourage more entrepreneurial behaviour, the greater the potential for the shadow side of entrepreneurship to prosper.

So far in this book we have extolled the virtues of entrepreneurship, suggested we need more entrepreneurs in all walks of life and used a wide range of examples to support our case. We have described our so-called 'well of talent' and argued that we must learn how we might better tap the rich seam of entrepreneurial talent that lies hidden. But, once we tap the seam we must also be able to control the flow. We cannot sensibly give every entrepreneur a totally 'free rein'. In some ways, this is a paradox, because entrepreneurship is encouraged by relaxing controls and constraints. Fewer regulations, less 'red tape', easier access to finance, and so on, are the accepted way forward. Yet these are the very constraints that regulate against excess by people whose ethics or honesty can be called into question. Metaphorically this is like an oil well – once the seam is found, the oil gushes up in free flow and the well must be capped to regulate the flow and exploit the yield most effectively.

Simply, there is a shadow side to entrepreneurship. In its extreme form it destroys capital as well as creating it. Some entrepreneurs direct their efforts to their own personal benefits at the expense of others who, as a result, suffer in some way. It is, of course, no coincidence that for many people the term 'entrepreneur' is synonymous with fictional characters like Arthur Daley and Derek Trotter – people we might call 'likeable rogues', 'wide-boys' or 'wheeler-dealers'. We read about property developers who appear to disregard the concerns of environmentalists and preservationists. We hear of 'cowboy' trades people who target vulnerable old people, take their money and fail to deliver an acceptable product or service in return. There has been no shortage of bogus mail-order businesses trading in counterfeit designer clothes and pirated music is widespread. The opportunities are always there for the people determined to find them – but that is no excuse for making it easy. The unpopular and heavily criticized rules for allocating tickets for the football World Cup in France in 1998 was an opportunity for the shadowy entrepreneur. England supporters, anxious to attend England's matches, were easily persuaded to hand money over to apparently legitimate ticket agencies with prestigious addresses as advance payments for tickets that would never materialize. Entrepreneurial ticket touts in France were able to buy and sell black market tickets at inflated prices when they realized that the football associations in the economically poorest countries in the competition, such as Cameroon, were being provided with tickets far in excess of the numbers they could hope to sell.

In addition, entrepreneurial journalists have been known to destroy people's lives with the way they have handled sensitive material. Terrorist bombers are entrepreneurs who destroy social and aesthetic capital at the same time. The organized football hooligans who can outsmart the police and engineer gang fights with local fans are proven project champions. Can we live comfortably with the entrepreneurial finance company manager in Japan who demanded that a client in arrears sell one of his eyes or kidneys on the black market in order to help pay off his debt? One important implication of this is that the whole notion of entrepreneurship needs redeeming to ensure people relate it to the beneficial financial, social, aesthetic and environmental capital it can generate.

People with the strongest entrepreneur life themes are very driven, very ambitious and very profit or achievement oriented. When the desire to succeed is particularly strong these entrepreneurs may well take exceptionally high risks – which sometimes do pay off. But not always – something 'boils over'. In a business context the company grows too quickly and the bubble bursts when there is no spare resource capacity to deal with the inevitable setbacks or crises. This can be made worse by an unrealistically optimistic belief in one's ability to handle the crisis and a refusal to seek help. Strategic errors can be made by egotistical entrepreneurs; shortfalls can be ignored or covered up. Sometimes this is accidental, but it can be negligent and, on occasions, dishonest. Some entrepreneurs do cut corners, bend rules, behave unethically and generally 'overstep the mark'. Some are fundamentally criminal.

In this chapter we look at examples of:

- opportunist entrepreneurs who either adopt a flawed strategy or fail to deliver
- inventors who become failed entrepreneurs as they lack key project championing capabilities
- empire-builders who grow too quickly and lose control – sometimes involving a creative cover-up strategy
- entrepreneurs who make mistakes, or whose business fails, but who determinedly make a comeback
- entrepreneurs who attract controversy
- dishonest entrepreneurs.

In the stories we see entrepreneurs who are extremely good at publicizing their activities in order to attract customers and finance, and entrepreneurs who believe their failure is not their fault. Other people, resentful of their success, have set out to destroy them. This is not uncommon in entrepreneurs and it helps explain why a number who have failed start all over again – determined not to fail a second (or even a third) time – the habitual, serial element. The real issue is whether they have been able to learn from their experiences.

We conclude the chapter with a section on criminal entrepreneurs. We have seen in earlier chapters how some individuals with strong entrepreneurial life themes are driven from a very young age to enterprising behaviour – such as a pocket-money business. Parental and other encouragement or discouragement affects their learning from this. Arguably some young people with these entrepreneurial life themes who also possess particular qualities such as impulsiveness, fearlessness, aggression and/or hyperactivity may seek to develop their enterprise 'in the shadows', at the expense of others. If they succeed, and if they are not discouraged, we have our shadow entrepreneurs in the making.

Some of the stories go back several years; they have been selected because the entrepreneurs they feature are well known and, often, very colourful characters. The failings in these stories will have been repeated in many other less well-publicized cases.

The failed entrepreneur

John de Lorean

The case of John de Lorean goes back some twenty years, but provides the ideal example for justifying the need to control the activities of entrepreneurs. In 1978 the UK (Labour) government was completely behind de Lorean's ambitious plan to build a radical new car in Northern Ireland. Whilst de Lorean was ultimately the architect of his own downfall, the appointed Receiver to the business later commented that 'a more robust project' could have succeeded. Anxious to secure the car plant for the troubled Belfast region, the government was pushed into acting quickly, arguably over-hastily, and failed to investigate all de Lorean's past business experiences. They were persuaded by his public image and salesmanship. In the event, £80 million of public money and 2600 newly created jobs were lost.

John de Lorean was born in 1925, the eldest son of a Detroit foundry worker. He obtained degrees in music, industrial engineering and business administration; his first employer was General Motors (GM), where he rose through the ranks. By 1970 he was General Manager of GM's Chevrolet division and he was being tipped by some as a future GM president. Tall, elegant, stylish and charismatic he was 'unparalleled as a salesman' and hugely popular with the company's extensive and powerful dealer network. Whilst his career progressed rapidly and seemingly was trouble-free, his high-profile personal life was different. In 1969 he was divorced from his first wife and quickly remarried to the nineteen-year-old daughter of a football star. Two years later he was divorced again and dating film stars from

Hollywood. He had been attracted by the glamour of the movie industry and his position in General Motors allowed him to socialize accordingly. His third wife was a New York fashion model. At this time he grew his hair and took to dressing in trendy clothes, which was seen as unusual for a prominent corporate executive. His whole lifestyle was 'expensive and flamboyant'.

Nevertheless, he was incredibly focused and worked long hours – and, partly for this reason, other 'skeletons in his cupboard' were largely ignored. Over a period of years he had made substantial personal investments in businesses which had all folded with acrimony and litigation. These activities, which included motor racing circuit franchising and car radiator manufacture, were related to automobiles. In 1973 he resigned from GM and announced his vision for an innovative and radical new car built in a state-of-the-art production facility. He blamed 'restrictive management controls' in General Motors for his move. There had been a number of signals and indicators that de Lorean might be a high-risk investment for the UK government, but they were largely overlooked.

The dream car would be built of stainless steel and feature distinctive gull-wing doors, hinged at the top. There were 'innovations to improve safety and drive-ability ... an emphasis on style and quality ... all at a reasonable price'. Part of its ultimate fame would come from its starring role as a time machine in the three *Back to the Future* films. John de Lorean was able to secure $175 million to finance the venture and finally chose Belfast in preference to Detroit, Puerto Rico and the Republic of Ireland – influenced by grants and a speedy decision. His outline concept was translated into a production model by Group Lotus under a subcontract arrangement. Both John de Lorean and Colin Chapman of Lotus agreed to handle the financial arrangements through a Swiss-based third party organization. It later transpired this company was in reality also a convenient vehicle for siphoning UK government funds and moving them back to the USA to cover personal loans to de Lorean himself.

The deal was struck in 1978, and within two years cars were coming off the line. A 72-acre field – with two rivers running through it – had been transformed into an advanced production facility. A dealer network was in place across the key market of North America, for where most of the cars were destined, and various personalities were signed up for endorsement advertising. De Lorean made things happen; but the controls were inadequate. Costs were escalating; production difficulties were emerging; and de Lorean began to talk about prices 20 per cent above the original estimate. He needed more money than he had forecast; and he began to seek funds from every source he could identify. Attempting to hide the severity of the problems, he continued to insist that the funding stream was secure. Flying across the Atlantic on Concorde on at least a weekly basis, and maintaining his expensive lifestyle, de Lorean successfully covered up the precarious state of his personal and business finances. The extra funding was never in place and the company went into receivership in 1982. The plant ultimately closed; the dream was over. Nevertheless, 8000 cars had been made and sold. Early in 1999 some 6000 of these were still on the road. Judged on the sales record after its launch, the car was clearly a success. Customers liked it and bought it. John de Lorean understood his market.

However, to compound matters further in 1982, de Lorean was charged with attempting to broker a $24 million cocaine deal in an endeavour to raise money. Whilst he was acquitted on the grounds of federal entrapment, his credibility was finally shattered. It seems an ultimate irony that de Lorean described his factory as 'the world's first ethical car company' and chastised GM managers as 'men of sound personal morality, but all too capable, as a group, of reaching business decisions which were irresponsible and of dubious morality'.

Inventor entrepreneurs

John Edgley

It is not the case that all inventors are entrepreneurial failures, simply that some never manage to establish and grow the business that their invention promises. The unique Optica spotter-plane was designed by John Edgley, who built the prototype in a house he owned in North London, before taking it for final assembly and testing to an airfield in Bedfordshire. The plane received substantial publicity when the first production model, under test by the Hampshire Police for observation duties, crashed on its maiden flight in May 1985. The subsequent investigation cleared the Optica of any design faults – but really the business never recovered from this slice of bad luck.

The Optica was revolutionary, having a three-seater observation cockpit at the very front, with the engine, propeller and wings all behind. It could cruise at slow speed and turn tightly. It was designed to compete with helicopters, and it promised a substantial cost advantage for both purchase and running. The business was design led, with the market investigated properly only after the prototype was flying. Forecasts for potential demand always proved overoptimistic. Throughout its history, interest in the aircraft and indications of possible future orders were frequently described as firm orders to imply an exaggerated and unrealistic level of acceptance and success. It is, of course, quite conceivable that Edgley actually believed they were orders and he was simply waiting for final confirmation.

In 1974 John Edgley was a thirty-year-old designer 'who wanted to build, own and run an aircraft factory'. Originally a civil engineer, he also had a postgraduate degree in aeronautical engineering. His company was begun with family savings, topped up with loans from relatives, and the first Optica was built on a shoestring budget. Its maiden flight was in 1979; one year later Mrs Thatcher described it as 'a triumph of British enterprise and technology'. At the Farnborough Air Show, painted in bright yellow, it was a 'show stopper'. Without any firm orders, Edgley set out to raise money to grow the venture. Using a network of friends and contacts in the City, he was successful.

Edgley and his institutional backers invested an estimated £8 million in building a sophisticated production facility, using computer-controlled machine tools, at Old Sarum Airfield near Salisbury, still before any definite orders were received. Hoping for interest to be translated into firm orders, they began building aircraft. Edgley had his factory. However, and typically, it had taken longer than he expected, and cost more than the original budget. Many obstacles had been overcome, such that Edgley commented they had become blasé about their ability to deal with problems and setbacks. The Optica won a major Design Council award in 1984 and a full airworthiness certificate at the beginning of 1985. Edgley had been committed for ten years by this stage. In October 1985, and just five months after the fatal crash, Edgley Aircraft (the company) went into receivership, was sold, and renamed Optica Industries. At this time John Edgley ceased to have any personal involvement in either the aircraft or the business – but there is more to the story.

The wisdom of building a capital-intensive production facility without orders for aircraft was questioned when the new owners had to accept subcontract and 'metal-bashing' work to utilize their spare capacity. The premises, however, were destroyed by a mysterious fire early in 1987, and subsequently rebuilt. The company was renamed Brooklands Aerospace. The first actual order for an Optica, in March 1988, came nine years after the prototype had first flown. In July 1989 an American order for 132 aircraft was received, and the company also diversified into manufacturing additional light aircraft under licence.

But in the end, the Optica has never been developed commercially – financial difficulties led to a second receivership in April 1990. It is another good idea that never came to fruition. Light aircraft manufacture is, by its very nature, a difficult and high-risk business to enter as substantial up-front investment is required to secure full certification to fly. Whether the Optica could have been successful if the unfortunate crash in 1985 had not occurred, or if the business had not accumulated huge overheads by building state-of-the-art production facilities, will never be known. Edgley appeared to know the risks and accepted them – but he failed. Afterwards he reflected that he had failed to realize that he was developing a product and building a business simultaneously, and that they are not one and the same. He was simply not a project champion. He was certainly an inventor, and maybe a good opportunity-spotter.

Clive Sinclair

Clive Sinclair also promised but never ultimately delivered. He is not remembered for his early successes but for his later failures. Like John Edgley, he is a mixture of the inventor and opportunity-spotter who never managed to build a successful long-term business. Sinclair was born in 1940 in Surrey; his father and grandfather had both been engineers. His grandfather was a renowned and innovative naval architect, and his father had started and run his own business. Whilst Clive was still at school, his father suffered a major business setback and had to start all over again. Entrepreneurship seemed to be in the blood.

Clive Sinclair was always a voracious learner – with 'ways of thought and speech beyond his years' – who preferred the company of adults to children. Keen on mathematics, he discovered electronics and began to experiment at home. Like the founders of Sony, he was naturally drawn to the challenge of miniaturization. He was still at school when his first articles were published in *Practical Wireless*. At the same time he was always looking for opportunities to supplement his pocket money and finance his experiments.

Despite being qualified, he chose not to go to university and instead found employment as an editor with *Practical Wireless*. Through the contacts he was able to nurture, he was next invited to work in publishing – writing, editing and commissioning books for hobbyists. But all the time he was dreaming of owning his own business once he had the financial resources to start it. In his early twenties, and thinking he had a private backer for a radio construction business, he resigned from his job. When the backer pulled out he had to return to technical writing – but this setback actually provided him with a valuable new expertise. In his new job he became knowledgeable about semiconductors. Eventually he was able to begin a business, initially designing and assembling miniature radios and amplifiers from bought-in components. His early successes were all down to innovative, breakthrough ideas and his natural tendency to seek and obtain publicity. Generally his success continued through the 1970s, but not without setbacks. He skimped on the quality of metal connectors in his calculators, for example, and they simply exploded and stopped working.

He established small assembly units in Boston, St Ives and Cambridge, where he based his headquarters; and in 1980 he launched the ZX80, 'the world's smallest and cheapest computer'. It measured just 9 inches by 7 inches and retailed at under £100. There were design issues – for example, the raised-surface touch keypad was difficult to use – but the 'person in the street' was attracted by the thought of ownership, and sales through both mail order and high street stores were buoyant. Although the rate of return for shoddy workmanship was relatively high, the low price continued to tempt customers. As a result, the ZX80 was followed by an improved version, the ZX81, and then the more sophisticated, but still low-price and miniature, Spectrum. At this stage in the company's development, the Timex factory in Dundee was a major subcontractor for much of Sinclair's assembly work. Without doubt, by 1983, the innovative, buccaneering and successful Clive Sinclair appeared to be the 'very epitome of the new Elizabethan technologist'. Moreover, 1984 was to be the year of the advanced, and much heralded, Sinclair QL miniature computer. QL was derived from quantum leap. Although the launch was announced and planned, the deliveries simply did not materialize. For the first time, the Sinclair bubble had been truly burst, and thereafter the story becomes one of largely unfulfilled promises.

Sinclair already had the technology and designs for flat screen televisions, which could potentially be mounted on walls and thus take up much less space in homes – but he has never been able to produce at a cost which would create a market. His real demise, however, came with the electronic tricycle, the C5. Promoted as the safe, easy and clean way to beat traffic congestion, its batteries were inadequate – it quickly ran out of power and stopped. Both Sinclair and the C5 were scorned and became the subject of comedians' jokes. Overwhelmed by debt and unsold stock, Sinclair sold his computer business – and all his patents – to Alan Sugar (Amstrad) for £5 million in 1986.

Clive Sinclair was an opportunity-spotter and, to a degree, an inventor. Although he had a business partner, this proved insufficient to overcome the relative failings that ultimately brought him down. Whilst cynics would dismiss him as an assembler, this seems unjust. He had obsessions (rather like social entrepreneurs have causes), but allowed these obsessions to push him into actions and decisions which were not sound business sense. He was not noted for accepting the blame when things went wrong or for learning from his misjudgements. He was willing to compromise on quality and engineering to keep his prices low, and this has to be an unsustainable strategy. He was not a businessman or true entrepreneur – because he was not a project champion. Sadly Sinclair is not the only loser. Some potentially great ideas have been lost because of his failings – customers and society are also losers.

In the next section we reflect on a wider range of business failures and consider the effect they have had on the entrepreneurs held responsible.

More business failures

John Ashcroft

John Ashcroft did not start Coloroll; he was recruited to be its Managing Director at the age of thirty in 1978, and he immediately set the business on a fast expansion path which ultimately would cause it to fail. After graduating, Ashcroft had started as a management trainee with Tube Investments before working in marketing management for Crown wall-coverings, the market leader in its field. Coloroll was a competitor to Crown. It was based in Manchester and after John Ashcroft became Managing Director (and subsequently Chairman) it first increased its share of the UK wallpaper market from 3 per cent to 30 per cent, and later diversified into pottery and earthenware, bed linen and finally carpets (Kosset) with the acquisition of John Crowther in 1988. Ashcroft deliberately recruited a new and youthful management team to support him – they were described by one analyst as 'MBA barrow boys'.

The company was very market oriented and concerned to give the customer 'what he wants when he wants it ... I've geared the business towards generic growth, which means exploiting market trends and knocking out competitors by pushing them off the shelf' (Ashcroft). There was a clear and coherent strategy. Coloroll targeted the growing do-it-yourself (DIY) retailers who were beginning to build large out-of-town units; delivery lead times (from stock) were reduced to a very competitive two days; and manufacturing costs were reduced with investments in new machinery. After securing market leadership for wall-coverings from Crown, Coloroll successfully identified and exploited an opportunity to provide a range of attractive and affordable household products for young consumers who were either first-time homeowners or removing for the first time. The Coloroll brand-name was now being stamped upon some famous and well- established products including Denby pottery and Edinburgh crystal glassware.

Acquisitions were implemented with a clear three-stage process: *assessment, reconstruction* and *rehabilitation*. Companies were acquired if Coloroll believed they could improve the performance, and they began by changing the culture.

> Symbols are regarded as important in making the change of culture. Staffordshire Potteries had a wood-panelled boardroom and a directors' snug complete

with bar. Both were ripped apart by Coloroll (alcohol is not allowed anywhere within the group) and turned into meeting rooms for the workforce. At Fogarty [duvets and bed linen], where there were three grades of toilet – one for the chairman, one for the other directors, and one for the ranks – there was a similar ritual demolition.

(Ashcroft)

Reconstruction was designed to simplify the job of management, accelerate decision-making and reduce unnecessary overheads. Structures were altered, and Coloroll ensured that managers understood the objectives they were being set, and offered incentives to make them worthy of achievement. The most senior managers from the acquired company were likely to be replaced, often by managers from within the company, and Coloroll introduced tight financial monitoring systems. Clear targets were set for key financial measures. Up-to-date sales and financial information was collected weekly, and any variations from budgets were acted upon quickly. His style was ruthless, radical and charismatic. He made a difference.

We have a very small head office team of four directors. The rest of the company is divided into businesses that all have their own managing directors [MDs] who operate autonomously. These MDs have big salaries, big bonuses, big cars and big prestige positions, and they are the people who make all the decisions . . . To operate smoothly, I need to have a clear perception of where the business is going. Every year we debate it, but once I decide, then everybody has to go along with it. There's a lot of nonsense talked about democracy. I believe management democracy is everybody agreeing to do what the leader wants.

(Ashcroft)

Sales of £6 million in the late 1970s increased 100 times in ten years. Profits grew at a comparable rate and exceeded £50 million in the 1988/99 financial year. There were misjudgements, nevertheless. A move into retailing – when Coloroll opened its own store in London in 1986 and planned another in Manchester – was abandoned when Marks & Spencer and other leading customers threatened to cancel orders. However, high rates of interest in 1989 led to a slowing down in the rate of growth of Coloroll's sales, aggressive pricing policies by both Coloroll and its competitors, and substantial increases in the cost of borrowings. The financial difficulties were compounded by Coloroll having paid too high a price for John Crowther. Interim profits for the six months to September 1989 collapsed. Ashcroft's strategy had proved extremely successful in buoyant market conditions, but growth was too fast. The company was not sufficiently robust financially to withstand adverse trading conditions. 'We got carried away with the concept and lost sight of the cash' (Ashcroft).

In March 1990 John Ashcroft resigned, and his replacement was described as a 'doctor handed an incurable patient'. Within weeks Coloroll was in receivership, and the business was subsequently offered for sale as either a whole or up to eleven separate parts. Finally five divisions were sold to their respective managers, three to other companies, and three were closed down.

Ashcroft himself started a new business – Survival Aid – in the Lake District in 1991, selling outdoor clothing by mail order, but with plans to expand into retailing. This again grew very fast and experienced cash difficulties. Ashcroft did not seem to have learned all the lessons from Coloroll. Once described by Mrs Thatcher as a 'shining example of British entrepreneurship', and appearing to be just that, he was actually an ambitious corporate empire-builder with a strong ego drive. Many of his decisions were sound strategically, but the growth was too rapid and too ambitious, and the company's resources were too overstretched to deal effectively with the inevitable crises.

Freddie Laker

Freddie Laker, who became Sir Freddie in 1978, was an entrepreneur and a pioneer in the competitive international air transport industry. He was a well-quoted self-publicist whose commercial exploits brought him fame and recognition. He introduced cheap transatlantic air travel, providing travel opportunities for many people who previously had not been able to afford the fares; but his business collapsed in the early 1980s. At the time he blamed others for his demise but, whilst there is substance in his argument, the fact remains that he had personally sown the seeds of his downfall with a flawed strategy. But he would later bounce back again.

Laker was born in 1922 in Canterbury. His trigger for a life in aviation was a sight of the *Hindenberg* and a Handley-Page biplane flying over his house when he was still a boy. He subsequently learned to fly and served with the Air Transport Auxiliary in the Second World War. In 1953 he began his first business, Channel Air Bridge Limited, to sell air transportation of vehicles, passengers and cargo (including live animals) on the same aircraft. He was involved in the design and development of Gatwick Airport, before he helped develop and run British United Airways (BUA) in 1960. At this time BUA was the largest aircraft company in the private sector. His next venture – Laker Airways in 1966 – was a small independent company 'operated on a shoestring' which offered inclusive package holidays and provided charter flights for organizations who could book all the seats on a plane and flights for tour companies who did not own their own airline. He was the first all-jet carrier in the UK. Laker's stated intention was to stay small: 'If we get any bigger than six planes you can kick my arse.' From a marketing perspective, Laker was always pioneering new ideas.

In the 1970s his ambitions changed and he became determined 'to try a new market and offer transport to a lot more people'. At this time the only cheap air fares across the Atlantic were charter flights, whereby travellers had to be a member of some sponsoring organization for at least six months before flying. The international carriers operated a price-fixing cartel organized by the International Air Transport Association (IATA) with the connivance of all governments concerned. Charter flight regulations tended to be abused, and consequently the major carriers fought for stricter monitoring which brought about a decline. Laker conceived Skytrain, a 'no booking, no frills' operation with prices significantly below those offered by the major airlines, who naturally opposed his idea.

Laker applied to the Civil Aviation Authority (CAA) for a licence first in 1971 and was refused. In late 1972 he was given permission as long as he flew out of Stansted, although his base was at Gatwick. Delaying tactics involving British and US airlines, the UK Labour government, the US government and the American equivalent of the CAA meant that the first flight did not take place until September 1977 when Skytrain was launched with enormous publicity, this time from Gatwick. In this period oil prices had increased dramatically and Skytrain, although still under £100 for a single fare, was double the price estimated in 1971. In turn the Skytrain fare was well under half the cost of the cheapest fare offered by IATA carriers who subsequently had to reduce their fares in the face of this new competition.

Although they claimed they did this reluctantly, it had a devastating impact on Laker – who accused them of adopting a predatory pricing strategy purely to try and drive him out of business. Skytrain's competitive strategy – and apparent advantage – was its low price resulting from its low-cost base; its service package was clearly inferior to that of the major carriers. When the price gap was narrowed, Skytrain became less attractive to customers; its early competitive advantage was not sustainable.

Skytrain made £2 million profits in its first year of operation, but difficulties experienced when it was extended to Los Angeles in 1978 effectively wiped out the profitability. In 1979 Laker became a fully licensed transatlantic carrier and for the first time was able to pre-sell reserved seats. Laker's confidence grew, and anticipating that he would be given permission to fly more routes around the world he ordered ten Airbus A-300s and five McDonnell Douglas DC10s at a total cost of £300 million. Eventually this was to bring his downfall. Laker was already using DC10s for Skytrain and when the US government grounded all DC10s for checks in 1979 Laker lost £13 million in revenue. In 1980 he failed to win licences to fly Skytrain in Europe and to Hong Kong, although he did begin services from Prestwick and Manchester and to Miami.

Profits of £2.2 million were reported for 1980/81, but significantly three-quarters of this came from favourable currency movements. By 1981 the pound was falling against the dollar, demand was declining, revenue was down but the debt interest payments, mostly in dollars, were rising. There were, in effect, too many planes and not enough passengers flying the Atlantic. The major airlines wanted fares to rise, but Skytrain remained the force that kept them low. Laker did manage to renegotiate some interest payments and a cash injection from McDonnell Douglas, but he also had to increase fares and sell his Airbuses. He was left with a breakeven level of virtually all the seats on every Skytrain, but was able to fill only one-third of them. When the receiver was called in (February 1982) Laker had debts of some £270 million.

Laker had pioneered cheap transatlantic airfares, which have stayed in different guises since his collapse, but he made the mistake of becoming overconfident. The man who originally intended to stay small went for growth. At the same time he was determined to retain total control of his company and, therefore, raised loan capital against very limited assets rather than seeking outside equity funding. The interest payments brought him down, particularly as he raised most of the money in dollars without adequate cover against currency fluctuations. Finally, as something of a buccaneering character described by one airline executive as a man who 'a few hundred years ago would have brass earrings, a beard and a cutlass', he underestimated the power of the vested interests who opposed him. Had their opposition not delayed the introduction of Skytrain by six years, perhaps things would have turned out differently.

A bitter Sir Freddie moved to Florida, but by the early 1990s he was back. In 1992 he began regular flights to and from the Bahamas from his new hub; and then, in 1996, he returned to the UK with return charter flights to Gatwick from Orlando. This time he intended to compete on service as well as discounted prices – he had learned a hard lesson. He negotiated convenient take-off and landing times and offered above-normal baggage allowances. His drinks (in crystal glasses) and food (served on china with stainless steel cutlery) were to be superior to most other charter flights. Would the package prove sufficiently different and would he be able to fly his small fleet of DC-10s reliably? Yet again, all would not go smoothly and he would be criticized for flights not taking off and landing on time.

Bill Rooney

Bill Rooney (born in 1941) created and built Spring Ram kitchens and bathrooms. Once dubbed the best manufacturing company in Britain, it became crisis prone and Rooney was ousted by the institutional shareholders when it became clear that financial and stock controls had collapsed. Before starting up on his own, Rooney had worked for Cavenham Foods (owned by the entrepreneurial James Goldsmith) and Hygena Kitchens. He began in 1980 in a disused mill in West Yorkshire. At this time he had a strong minority partner, Bill Murray, who stayed with the company until 1990. Whilst Rooney was always the power behind the ideas and the marketing, Murray maintained effective controls. Murray's successor as financial director was never as able to restrain both Rooney and the business's propensity to grow.

When Murray departed Spring Ram had built a 20 per cent share of the bathrooms market (second only to Armitage Shanks) and 12 per cent of kitchens, where it was outperforming all its main rivals. There had been a mixture of organic growth and acquisitions. Pre-tax profits had been growing at an annual rate of 50 per cent whilst most rivals had seen profits decline; Spring Ram seemed to be resistant to the forces of the economic recession which was gripping Britain. Analysts concluded that Spring Ram was simply able to produce market-led products with guaranteed quality and lower prices. Its delivery times of forty-eight hours were uncharacteristically short. Its plants were heavily automated and featured the most advanced technology; Spring Ram had bought land at favourable prices and, paying only low dividends, had invested its past profits in new factories. Good at forecasting both sales and supply requirements, Spring Ram took seventy days' credit but gave its customers just twenty-eight days. The product ranges and their distribution were wide and comprehensive. The products appealed to the cost-conscious and the quality-conscious segments of the market and were available from DIY superstores, builders' merchants and specialist independent retailers. Bill Rooney and the company had accomplished a great deal and had made a number of sound decisions, but future problems were already rooted inside the business. Spring Ram had decided to expand into related products such as Artisan ceramic tiles and interior doors (Regency Doors) and again committed investments in large, new factories. With these new activities in the early 1990s, Spring Ram 'began trading without definite business plans, and without adequate appreciation of the technical, production and marketing issues surrounding the early development of a business'. In addition Stag Furniture had been acquired – realistically an unrelated product dependent largely on a separate distribution channel.

The 'bad news' began to emerge in November 1992 when it came to light that the accounts for a Spring Ram subsidiary business (Balterley Bathrooms, which had been acquired in 1986) overstated both stocks and sales. Order bookings, rather than deliveries, constituted the sales figures; and distributor returns were not being recorded. In spring 1993 Spring Ram asked for its shares to be suspended – in advance of an announcement that profits had fallen, mainly because previous result-boosting presentations in the figures had been prohibited but also because the new activities were losing money. Typically grants had been booked earlier than was legitimate; product developments costs had been recorded as assets; and depreciation was being understated. Spring Ram had always made a virtue of the way it 'motivated the entrepreneurs who ran its subsidiaries'. Rooney had always operated a very devolved structure; each subsidiary had its own directors and considerable independence. When the head office had continued to demand growth results when the housing market was clearly in recession, essential to maintain its 'good news culture', 'aggressive accounting' had become more commonplace throughout the whole business. The institutional investors pressed for Rooney's resignation. He was joined by forty of the sixty subsidiary directors and the company's auditors. Rooney commented wryly: 'There was a hiccup at the time institutional shareholders generally were getting macho.'

Despite management changes and new systems, the company has never recovered. Attempts to properly turn it around have failed. Artisan Tiles was closed in 1994; Regency Doors was sold to a competitor. Factories have closed, with resultant job losses. The housing market continues to rise and fall; Spring Ram, after all, was not recession-proof. In 1999 the business was sold to US Industries for £82 million; at its peak in 1992 the company was valued at ten times this amount.

Meanwhile, Bill Rooney, a habitual entrepreneur, has prospered. He resettled in Barbados, where he already owned property, and he has begun to develop a prestigious golf and leisure complex which is attracting both golf and media celebrities. Alongside the championship golf course are villas that sell for between US$700 000 and US$2.5 million. He has planning permission for 270 units on land he owns. He originally invested £2 million to buy 75 per cent of a sugar plantation while has was still with Spring Ram, and has subsequently bought the remainder. As well as the villas, he is building a new hotel with 950 bedrooms, the largest on the island. He has a parallel property rental organization. The villa owners typically stay in their properties for about two months every year. For a commission, Rooney organizes lets for the remaining ten months.

Estimates of Rooney's personal wealth come out at around £200 million; and three of his sons are involved with him in the property business. Again he saw an opportunity and he has made it happen. He has been able to attract wealthy British tourists to Barbados – important because Americans prefer the Bahamas. He claims to be 'the catalyst who helped restore Barbados's flagging tourist industry'. He is a popular figure there.

Gerald Ratner

The story of Ratner's recounts another business that has managed to survive the fall from grace of a high-profile entrepreneur, who has himself again made a come-back. This time the company did not suffer as significantly as did Spring Ram.

Gerald Ratner was born in 1949 and became Joint Managing Director of the family business (jewellery retailers) in 1978. By 1984 he was sole Managing Director, and Chairman in 1986. He saw a real opportunity in critical mass and in product standardization across a range of stores for low-cost, lower-quality fashion jewellery. He realized that some people, with some products, will treat jewellery as discard-able rather than a lifelong investment. A major competitor, H. Samuel, was acquired to yield the critical mass. To ensure standardization everything was sourced centrally. Staff at head office experimented with window designs and layouts, and when they were satisfied they took photographs which were sent to every branch. The exact same layout, down to the position of an individual ring on a tray, must be replicated in every branch. The business invested in advertising and promotion. Later Ratner's bought other retail outlets – such as Zales (jewellers) and Salisbury's (principally leather goods) which were acquired from Next. Ratner was very aggres-sive. 'I was a complete megalomaniac, very ambitious, very competitive. If another jeweller opened, I'd do anything to put him out of business.' The strategy worked, but it was always replicable. His rivals could follow – and some did, even if they were smaller and less profitable. He was never a major threat to the expensive and exclusive specialist, of course.

Speaking at an Institute of Directors' Conference in 1991 Gerald Ratner claimed that his company was able to sell sherry decanters at really low prices because they were 'total crap'. Ratner's continued success relied on its reputation for slickness and efficiency; denigrating his company's products in this way would prove a 'bridge too far'. The tabloid newspapers seized on the comment, were very critical and the company's previously strong image was damaged. The group name has subsequently been changed to Signet and, although the company still trades prof-itably, the name Ratner's has disappeared from the high street. Gerald himself was forced to resign, devastated by the reaction to what he saw as a light-hearted, throwaway comment.

He spent four years recovering from this setback – 'my esteem was low for a long time'. He did find work, though. One job was letting office space for a property developer in Canary Wharf. In 1996 he spotted that one of the richest towns in the country, Henley-on-Thames, did not have a health club. The sixth bank that he approached was willing to back his proposed new venture; he also had financial support from friends. Reflecting his project championing skills, he advertised for members and signed up 500 prospects before he committed himself to a lease on a warehouse he planned to convert. He planned a luxury, up-market health club

– and he knew he needed to open without delay. Once other property developers realized there was a gap in the market they might try and beat him by being first to open. He began work with a colleague/partner, who was destined to be the General Manager after it opened. In the end there were tensions, and Ratner took over control of day-to-day responsibilities. Changes to the specification were made as the conversion progressed; Ratner decided to add both a crèche and a pool. The target breakeven increased from 700 to 900 members. On the day of the official opening the complex was not completely ready, but Ratner went ahead anyway. It was reopened two months later, when it was fully complete; and very quickly the membership topped the thousand mark.

Ratner said he was determined that this time his style and approach would be more restrained. 'My ambition has gone', he claimed. Well, maybe not altogether, because he was soon talking about the prospect of opening more clubs.

Petra Doring

The story of Petra Doring and Cabouchon is different. This is the story of a business collapsing and being resurrected (legitimately) by the same entrepreneur. Cabouchon first began in 1990 without any debt financing. Petra Doring was a German-born entrepreneur with an MBA who saw an opportunity for direct sale costume jewellery, sold through catalogues and jewellery parties. She was able to establish a network of independent distributors across Europe, but mainly in England, who advertised for and recruited individuals who would work from their homes and sell in their local neighbourhood. Cabouchon main distributors were able to generate revenues of up to £200 000 a year in this way. When Cabouchon collapsed in 1998, with debts of £7 million, it was turning over £40 million a year. The company had simply not got an adequate cash flow or control systems in place. Once one of Britain's richest women, Doring was declared bankrupt at the end of 1998. There was never any suggestion that she had managed to stash away a fortune. Yet she and Cabouchon were soon to start again. Petra Doring was, of course, prohibited from being a director. The organization was officially controlled by her jewellery designer and they employed a chief executive. In fact they employed several chief executives, one after the other. People did not stay. Many of her creditors, who had lost money, were incensed, but realistically powerless. Some of the distributors were wary of signing up for a second time, but others were enthusiastic, believing that at the heart of the business was a good product. A BBC television documentary[1] featured a public relations executive who claimed she had been dismissed and was owed £10 000.

Distribution problems arose for a second time when the cash flow appeared inadequate; suppliers were pressed for extended credit. Petra Doring staged high-profile sales events to try and sign up new distributors – upon which the whole venture really depends. Strapped for cash, Doring and her designer flew to Hong Kong by using accumulated air miles in order to discuss new designs and supplies, particularly of related products such as leather wallets and handbags. Somehow, and on a real shoestring budget, the business was hanging together. The BBC documentary suggested that Petra Doring's methods were sometimes 'less than wholesome' and that many previous colleagues and distributors 'would not go near her with a barge-pole'.

The controversial entrepreneur

Bernie Ecclestone

Bernie Ecclestone is sometimes called 'Mr Formula One' to reflect his status and power in this high-profile, highly funded motor sport. His story is one of power and control. Using his project-championing skills he has 'taken over' Formula One, having realized the marketing opportunity that was always there. Without an ability to select the right people to deal with, he would not be the extraordinary fixer that he is. For all his achievements, though, he remains a controversial figure. Late in 1999 he remained the commercial rights owner for Formula One, controlling where races are held around the world and the lucrative television rights. His personal earnings from motor sport exceed £50 million per year – and he is credited with ensuring that team owners and drivers are also predominantly millionaires. Ironically he really became a public figure when he was seen to have donated £1 million to the UK Labour Party around the time when possible bans on tobacco advertising throughout Europe were under discussion. The tobacco companies are, of course, major sponsors of motor sport.

Ecclestone was born in 1930 and he is just a little over 5 feet tall. Initially a used-car dealer, but a racing driver himself in the 1950s, he went into driver management, acting as manager/agent for successful drivers such as Jochen Rindt. By the late 1970s he had become the acknowledged spokesman and representative of the constructors through the Formula One Constructors' Association (FOCA). His business partner was Max Mosley, who features prominently in this story. Following a dispute with the Formula One Association (FOA), the governing body for all motor sport, Ecclestone organized a 'pirate Grand Prix' in South Africa in 1981, which helped parachute him into a key position in the FOA. It has been argued by some commentators that his dual roles in FOCA and the FOA will always imply a conflict of interest, something he would inevitably deny. He is quoted as saying: 'You can buy anything in the world – as long as you are prepared to pay too much for it.' He has demonstrated that he is willing to take huge financial risks and then look to extract maximum advantage from his deals.

Late in the 1990s Ecclestone was looking to float his own Formula One business, really to capitalize on its potential. But he experienced a setback because of controversy over the current fifteen-year contract (1995–2010) for television rights he has with the FOA. As a background to the deal, it is important to realize that as governing body for all motorsport, and with a role of championing safety, the FOA has a need for a regular cash flow.

The story really began in 1987 when Ecclestone first brokered a deal between the television companies, the FOA, the racing teams and himself. He would control the promotion and televising of Formula One racing around the world, including race locations. Thirty per cent of the negotiated fees would go to the FOA, with the racing teams receiving 47 per cent and Ecclestone the remaining 23 per cent. At this time there was only limited interest in the sport and the contract was thought to be worth about $1 million a year to the FOA.

In 1990 the French television broadcaster involved in the contract, Canal +, experienced a number of problems and the FOA grew nervous of the existing arrangements and its potential for regular income. The 'ageing, risk-averse and pessimistic' President of the FOA, Jean-Marie Balestre, turned to Patrick McNally, a businessman who had previously worked for Marlboro (cigarettes) and who was a friend of Ecclestone. The FOA sold to McNally's Irish company (which sold space on advertising hoardings at Grand Prix circuits) its 30 per cent of the television rights in exchange for a guaranteed annual royalty. This was estimated to yield the FOA some $5.6 million in 1992 rising to $9.0 million in 1996.

But, largely thanks to Ecclestone's tireless promotion of the sport, the popularity of Formula One racing soared and Ecclestone is rumoured to have generated television income of $341 million during the 1992 to 1996 period. McNally's company, APM, thus 'made some $65 million out of the FOA'. By this time Balestre had been succeeded as President of the FOA by Max Mosley. Bernie Ecclestone was one of a number of Vice-Presidents.

Mosley decided he would once more deal directly with Bernie Ecclestone over television rights for the next contract, to cover the early years of the new millennium. For the first years of the agreement, covering 1997 to 2001, Mosley again agreed a fixed dollar royalty fee. In 1997 the FOA received its $9 million and Formula One as a whole received $225 million for television rights. To sweeten the deal, the FOA were to be given 10 per cent of the equity when Bernie Ecclestone's Formula One business was floated. Mosley is reported to believe the original 30 per cent was 'lost forever' as the teams would fight to retain their 47 per cent stake and Bernie Ecclestone could not 'run' Formula One if his income was substantially reduced. It is Ecclestone who organizes and pays for the two jumbo jets which ferry the teams and their equipment from country to country throughout the competition season and negotiates with every circuit owner.

Unfortunately the European Union Competition Commission had been alerted to the fifteen-year deal and, apparently, instinctively felt it was too long a period to keep it clear of investigation. Rumours and statements have circulated. Ecclestone has gone on record to say that all concerns 'are [or are being] dealt with'. The European Union (EU) Commission has not confirmed this view and in mid-1999 accused the organizers and promoters of Formula One of 'abusing their dominance of the sport'. The law had been broken, they suggested, in these preliminary findings. It was soon rumoured that Formula One had threatened to pull Grand Prix racing out of Europe completely if it is unduly restricted, say, through tobacco sponsorship and the accompanying advertising being outlawed. Ecclestone by this time had switched his focus from a flotation to a $2 billion Eurobond deal, but this could not realistically go ahead until the television rights (which would pay back the bonds) could be seen as guaranteed income, safe from interference by the Commission.

Two others issues or controversies are embroiled. First, through a family company in his wife's name, Ecclestone actually promotes and runs the Belgian Grand Prix at Spa. He gets to keep most of the receipts. The relevant Belgian local authority is not unhappy with the arrangement, anxious not to lose the Belgian Grand Prix to another country. Second, Ecclestone has the television rights to other motor sports under the wing of the FOA. GT sports car racing is one. Critics argue that Ecclestone's television deal deliberately holds back the sport by protecting Formula One and giving it preference for times and schedules over GT racing. Another motor sport, European truck (cabs) racing, has traditionally encouraged television coverage by making the films itself and giving them away free to any broadcaster who would use them. As a consequence, the sport's popularity has soared. Ecclestone again sought to intervene and control the deal, to the extent the existing German film-maker used by the truck racers decided to take the FOA to court, and thus provoked a threat from the FOA to cancel the races altogether. In the event, the film-maker lost the case.

During 1999 the FOA deliberately moved its headquarters out of the EU into Switzerland, and in October, Morgan Grenfell Private Equity agreed to buy a 50 per cent stake in Formula One from Ecclestone for $1.3 billion. While this partic- ular deal subsequently fell through, Ecclestone has now sold a substantial stake to a private equity firm based in San Francisco. Whatever the EU Commissioners might finally decide, some believe the downside risk is acceptable.

Dishonest entrepreneurs

Robert Maxwell

The story of Robert Maxwell is too complex to recount in full, but a number of key points show how he was a successful and extremely able entrepreneur, but uneth- ical and dishonest. Physically a big man, he had a matching ego and reputation; even in death he remains mysterious.

Maxwell was born in real poverty in a small village on the Czech-Romanian border in 1923. His real name was Jan Hoch, and he was Jewish. His father, like his father in turn, 'wheeled and dealed in cattle'. Separated from his family at the outbreak of the Second World War Jan Hoch somehow found his way to England, where he joined the Pioneer Corps. He was useful because he spoke fluent German. During the war he adopted a number of different aliases before adopting Robert Maxwell for his new name. A brave soldier, he won several promotions and deco- rations. At the end of the war he was determined to become 'rich and famous – and to belong'. He began trading scarce commodities; and in 1947 he secured a position, and later a partnership, with the German scientific publisher, Springer Verlag, which was struggling to find export markets for its scientific books and journals. Even at this time, Maxwell was always involved in several simultaneous activities, which he generally managed to separate and compartmentalize. Whilst the constant disarray that seemed to surround his activities might have suggested he was more an opportunity-spotter than a project champion, he was able to get things done. In the end, however, his business affairs became too complex.

Maxwell soon established a publishing house of his own, which he called Pergamon, and which he used to publish some of the valuable scientific work he was beginning to acquire, much of it from Russia. Breaking with Springer, after agreeing certain concessions for Pergamon, he immediately broke his agreement and poached work from his previous partner. Charging unpopular high prices for his journals, he was a millionaire by the early 1960s. He was elected as a Labour MP in 1964 but, much to his disappointment, he was not offered an immediate ministerial post. When Rupert Murdoch 'pipped him to the post' in an acquisition battle for the *News of the World* he commented that 'the British will never let me succeed'.

His first major setback came when he sought to merge Pergamon with an American publisher. Creative accounting practices which overstated profits were discovered during due diligence. The eventual outcomes were that Pergamon was sold to America, Maxwell lost his parliamentary seat and a Department of Trade and Industry (DTI) enquiry concluded that his 'fixation with his own abilities causes him to ignore the views of others . . . the concept of being responsible to a Board was alien to him . . . he could not be relied on to exercise proper stewardship of a public company'.

But he did not earn the nickname 'the bouncing Czech' for nothing. One year later (in 1974) he controlled Pergamon again, having ingratiated himself with its new owners, the Scottish Daily Express. Pergamon now grew rapidly, and on the back of its success, Maxwell first regained full ownership and then used it as collateral to acquire the leading, but troubled, printer British Printing Corporation (BPC) in 1980. The vendors commented: 'he was the greatest wheeler-dealer we'd ever met'. Although closure of this struggling business had earlier seemed a real possibility, Maxwell's autocratic and robust style quickly returned it to profit. In 1982, and allegedly bored, he began juggling and trading a whole network of businesses. Amongst other things, he bought a stake in Central Television and acquired Oxford United Football Club. In 1984, and fulfilling his dream of owning a newspaper, he bought the *Daily Mirror*. The paper was in trouble, but its owners, its employees and the Labour government (which the paper supported) all expressed dismay at the news. Despite protestations to the contrary, he interfered with the editorial policy and content. By this time, five of his seven children were working in managerial positions in one or other of his companies – but under his tight control and authority.

A bid for Waddington's (games) foundered when details emerged about the complex ownership arrangements of the companies that Maxwell controlled. It transpired that they were ultimately registered in Liechtenstein, where disclosure requirements are more limited. It did not seem to matter to Maxwell that some of these were public companies with shareholders. At his death in 1991 there were 400 registered businesses in the Maxwell empire. His companies constantly traded in each other's shares, a convenient method of moving money around and, at the same time, propping up share prices and inflating their worth.

Maxwell was now rich and famous but he still felt he was not accepted. He became even more determined to satisfy this outstanding ambition by building a global communications business. He set out to purchase the American publisher, Macmillan. Trading shares between his various businesses, he was able to boost the paper value of Maxwell Communications (the new name for BPC) and thus guarantee a bank loan for the acquisition. After his early bids were all refused, he eventually triumphed, but he had paid a very high price. 'The battle had not been about commercial sense, but over a man's place in history.' This all took place in 1988. When the cash needs of his various businesses began to soar in the following economic recession, Maxwell was forced to adopt increasingly desperate strategies. The sale of Pergamon in 1991 helped, but it was not enough. Maxwell secretly transferred shares held by the Mirror Group Pension Fund and pledged them as collateral for further loans. They did not belong to him, of course. He simply knew of their existence and whereabouts and was initially able to cover up his clandestine activity.

In 1991 a BBC *Panorama* team began to investigate some of his activities, not appreciating at first what they would uncover. They had been tipped off that his high-profile Bingo game in the Mirror was rigged to prevent anyone winning the main prize. The public was at last beginning to learn the truth about Robert Maxwell. In November 1991 his body was found floating in the sea alongside his yacht. His death has never been fully explained. It soon became apparent that his cumulative business debts were unrepayable and his empire was in a 'meltdown situation'. Once he was no longer in a position to cover up his wheeler-dealing, more and more of the facts came out.

How had he got away with it? Alongside his huge ego, he had real ability. He was able to overcome obstacles. He was also hugely charismatic and – when he wanted to be – charming. Determined and plausible, he told people what they wanted to hear, regardless of whether or not it was true. When haggling and dealing he simply made promises he had no intention of keeping. Had he been driven only by a profit motive, maybe he would have been more restrained, but he wanted, it seemed, unlimited power and prestige. His background – he never ceased to trade on his reputation for being 'a Jew who had escaped the holocaust' – and his perception that he was rejected by the British Establishment, were instrumental in his behavioural extremes. Yet he was always able to court other famous and influential people and trap them in his web. Life with Maxwell could be highly rewarded, and it was certainly exciting. Ideas flowed from him continuously, but he failed to build strong and robust businesses for all his activities. Senior managers who worked for him, and who suspected at least some of the truth, were very clearly afraid to expose him.

Nick Leeson

Rogue-trader Nick Leeson is the plasterer's son from Watford who brought down Baring's Bank. Initially a City settlement clerk, he had moved to Baring's and transferred first to Jakarta and then to Singapore in 1992. He enjoyed a 'star trader' image and reputation and he was noted for his high-risk deals. By 1994, at the age of twenty-eight, he was General Manager of Futures Trading for Baring's in Singapore. Convinced the currently depressed Japanese market was about to turn the corner and start to rise, he began investing heavily. His guess was wrong, and the Japanese market actually continued to fall. Leeson increased his investment – some would say naïvely – still believing in the upswing. Dealer losses are not, of course, unusual in this speculative business – the problem here was that he had no trouble covering up the truth about his predicament. Unusually, he was allowed by Baring's to control his own 'back office' where all the deals were settled, and where he simply set up dummy client accounts into which money was able to disappear. He was empowered with too much freedom and he exploited it. He deceived his employer. Of course, if the market had turned upwards, Baring's would have made huge profits and Leeson would have been in line for a substantial bonus. In the event, he was regarded as a criminal and not a hero of the dealing floor.

In January 1995 an earthquake in the Kobe and Osaka regions caused the Japanese market to plunge even further and very rapidly. At last it came to light that Leeson had accumulated losses of $1.3 billion, over twice the level of reserves held by Baring's. Leeson went on the run with his wife, but he was caught in Germany, extradited back to Singapore and sentenced to a period of imprisonment for fraud and perjury. Now released he is able to earn money for his story, and he may have managed to stash away some money. At the same time, he has suffered from colon cancer during his spell in jail and his wife has divorced him.

The world of crime

Nick Leeson became dishonest as he became increasingly desperate; Robert Maxwell turned from unethical and questionable practice to dishonesty in his increasingly desperate attempts to save his cracking business empire. In this section we look at a different group of dishonest entrepreneurs – those for whom crime is their business. Entrepreneurs have long been a feature of criminal fiction. Arguably both Sherlock Holmes and James Bond possessed a number of obvious entrepreneur life themes; and many of James Bond's adversaries were unquestionably entrepreneurs. Auric Goldfinger, for example, was an opportunity-spotter and a project champion. He did not intend to steal the gold from Fort Knox – he would never have been able to move it all! Instead, he planned to contaminate it with a small nuclear device. If it were untouchable for several years, his own stock of gold would increase in value. Poisoning the guards with spray from light aircraft – to facilitate the break-in – was creative and innovative.

In the story of *The Godfather* we can again see clear evidence of entrepreneurship. The story is about Mafia control of rackets, gambling, bookmaking and labour unions. The Godfather himself, Don Vito Corleone, carefully avoids drugs – 'society does not accept drugs as readily as it does liquor, gambling and prostitution.' The family-based network of contacts brings in all the necessary resources – and there is superb succession planning. The profit orientation is clearly visible. Things are made to happen; setbacks are not allowed. Anything or anyone who stands in the way of the Godfather is dealt with. There are no barriers that cannot be surmounted.

The Godfather is a popular book and movie. People even feel sympathy for the Don, because there is visible evidence of worldly wisdom, insight and relative good in activity that is fundamentally evil. And, is it wholly fictional? The Mafia exists. Moreover, it is not the only manifestation of organized crime. Successful criminals are invariably successful entrepreneurs. To spot a criminal opportunity – and to carry it out successfully – needs an entrepreneur with project-championing skills. It implies someone with strong entrepreneurial life themes who simply chooses to deploy these talents in illegal acts. In addition, legitimate businesses have to learn how to deal with both organized crime and more random corruption if they wish to trade with many developing – and some developed – countries in the world. It has been estimated that at the very least, European and American businesses spent $45 billion on dealing with criminal activity and corrupt officials in 1998 alone.

Sometimes, of course, entrepreneurial criminals are countered by equally talented entrepreneurs working on the side of law and order. The true story of Al Capone (who found his most valuable opportunity in bootlegging and illicit brewing during the years of prohibition in America) and Eliot Ness is an excellent illustration of this point.

Al Capone and Eliot Ness

In the late 1920s Al Capone was one of the best-known, most feared and most successful criminals in America. 'His power in the Chicago area was as awesome as his intrinsic cruelty.' Involved in a wide range of criminal activities, most notably his illicit brewing, he nevertheless wanted to be seen as a legitimate businessman. Somewhat ironically, he was recruited by the President of the Chicago Crime Commission to ensure an honest mayoral election in a local county. In accomplishing this Capone, achieved something most observers had believed was an impossible task. Outraged at being labelled 'Public Enemy Number One', in the Depression he opened a soup kitchen for people without jobs. He was an entrepreneur as well as a crook. He understood profit. But to call him a social entrepreneur would not be realistic. It took three other enterprising men, and a series of creative and innovative moves, to finally bring him to justice.

Eliot Ness was totally focused and dedicated to the fight against organized crime and in 1928 he was invited to focus his energies on defeating Capone. He had been born in 1903, the son of a Norwegian immigrant who had become an entrepreneur in the bakery business. After graduating in business and law, he surprised his family and friends by choosing a career in federal law enforcement. Apparently he had 'always admired the resourceful, albeit fictional, Sherlock Holmes'. To some he was an egomaniac who craved attention – but the more popular view is that he was motivated by risk, excitement and danger. Taking on the most ruthless criminals provided the ideal opportunity for him to prosper.

The arrogant and egocentric Capone felt he was outside the grasp of the law. The city law enforcement officials in Chicago were not actively seeking his prosecution. They tolerated his activity – after all, most of them were on his payroll. The President, Herbert Hoover, however, had a different view, and in an enterprising move, chose to target Capone for federal offences and ignore city and state issues. Capone was leading an extravagant lifestyle and appeared to be wealthy – yet he had no apparent means of support and had not filed an income tax return for several years. The Federal authorities believed that this offence, together with his bootlegging activities – both Federal offences – could be used to nail him.

Employed by the Federal Prohibition Bureau, Ness was invited to build a team of agents to tackle Capone – a group that became known as 'The Untouchables'. Every member of this team had to be unquestionably honest and reliable – as well as dedicated and brave. Whilst Ness's Untouchables started to look for the illegal breweries, the Internal Revenue Service (IRS) officials started digging for firm evidence of his real sources of income. There were, in fact, over twenty breweries yielding a weekly sales revenue in excess of $1.5 million. Hard liquor, purchased from the Mafia, was also being delivered through Capone's extensive distribution system. Ness started to gather information via phone tapping, but on his first brewery raid, the staff managed to escape. It had taken too long to break through the security protection system. Undeterred, and learning from this experience, Ness fixed a snowplough on to the front of a ten-ton truck and ram-raided the other breweries he was able to identify. His approach was that of the 'Wild West frontier lawman'.

At the same time, Elmer Irey, senior IRS investigator, managed to implant two undercover agents in Capone's organization; and they were able to gather priceless intelligence. At the time, this was seen as a remarkable achievement. Ness then deliberately baited Capone by publicly parading the forty-five brewery trucks he had systematically captured and impounded. Capone's brewing empire was being destroyed and he seemed unable to counter Ness's daring and enterprise. As his breweries closed and his income fell he had fewer resources for bribing key officials.

Meanwhile, and due largely to the leads provided by the undercover agents, sufficient evidence was gathered to bring Capone to trial for several counts of tax evasion. A wholly successful prosecution could net him a thirty-four year jail sentence, but this looked very optimistic. A confident Al Capone and his lawyers attempted to plea bargain for a confession and light sentence. He even let it be known he was discussing the script for a movie of his life. The government was actually willing to accept the proposed deal – but Judge James Wilkerson was not, and the trial went ahead. Demonstrating his enterprise, and exploiting his network of contacts, Al Capone was able to bribe every prospective juror sequestered for the case. The equally enterprising judge – when he heard rumours of this achievement – waited until the very last moment and then switched juries with a fellow judge who was trying a similar case. Capone was found guilty and sentenced to eleven years' imprisonment. Already ill with syphilis, he 'finally emerged from jail little more than a cabbage'. His career was over.

Having made his contribution, Eliot Ness later took over – and systematically cleaned up – the corrupt and apparently incompetent police force in Cleveland, Ohio, another haven for gangsters. Again he was able to build a team of trusted undercover agents who were dedicated to the task in hand. Eliot Ness clearly possessed many leadership life themes, but he was an entrepreneur because he made a difference by being different. His tactics – his daring raids on illegal gambling joints and his willingness to go head to head with the most hardened criminals – were innovative and imaginative. He was always an above-average risk-taker as his life was constantly in danger – but he was able to cope with this.

The next two stories of less well-known contemporary criminal entrepreneurs are merely indicative of this active sector.

James Munroe

In 1999 James Munroe launched a new motor racing team in the UK at a well-publicized and lavish press reception. Apparently a multimillionaire, he actually worked in the finance department at publishers, McGraw-Hill. Munroe had set up a series of companies, which were regularly sending invoices to McGraw-Hill, where he was in a position to ensure they were paid. Estimates for his scam varied from £2 million to £3 million. Initially he used the money to fund a lavish personal lifestyle before moving on to racing car ownership. He courted publicity for his racing activities and was featured in magazines and on television. He was also noted for organizing lavish corporate hospitality events, which he did in his spare time through one of his illegally funded companies.

Martin Frankel

In September 1999, America's most wanted financial fugitive, Martin Frankel, was arrested in a Hamburg hotel, 'surrounded by a bank of computers, a bag of diamonds and a female accomplice'. Previously at odds with the regulatory authorities, Frankel had managed to set up a bogus securities business that he ran from his house in Connecticut. He had been able to obtain control of eight small insurance companies – across six Southern states – and then siphon money from these businesses, apparently as legitimate investments in funds he managed. His capture came down to a lucky tip-off; he had effectively escaped the detection of the Federal Bureau of Investigation (FBI).

George Reynolds

Our final story concerns a criminal who changed. George Reynolds manufactures chipboard in County Durham. He is a reformed criminal who now uses his entrepreneurial talents for more legitimate – and lucrative – ends. Sixty-three years old in 1999 he was born in Sunderland; his father was a deep-sea fisherman. He describes himself as 'dyslexic, illiterate, backward and brainless'. The first may be true, and the second partially correct, but he is neither backward nor brainless. His childhood was deprived, and he followed years in institutional care with three jail sentences, the last for safe-breaking. In prison he was a 'bootlegger and bookmaker, lucky not to be caught'. A trigger happened during his last jail sentence when a Catholic priest asked him: 'If you are such a good thief, how is it you were caught yet again?' The priest suggested he should go into business, and he heeded the advice. It turned out to be good advice; Reynolds does possess strong entrepreneur life themes.

Borrowing money from his mother (which he was initially able to supplement with some illegally earned savings) he opened an ice cream business, a nightclub and a shop before he began manufacturing. As well as chipboard (which he started in 1981) he has an engineering business and a share in a shipping company. Worth over £250 million, he also owns Darlington Football Club. His managers work closely together with no secretaries – a 'type of prisoner cameraderie'. Long hours are the norm and Reynolds is proud of his reputation for being a fast and decisive decision-maker. Employee discipline is tight, misdemeanours are fined but the rewards are high. Reynolds is reputed to be a tough negotiator and 'intolerant of suppliers who let him down'. One close colleague comments: 'In 1981 he would have made rash decisions ... now he makes devastating decisions ... he has learned a lot.'

In this chapter we have looked at a wide range of entrepreneurs who operate in the shadows. Some are unlucky, some are rash and overreach themselves – but others are dishonest. In the context of talent, temperament and technique we have seen a number of cases where an overabundance of certain aspects of temperament – a particularly strong ego and a real desire for recognition, for example – mean that, on the one hand, natural talents are not exploited as effectively as they might be and, on the other hand, important techniques and controls are ignored. The relative weightings of talent, temperament and technique are simply inappropriate. In every case we have considered, the mistakes were realized and a penalty was paid. There are many similar stories that have passed largely unreported, and other entrepreneurs whose crimes and misdemeanours have so far not been detected. Sometimes these people are colourful, fun characters; on other occasions they are, to some degree, evil. They will always exist. They will always find opportunities. For them, shadowy or even illegal behaviour becomes unsuppressible. But we must never make things too easy for them by misjudging the controls we need.

In the next two chapters we consider two related sectors where entrepreneurs have flourished: Silicon Valley, where we look at its history and development as a powerful cluster of entrepreneurial activities, followed by the new Internet entrepreneurs who are constantly realizing new opportunities. Although we do not develop the issue, the World Wide Web has spawned shadowy activity as well as bringing many positive developments. There are several pornography millionaires and 'piracy on a scale not seen since Long John Silver rode the waves'.

Note

1. *Trouble At The Top*, screened on BBC2 on 10 March 1999.

8 The entrepreneurs of Silicon Valley

Silicon Valley is unique. Although the computer industry has emerged and developed in different places, and not exclusively in America, we typically think of Silicon Valley as its natural home. This story of the entrepreneurs who have started up and grown both computer and semi-conductor businesses in this part of California shows how a community or region can become a collective entrepreneur – where the whole region behaves as if it was itself an entrepreneur. It also demonstrates the potential synergy when ideas, finance and talented people come together.

In principle we believe that all regions have this potential because of the entre-preneurial talent that resides within its inhabitants. But just as this talent can lie buried within the individual entrepreneur, so it can also remain dormant within a community. Silicon Valley is the story of a number of individual entrepreneurs who were able to produce an environment that stimulated the emergence of entre-preneurial talent and, most importantly, attracted more of this same talent into the area.

The Silicon Valley story is not just about *individual entrepreneurs,* important though they were. It is also about the development of *mechanisms* and *infrastructure* within an *opportunity setting.* When these factors were focused to serve the entrepreneurs in the community the collective entrepreneur was formed.

Regions that attempt to replicate the Silicon Valley experience often fail because the *mechanisms* and *infrastructure* that have been put in place have not been within an *opportunity setting,* nor has there been a strong focus on encouraging and serving the *entrepreneurs.* These issues are dealt with in Part Three of this book; our purpose now is to show how they combined in a small valley just south of San Francisco so that within one generation a vibrant economy was generated. Silicon Valley is an example of what happens when a community taps into its well of entre-preneurial talent – it simply takes off!

The industrial milieu or district itself can be seen as a community or collec-tive entrepreneur with not only firms, but inter-firm associations, worker organizations, financial institutions and government agencies also playing important roles.

(Malecki, 1997 – an economic geographer)

There is nowhere else in the world we could have started this company. Silicon Valley is an attitude. We found risk capital, we found suppliers and vendors who wanted us to succeed and we found people with an attitude that made us succeed.

(James Treybig, founder of Tandem Computers,
quoted in Larson and Rogers, 1986)

Silicon Valley is different from anything else I've experienced. It's like Florence must have been at the Renaissance. It's where all the bright minds are coming together and it's a place where wonderful things are going to happen.

(Corporate head-hunter Gerry Roche, Chairman,
Heidrick and Struggles Inc., quoted in Sculley, 1987)

The issues behind the story

The entrepreneurs

'Without Fred Terman Silicon Valley might never have happened' (Larson and Rogers, 1986.) Fred Terman of Stanford University, first as professor of radio engineering in 1926 and subsequently as Provost and Vice-President in the 1950s, was a key figure in the early days of Silicon Valley. He always encouraged his students to go into business, personally playing the role of coach to a generation of potential entrepreneurs, that included Bill Hewlett and Dave Packard. The now world famous Hewlett-Packard company began life in 1938 in a garage with money loaned by Fred Terman. In 1951 Fred Terman founded what became the Stanford Research Park.

'Without Bell Labs there would be no Silicon Valley' (Arno Penzias, Vice-President of Bell Laboratories, quoted in Larson and Rogers, 1986). Certainly it was at Bell Labs in New Jersey that Bill Shockley co-invented the transistor, but it was his decision to set up his new company in Palo Alto in Silicon Valley that brought the technology of the silicon chip to the area.

The 'Traitorous Eight' (Jackson, 1998) were eight young engineers who left Shockley's new company after a year to form Fairchild Semiconductor. Amongst these eight were entrepreneurs Bob Noyce and Gordon Moore who were later to found Intel Corporation, the world's leading manufacturer of microprocessors for personal computers.

From this point on the entrepreneurs seem to emerge all over Silicon Valley. Among the legendary names are Steve Jobs of Apple Computers, Gene Amdahl of the Amdahl Corporation, Nolan Bushnell of Atari, Jerry Saunders of AMD, Larry Ellison of Oracle, John Chambers of Cisco and Scott McNealy of Sun Microsystems. Other legends are still being made – like Linus Torvalds, who, at the age of twenty-one and when still in his native Finland, wrote the Linux operating system for personal computers. Torvalds now lives and works in Silicon Valley. What makes

Torvalds different is the fact that he is essentially an inventor who is more concerned with achievement than a personal fortune. He has made his system freely available through the Internet; around the world a team of like-minded technocrats continue to work on refinements and developments – all without charge.

The mechanisms

From the very early days, two essential mechanisms – spin-offs and networking – have operated consistently in Silicon Valley

Spin-offs occur when an individual or team leaves an existing business or institution to set up a new business. Thus Fairchild Semiconductor was a spin-off from Shockley Laboratories when the 'Traitorous Eight' left to form their own company. An effective spin-off mechanism comprises a number of *spin-off points*, which generate a flow of new companies. We can identify three major spin-off points for Silicon Valley:

- Stanford University as early as 1912
- Fairchild Semiconductor in the 1960s
- the Home Brew Computer Club in the 1970s.

From the 1980s onward the process of new business generation was self-sustaining as spin-offs begat spin-offs. We elaborate later on how these spin-off points worked, but it is important to note that these three spin-off points were sufficient to get the ball rolling. This is because each was able to produce a further stream of spin-offs that multiplied themselves.

Networking is a second important mechanism. This developed naturally around people like Fred Terman and his students and then around the companies they formed. Silicon Valley, particularly in the early days, was like a big village where people networked easily. As time went on informal groups like the Home Brew Computer Club were formed. The main talking point in these networks was the latest technology, so that they served as a very effective way of transferring and dispersing technical information. 'If a Home Brew member knew about a secret chip design at Intel, he'd be happy to share the details' (Rose, 1989).

Networking also encouraged the spin-off process as ideas were born and developed. 'The Fairchild spin-offs were often projected, discussed and decided in a nearby restaurant in Mountain View, Walker's Wagon Wheel Bar and Grill, frequented by the company's engineers' (Castells and Hall, 1994).

The infrastructure

The most important part of the infrastructure in the Silicon Valley story is Stanford University itself, but the development of part of the land owned by the university as a research park in 1951 was crucial in stimulating and supporting the entrepreneurial activities. Venture capitalists then moved into the area in the early 1960s and grew steadily, so that by the 1980s they were a major part of the infrastructure. They had enough money available to be able to support the growth of significant businesses – this story is not just about small business start-ups. These Californian venture capitalists have typically contributed far more than dollars and cheques to the growth of Silicon Valley. They have provided expert advice on strategy, recruitment and future financing.

As early as the 1950s, major clients and a network of subcontractors began to develop as the Lockheed Missiles and Space Company set up in Northern California and the US Defense Department placed major contracts for semiconductors. IBM and Xerox also moved into the area and enhanced the research base.

Whilst a major university and research park, venture capital companies, customers and subcontractors were all key parts of the infrastructure, it was really the bars and restaurants that grew up in Silicon Valley that enabled a community of entrepreneurs to develop. This we see as the distinguishing mark of Silicon Valley and it is the part that is so often missed by those who try to replicate what happened. It was in these places, the bars and the restaurants, that the entrepreneurs met – those who were already in business and those who were thinking about it. There was a cross-fertilization of ideas and opportunity as entrepreneurs and the engineers talked together. These meeting places were essential to the development of networks and the building of an entrepreneurial community and formed an important part of the infrastructure.

The opportunity

Silicon Valley owes its remarkable growth to two technological opportunities. The general background to both was electronics, in which Stanford University had a strong reputation; but it was the silicon chip and the personal computer (including its software) that provided the two key opportunities. Although the Internet is now providing a new impetus, it was these earlier opportunities that enabled Silicon Valley to become what it is today.

The transistor had been co-invented by Shockley, who moved to Silicon Valley in 1955. Two years later Bob Noyce at Fairchild Semiconductor patented the integrated circuit. These inventions resulted in the first wave of companies whose business was built around the silicon chip that was to give the valley its name.

The second wave came out of Intel when Ted Hoff invented the microprocessor in 1971 and began the personal computer industry. This led to opportunities in software, computer games and now the Internet.

Without these opportunities and their enormous commercial potential Silicon Valley would not be what it is today, namely the largest concentration of technology-based businesses in the world, with an economy greater than that of many a nation. Nevertheless, there have been disappointments and setbacks amongst the many successes. 'Silicon Valley probably produces more spin-offs than it really should. Whilst it's great to believe that anything is possible, anything ISN'T possible. But [this belief] allows some things that are possible to be realized more quickly than they otherwise would be.'

The Silicon Valley story

If you drive south down the main highway from San Francisco, in just over half an hour, depending on traffic conditions, you will come to Palo Alto and Menlo Park. This is the start of Silicon Valley and the home of Stanford University and Hewlett-Packard. The next thirty to forty miles are all Silicon Valley, with place names that will be heard later in the story. Mountain View, the home of Fairchild Semiconductor, Sunnyvale, where there were almost 800 electronic firms in 1982, Cupertino, the home of Apple Computers and Santa Clara, Intel's headquarters. At the south end of the valley is San Jose, an urban sprawl that has now spread out to extend the valley further.

Had you driven this route in 1950, you would simply have been heading for Santa Clara County, then acknowledged to be the prune capital of America. You would have seen orchards and an agricultural community. There would have been some electronic firms around in those days; indeed there were spin-offs from Stanford happening as early as 1912. Hewlett-Packard, which was formed in 1938, would also have been there – but these were all small activities compared with what was about to happen.

There are many strands that continue throughout the story of Silicon Valley, but it is possible to identify four discrete periods, each of which moved the economic activity into a higher gear. The first period takes us to the mid-1950s and lays important foundations. The second period brings the silicon chip to the valley, and the first real economic growth is seen. It was at the end of this second period in 1971 that Don Hoefler of Microelectronics News coined the name 'Silicon Valley'. The third period from 1972 to 1985 saw the arrival of the personal computer and this is when the economy really took off. By the end of this period more people were employed in this sector than in any other. Since 1986 companies like Intel and Sun Microsystems have become world leaders and the arrival of the Internet in the early 1990s has stimulated the emergence of a new generation of entrepreneurs.

Each period built on the previous one, such that the accumulative effect was truly remarkable. In 1959 around 7000 people worked in high technology; by 1970 this number had increased to some 52 000; and by 1980 the total was close to 180 000. Hewlett-Packard, the oldest Silicon Valley company, has remained ahead of the pack, and was the largest company in 1998 with sales of $47 billion. Intel was second, with sales of over $26 billion. In third place was Sun Microsystems, which produces servers and high-performance workstations. Oracle (world leader in database software) was fifth, with the Apple Corporation still in seventh place despite several setbacks. Two key Internet companies, Cisco and 3Com, were in fourth and ninth places respectively (*San Jose Mercury News*, 1999).

The foundation period: 1930s to 1955

In reality it is difficult to say when this period actually began because electronics was always a subject of interest in Stanford University. In 1909 a Stanford graduate set up Poulson Wireless Telephone and Telegraph Company in Palo Alto. It was funded by the school's President and based on a wireless telephone invented by a local teenager. A year later two engineers spun-off from Poulson's and founded Magnavox to exploit a loudspeaker they had invented (Rose, 1989). In 1912, Lee de Forest, a researcher at Poulson's, by then renamed the Federal Telegraph Company, discovered that the vacuum tube could be used to amplify an electrical signal. This proved to be a discovery of profound significance to the future development of electronics. With this level of invention and innovation happening, and with professors such as Harris Ryan, who was in many ways similar to Fred Terman, it is perhaps surprising that more progress was not made at that time. But the situation was some way from reaching critical mass and it took a further thirty years before things began to move.

It is from this background of opportunity that the hero of the Silicon Valley story, Fred Terman, emerged. Terman was born into an academic family. His father was a professor of psychology at Stanford College (as it was known in the 1920s) with a special interest in gifted children. Terman Sr developed the world's first IQ test; and its use in the evaluation of two million American service personnel in the First World War made it famous. The academic yet practical approach of his father is something that Fred Terman always exemplified. He studied chemistry and electrical engineering at Stanford, graduating in 1920. It would appear that he caught something of the entrepreneurial approach at Stanford and was aware of the way in which electronics companies were being set up from the university.

Terman's next step took him east, to the research excellence of the Massachusetts Institute of Technology (MIT). Here he studied for his PhD under Vannevar Bush, an outstanding academic who was also closely involved with industry and was later to be one of the four founders of the renowned electronics company, Raytheon Corporation, as well as becoming the Vice-President of MIT. In many ways, as we shall see, Terman himself emulated his mentor, Bush. For both men, research excellence and commercial application always went together, each reinforcing the other.

But for an event in 1924, Fred Terman may have stayed on at MIT and 'left his footprints' there. Perhaps he would have become the father of the high-technology developments along Route 128 in Boston, rather than of Silicon Valley. There were, of course, others who could – and did – make Route 128 happen, but only one person was available in Silicon Valley, and that was Fred Terman. This came about in a remarkable way.

After completing his PhD Terman accepted a professorship at MIT but returned home to Stanford for a vacation before he took up his new post. It was whilst he was at home that he contracted tuberculosis, which in those days was a very serious illness. It put Terman out of action for a year, at the end of which he decided it would be better for his health if he stayed in the warmer climate of California. Consequently he took the position of Professor of Radio Engineering at Stanford University. Apart from a spell at MIT working on a military project during the Second World War, Terman then spent his whole career at Stanford University, rising to the position of Provost and Vice-President.

Fred Terman was no ordinary man. He was a visionary leader with an entrepreneurial heart. Terman influenced people to think in a different way – he set his students thinking about having their own business, based around the technology that he was teaching them in the classroom. His student laboratory became a place where students could put their ideas into practice. When Bill Hewlett, later of Hewlett-Packard fame, was a student he built a portable radio transmitter and receiver in this laboratory.

This 'maybe I could be an entrepreneur attitude' that Terman instilled was to permeate the thinking of Silicon Valley. Bob Noyce, who co-founded Intel, came to Silicon Valley from the East Coast in 1956, and caught this same thinking. 'Suddenly it became apparent to people like myself, who had always assumed that they would be working for a salary for the rest of their lives, that they could get some equity in a start-up company. That was a great revelation and a great motivation too' (Hanson, 1982).

Fred Terman's contribution to Silicon Valley is often measured in what he achieved, most notably in helping Hewlett-Packard to get started and then in establishing the Stanford Research Park. Whilst we discuss these achievements we believe that his greatest contribution was in getting academics and students to think differently – to think entrepreneurially. He made entrepreneurship both academically respectable and socially acceptable. In that way he started to 'dig the well' so that the entrepreneurial talent in the community could be tapped and developed.

Terman assumed that the argument between pure and applied research was over, and that subjects like engineering had to be linked with the world of industry. He therefore concentrated on what to him was the next logical step, which was spinning-off businesses from the university and the technology that it was developing. It is important to remind ourselves that this was in the 1920s and 1930s, and that Silicon Valley was grown on this foundation. Similar experiences around MIT, with Route 128, and Cambridge University in the UK, with the 'Cambridge Phenomenon', demonstrate that research excellence and commercial application are friends and not enemies, and also that spin-offs from the university sector can generate an entrepreneurial culture.

We now turn to consider Fred Terman's role in Hewlett-Packard and in the Stanford Research Park. The Hewlett-Packard Company (H-P) is the classic Silicon Valley story of two young men who start their business in a garage and become millionaires. Bill Hewlett and Dave Packard met at Stanford in 1931 and their shared interest in ham radio took them to Fred Terman's classes. Terman got to know his students well and encouraged their interest in starting their own business. The opportunity came in 1938, four years after they had graduated, when Terman arranged fellowships for them so that they could return for a further year at Stanford. It was at this time that they set up a small workshop in a garage behind their lodging house, no doubt developing various electronic gadgets. The real product opportunity came from Hewlett's end of year project to build and evaluate a variable frequency oscillator using some of the novel ideas Terman had presented in his lectures. The result was a device that was better than others that were available commercially and which cost just one-tenth of the price. Terman encouraged Hewlett to join up with Packard to exploit this opportunity and organized the finance of around $1500 to get them started. After a shaky first year they landed a big order from Walt Disney Studios to build eight audio oscillators to produce the soundtrack for the film *Fantasia*. In 1940 they were able to move to larger premises and by 1942 their annual sales reached $1 million.

The Second World War helped H-P to grow steadily. By 1950 they had doubled their sales to about $2 million and employed 200 people. Whilst this does not compare with the spectacular growth of some later Silicon Valley companies, H-P was still in business and well set for the future. By the mid-1980s things had really taken off. They employed almost 70 000 people worldwide and had sales of $4.4 billion. More importantly, they were the role model for other Silicon Valley companies. The 'H-P Way' of suits, ties and professionalism might be ridiculed by some, but their personnel policies which provided stock options and other employee benefits were copied by many and is the reason why there are more millionaires per head of population in Silicon Valley than anywhere else in the world.

Fred Terman had few doubts about the talents of Hewlett and Packard. As their coach and mentor he commented,

> any place in which you put them in a new environment they somehow learned what they needed to know very quickly . . . at a really superior level. So when they got into business they didn't need a teacher; they somehow learned as they went along. They always learned faster than the problems built up.
>
> (Brown, 1973)

Hewlett-Packard was not the only company that Terman helped to get on the road, but it is by far the most well known and, obviously, was important to him and to them. In 1977 Hewlett and Packard made a donation to Stanford University of almost $10 million for the construction of the Frederick Terman Engineering Center.

Fred Terman's masterstroke, however, was the founding of the Stanford Research Park, an opportunity that owes much to the history of Stanford University itself. The university and the land that surrounds it, is the result of a bequest by the parents of Leland Stanford Jr, who tragically died of typhoid in 1884, when he was just fifteen years old. His father was a self-made man who had risen from being a grocer selling food to the hungry miners of the Gold Rush days, to the position of Governor of California during America's Civil War. He was a man of vision who was involved in the completion of the transcontinental railway. Although motivated by the death of his son, the establishment of the Leland Stanford Jr University was also a visionary step, without which the Silicon Valley story would not even have started.

Stanford left the whole of his 8800-acre estate to the university with the stipulation that it would never be sold. In the late 1940s Fred Terman, now Vice-President, and Wallace Sterling, the President, were considering how they could move Stanford up into the university superleague to be comparable with places like MIT. It may be that Terman's time at MIT during the Second World War made him see the need for such a strategy. Within the American university system the answer was a simple one – you needed enough money to attract the best people. The only asset that Terman and Sterling could turn to was the land around the university, but this was not able to be sold, and so they did the next best thing, which was to lease the land. They decided to designate 655 acres of their land as an industrial park. Industrial estates were not new, but what was novel here was the use of the word 'park' and its proximity to a university. As Terman himself put it, 'this idea of an industrial park near a university was completely foreign'.

When it was realized that such a park could promote technology transfer and stimulate university research, the name was changed to the Stanford Research Park. The first company on the park in 1951 was Varian Associates, itself a Stanford spin-off which had Terman as a board member. Their deal of $4000 per acre for a ninety-nine year lease on four acres has been criticized as a 'give-away', but companies in those days were not 'falling over themselves' to come on to the park and it was important to get at least one tenant. The real breakthrough came three years later in 1954 when Hewlett-Packard took a lease and made the park their head-quarters. Hewlett-Packard became an excellent reference site that could explain the advantages of being close to the university. By 1955 the park had seven compa-nies, and growth continued steadily rather than dramatically. By 1960 there were thirty-two companies and by 1970 there were seventy companies. By the mid-1980s the park was full with ninety companies in all.

The Stanford Research Park became an important flagship for Silicon Valley and the companies it attracted played an important part in building the attitudes and level of research competence that typifies the valley. The next period in the devel-opment of Silicon Valley would almost certainly not have taken place had a division of Beckman Instruments not moved in to the park.

The silicon chip period: 1956 to 1970

In 1956, British-born Dr William Shockley received a Nobel Prize for Physics and set up his own company, Shockley Semiconductor Laboratory, in Silicon Valley. Shockley shared the Nobel Prize with two colleagues for their invention, nine years earlier, of a small device called a transistor. A transistor is an electronic switch that uses the semiconducting properties of certain materials such as silicon. The tran-sistor did the same job as an electronic valve but was more than 100 times smaller, more reliable and used much less power. This was the key invention that opened up the world of electronics to a mass of applications that today we take for granted. It has been called 'the major invention of the century'. Bill Shockley was the leader of the team at the world-renowned Bell Laboratories (Bell Labs) in New Jersey that developed this fundamental device.

His own business came about when he left Bell Labs in 1954 to exploit his inven-tion. His first thought was to set up in the Boston area, but the larger firms there, such as Raytheon, were not interested, and so he looked elsewhere. Palo Alto in Silicon Valley was his second choice. It was his hometown and where his mother still lived. On the business side there was also an important connection. Shockley's former chemistry professor at the California Institute of Technology, Arnold Beckman, had a division of his company on the Stanford Research Park. Beckman, who had spun off a successful business just as Shockley planned to do, was keen to help Shockley get started and provided him with financial backing.

The Shockley Semiconductor Laboratory was set up in Mountain View, in Silicon Valley, in 1956. Shockley's reputation enabled him to attract high-quality staff, some of whom came across America from the East Coast to join him. In this first year, as they were setting the research direction of the new company, a major disagree-ment arose. Eight of the team wanted to work on silicon transistors and saw this as the way forward. Shockley strongly disagreed and insisted on imposing his own views, namely that they should concentrate on diodes. The eight who Shockley was to call the 'Traitorous Eight' (Jackson, 1998) decided to ignore Shockley and do their own thing. They approached a wealthy businessman on the East Coast, Sherman Fairchild, with their ideas. He backed them to the tune of $1.5 million in setting up Fairchild Semiconductor in 1957, as a subsidiary of his Fairchild Camera and Instrument Company.

Shockley Semiconductor never recovered from this defection and was eventually closed down. Shockley took an endowed professorship at Stanford in 1964. Fairchild Semiconductors, on the other hand, went from strength to strength. In 1959 one of the 'Eight', Robert Noyce, later of Intel fame, put forward his ideas of having more than one transistor on a small piece or chip of silicon and so came up with the 'integrated circuit'. In 1960, another of the 'Eight', Jean Hoerni, invented a manufacturing process that significantly increased the efficiency of silicon chip production. This made true volume production possible and put Fairchild well ahead of the competition. With these innovations, Fairchild soon established itself as a leading semiconductor company. The timing was also right as the American space programme was getting under way, spurred on by the success of the then USSR. In 1957 the Soviets succeeded in putting man's first satellite into space to orbit the earth. Spending by NASA and the American Defense Department effectively bankrolled the dramatic growth of companies like Fairchild, by funding their research and development and paying them well for the products they produced.

Whilst this gave Fairchild and the rest of Silicon Valley its financial and commercial impetus, something equally important was happening – a network of spin-off companies was developing out of Fairchild and spreading across the valley. Somehow Fairchild just replicated its own origins as a spin-off from Shockley Semiconductor. In 1961, just four years after leaving Shockley, four of the original 'Eight', including Hoerni, moved on to found Anelco. In 1964 Hoerni left Anelco to found Union Carbide Electronics, and moved on once more in 1967 to Intersil.

This spin-off from spin-off characterized Fairchild. By 1965 there had been ten spin-offs and in 1967 they experienced the same kind of treatment that they had given to Shockley. Their key manufacturing specialist left to form National Semiconductor. Not only did he 'hire away busloads of his former colleagues' (Jackson, 1998) he established a serious competitor. The spin-off process still continued so that now about half of America's semiconductor firms are either direct or indirect spin-offs from Fairchild (Larson and Rogers, 1986; Saxenian, 1990). Many young engineers would get their first a job in the industry at Fairchild and then move on. Larson and Rogers (1986) report a conference of semiconductor engineers held in Silicon Valley in 1969 at which 'less than two dozen of the 400 present had never worked for Fairchild'. Amongst the many passing in and out of Fairchild were some with entrepreneurial ambitions, and the conditions were right for them to at least try. An entrepreneurial culture was beginning to take root.

Intel is perhaps the most famous spin-off from Fairchild. Intel's origins lie in the deal by which Sherman Fairchild put his money in to found the company. If the company succeeded then he had the right to buy out the eight founders at $300 000 each. He exercised this right in 1959 when the company was just two years old. Whilst this gave the eight some real money, it took away their stake in the company and meant they were no longer in control. After a while this began to tell and in due course six of the original eight founders left to start their own businesses. The two remaining founders were Noyce and Moore. Noyce was promoted from General Manager to be Group Vice-President of the parent company, and a successful career within Fairchild looked to be the way ahead. Gordon Moore, a close friend of Noyce, and in charge of research and development, also stayed on. Business, however, was slowing down, and the parent company began to impose controls that were alien to the Silicon Valley culture. This, of course, only made matters worse. Noyce and Moore decided that the time had come for them to move on, and so they planned to set up NM Electronics, using Moore's many innovative ideas and Noyce's management skills. The name was soon changed to Integrated Electronics, abbreviated to Intel.

With their excellent track record at Fairchild Semiconductor, it was not difficult to raise the $2.5 million required. By this time, 1968, the venture capital industry was beginning to develop. They contacted Noyce's friend, Arthur Rock, the investment banker in New York who had found Sherman Fairchild for the 'Traitorous Eight' ten years before. Since then Rock had invented the term 'venture capital' and moved to San Francisco. With his contacts and the reputation of Noyce and Moore, Rock was able to raise the $2.5 million over the telephone in just one afternoon (Jackson ,1998).

Intel's main business was planned to be in memory chips. At that time, silicon chip technology had been applied to the integrated circuit that performed the calculations in a computer but not to the storage of information in the computer's memory. Intel was not the only company trying to produce a memory chip, but its funding enabled it to make real progress. The difficulty, however, was as much in the manufacturing process as in the technology itself. Tiny circuits were etched on to silicon, and in those early days only about 10 per cent of these circuits actually worked. It was essential to have a person in charge of manufacturing who could instil disciplines and give attention to detail. One of Noyce and Moore's first recruits was Andy Grove to be Director of Operations. This proved to be an outstanding appointment, and over the years Grove was to make Intel into the powerful company it is today. It is Grove's stamp on the company that we see today, and not that of Noyce or Moore. The *laissez-faire* of the Silicon Valley entrepreneurial business has been replaced by a tough, professional regime.

The story of Intel is about microprocessors. Apart from the manufacture of memory chips, Intel was doing contract work to produce custom chips to meet special requirements. One of these was a calculator for the Japanese company, Busicom. In 1971 this led to Ted Hoff's great idea for combining the logic and memory functions required for a simple computer on the same silicon chip. Ted Hoff had invented the microprocessor. Intel's first microprocessor chip was the 4004. It was normal to assign customers the exclusive rights on the chips designed especially for them, but Intel had designed a general-purpose chip that would do more than just run a calculator. This involved some rapid renegotiating of the contract with Busicom so that Intel could sell the 4004 to other customers.

The industry was not ready for this new innovation, nor was Intel's marketing team. Ted Hoff and his group had to spend most of 1972 selling the idea both internally and externally. In August 1973, a new, improved and faster, version of the chip, the 8080, came out. This answered all the earlier criticism and sales just took off. This innovation made Intel what it is today, but it also spawned the personal computer industry, the third phase of Silicon Valley's growth.

The personal computer: 1971 to 1985

IBM had been king of the mainframe computer business in the 1950s. Their competitors were known as the seven dwarfs (Wallace and Erickson, 1993). The machines they built were huge and had rooms to themselves. Then came the semiconductors and integrated circuits that we have already described, such that it became possible to provide the same computing capability with much smaller machines. When IBM decided initially not to enter this minicomputer market, it was left to new companies such as the Digital Equipment Corporation (DEC). DEC is an East Coast company that spun out from MIT in 1957 – the same year that Fairchild Semiconductors spun out of Shockley. Spin-offs in this industry were not exclusive to Silicon Valley! DEC latched on to this minicomputer opportunity and its PDP-8, launched in 1965, established it as the market leader. Apart from offering a machine that was much cheaper and smaller than the mainframe computers, it introduced the idea of using a keyboard to input data in to the machine rather than the traditional punched cards.

The minicomputer spread across the USA into schools and colleges as well as industry. In 1968 an exclusive private boy's school in Seattle raised enough money to buy time on a PDP-10 owned by General Electric. This gave a thirteen-year-old Bill Gates his first access to a computer. From that time, like so many other youngsters in the USA, Gates became a computer addict and wanted a computer of his own. When Intel put the computer's central processing unit on to a small piece of silicon in 1971, and invented the microprocessor, the dream of a small computer became a real possibility.

This opportunity was not taken up by either IBM or DEC. Instead it was the computer hobbyists who made the running. One such enthusiast was Ed Roberts, who had a small electronics company in Albuquerque, New Mexico, called MITS. Roberts designed a small computer around Intel's new and much improved microprocessor, the 8080. He did a deal with Intel on the price of the chip and arranged for his 'personal computer' to be featured in the January 1975 issue of *Popular Electronics* at a price of $397. The response from the half a million readers of this magazine was overwhelming.

Back in Silicon Valley, the computer hobbyists responded with a similar enthusiasm. In March 1975 about thirty people turned up to the first meeting of the Home Brew Computer Club, held in the garage of one of the enthusiasts in Menlo Park, close to Palo Alto and Stanford. The club soon had a membership of 500 and became the driver for the microcomputer industry in Silicon Valley. By the mid-1980s twenty-two computer companies had been set up by club members, Apple being the most famous.

The Home Brew Club captured all that Silicon Valley stood for. It brought together an exciting and innovative group of people who networked extensively and saw all knowledge as something you shared. They saw nothing wrong with passing around copies of the BASIC computer language that Bill Gates had written for Roberts's personal computer. The latest microprocessor chips from Intel could be *obtained* and when Steve Wozniak designed the Apple Computer he passed out copies of the circuit to members. It was a club without rules and without formality. As the microcomputer industry began to grow, this free exchange of information gradually died away and the club was never quite the same again.

The industry itself thrived as the entrepreneurs came forward and made things happen. Steve Jobs is the classic entrepreneur of this time. He saw himself as an outlaw, a maverick, who was going to change the world by giving everybody the possibility of owning their own computer. For him, the computer was an extension of man's intellectual capabilities. It was not just a box of electronics (Sculley, 1987). For Jobs, and the team he built around him, Apple was more of a crusade than a company. Their original mission, now largely fulfilled, was 'to change the way people use information to work, learn and play'.

Jobs, the potential entrepreneur, teamed up with Wozniak, a computer 'nerd' to build a computer of their own because they could not afford the kit computer being sold by Roberts. They built their first machine in the garage at Jobs's home for their own use. When they showed it at the Home Brew Computer Club, everybody wanted one, and they realized they had a business on their hands.

The Silicon Valley network enabled Jobs to find a market outlet, The Byte Shop, and to build a team. He linked up with Mark Markkula, a millionaire at the age of thirty-eight and former marketing manager at Intel, to finance the new venture. He also recruited Michael Scott, aged thirty-three, the manufacturing director of National Semiconductor, to be President of Apple. The Apple I was replaced by Apple II in 1977 and the company really took off. Their sales growth was the fastest that US business had ever seen. In 1977 sales were $2.5 million, in 1978 $15 million, in 1979 $70 million, in 1980 $117 million, in 1981 $335 million and in 1982 $583 million.

This success alerted IBM and the competition really began. IBM released its first competing personal computer in 1981. By 1983 the IBM PC and the Apple II were neck and neck, with sales of $1 billion each. Based on technology that Steve Jobs had seen on a visit to Xerox PARC in 1978, the Apple Mac was launched in 1984. The Macintosh featured a mouse-driven screen graphics interface and a windows-based operating system, which allowed users to view what they were doing and to switch between applications. It was launched with a sixty-second commercial during the US Super Bowl. The commercial adopted an Orwellian scene depicting the world of IBM being shattered by a newcomer and, although it cost Apple $1.6 million, it made a huge impact. Steve Jobs, however, had involved Bill Gates and others in the development of the software for the Macintosh (Mac). Jobs saw IBM, and not Microsoft, as its key rival. When Apple launched the Mac with a premium price – which it subsequently maintained – it adopted a misjudged niche strategy and provided Gates with the mass-market opportunity he would exploit with his Windows software. In 1985 Apple revenues reached $2 billion, but in that year sales began to slide, partially because the Mac's limited memory was restricting sales growth. This resulted in the departure of Steve Jobs, the entrepreneur and co-founder. In due course the Apple Mac was to fulfil all the hopes that Jobs had had for it; and Apple sales reached $2.7 billion and gave the company a stock valuation of $7.7 billion. Apple was able to link up with Adobe to pioneer desktop publishing – Adobe had the software that would put out on a laser printer whatever appeared on a screen. To this day, the Apple Mac remains the standard equipment for designers. For many subsequent years the Apple story is one of steady erosion of market share to the IBM PC and its clones. A decade without entrepreneurial leadership almost killed the company; and in 1997 Steve Jobs returned.[1] Almost immediately, exciting new products like the iMac began to appear.

Apple was important to Silicon Valley because it represented a new kind of exciting entrepreneurial business which others copied. It was what we call in Part Three a 'third wave' company. It also spawned a whole host of businesses and new sectors such as desktop publishing that fed off Apple's success.

The first real growth in the computer industry in Silicon Valley took place between 1970 and 1980. The number employed in the industry rose from about 9000 to almost 53 000, making the computer industry the biggest employer in Silicon Valley. The semiconductor industry was second with 34 500 employees. Total high-technology employment stood at almost 180 000 in 1980.

Two other industries made important contributions to the Silicon Valley scene in this period. The video games industry, which led the microcomputer industry by about five years, and the computer software industry that lagged it by about five years. The games industry was able to take the lead because it used the television set and did not have to wait for the low-cost computer. Nolan Bushnell started Atari in 1972 and gave the general public its first video game, Pong – an addictive electronic table tennis game. Atari experienced instantaneous growth, shipping 200 000 home versions of Pong in its first year. By 1974 the Pong craze was over and Atari was in trouble. In 1976 the entertainment group Warner Communications (now Time Warner) bought Atari, and Bushnell collected $15 million. Prior to starting Apple, Steve Jobs worked for Nolan Bushnell at Atari – whilst his partner, Steve Wozniak, was employed by Hewlett-Packard. Atari's notorious wild style, coupled with its rapid success, gave a 'California Gold Rush feel' to Silicon Valley, and this was captured by the Home Brew Club and by companies like Apple. More recently the Gold Rush comparison has been applied to the time in early 1990s when the Internet arrived on the scene – but in truth it has never really left the valley since it began in the early 1970s. The culture of fun and irreverence has been fundamental in driving the creativity and innovation that remains at the heart of the story and the experience.

The computer software industry developed from zero in 1970 to employing 4000 people in 1975. Thereafter it doubled every five years to reach over 15 000 in 1985. Larry Ellison founded Oracle in 1977 to develop relational database software. Ten years later sales reached $131 million, relatively modest by Silicon Valley standards, but since then Oracle has achieved a leading position in the market. Sales in 1996 were $402 billion. With a personal stockholding in Oracle worth some $6 billion, Ellison is one of the world's richest software tycoons after Bill Gates and Paul Allen of Microsoft.

The Internet period: 1986 to the present day

The beginning of this period coincided with a major shift in the fortunes of companies like Apple and Intel. Here people were being laid off and sales were falling. This sent shock waves through the Valley, with many thinking that the bubble must have finally burst. In addition, there were some notable changes to the culture and physical appearance of the valley. Ties and suits began to appear at places like Apple when executives with MBAs became omnipresent, and venture capitalists began to control more and more decisions and events. A transition from the dominant entrepreneur to the professional manager was taking place.

At Intel, Andy Grove became Chief Executive and took the company from a loss-making position in 1986, a year when 7200 workers were laid off, to a position of complete dominance of the microprocessor industry, with an 80 per cent market share, ten years later. Apple were less successful in achieving their move to professionalism and struggled throughout this period. They finally reached a performance rock bottom in 1996, though even at that time their sales were still around $8 billion. Their recent revival under a returned, and more mature, Steve Jobs has brought the entrepreneurial spirit back to Apple, and it now has exciting new competitive products.

Companies like Sun Microsystems (started in 1982) and Oracle Corporation have been the Silicon Valley success stories of this period and they are now established world leaders in their fields. By the late 1990s they were the third and fifth largest companies in the valley. In 1995, *Industry Week* had placed Sun Microsystems among the top 100 best-managed companies in the world.

Whilst it would have been easy to conclude on the evidence of the late 1980s and early 1990s that the Silicon Valley phenomenon had run its course, and that it had now entered the ranks of the professional establishment, this was not the case – for two main reasons. First, the valley continues to attract young talent from all over the world, thus sustaining the entrepreneurial dynamic. For them it is still an exciting place to be; it is where the technology is leading edge and fortunes can be made. Linus Torvalds, the inventor of the Linux operating system put out over the Internet, left his native Finland and moved to Silicon Valley because it was a 'high-tech Mecca' and because of the distinctive culture. 'Here, if you are successful, people tend to respect you. In Europe, if you're successful, people tend to envy you. Here it's easier to be rich and successful and that motivates people' (*San Jose Mercury News*, 1999).

The second reason why Silicon Valley has retained its entrepreneurial dynamic is the emergence of the Internet. The Internet was to provide a new, exciting opportunity where visionary entrepreneurs would create and drive a new future. Its development needed – and found – both the backing and the will to succeed. It was actually in October 1969 that a computer at the University of California at Los Angeles first linked up by telephone line with a computer in Menlo Park in Silicon Valley. Though this experiment proved it could be done, it was not until 1986 that things began to move. This was when the US National Science Foundation (NSF) set up the NSF net, which allowed universities to access the computing resources of supercomputers in five selected universities. By 1988 there were 60 000 host computers on the Internet. With the emergence of the World Wide Web in the early 1990s, a development proposed in 1989 by Tim Berners-Lee in Switzerland, the Internet moved into the public domain.

The Internet we know today, however, needed other parallel developments, many of which have their roots in Silicon Valley. Users need web browsers, or programs that enable PC owners to view and access data on the web. The main pioneer of web browser software was Netscape, with Navigator, but its success attracted competition from Microsoft. Bill Gates linked his browser – Explorer – to Windows, and provided it as a free extra. The third pillar was provided by Java, a programming language that enables web pages to contain imaginative programs and materials which appear as animation, sound, scrolling text and interactive features. The inventor of Java, James Gosling, was provided with development funds and working space by Sun Microsystems. The final pillar comprises access gateways or portals.

As an exciting new technology, the Internet was of huge interest to the programmers and entrepreneurs of Silicon Valley and many new companies were spawned, each seeking to predict and influence the direction in which the Internet would move. One of these was 3Com Corporation, the networking company with sales of around $5.5 billion in 1999, helped recently by the success of its Palm Pilot pocket computer and its acquisition of the modem company, US Robotics. Ahead of 3Com, and still growing fast, is Cisco Systems, with sales of $12 billion in the year 1998/99. The driving force behind Cisco is John Chambers, who joined the company in 1991, and who has presided over a stock growth of 2356 per cent in the last five years. Chambers has seen the opportunity for building a portfolio of Internet-related companies. By 1999 he had acquired forty young innovative companies, many of which are located in Silicon Valley. His most costly purchase to date was a two-year old start-up, Cerent Corporation, with sales of a mere $10 million and for which he paid $6.9 billion in August 1999.

Yahoo!, probably the best-known provider of Internet portals, is also a resident of Santa Clara in the Valley. Yahoo! provides shopping and e-mail facilities alongside games, financial information and news, and of course its vitally important search facilities. Search engines enable users to track down information and sites on specific topics. Yahoo! is 'about helping people find what they want and where they want to go'. Like Amazon.com (Chapter 9), Yahoo! is a brand, which can be applied successfully to several related services. It began when two Stanford PhD students produced a directory of their favourite web sites in their spare time. They did not set out to build a business. Founders Jerry Yang (born in Taiwan, and an immigrant at the age of ten with his widowed mother) and David Filo were both technocrats. Reflecting the pace of growth for the Internet, Yahoo! had eleven employees in 1995 and 1600 in 1999 – at which time it was valued at $44 billion. Its site is visited every month by 32 million people – over half of all American Internet users. It is the leader in Japan and much of Europe. Research also significantly confirms that users spend longer on the Yahoo! site than on the sites of any of its main rivals.

The company is run by a team of three entrepreneurs – the two founders and Jeff Mallett, an MBA graduate they recruited from Novell. Recognizing their own strengths and limitations, Yang and Filo were always keen to recruit the professional senior managers they knew they needed. The three work in neighbouring cubicles and get together about three times a week to discuss strategy – their acknowledged challenge lies in

> finding a structure that allows Yahoo! to operate with the speed and flexibility of the myriad of start-ups that challenge it and every one of its main activities. The culture [of Silicon Valley] has become unforgiving. If people are not comfortable with having their ideas and practices constantly tested, they will not fit in.

> (Mallett)

A second challenge lies in finding more creative and innovative ways of helping meet users' information and communication needs, and linking this with new technologies. Reinforcing the significance of this last point, Oracle is one Valley organization currently seeking to play a lead role when stronger links are forged between mobile telephones and the Internet seen by many as the next key stage of development – mobile phones can enable easy Internet access from anywhere in the world. Larry Ellison has identified that there are 300 million people worldwide who own mobile phones but only 120 million owners of Internet-connected computers. In 1999 Oracle launched software which enables web pages to be translated into a format which allows them to be displayed on the screens of mobile phones and handheld computers. Valley resident 3Com, manufacturer of Palm pocket-size computers, has formed an alliance with Nokia, the Finnish manufacturer of mobile phones to compete with the rival alliance of Microsoft and Ericsson to develop products for this growth sector of the Internet market. Also in 1999, Oracle joined with Cisco, Sun Microsystems and Exodus (a web-hosting business) to provide subsidized incubation facilities for new web companies in the UK. The alliance provides a complete hardware, software and consultancy package for three months at a cost of £15 000.

Meanwhile, Sherwin Pishevar had graduated from the University of California, Berkeley, in 1997. He was twenty-three years old. His new company, WebOSinc, now has ten employees – he is the oldest – and offers a web-based operating system which can be blended with a full suite of office applications, all hosted on a web server. Oracle and Sun Microsystems also believe in 'software as services', bringing them all into conflict with the Microsoft approach of having all the relevant software in every personal computer. Pishevar describes himself as an 'entrepreneurial activist' and his WebOS system as 'disruptive technology' that he hopes will change the dominant distribution system for software. Things never stand still in the valley!

Silicon Valley, then, attracts both talented young people and experienced professionals such as Cisco's Chambers, now fifty years old and with experience at IBM and Wang. This is a powerful combination and one of the secrets of the valley's continued success. Its mature and extensive venture capital system is another of its secrets. There are no small business attitudes in Silicon Valley. As Don Valentine, one of the valley's most successful venture capitalists, told us some years ago: 'I only back a start-up if I am convinced it can become a billion-dollar business. I then put together the financial resources to make that possible.'

Silicon Valley today

More than fifty years on Silicon Valley has shown the world that there is such a thing as a *collective entrepreneur* and that it is sustainable. The future challenge for its entrepreneurs is to maintain a leading role as the Internet opens up more and more opportunities – whilst being ready for the next, discontinuous wave of developments. Just as the Silicon Valley venture capitalists spread their risk by investing in several companies, accepting that more are likely to fail than succeed, many of the entrepreneurs work on several new projects simultaneously – always on the lookout for the 'next big one'. They may well have a main project, but the serial element is persistent and habitual.

Yet, for all its economic success and entrepreneurial spirit, Silicon Valley is fundamentally an urban sprawl. Silicon Valley is not one, single organized and obvious business park in an obvious location. Instead, there are office parks with car parking everywhere, and many of the spawning businesses seem anonymous – simply people seem to know who they need to know, and where they can be found. The activity and the 'buzz' are there, but it is partially hidden. The area is clogged by traffic; and house prices are hugely inflated. 'Ordinary employees' are finding it is becoming excessively expensive. Even the richest entrepreneurs often work in cubicles. They may enjoy large houses, Porsche's and Ferrari's – and stickers that claim 'My other car is a plane' – but money is not their only driver. If it were, the multi-millionaires would not keep working, perpetually searching for the excitement of the next big opportunity.

The Valley itself has really become the opportunity – to become a millionaire and to achieve something unusual and different. People have realized that equity and ownership, rather than salaried employment, holds the key to personal wealth. The Valley attracts (and sometimes, but not always, rewards) young people who are willing to take risks with their lives, or who are in search of unusual lives. 'They have given up lives elsewhere to come. They come for the tremendous opportunity, believing that in no other place in the world can one person accomplish so much with talent, initiative and a good idea' (Bronson, 1999). They see the other people that have made it and conclude 'they are nothing special'. They believe that they too can do it!

For many, however, whilst Silicon Valley is a magnet and a good, creative place to work, it is not automatically a nice place. It could also be described as a multitude of cramped cubicles where people spend hours staring at screens and trying to come up with something which has never before existed. Dedication, creativity, uncertainty and the risk of failure are the essences of the lifestyle. Companies that do succeed often grow very rapidly – and then key people leave to spin-off a new venture. There is little employee loyalty – compounded by some very entrepreneurial headhunters whose tactics for luring people away from their existing employers are ethically questionable. Many people work for performance-related pay – linked to sales they can generate or venture capital they can raise – and with a very low basic salary, but jobs are still hard to find and easy to fill. We might ask why. Arguably Silicon Valley needs an injection of social and aesthetic entrepreneurs to improve the overall quality of life.

Although Silicon Valley has spawned business upon business, and millionaire entrepreneur upon millionaire entrepreneur (sixty-four every day), Yahoo!'s Jeff Mallett believes 'people do not come here for the best salary. They come here for no bureaucracy, to get their ideas heard by good people and to create something'. Clearly the very success of the valley, intertwined with its unique culture and promise, will be a magnet for the best people and sustain the virtuous circle of growth – as long as it lasts. In the next chapter we look further at a number of the issues we have raised when we examine the new Internet businesses and entrepreneurs.

Note

1. The contribution to Apple of Steve Jobs, his departure and return, was discussed in Chapter 4.

References

Bronson, P. (1999). *The Nudist on the Late Shift – and Other Tales of Silicon Valley*. Secker and Warburg.
Brown, G. (1973). Interview with Fred Terman, Hewlett-Packard Archives. (Referenced in Larson, J. K. and Rogers, E. M. (1986). *Silicon Valley Fever*. Unwin Counterpoint.)
Castells, M. and Hall, P. (1994). *Technopoles of the World*. Routledge.
Hanson, D. (1982). *The New Alchemists: Silicon Valley and the Microelectronics Revolution*. Little, Brown.
Jackson, T. (1998). *Inside Intel*. HarperCollins.
Larson, J. K. and Rogers, E. M. (1986). *Silicon Valley Fever*. Unwin Counterpoint.
Malecki, E. J. (1997). *Technology and Economic Development*. 2nd edn. Longman.
Rose, F. (1989). *West of Eden*. Business Books.
San Jose Mercury News (1999). Linus the Liberator. Special report: Linus Torvalds, September, www. mercurycenter.com
Saxenian, A. L. (1990). Regional networks and the resurgence of Silicon Valley. *California Management Review*, **33**, 89–112.
Sculley, J. (1987). *Odyssey: Pepsi to Apple*. Collins.
Wallace, J. and Erickson, J. (1993). *Hard Drive*. John Wiley.

9 The new Internet entrepreneurs

Internet-related businesses are now starting and growing all round the world. At one level electronic commerce (e-commerce) businesses require only limited start-up capital. Developing the idea and a web site is not prohibitively expensive; the problem – and the expense – lies in establishing the procurement and distribution systems. The other key issue is making sure web users visit the site of the business, a problem that intensifies all the time as more and more sites are put up. However, venture capitalists are investing in these businesses, often accepting risks and uncertainty not normally associated with venture capitalists. A number of professional firms (consultants, lawyers and public relations specialists) opt to waive their fees in exchange for equity in these new ventures. The reason – things are moving very quickly and people are afraid of being left behind in the race!

In this chapter we pick up and develop a number of themes we introduced in Chapter 8. Although Silicon Valley is home to many new Internet entrepreneurs, it is not the only place where they can be found. After all, the Internet itself is virtual. We concentrate mainly on e-commerce businesses and feature an extended analysis of the world's leading e-commerce retailer, Amazon.com, written in a form that allows it to be used as a case study; but we also consider how these uncertain and high-risk businesses might be evaluated and look at a number of British stories.

As we start the new, third millennium, cyberspace and e-commerce is 'providing another Klondike gold rush . . . it is not just another fad'. The use of the gold rush metaphor is both interesting and meaningful. It conjures up thoughts of huge fortunes and, as we saw in the last chapter, these fortunes are being made – sixty-four new millionaires every day in Silicon Valley alone. But we must not forget that only a small percentage of those prospectors attracted to Alaska really made their fortune. Most failed to find very much gold – and many perished in the harsh conditions. The Internet is a wonderful and attractive opportunity, but it will prove disappointing, even cruel, to many of those would-be entrepreneurs it attracts. The commercial potential of new creative, innovative ideas is difficult to evaluate, and consequently the ability to persuade a venture capitalist to back a venture – difficult as this may prove to be – is certainly no guarantee of success. An infrastructure and a market both have to be built.

The USA is well ahead of the UK for both Internet access and the popularity of e-commerce, but in turn the UK is regarded as the leader in Europe. Over a quarter of the UK population now has Internet access, but the penetration varies regionally. It is lowest in the North-East and highest in the South-East, where it is over 35 per cent. On-line sales of £750 million in 1999 were forecast to triple to £2250 million in 2001. Britain's first Internet millionaires have already arrived. As these businesses are knowledge-based and often begin with a creative, innovative, novel idea, market entry can seem tantalizingly simple. After all, there are no effective barriers against putting up a web site. But attracting adequate finance to develop the idea, buy the necessary powerful web servers, establish a supply chain and then attract customers from the 'busy electronic highways' is not quite so straightforward. 'The net is all about execution . . . things being done on time and with great service.' Shoeless Joe, in the film *Field of Dreams*, said 'If you build it, they will come' – but whilst new web sites may attract interest, the implementation and project management of a new e-commerce business is complex, expensive and hazardous.

The low entry barriers and customer capture issues were illustrated wonderfully in 1999 when an enterprising businessman in County Durham sold the web address 'www.inlandrevenue.org.uk', which he had registered properly, to the Inland Revenue for £194. The address was sufficiently similar to the Inland Revenue's actual web address to be causing confusion amongst clients trying to access the real site and using search engines. Instead of tax information they were finding they were being offered rail tickets. The entrepreneur (Alex Nelson) has registered over 700 domain names using similar principles, every one of them close to the real web address of a large and well-known organization. As a result he is successfully attracting some 8000 visitors to his own transport ticket sales site every day. Whilst we might genuinely see him as entrepreneurial, others see him as a nuisance.

Electronic commerce can change the economics and customer proposition of an industry; exploiting this real opportunity is the challenge for many Internet entrepreneurs. Distribution costs can be reduced as less stock is required in the system. Prices can be truly flexible, ideal if last minute price reductions are being considered for non-storable services such as airline and theatre seats and hotel rooms. Demand can be matched with supply more effectively for the benefit of both suppliers and customers who are willing – or need – to wait until the last minute. The range of choice can be improved dramatically – a virtual store can have almost limitless size whereas physical stores are inevitably restricted. Extensive background information can be provided very easily. In addition, suppliers can use the information they acquire about their customers to carefully target special promotions. However, e-commerce can only work properly if the goods or parcels can be delivered efficiently and effectively. Amazon.com, for example, has a marketing partnership with the US Postal Service, and similarly valuable opportunities have arisen for specialist parcel carriers such as Federal Express who we discussed in Chapter 4.

This chapter, then, focuses on the stories of two American Internet successes – Sabeer Bhatia with Hotmail and Jeff Bezos with Amazon.com. However, we also include a series of shorter stories about a number of British beneficiaries of Internet wealth. With Hotmail (which is an Internet business but not e-commerce) we concentrate on the entrepreneur and the start-up process; but with Amazon we deliberately look in greater detail at the strategic issues we introduced in Chapter 2. What we see in our examples are many degree-educated entrepreneurs, a pattern that differs from the successful people we have discussed in earlier chapters. As this sector is still in its infancy it is not realistic to draw any firm conclusions from this nevertheless interesting fact.

Sabeer Bhatia and Hotmail

Sabeer Bhatia arrived in America – Los Angeles – in 1988. His father had served as an officer in the Indian army before entering public service; his mother worked as an accountant for the Bank of India. Sabeer had won a scholarship to study in America and possessed just $250, the maximum he had been allowed to bring out of India. His scholarship for Cal Tech was no ordinary scholarship – he was the only student in the world that year to have reached the qualifying threshold on the brainteaser tests. In a typical year, 150 people try and the best scores above the threshold qualify for a scholarship. He came with no intention of staying; he assumed he would obtain his degree and return to India to work as an engineer in a large corporation. At the time he had not realized that America is the land of opportunity!

An enthusiastic student, he regularly attended lunchtime seminars at Stanford, when entrepreneurs from Silicon Valley came in to talk about their experiences. They all told their audiences: 'You can do it too.' Sabeer began to listen. After all, they seemed like ordinary people to him – something he had not expected to find. Eventually, after successfully completing his Master's degree, and freshly armed with a Green Card, he took a job at Apple, at the time thinking that he would pursue a career path in a large American corporation. At the same time he began to network extensively; he joined an association of Indian entrepreneurs, most of them much older than he was. Soon they began to seem like men he could emulate. Amongst the people he met was Farouk Arjani, who became his mentor, and who later became intrigued by Sabeer's overwhelming belief that he could build a million-dollar business.

His best friend at Apple was fellow hardware engineer, Jack Smith, a shy young American with a wife and two children. Sabeer was single. Sabeer kept telling Smith that if they worked together closely they could make it on their own. On the face of it, he had less to lose. But Smith was finally persuaded. Now all they needed was a good idea.

Their first idea (in 1995, when they were both twenty-six years old) was for a net-based personal database, which they called Javasoft. They wrote a business plan, but every time they approached a venture capitalist they were rejected. Their plan contained flaws, a reality they began to accept when the same shortfalls were repeatedly pointed out to them. In December 1995 Smith had the germ of an idea for a free-of-charge e-mail network that users could access anonymously on the Internet from anywhere they were in the world. The moment he shared the idea with Sabeer and they began to discuss its potential, they knew they were on to 'something special'. They believed the idea was so powerful, but easily copied, that they needed to keep it under wraps until all the necessary funding was in place. Both Sabeer and Smith had personal e-mail accounts with American Online (AOL) but they were unable to use this system from their computers at work, which meant that any personal e-mail messages they shared during working hours were on an organizational intranet and therefore insecure. They drafted their business plan – and deliberately avoided making any spare copies.

In the next two years they would build a company's subscriber base at a faster rate than any other media company had ever achieved. By 1998 they would reach 25 million active e-mail accounts and 125 000 new members every day. Sabeer's personal wealth was about to reach $200 million. At this time he was still single and living in a rented apartment. 'Houses [here] are overpriced . . . I think I'll save a little money if I wait until they come down.' Simply, they had found a way to overcome a problem they were facing. Like many good ideas, it had been under their noses all the time.

Early in 1996 Sabeer, sometimes on his own, sometimes with Jack Smith, continued to seek appointments with venture capitalists. Still obsessed with secrecy, Sabeer cannily presented his Javasoft business plan and waited for a reaction. If he felt he was being treated dismissively, he simply went way. If he received objective and helpful feedback on the Javasoft flaws, he followed up with the business plan for Hotmail. Whilst Sabeer was doing this, Smith fixed them a fall-back seed capital fund of $100 000 from his friends and family, although they were always realistic that this would never be enough to bring the project to fruition. Their twenty-first venture capitalist was interested. Nevertheless, Steve Jurvetson of Draper, Fisher, Jurvetson, regarded Sabeer's growth projections as totally unrealistic. In the event, Sabeer would be proved correct. His instincts for Hotmail were right, but he was always in danger of being seen as 'arrogantly optimistic'.

Jurvetson was genuinely interested in a deal, although so far there was nothing beyond a well-documented idea committed to paper. There was no proof of concept or confirmation of early customer interest. Despite the fact that nobody else was expressing any interest, Sabeer was determined to hold out for the deal he wanted. He was willing to release up to 15 per cent of the equity; the bankers first demanded 30 per cent. At one stage, he simply walked out of the negotiations. Hiding the real business plan, and walking away when someone is offering a considerable sum of money to a completely unproven entrepreneur with an untested idea, reflect true self-belief and a substantial ego. But having been rejected over twenty times, Sabeer and Smith were even more determined to prove they could succeed.

Sabeer and Smith persisted with the name Javasoft for their business – they continued to believe the Hotmail idea was worth stealing and someone could beat them to launch. Every day for six months they checked the Internet to make sure someone else had not marketed the idea ahead of them. They also worked from nondescript offices with the name Javasoft on the door to try to avoid any unwanted attention. In exchange for 15 per cent of their equity Juvetson had provided $300 000, ostensibly for proof-of-concept work. Sabeer and Smith began to employ people and to build their embryo business. Fearful of having to release more equity to financiers, they were determined to stretch the $300 000 as far as it could possibly stretch. They bought cheap or second-hand equipment wherever this was feasible. Their essential paper shredder cost just $15. But by June 1996 money was very tight. Sabeer somehow managed to persuade a bank to loan them a further $100 000 unsecured and a public relations agency to represent them in exchange for stock options. Sabeer was also taking advice from Farouk Arjani and followed up his suggestion to persuade his first fifteen employees to also accept stock options in lieu of wages.

They launched Hotmail on 4 July 1996, Independence Day, a public holiday. Although e-mail was well established, computer users immediately saw the value of being able to access their e-mail from any remote terminal anywhere in the world. Word-of-mouth recommendations were instantaneous. One hundred subscribers in the first hour Hotmail was available were joined by 200 more in the second hour. Simply, as soon as someone received a Hotmail message they became a subscriber themselves. The growth was so rapid no advertising of any consequence was required. Hotmail began to deliver news and promotional material directly to its subscriber mailboxes – always for a fee. Sabeer had no intention of paying for the news, which was the normal procedure. He argued his users would read the news and then visit the relevant origination site – so he was providing a gateway service. He began to convince everyone of his vision.

The company was now growing quickly – and its people were growing with it. Sabeer and Smith continued to recruit 'strong, smart people' and give them all the responsibility they would accept. 'Sabeer got everyone in the company totally focused . . . harmonized . . . telling the same story. People trusted each other and believed in the business.' Hotmail enjoyed a six-month window before anyone attempted to compete with it directly. Serious competition, in the form of Rocketmail, took a full year. Sabeer and Smith continued with their external networking with renewed energy and vigour – and the momentum increased. More capital was raised and used to develop both the concept and the business. Jack Smith's invaluable contribution from behind the scenes was a system which did not crash as it absorbed more and more users and activity.

For some reason, Microsoft – who many had predicted would launch a rival service – left Hotmail alone for eighteen months. By this time Hotmail, with twenty-five employees, had signed up 6 million subscribers and was clearly entrenched as market leader. A rumour grew that Microsoft would invest in Hotmail and offer it to Microsoft Network subscribers, but in autumn 1997 Microsoft offered Sabeer and Smith $350 million to take over Hotmail. The partners would have made 'tens of millions each' but they turned it down as inadequate. They were invited to Seattle to meet Bill Gates. Initially in awe, Sabeer grew in confidence when he realized that Gates was asking him 'very predictable questions about the strategy'. He realized Gates was 'smart but not superhuman'. Now supremely confident, Sabeer demanded $500 million for the business. Angry Microsoft negotiators responded that he was 'crazy'. External analysts agreed, convinced that Microsoft was also negotiating to buy Rocketmail as an alternative. Urged to settle by most of his employees, and advised to be careful by his financial backers, Sabeer continued to hold out for more money. Steve Juvetson even began to joke that he should wait until he was big enough to counter-bid for Microsoft. Whilst the negotiations continued, the subscriber base grew remorselessly. Finally, on 31 December 1997, Microsoft acquired Hotmail in exchange for shares valued at around $400 million.

Some analysts and journalists seemed truly amazed that a two-year-old e-mail company could be worth this amount of money. Sabeer and Smith 'did not deserve their success and wealth'. Ex-Apple colleagues were said to be particularly resentful. Mentor Arjani, however, reached a different conclusion. 'Sabeer had never had an opportunity to raise money . . . to run a company or even a division. But . . . he did an outstanding job. Nothing in his background prepared him for it . . . it must be something innate in him'. Specifically he had the talent and the temperament.

Together with Smith, Sabeer stayed on to run Hotmail, which now has around 150 employees and 45 million subscribers, boosted by the infusion of Microsoft resources. Sabeer was appointed as General Manager of Hotmail, Jack Smith as Director of Engineering. Sabeer went straight on to level three in the Microsoft hierarchy, 'reporting to someone who reported to Bill'. The company remains devolved and empowered. Some have even dared to argue that the selling price of $400 million was still too low.

In March 1999, having at last bought an apartment and a Ferrari, Sabeer Bahtia left Microsoft and Hotmail. He has started a new venture in Silicon Valley but has been overheard articulating a new vision for his home country. India has one-fifth of the world's population but only 150 000 Internet connections. None the less Hotmail has 560 000 subscribers in India. Ownership of a television remains far more popular than owning a telephone, which is very expensive to have installed. Sabeer envisions a fibre-optic cable linking London and Bombay, providing Internet access via cable television with a $50 device. The project would need a capital injection of $200 million. 'It's a Herculean task . . . but the prospect of changing the destiny of a country motivates me.' He has a sense of destiny now and he feels he is too young to retire.

E-commerce businesses

The fundamental principle behind many new e-commerce businesses is trading without either manufacture or long-term inventory. E-commerce cuts out the retail store element. New organizations dedicated to e-commerce are similar in principle but yet distinctly different from the situation where established organizations (including, for example, Tesco and Waterstone's) sell via the World Wide Web as well as through their own high street outlets. The large retailers are, of course, increasingly moving in this direction because of the impact the specialist e-commerce companies have had on customer buying habits. Whilst the new businesses may own warehouses for collecting stock for onward transmission and holding limited numbers of fast-moving items, there will rarely be any need for them to employ either sales or production staff – and, of course, this element can be outsourced to specialists in logistics, leaving the e-commerce company to focus on creating and maintaining a successful web site once the supply chain is set up. Simply, they are a virtual company, as we can see in Figure 9.1.

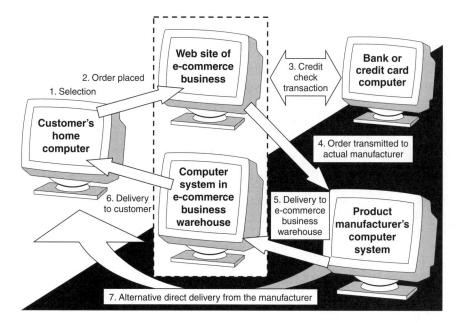

Figure 9.1   *A typical e-commerce business network*

The transaction begins when a potential customer uses his or her home computer to check out the web site of the e-commerce business, selects what he or she wants and places an order electronically. Typically credit card information will be requested – and an instant credit check will be carried out by contacting the computer system of the relevant credit card company. Once the payment details are confirmed, an order is transmitted to the manufacturer of the product in question. If the e-commerce company is holding the product in stock, of course, this would be replaced by an order to the company's own warehouse – who will later reorder from the manufacturer. Delivery to the customer can be direct from the manufacturer or via the e-commerce business, which will receive bulk supplies and post out individual parcels.

Their fundamental advantage is their ability to reach a wide customer audience at low cost – as long as they can be attracted in the first place and then retained as a regular customer. Relatively specialist items can thus be made available to people who find it difficult to visit the shops which actually sell them directly. One key disadvantage is that the goods cannot be touched and inspected, which matters more for some customers and products than it does for others. The main infrastructure requirements for a successful e-commerce business are appropriate managerial and technical skills, venture capital to set up a sophisticated supply chain and secure payment systems. They also need customers who can and do access their site, recognize the convenience and benefits being offered, and believe the payment systems are private and secure.

Brady (1999) argues that the success of any e-commerce business is dependent upon several factors. The idea must be innovatory, and whilst the business should be clearly focused it must be able to change and evolve speedily if it is to sustain growth. The people behind the business, their plans and their grasp of the issues, together with their ability to raise the necessary finance, are obviously critical issues. It is also essential that they develop a strong brand and, on the back of this, create and maintain very high levels of service. The site must be readily accessible, orders must be simple to place and then easily tracked whilst they are in the system. It goes without saying that deliveries should be on time.

How, then, might we evaluate these new businesses, remembering that at the moment only a minority are profitable? Partly concerned not to be left behind in this new 'gold rush', some financiers and venture capitalists seem willing to back some very high-risk proposals if they believe in the idea and the entrepreneur. Amazon.com, the most substantial and famous e-commerce company in the world, has secured enormous funding but has yet to declare a profit, as we shall see later. Customer numbers are growing dramatically, as are revenues, but all cash generated goes back into the business.

Management Today (see Gwyther, 1999) offers the following set of evaluation criteria, which we have annotated:

Three factors which determine the extent and value of the opportunity

1 *The concept or idea*

- How *value* is created and built
- The potential for profit, based on costs and revenues
- The size of the potential market
- The potential to establish an advantage and reap the rewards – specifically the presence of effective barriers to entry by direct competitors

2 *Innovation*

- The initial difference and the potential to build new values and thus sustain any early advantage

3 *Engagement and implementation*

- The ability to set up the infrastructure and the business – which inevitably depends upon the people behind the business

Three further factors which reflect the project or business outcomes:

4 *Traffic*

- Numbers of customers generated – linked to the extent of repeat business, which in turn is dependent upon service levels achieved.
- Although web congestion can be a constraint, the fact that people recommend web sites by word of mouth is a major opportunity.

5 *Financing*

- Financial resources secured, to fund continued expansion as well as start-up.
- Setting up a robust business and infrastructure on the web is expensive.

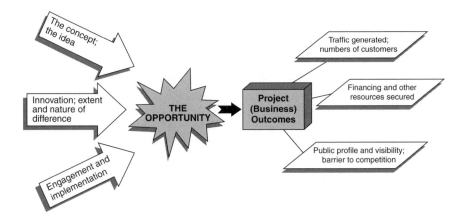

Figure 9.2 *The new Internet businesses*

6 *Visibility*

- The critically important brand identity and image.
- Public profile and visibility – which can also act as a barrier to entry. This will often be in the form of media coverage for either an exciting new idea or the recognition of a new, successful entrepreneur or even web millionaire.

These six factors are illustrated in Figure 9.2.

Although Hotmail is not an e-commerce business, these criteria can be readily applied to the business. The idea and the concept were simple but very powerful. People use e-mail extensively and Hotmail provides them with privacy and access anywhere in the world. It is clearly innovative. It is incrementally different, but not so different that potential users were not able to see and realize the benefits immediately. The business grew with word of mouth recommendations and through Sabeer being able to sell advertising space on the site. It also needed Smith to make sure it never seriously crashed as it continued to grow. The traffic generated was huge – six million in the eighteen months before Microsoft bought the company. Extensive finance was needed to set up the business, which Sabeer Bhatia was able to raise. He then set about conserving this and spending only what was essential. The public profile was high from the very beginning; this was an idea that caught on. Interestingly, and despite the fact that the idea could be copied, competition was relatively slow to materialize. In essence, Hotmail passes all six tests.

British stories

Boo.com

Boo.com has a physical base in London's Carnaby Street, home of 1960s fashion, and it was set up to sell sportswear. The idea is to widen the availability of the more exclusive designer-label items, which are typically only available in large cities. Two of its three founders (who are all in their twenties) had previously created Books.com, an early on-line bookseller; the third is an ex-model. It has been estimated that Boo.com has been able to raise £75 million in venture capital, but this is still far less than the amount required to set up a physical retail infrastructure which could provide customers with these items on a wide scale. After a number of well-publicized false starts, the company went on-line in November 1999, offering deliveries in eighteen countries from warehouses in Cologne and Kentucky. Boo.com does not own these warehouses but has a dedicated staff working there and an alliance with the actual owners. Goods are delivered to the warehouses by their manufacturers and then repackaged in distinctive Boo boxes before being posted on.

The web site offers 40 000 items. Each has been photographed at least twenty-four times such that browsers can examine them from every angle. Clothes can be seen on their own and on particular mannequin figures. Product descriptions are available in eight languages and sales are in local currencies. There is a sophisticated internal checking system to ensure customers are never sold anything that is not immediately available from the relevant manufacturer. However, the site has been criticized for its complexity and the business was soon in trouble.

Lastminute.com

Lastminute.com deals in products and services with a finite shelf-life that are close to their sell-by date and are sometimes candidates for distress pricing. Seats for flights, sporting events, theatres and holidays would all qualify. Events in the UK, France and Germany are included. Lastminute.com brokers a deal and then takes a commission. Clearly this web company is not the only potential outlet for the products in question, and consequently its success will depend on the variety it can offer, the extent of the business it can generate through its site and its ability to finally bring buyer and seller together. The target market is cash-rich, time-constrained professionals who would like a bargain but who cannot invest the time and effort to find it personally. In 1999 Lastminute.com claimed 300 000 registered subscribers with an average of almost fifteen site visits per month each. Revenues amounted to some £6 million; and no direct American equivalent has been identified.

The company was founded in November 1998 by two ex-consultants in their late twenties, Brent Hoberman and Martha Lane Fox. The basic idea was Hoberman's – he had become increasingly irritated with the process of price haggling with individual hotels and airlines when he was travelling. In 1999 it was being anticipated that the company – which has yet to make a profit – would be floated in 2000. A potential valuation of £400 million was featured in the reports. In the event, the flotation value was £732 million, making instant millionaires of the two partners who have retained 45 per cent of the equity. Martha Lane Fox has become a high profile media figure and *Management Today* (April 2000) described her as the fifth most powerful woman in the UK. However, the shares have not been able to sustain their flotation price and have fallen dramatically to one-third of their post-issue high.

Thinknatural.com

Carol Dukes is the creator of Thinknatural.com. Dukes graduated from Oxford in 1983 and then, unusually, embarked on a secretarial course. She later worked as a strategic planner for Emap and at Carlton, where she was involved in Internet developments. Specifically she helped launch three on-line businesses in film, food and entertainment. Before these large companies she had worked for IUS, a five-person microbusiness supplying in-house movie systems to hotels in the Middle East. When IUS was an early mover into cable franchising in the UK, Dukes was involved in raising money from venture capitalists. Her experience then was already helping map the route ahead for her. At the end of the 1980s she completed an MBA at London Business School.

In 1999 Carol Dukes raised substantial venture capital funding to start Thinknatural.com, Europe's first site for natural health and beauty products. The money, again unusually, but similar to the experience of Hotmail, was secured on the strength of the business plan and a confidence that she was 'the right person' for this sector. 'Thinknatural will make money because we have this weird business model where we sell things for slightly more than we pay for them.' Dukes has a partner, Emma Crowe, who worked with her on Internet projects at Carlton.

Unlike Amazon.com, which we discuss later, where discounting is essential for building sales, Thinknatural can charge full prices for its distinctive products, ranging from vitamins to aromatherapy oils and beauty products. Whilst the range is far wider than that of Body Shop, Thinknatural.com has adopted one of Anita Roddick's key strategies. The web site offers a wealth of information on products and therapies and a facility for customers to exchange ideas. As well as funding the development of the site, the venture capital will fund a physical warehouse for over 5000 different lines.

Dukes sums up her views on collateral and risk as follows: 'my flat was not available as security . . . there is an old-fashioned attitude among *some* UK venture capitalists that things have got to hurt . . . remortgaging my home would have made me risk averse, whereas with the Internet you really have to go for it'. The reality for many start-ups is, of course, double jeopardy. The founders' business loans are secured against their main assets, and yet the business remains their only source of income. To overcome this, venture capitalists will need a deep-seated belief in the ability, talent and temperament of the potential entrepreneur.

Peoplesound.co.uk

Peoplesound.co.uk was founded by Ernesto Schmitt, another ex-consultant in his late twenties with an MBA from European Institute of Administrative Affairs (INSEAD). Schmitt is reputedly worth £4 million but does not own a car, and instead travels on the London Underground. Schmitt cleverly brings together musicians and music buyers. Every year 15 000 new albums are launched in the UK – and they do not all find their way on to the shelves of the main high street retailers. Schmitt has persuaded over 1000 bands to each pay him £100, and in return he provides them with an individual web page on his site, and plays tracks that each band selects.

The artists retain full copyright, but music can be downloaded free and customized collection CDs can be produced and sold to order. Peoplesound retains 50 per cent of the price and splits the remainder among the relevant artists. Advertising and sponsorship is also important because the site has really become a powerful meeting point for musicians, buyers, record industry executives and journalists.

Schmitt has built a strong team of executives, recruiting the two people who built the on-line site for the Ministry of Sound, one of London's leading nightclubs. One of the two was also being headhunted by an investment bank that was offering a Ferrari in the package – but he joined Schmitt because 'he didn't like red'.

Gameplay.com

Although relative youth, good qualifications and something of a privileged background seem to characterize many of the new Internet entrepreneurs, there are notable exceptions. Dylan Wilk was brought up on a council estate in Batley, West Yorkshire, and he left school at the earliest opportunity to work for a mail-order fish products company. In 1994, aged twenty, he was given a grant of £2000 by the Prince's Youth Business Trust to start a small business selling computer games. Whilst the business was still in its infancy he failed properly to proof-check an advertisement and offered a game at £42.99 instead of the proper price of £47.99. He had to persuade – beg – the supplier involved to help bale him out. But he learned and the business that evolved, Gameplay.com was eventually floated, yielding Wilk a cash payment of £2.6 million and shares worth over £4 million.

To conclude this part of the chapter we return to Silicon Valley to find our 'older' Internet entrepreneur. 'At sixty-two (in 1999), Kelly Blanton is probably the oldest Internet whizz-kid'. His career has largely been spent in public service, in the employment of the US government. His company, Epylon, wants to take the $859 billion spent on non-defence procurement every year by state and federal governments on to the Internet – and he understands both the business and the politics. He has the necessary network of contacts to make this seem plausible.

As e-commerce grows in this new millennium, an increasing number of new opportunities will require this type of deep-seated industry knowledge and insight. The challenge will be to find and encourage the relevant entrepreneurs who have the latent talent and required temperament but who have become 'buried and lost in our well of talent'.

Our last story describes in detail the most famous Internet business so far, Amazon.com.

Amazon.com

Amazon.com, the 'Earth's largest bookstore', pioneered book-selling via the Internet and, in the process, changed consumer buying habits and forced the existing major booksellers to react and also offer electronic sales and postal deliveries. Paradoxically this has happened in an environment where – in parallel – 'good bookstores have become the community centres of the late twentieth century' by providing comfortable seats, staying open late and incorporating good coffee bars.

The Amazon site allows bibliophiles to exchange views and reviews as well as place orders – and some browsers apparently spend hours searching through the catalogues for titles they think will interest them. Amazon.com can never replace the hands-on element of a physical bookshop, nor engage authors for meet-the-customer signing sessions, but it can, and does, offer a far wider choice. The number of people around the world who are connected to the Internet – and buying goods electronically – is now growing rapidly. And the number of people who buy at least one book a year is huge. Many of them are willing to buy on the strength of an author's reputation or a good review of the content and style, sacrificing an insistence to inspect the book beforehand. Because of the different time zones around the world, Amazon.com can sell twenty-four hours every day.

Book-selling

Books are bought and read all round the world; and they are published in various different languages. The UK market is worth some £2 billion per year, but the American market is about ten times this size. Sales of best-selling paperback fiction titles can be huge, but other more specialized books may only sell a few hundred copies during the time they are in print. Whilst many people buy books regularly, others rely more on libraries. The industry risk lies with the publishers, who pay royalties to their authors on confirmed sales and who accept unsold books back from their wholesalers and retailers. Publishers can reprint books that sell consistently well, of course, but generally they will always carry surplus stock because of time lags. Final returns of 30 per cent are not exceptional, but the average is something below 20 per cent.

Distribution is fragmented and comprises the following channels:

- Specialist book 'superstores' – which often also sell music. The largest chains are Barnes and Noble, and Borders, American-based businesses which are now expanding into the UK. Waterstone's/Dillons is the market leader in the UK. All these are still growing in size and opening new stores. WH Smith has the second largest market share in the UK and is the leading travel (airports and railway stations) bookstore.
- Smaller independent bookshops, both single outlets and small chains. These are generally served by wholesalers as well as directly by publishers.
- Supermarkets – who typically sell only a limited range at discounted prices.
- Book clubs.
- Supplies to libraries – sometimes via specialist library wholesalers.
- Sales through university bookshops and to schools. In the UK, Waterstone's is a leading university campus retailer.
- Virtual bookstores. As well as Amazon.com, Barnes and Noble, Borders, Waterstone's and WH Smith all sell electronically via the web, and there are several other specialist e-commerce booksellers.

Since the abolition of the NBA (the net book agreement, which allowed publishers to set prices and reduced the incidence of discounting) in the UK in the mid-1990s, price discounting has been a major feature of the industry, as it is in the USA. The scope for this is significant as full retail prices are often twice the amount the publisher receives. This latter amount typically breaks down as follows:

- Direct manufacturing costs: 20 per cent
- Overheads (including marketing): 30 per cent
- Returns and allowances: 25 per cent
- Author royalties: 10–20 per cent
- Operating profit: 5–15 per cent.

The market overall has been growing throughout the 1990s, but some forecasters predict it will be more stagnant in the early years of the new millennium.

Jeff Bezos: the entrepreneur

Amazon.com was founded in 1994 by Jeff Bezos. The son of a Cuban immigrant, Bezos once dreamt of being an astronaut and consequently went on to graduate in electrical engineering and computer science from Princeton. Whilst a teenager, a paper he wrote on the effect of zero gravity on the common housefly won him a trip to the Marshall Space Flight Center in Alabama. But after Princeton he became a successful investment banker on Wall Street. He was, in fact, the youngest senior vice-president ever at D. E. Shaw, which he joined from Bankers Trust. Intrigued by the speed of growth of the Internet in the early 1990s, which he had investigated for Shaw, he decided to 'seize the moment'. He had experienced his trigger and he left the bank with the straightforward intention of starting an e-commerce business.

At this stage he had no specific product or service in mind, and so he began by drawing up a list of possible activities. He narrowed down his first list of twenty to two – music and books – before choosing books. In both cases, the range of titles available was far in excess of the number any physical store could realistically stock. In 1994 there were 1.5 million English language books in print, and another 1.5 million in other languages. Yet the largest bookstore carried 'only' 175 000 titles. Moreover, Bezos appreciated that the distribution was fragmented. He believed there was scope to offer books at discounted prices and wafer-thin margins to seize sales from existing retailers, whilst also boosting the overall size of the market.

His second decision was location. He quickly narrowed the field to Boulder, Portland and Seattle before selecting Seattle. In theory, he could have picked anywhere, but he believed there were a number of important criteria that had to be met. A ready supply of people with technical ability was essential – and other key members of his management team would need to find it an attractive place to live and work. As the firm has grown, a number of experienced people have been recruited from nearby Microsoft. In addition, it had to be a relatively small state. Bezos would have to charge a relevant sales tax to residents of any state where Amazon.com had a physical presence, but others would be exempt.

He rented a house and started in the garage, using the coffee shop in the nearby Barnes and Noble bookstore to interview potential staff. He personally made the first desks they used from old, recycled doors. After raising several million dollars from venture capitalists and private investors he knew, he moved into a 400 square foot office and began trading on the Internet in July 1995. Bezos is adamant that he warned his investors of the inherent risks in his ambitious venture. Sales began immediately, and within six weeks he moved to a 2000 square foot warehouse. Six months later he moved again. This time he set up Amazon's headquarters in a twelve-storey former hospital.

Within its first year, Amazon.com earned revenues of $5 million, equivalent to a large Barnes and Noble superstore. Sales have since grown dramatically as the company has expanded rapidly – but so too have the costs. After four and a half years the company is still trading at a loss, and profits are not in the forecast time horizon. The company went public in May 1997. Not unexpectedly, its share price and market valuation are very volatile, but Amazon has been valued at $27 billion, some $2 billion more than Wal-Mart. Bezos, himself, remains infectiously enthusiastic. He is noted for two personal quirks – his loud and frequent laugh and his tendency to always have to hand a small camera. His closest colleagues confirm he is 'sometimes goofy'.

The virtual bookstore

There are four value propositions to Amazon.com: convenience, selection, service and price.

Clearly there are no books to touch, open and read. All communications are through the World Wide Web site pages or via e-mail. The web site allows customers to search the extensive (one million plus titles) book catalogue by topic and author, to read explanations and summaries from authors as well as reviews from other readers, specialist reviewers and Amazon's own staff – and to order with a credit card. Those who prefer can reserve books via the web and then telephone Amazon with their credit card details. Orders are processed immediately. Amazon holds limited stocks of its best-selling titles, which it can post out immediately it receives an on-line order from a customer and credit card details have been confirmed. Otherwise the customer order triggers an order to the relevant publisher or a specialist wholesaler. These books are redispatched very quickly after Amazon receives them into stock. Delivery to the customer of a non-best seller, therefore, is normally around a week, with more unusual titles taking longer.

The site can also provide information on any books that are similar to any title a customer nominates; and Amazon.com will also keep customers up to date with new publications from selected authors. Readers are encouraged to post their own book reviews – and, if they wish, they can communicate electronically with any other readers looking at the same book or topic at the same time. This allows an instantaneous exchange of views and opinions.

All books are discounted – bestsellers typically by 30 per cent and others by at least 10 per cent of the jacket price. For special promotions, and to compete with the web sites of Barnes and Noble and of Borders, bestselling titles have occasionally been discounted by as much as 50 per cent. Amazon.com can do this because a book is held in stock for just two days; a high street bookseller is holding the equivalent of at least three months' sales in stock at any time. Of course, increased marketing expenditure (mostly on the Internet) for a virtual bookstore partially offsets this relative cost advantage. Moreover, the price gap is narrowed again when packing, postage and administrative charges are added back to the discounted price. These vary and depend on the point of delivery. There are no salespeople. The 'store' is open twenty-four hours every day and is accessible from anywhere in the world.

The combination of price and service are instrumental in attempting to persuade customers to return to the web site and to Amazon.com. After all, the most committed book-buyers do buy several titles at different times through the year. Finally, there is an element of fun and irreverence. Every week Amazon makes an award for the most amusing and obscure book on order at the time. Past winners include *Training Goldfish Using Dolphin Training Techniques* and *How To Start Your Own Country.* Bezos, however, maintains that

> people don't understand how hard it is to be an electronic merchant . . . most correspondence is by e-mail . . . some people do nothing but answer customer e-mails . . . we have to develop our own technologies . . . no one sells soft-ware for managing e-mail centres. There are lots of barriers to entry.

Behind the success

> We always wanted to build something the world has never seen.

Bezos is allegedly obsessed by customers and service. 'The Internet is this big, huge hurricane . . . the only constant in that storm is the customers.' Bezos was not the first Internet bookseller, but he was always determined to be the most customer-friendly. When interviewed, he talks about his customers constantly; they have clearly been a major focus for the business. In many respects, this view contradicts a belief held by many that there is no customer loyalty on the Internet. His efforts have paid off – 70 per cent of Amazon shoppers are regular customers.

In reality, Amazon.com should not be seen as a bookselling operation but as an 'e-commerce customer relationship business' because it has successfully used its web site, its image and reputation and its network to expand into other areas such as electronic greeting cards, music, videos, pharmaceuticals and pet supplies. Amazon.com also hosts Internet auctions. Some of this diversification has been achieved by the acquisition and absorbtion of other e-commerce businesses. Amazon's core competencies are in generating site traffic and potential customers, persuading them to order and then satisfying them with excellent service. An innovative and robust web site, and a distinctive brand, have always been critical elements of the Amazon strategy. The company has been at the forefront in a number of ways, many of which have been copied by other Internet businesses. It pioneered numbered steps in the purchasing operation, proactive order confirmations, credit cards sales and the single-click transaction. In the case of the single-click transaction Amazon has obtained a temporary injunction against Barnes and Noble for copyright infringement.

Bezos clearly understands web technology and knew the type of people he would need to recruit to build a strong central team. As an organization, Amazon.com is structured into five divisions: marketing; operations (order processing and warehousing); business expansion (new products and services); development (software innovations); and editorial (web site design and content). He was willing to offer generous stock options; his strong and expert top management team has stayed intact. There are four vice-presidents (VPs) who report directly to Bezos. The Marketing VP was recruited from Cinnabon World Famous Cinnamon Rolls – and prior to this he had several years' experience in a variety of other fast-moving consumer goods businesses and an MBA degree. The Business Expansion VP was experienced in book retailing. Originally the founder of a software business, Omni Information systems, he was working for Barnes and Noble before he joined Amazon. The Development VP was a mathematics graduate with over twenty years' experience in designing both hardware and software systems. The Executive Editor, the fourth VP, was a PhD graduate who had had a similar post at *PC Magazine*, which he had also launched on the web. Clearly Bezos wanted a team that was both intellectually strong and experienced in areas that would be critical for the success of the business.

Bezos always recognized the importance of the supply chain. His second and third warehouses in Delaware and Nevada were again located to reduce the impact of sales tax on purchases. At the end of 1999 there were five warehouses in the USA and one in the UK. Specialist web sites in the UK (Amazon.co.uk) and Germany supplement the main web site.

Growth and success

Without question, Amazon.com has grown dramatically to become the world's third largest bookseller through constant change and innovation. But with 12 million customer accounts and a brand-name recognized by 118 million adults in America (1999) it is far more than a bookseller. Bezos maintains he now offers 'the earth's biggest selection of goods'.

Sales began by doubling in size every ten weeks. In 1996, revenues amounted to $16 million; by 1997 they had increased to $150 million; and in 1998 they almost quadrupled again. The 1999 figures were $1.64 billion sales and $390 million losses. In comparison, the leading players in bookselling, Barnes and Noble and Borders earn approximately $3 billion and $2.5 billion respectively. Tables 9.1 and 9.2 use indices to illustrate the costs, profits and losses as a percentage of sales revenue for Amazon over a period of five years and for Amazon compared with

Table 9.1 *Amazon profitability shown as an index of revenues*

Indices for	1995 (part-year)	1996	1997	1998	1999
Revenue	100.0	100.0	100.0	100.0	100
Cost of goods sold	80.4	77.8	80.5	77.1	79
Gross margin	19.6	22.2	19.5	22.9	21
Overheads	80.4	59.9	39.3	40.3	45*
Loss as percentage	(60.8)	(37.7)	(19.8)	(17.4)	(24)

Note: * Increasing because of new developments requiring additional investments.

Table 9.2   *Amazon compared with Barnes and Noble and with Borders, 1997*

	Amazon.com	Borders	Barnes and Noble
Revenue	100.0	100.0	100.0
Cost of goods sold	80.5	72.1	72.2
Gross margin percentage	19.5	27.9	27.8
Overheads*	39.3	24.3	22.0
Profit/(loss) percentage	(19.8)	3.6	5.8

Note: * Mainly marketing and product development.

its two main competitors in 1997. When it was launched, it was thought that Amazon.com could be profitable within five years, but this has been abandoned. 'If we are profitable anytime in the short term it will just be an accident' (Bezos).

Strategic developments

The key people at Amazon realized some years ago that the Internet would generate a proliferation of new enterprises, many of them small and specialist – and that a network would offer enhanced distribution and selling opportunities. Consequently, in 1996 Amazon.com pioneered the idea of strategic alliances with other web sites. Visitors to the sites of any Amazon associate company can hyperlink and buy relevant books from the Amazon catalogue. There are now over 60 000 associate companies. Typical examples would include a food-oriented site linked to cookery books, a horticulture site and gardening books, an outdoor clothing site and guide-books. Amazon pays a referral fee of between 5 per cent and 15 per cent of sales revenues for the introduction and sales. The Amazon site is set up to provide a unique, customized collection of relevant titles for each associate.

Music and video were added to books on the web site after Amazon bought Junglee Corporation in 1998, a company which had developed innovative compar-ison shopping technologies. Consumer electronics, games, toys and pharmaceuticals – a market six times as big as books – have followed at various times. Simply, Amazon.com became increasingly concerned with lucrative electronic sales of almost anything to a vast number of customers rather than specializing as a bookseller. It is a brand.

The next step from this was almost inevitable. Late in 1999 Amazon opened its site and customers to products being sold by other companies, for whom it essen-tially provides an electronic shop-front. Amazon charges a small monthly fee and a percentage of sales revenue – in the region of 2–5 per cent. Beauty products, pet foods, branded sportswear and antiquarian books were early subscribers to this opportunity. Amazon bought equity stakes in most of these partner businesses to strengthen the alliance. In 1999 Amazon also entered the electronic auction market, another area of rapid growth, in a further attempt to exploit its customer base. Simply, it provides access to its site for companies who want to auction goods over the Internet. To support these strategic developments, Amazon earlier (1998) bought PlanetAll, a business that had built a site that allows people to maintain their personal calendars and web directories. The intention was to use it to develop a reminder service to prompt people to buy birthday and other presents.

Challenges and risks

Amazon.com is a pioneer and 'the quintessential Internet company'. Its customer base and its range of products continue to grow and diversify. But each new development appears to require additional investment. In the end, Amazon may be profitable – but it might also be a disaster waiting to happen.

There is no shortage of direct competition to its main business from other Internet book retailers, which keeps margins very low. Establishing an efficient, effective supply chain is a barrier to entry, but setting up a web site is relatively easy. As the range of activities becomes more extensive, and the company's site becomes more diverse, it is conceivable that the more serious book-buyers will select a more focused competitor such as Barnes and Noble, Borders, Waterstone's or WH Smith, all recognized brands with an e-commerce presence. This switching could even be encouraged if Amazon is too aggressive at targeting its promotions of non-book products and services at customers whose buying profile has been tracked and analysed – or if it allows other partner companies access to this information. After all, Jeff Bezos has said: 'customers are loyal right up to the point somebody offers them a better service'.

Although Amazon invests considerably in developing and improving its site, it is not inconceivable in this dynamic and turbulent industry that some form of technological breakthrough by a rival could make Amazon appear much less attractive and innovative.

In this chapter we have looked at a handful of successful new, Internet businesses. Those in e-commerce often 'exist on a precarious precipice'. However good the idea and the opportunity, championing the project is essential. Establishing the supply chain and maintaining the marketing expenditure in a dynamic and competitive environment absorbs enormous sums of money. Venture capitalists have been willing to back these start-up businesses, accepting that some will fail and assuming that a few will earn huge returns and fortunes. If there are more and more success stories, and genuine profits earned, this investment capital will continue to flow. If there are too many failures because of the industry dynamics and uncertainty, the situation could become increasingly sticky. Without substantial sums of money, these businesses can never build a realistic base from which to launch a potentially successful venture. Amazingly large sums of money do seem to be available at the moment but the share prices of the floated businesses are extremely volatile. Company valuations can change dramatically in a short space of time. The key question for e-commerce in the retail sector is whether enough people will change their buying habits and move over to the Internet. On this question, the jury is still out.

References

Brady, G. (1999). The new rules for start-ups. *e-business*, December.
Gwyther, M .(1999). Jewels in the web. *Management Today*, November.

The following publications have been used for some source material:

Bronson, P. (1999). *The Nudist on the Late Shift – and Other Tales of Silicon Valley*. Secker and
    Warburg.
Kotha, S. and Dooley, E. Amazon.com. Case study quoted in Hill, C. W. L. and Jones, G. R.
    (1998). *Strategic Management: An Integrated Approach*. 4th edn. Houghton Mifflin.
Saunders, R. (1999). *Business the Amazon.com Way*. Capstone.

Part Three
Entrepreneurs and enterprise

The link between entrepreneurs and enterprise might sound like a simple case of cause and effect. Entrepreneurs produce enterprises. If only this was true! Sadly many would-be entrepreneurs never succeed in building an enterprise. As with Cyril in our Introduction there can be a host of reasons for this. There may be shortcomings in the entrepreneur's make-up; his or her talent may be limited or their temperament unsuitable. Or it may be lack of training and know-how; his or her technique.

Equally the reasons may not be of the entrepreneur's making. The business support infrastructure may be weak so that finding start-up money and getting help is very difficult, with the result that few entrepreneurs emerge and many that do never quite make it. There can be practical things in the infrastructure that are just not there or are at least not of the quality or in the quantity needed. The educational and financial sectors may not be geared to the needs of the new enterprise. Basic facilities like transport, the postal system and telecommunications can be a major problem for start-up entrepreneurs who have to learn their way around before they can find out the best deal. There is the simple Catch 22 situation of organizing credit accounts with suppliers. In the UK a supplier will not set up a credit account with a new business unless it has references from other suppliers where the new business already has a credit account. As a new business has no suppliers when it starts, it has no credit accounts either so cannot provide any references. Whilst the new business is resolving this problem it has to pay cash on delivery and its cash flow is hit immediately.

Most likely the environment in which the entrepreneur has to operate is hostile. Despite all the regulations and controls the marketplace still has its cartels that shut out new entrants. Government bureaucracy and taxation systems and the economic situation can strangle a business before it starts, not to mention problems of corruption and extortion. Worst of all there can be a culture that rewards dependency and discourages risk-taking.

With all these problems to cope with it is no wonder that the link between the entrepreneur and the enterprise cannot be taken for granted.

Even in the other direction there are difficulties. Just because there is an enterprise it does not mean that there is an entrepreneur around. There may have been in the early days but when the entrepreneur goes he or she leaves behind an enterprise that is soon intellectually bankrupt even if it is not financially bankrupt. Such businesses join the ranks of the business community run by well-meaning people of moderate competence but without the innovation and dynamic of the entrepreneur. Apple Computers was never the same once Steve Jobs had been ousted (Carlton, 1998).

In the Introduction to the book we defined an entrepreneur as 'a person who habitually creates and innovates to build something of recognized value around perceived opportunities'. It is our belief that entrepreneurs are the people who possess the imagination and flexibility to ensure that there is a causal link between them and the enterprise. They are the ones best suited by talent and temperament to deal with the challenges of today's turbulent and uncertain world. Their minds and behaviours are agile, and they are willing to experiment with new ideas in their attempt to make a difference. In an entrepreneurial society – just as we saw in the story of Silicon Valley (Chapter 8) – ideas, talented people, finance and opportunity all come together. In this part of the book we explore the challenge for us all if this potent combination of forces is to be brought and fused together.

However, it is also important to remember that entrepreneurial behaviour in established organizations, or intrapreneurship, needs the same synergistic forces – as we discussed in Chapter 2. There is really no reason why this should not happen in large companies – if those who run the business are willing to sponsor and champion it. People everywhere in the organization can be encouraged to contribute ideas, as we saw with the stories of Asda, Wal-Mart and Richer Sounds in Chapter 4. There is rarely a monopoly of good strategic ideas at the most senior levels in the hierarchy. Within most, if not all, organizations, if they are sought, identified and encouraged, there are people with the talent and temperament to be an internal entrepreneur. The organization simply has to create the mechanisms and opportunities for exploiting this talent and provide the necessary resources to finance and implement their projects.

In reality, intrapreneurs ought to be able to find the resources from inside a large, established and successful organization more easily than an entrepreneur trying to start up a new business from scratch; but the culture has to be right. Moreover, the larger companies should be ensuring they retain and reward their most talented people (in this context) if they are going to foster this intrapreneurship. A hostile or unwelcoming culture, which demands conformity and fails to recognize or reward initiative, will have the opposite effect. People with entrepreneurial talent will underachieve, and they may very well leave.

In the remaining chapters of this book, we focus mainly on the start-up situation and consider the key issues. However the principles and lessons are easily transferred to the creation and championing of innovative new ventures and projects inside the established organization. The stages of the process are broadly similar. Simply the relevant environment is internal to the organization itself rather than external.

Creativity and innovation

Before we explain the structure of Part Three it is important to clarify further certain key terms in our definition, and the links between them.

Creativity

Creativity implies conceptualizing, visualizing or bringing into being something that does not yet exist. It is about curiosity and observation. In the history of science there are interesting examples of creativity occurring at the same time with no contact between the individuals involved. The mathematics of calculus was created by Newton and Leibniz in the seventeenth century quite independently of each other, despite their allegations of plagiarism. Creativity seems to come 'out of the blue' triggered by a problem to be solved or an idea to be expressed. Its roots and origins are mysterious and unknown but its existence cannot be denied. This meta-physical aspect has meant that science has shied away from the topic though it is now becoming a subject 'of serious study among cognitive scientists and experi-mental psychologists' (Finke, Ward and Smith, 1996).

Entrepreneurs are familiar with ideas that suddenly come to mind and are not too concerned with their origins. This is the starting point of the entrepreneurial process. We see creativity as a talent, an innate ability, though we recognize that it can be developed and that there are techniques that promote creativity and problem-solving. Creativity is also a function of how people feel. Some are more creative under pressure whilst others need complete relaxation. Some use diver-gent thinking in their creativity whilst others prefer convergent thinking.

One thing that seems common to all forms of creativity is joy. Einstein comments that the idea that 'the gravitational field has only a relative existence was the happiest thought of my life' (Pais, 1982). His creative genius had come up with the idea of relativity and it made him happy. There is an intense personal satisfaction in having come up with something new and novel.

This is one reason why entrepreneurs see their activities as fun. There is the joy of creativity all around them. For the entrepreneur, creativity is both the starting point and the reason for continued success. It is the secret formula by which he or she overcomes obstacles and outsmarts the competition.

Arguably every one of us has the ability to be creative – but do we all use and exploit this ability? Many of us simply do not act creatively much of the time. Possibly we are not motivated and encouraged; perhaps we do not believe in ourselves and the contribution and difference we could make. There is certainly a skills and technique element to creativity – in a business context, for example, we can be taught creative thinking and behaviour in the context of decision-making – but this is clearly only part of the explanation. The issue of meaning is also a critical element.

Many people have the ability to play a musical instrument. They have a skill – and possibly natural talent – and they can be taught more skills and techniques, whilst they are willing to persevere and practice. Furthermore, some people who play music naturally appreciate the meaning the composer was trying to convey when the work was written. Others have to be taught this interpretation. Some people simply see things that others cannot until they are given a detailed expla-nation. The same applies to opportunity-spotting. People who miss the valuable opportunities that others see first often have access to the same information – but it means something different to them.

> Discovery consists of looking at the same thing as everyone else and thinking something different.
>
> (Albert Szent-Gyorghi, physician and Nobel Prize winner)

In just the same way, many young people can dribble, head and pass a football, and their skills can be improved with coaching. But when they watch a football match – or play in one – are they able to 'see the whole game'? Can they spot goal-scoring opportunities and positions, and get there ahead of a defender? Most people who watch team sports such as football simply follow the movement of the ball, exactly as the television camera tends to do. They ignore or miss the emerging patterns as the other players move off the ball in search of good positions. This partially explains why we do not all seem to see the same game evolve, even though we were present at the same match.

Innovation

Innovation builds on creativity when something new, tangible and value-creating is developed from the ideas. Innovation can be focused on the theme of being 'better' – incremental improvements – as well as the theme of being radically different. The former will often form the world of the intrapreneur, who is attempting to make his or her organization better and stronger than its rivals. The latter is often, but certainly not always, reserved for the true entrepreneur, who is more concerned with doing something genuinely new and different rather than improving on ideas which have gone before.

Innovation is about seeing the creative new idea through to completion, to final application but, of course, this will not necessarily be a business. It is the *entrepreneur* who builds a business around the idea and the innovation. Both can be difficult roads and require courage and perseverance as well as creativity and imagination. These are attributes that the entrepreneur brings and his or her role in innovation is crucial.

There are three basic approaches with innovation, which are not mutually exclusive, and which we have seen illustrated in the stories in Part Two. First, it is possible to have a problem and to be seeking a solution, or at least a resolution. Edwin Land invented the Polaroid camera because his young daughter could not understand why she had to wait for the pictures to be printed when he took her photograph. Second, we might have an idea – in effect a solution – and be searching for a problem to which it can be applied. 3M's Post-it notes happened (as we saw in Chapter 4) when a 3M employee created a glue with only loose sticking properties, and a colleague applied it to a need he had for marking pages in a manuscript. Third, we might identify a need and design something that fits. James Dyson's dual cyclone cleaner came about because of his frustration with his existing machine, which was proving inadequate for cleaning up the dirt and dust he generated when he converted an old property.

Generating opportunities from ideas requires us to attribute meaning to the ideas. Ideas form in our minds and at this stage they mean something to us, personally. Typically, they become a real opportunity when we expose the ideas and share them with other people, who may well have different perceptions, attribute different meanings and see something we miss initially. This process of exploration is fundamental for determining where the opportunities for building new values are. In other words, innovation comes from the way we use our ideas. Crucially the person with the initial idea may not be the person who realizes where the real opportunity lies. An inventor is not always an opportunity-spotter, and often not a natural project champion. Picasso claimed that 'great people steal ideas and create opportunities where others cannot see the potential'.

Creativity is the talent of the inventor and innovation is the talent of the project champion who turns ideas into reality. Entrepreneurs do both these things but they do more. They do not just complete the successful application of an idea; they build something of value in the process.

The Sony Walkman provides an excellent illustration of what happens. The idea came to Sony co-founder Akio Morita when he was questioning why he was finding it difficult to listen to music when he was in public places or walking round a golf course. The idea became an innovative new product – and a valuable opportunity – when Morita shared his idea with other colleagues in Sony, and existing technologies and competencies were used to develop the compact personal radio with adequate playing time from its batteries and individual headphones. The project was championed, resourced and implemented. The original radio has systematically been joined by personal cassette and CD players. It was simply a great idea that rejuvenated Sony at the time it was conceived; and it has brought value and affected the lives of millions of people around the world.

Figure P3.1 endeavours to pull these strands together. Creativity (the idea) is the starting point whether it is associated with invention or opportunity spotting. This creativity is turned to a practical reality (a product, for example) through innovation. Entrepreneurship then sets that innovation in the context of an enterprise (the actual business), which is something of recognized value.

To be exploited fully and effectively, creativity and innovation need to be supported by certain talents and aspects of temperament. We also need a base of knowledge, which we use to help generate and develop our new ideas. In part this is developed through our experiences but it also needs to be supplemented further by certain key skills.

In very simple terms:

- talent and temperament combined with
- knowledge helps us find out and discover new possibilities
- key skills can enhance the discovery process, whilst other skills help us design and craft new opportunities from the ideas.

The enterprise process

To repeat our definition, 'an entrepreneur is a person who habitually creates and innovates to build something of recognized value around perceived opportunities'. In Part Three we look at how the entrepreneur actually does this. As the earlier

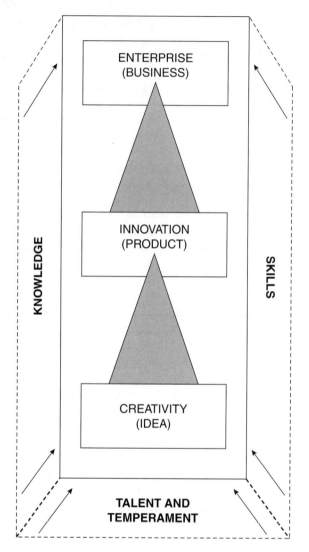

Figure P3.1   *Creativity, innovation and entrepreneurship*

comments show, the link between the entrepreneur and the enterprise cannot be taken for granted. We therefore set the actions of the entrepreneur within a process model that captures this link. In Part One we spoke of the entrepreneur process and now we turn to consider the enterprise process. This is an important distinction. The former is concerned with the entrepreneur and how his or her attributes and personal qualities contribute to the things that he or she does. The latter is concerned with the process whereby the entrepreneur builds the enterprise.

The *enterprise process* has as its setting what we have called the *enterprise paradigm*. Figure P3.2 illustrates this setting and gives some of its characteristics. In many ways this is the natural habitat of the entrepreneur. He or she is at home with its

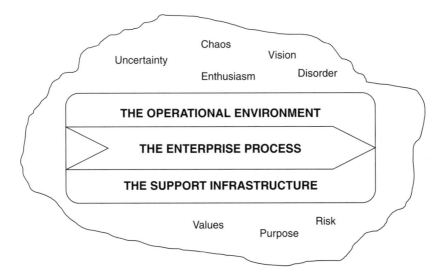

Figure P3.2   *The enterprise paradigm*

fuzzy boundary and its uncertainty and chaos, seeing them as the fertile soil of new opportunities. The vision and values of this new paradigm emphasize that it is the domain of the social and aesthetic entrepreneur as well as the economic entrepreneur, though for him or her, too, issues of vision and values are becoming increasingly important. All this is a refreshing change for the entrepreneur who for centuries has had to live within a deterministic world that is suspicious of the new and hates risk. In Chapter 10 we consider the entrepreneur's world and show how today's world of the enterprise paradigm is moving in his or her direction. Hopefully this will mean that more of the latent entrepreneurial talent will emerge and we will learn to value the entrepreneur more highly in our society.

The centre and focus of the model is the enterprise process. It is this process that is served and promoted whether by the entrepreneurs themselves or those who are trying to educate, encourage and support them. In Chapter 11 the enterprise process is broken down into its component parts as we consider how the entrepreneur operates. The *getting ready* stage prior to start-up is considered first followed by the *building* stage in which the enterprise grows and develops. Although we deal mainly with the entrepreneur who creates economic capital the principles are similar for those who employ their talent in other areas such as society and the arts. We therefore use 'enterprise' in its widest sense to mean 'a piece of work taken in hand, an undertaking; especially one that is bold, hazardous or arduous' rather than as simply a 'business firm, company'.[1]

In Figure P3.2 the 'support infrastructure' is set beneath the 'enterprise process' because it is the infrastructure that supports the process and carries it forward. This can be thought of as a boat that carries its passengers or freight to its destination. A boat that is not strong or large enough or takes in water will hinder the process and may even sink. The elements that comprise the support infrastructure are the subject of Chapter 12 as we consider how the entrepreneur can be helped and supported. Each element of the infrastructure has a specific job to do and must link together effectively. Thus if a university or research laboratory is a source of business ideas then there has to be a means of accessing that technology. There must be mechanisms for capturing the intellectual property and funding resources for its commercialization.

The 'operational environment' is placed above the enterprise process in Figure P3.2 because the process has to operate under this environment and be subject to it. In our analogy it is the weather or climate through which the boat has to sail. If the weather is hostile the boat will have a difficult journey and may not survive, but if there are sunshine and gentle seas then progress will be rapid and the mission successful. In Chapter 13 we review the main elements that make up this environment. It includes elements such as the market and the economy that the entrepreneur cannot influence in the short term. These are things that he or she has to learn to live if he or she is to *survive and win*.

The distinction between infrastructure and environment is based upon the degree to which the entrepreneur or the economic developer can control the elements involved. The infrastructure is under short to medium control but the environment takes much longer to change. It may be possible to set up a seed capital fund or build a business incubator but there is little that can done about interest and inflation rates.

In terms of our analogy it is possible to design and construct a boat that is seaworthy. This kind of activity can be organized. Mechanisms and facilities can be put in place in the short and medium term. Even if it is not be possible to do everything at once a strategy can be developed for a region that puts the most important elements in place first. On the other hand there is little that can be done about the weather. We can watch the weather forecast and either steer out of the way or take precautions as best we can. A company that is holding on to its cash in a recession is taking the right precautions. It is battening down the hatches.

Chapter 14 considers *techniques for the entrepreneur* and presents a number of basic concepts and techniques for running a successful business and *making it happen*.

In summary, then, Part Three considers how the entrepreneur:

- sees the world
- operates
- can be helped and supported
- survives and win
- makes it happen.

Underlying all these 'How' questions is the make-up of the entrepreneur – his or her talent and temperament. Two of the questions considered are more specifically about technique and know-how and have a body of knowledge and experience associated with them. These are *how the entrepreneur can be helped and supported* and *how the entrepreneur makes it happen*. In presenting this material we want to repeat the point that the acquisition of this knowledge does not make a person an entrepreneur. We acknowledge that someone may be able to turn a failing business into a successful one when they have learnt about cash flow and market share, but unless the right talents and temperament are there to be developed they will never be able to 'build something of recognized value'.

Most of us are able to run. Some can sprint to catch a train, others are fitter and jog regularly or even run a half or full marathon. But we reserve the word 'athlete' for the person who runs competitively on a regular basis and we describe the outstanding performer as an 'élite athlete'. We believe that the word 'entrepreneur' should be used in a similar way – it is too important an issue to apply the word generally to the enterprising businessperson or, worse still, to the small businessperson.

Notes

1. Definitions from the *Shorter Oxford English Dictionary*.

References

Carlton, J. (1998). *Apple*. HarperCollins.
Finke, R. A., Ward, T. B. and Smith, S. M. (1996). *Creative Cognition*, MIT Press.
Pais, A. (1982). *'Subtle is the Lord': The Science and the Life of Albert Einstein*, Oxford University Press.

10 The entrepreneur's world

Today the entrepreneur is in a world that perhaps for the first time ever has close resonances with his or her own. Uncertainty and opportunity have come together. Here we examine and critique today's world to arrive at an intellectual framework that helps us to understand why the entrepreneur has such a central role, both economic and social, to play in the society of the future. We conclude by considering the factors that present the entrepreneur with a unique opportunity to realize his or her true destiny as an agent for positive and creative change.

Opportunity and action

How we see the world is important. Some see threats where others see opportunities; for some the cup is always half-empty for others it is half-full. The entrepreneur has two linked perceptions of the world. First, he or she sees it is a world full of opportunities and, second, as a world of actions in which he or she can make things happen. It is as if the entrepreneur has two eyes seeing *opportunities to grasp* and *actions to take* as illustrated in Figure 10.1. The brain links these perceptions to give a single view of the world. If the opportunity side is not linked with focused action then in the worst case we have a *butterfly* that hops from one opportunity to another, never settling for very long. If the action side is not linked with the right opportunity then we have a *beaver* that digs a perfect hole but in the wrong place.

The link between these two perceptions is important. The mature entrepreneur moves from opportunity to action without difficulty but for the potential entrepreneur the link may not be so straightforward. The first sign of entrepreneurial talent is generally the ability to spot opportunities, but the circumstances may be such that the potential entrepreneur does not have the confidence to go forward and take action. Lack of confidence in the early days is not a sign of lack of talent. This is seen in other areas when a talent is discovered. Gifted public speakers often admit that they found it extremely difficult when they first addressed an audience. After a while they discover that public speaking comes naturally to them and they begin to enjoy

Figure 10.1 *Linked perceptions*

it as their talent blossoms. It is the same with entrepreneurs when they discover that they are able to spot an opportunity and take it to fruition. Once they find they can do this they gain confidence and very soon it becomes something that they do naturally, even habitually – they have discovered that they are entrepreneurs.

The challenge then is how to create an environment in which people are able to come forward and test their abilities as an entrepreneur. The educational approach would suggest some form of school or academy, such as are found in cricket and tennis that are geared to identifying and developing talent in those sports at an early age. Although this is a possible approach the world view of the entrepreneur is often anti-academic – they are doers rather than thinkers. There is certainly no correlation between IQ level and success as an entrepreneur. Entrepreneurs are often strongly individualistic and difficult to work with in groups. They learn best by doing and not talking.

Whilst the entrepreneur-school approach is discussed under 'developing and supporting' the entrepreneur in Chapter 12 hopes of tapping the well of talent lie much more with the developments that are taking place in the world around us. Today's world is characterized by change and uncertainty, and for the entrepreneur this is fertile soil. It is an opportunity generator in which nothing is impossible. The 'Berlin Walls' of the large multinational are no longer as impregnable as they once appeared. Richard Branson has championed the cause of the entrepreneur against the big monolithic business empires by first taking on the record companies and, more recently, the might of British Airways. Many of these same organizations are now seeking ways of being like the entrepreneurial start-up themselves. Even British Airways has put together an entrepreneurial team in their GO company in order to compete with the low-cost airlines. The title of Rosabeth Moss Kanter's book (1990), *When Giants Learn to Dance*, captures this point well. At that time, now more than a decade ago, she saw a revolution taking place in business management which she termed 'post-entrepreneurial because it is taking entrepreneurship a step further, applying entrepreneurial principles to the traditional corporation'.

Tom Peters's books have targeted the same area. His *Thriving on Chaos : Handbook for a Management Revolution* (1989) became a bestseller as the corporate world tried to come to terms with uncertainty in which markets changed almost overnight and competitors emerged out of nowhere. As reported in the Silicon Valley story in Chapter 8, IBM disregarded the idea of the minicomputer allowing a new start-up, DEC, to make the running. Both companies then disregarded the PC opportunity allowing Apple and others to take the lead. It was a credit to the new thinking in IBM that they later put together an entrepreneurial team to develop the IBM PC that caught up and overtook the early leaders.

Entrepreneurs are at home in this turbulent world where they can see opportunities and can take action. It is not a matter of being *post-entrepreneurial* but rather of being entrepreneurial in a business environment that has suddenly become uncertain and turbulent, whether that is in the large corporation or the start-up company. The dynamic of the entrepreneur has not changed. It is simply that the business environment has now moved on, enabling the entrepreneur to make the difference. Sadly many years of neglect have resulted in entrepreneurs either staying away from the large corporation or having their talent unrecognized and undeveloped, but times are changing and the intrapreneur is now seen as a valuable asset.

The situation with small businesses has not been a great deal better. This is partly because they serve the large company and end up very like them in attitude, or become so disillusioned that they never want to work for a big company again. Some big name companies take a year to pay their bills and believe that their suppliers should regard it as a privilege to have their business!

The importance of the small business sector has been championed in the UK since the Bolton Committee of Enquiry on Small Firms published its report in the early 1970s (Bolton, 1971). The contribution of the small business is the same in most of the world's developed economies. Ninety-nine per cent of all businesses employ 100 people or less and 95 per cent of them employ less than ten people. Half of the entire workforce and half of the sales come from firms with 100 people or less. These figures make the importance of the small business sector no longer a matter of debate.

With the recognition of the importance of the small firm the UK government introduced schemes to encourage their growth and development. Despite the money spent, firms have not grown and small firms have remained small. The reasons for this are at the centre of our theme. The schemes are focused on almost everything except the entrepreneur. They look at product development and innovation, at new manufacturing initiatives, at quality improvement, at providing advice on marketing and IT and so on. To the real entrepreneur all these issues are peripheral. Entrepreneurs know when they need help and they know where to get it. In principle they just want to be left alone to get on with the job. It would be better if governments made greater efforts to reduce the bureaucracy that start-up businesses have to deal with.

The small business has stifled the potential entrepreneur almost as much as the big firm, but times are changing thanks to the turbulence in technology and markets. The young entrepreneur who sees an opportunity and is told by his or her boss that promotion in a couple of years can be almost guaranteed is no longer prepared to wait. He or she leaves and sets up his or her own business using the opportunity that the previous employer refused to take up. It is these kinds of entrepreneurial aspirations that government schemes should encourage. The challenge is to unlock the entrepreneurial potential. The Thatcher government did this to some extent when it withdrew the exclusive rights held by the British Technology Group to the commercialization of government funded research in British universities. Unfortunately in most cases this control was then taken over by the universities themselves, showing a complete failure to recognize the importance of the role of the entrepreneur in the process of commercialization. Cambridge University has been an important exception to this, and its liberal policy on intellectual property has certainly been one of the factors behind the remarkable growth of technology-based businesses in the Cambridge area over the last fifteen or so years.

These comments reflect the situation in the UK and Europe. In the USA the role of the entrepreneur is well recognized and some of the government schemes to help small business growth have been excellent. The important contribution of the US Space Race budget to the rise of Silicon Valley has already been noted. The requirement that a percentage of all defence contracts should be placed with small firms has also been an important driver. This experience suggests that a main task of government is to open up opportunities that entrepreneurs then identify and exploit.

The situation in those economies that have had years of central control are particularly difficult for the entrepreneur. The countries that previously composed the USSR, including Russia itself, have a huge task before them. Speaking to a young Russian entrepreneur on an internal flight, we were told that it was impossible to grow a business in that country because if there was any degree of success there would be a visit from the Mafia and the government tax police would take the rest. So it is not surprising to find that some people use their entrepreneurial talents on the dark side of that society. It is the easiest route, if somewhat risky!

The Third World is an interesting place for the entrepreneur. Although most businesses are small and serve a local market the owner-managers seem to show more entrepreneurial characteristics than their counterparts in the developed world. Many of the new aid programmes are linking in to this entrepreneurial talent and provide start-up funding and resources. In 1998 a fish-farming project in Cambodia provided 800 000 baby fish to eight local villages and thereby enabled them to take a significant step out of poverty and into self-sufficiency. Run by a Christian charity on a not-for-profit basis the project was set up as a commercial venture. The local farmers had to pay for their fish, often on credit terms, but then were given help and advice so that they could learn how to run their farm as a profit-making business. This type of project provides an excellent opportunity for entrepreneurs to come forward and develop their talent for the benefit of the rest of their community.

The next section develops further the idea that we are moving into a world that puts the entrepreneur centre-stage but before that an important distinction has to be made between the way the entrepreneur sees things and the prevailing world view in a culture. Entrepreneurs, like Jacob and the artistic entrepreneurs of the Renaissance mentioned in the Introduction, are no different from the entrepreneurs of the Industrial Revolution or of Silicon Valley. They all see opportunities and build upon them. Jacob's world of sheep and goats was very different from the sophisticated world of the Renaissance and, yet, the essential characteristics of the entrepreneur remain the same. We have found that entrepreneurs are the same the world over, from the Central African Republic to Silicon Valley. Entrepreneurs have a particular view of the world that they see through the two lenses of opportunity and action, and are independent of the world in which they find themselves. The world around them simply determines the opportunities that are there for them to see and the resources that are available for them to use.

The enterprise paradigm

A young concert pianist from Latin America once won a scholarship to the USA. There she met Dizzy Gillespie and was impressed by his amazing ability to improvise his music. To her his music was alive and exciting and when Gillespie asked her why she played 'dead music' she abandoned her musical career. She saw no hope that she could be so spontaneous and creative. Later on she began to study how jazz musicians like Gillespie made their music and learnt that they improvise within a structured framework. It might appear spontaneous, and it is, but there is a framework behind it. Today's world of uncertainty and turbulence is a place where the creativity and improvisation of the entrepreneur can flourish but it does so within a framework that is both conceptual and practical. This chapter deals with the conceptual aspects and Chapters 11 and 12 with the practical.

The term 'enterprise paradigm' is chosen to describe this framework. The word enterprise catches its spirit and provides positive focus towards a more prosperous society. It is a paradigm in which the entrepreneur has a central role to play, but it is not his or her paradigm, it belongs to all of us. The word 'paradigm' is used because the framework has content and embodies a new way of thinking. This is done with some hesitation because the word 'paradigm' is now overused and often misapplied. The word should be restricted to the sense developed by Thomas Kuhn (1975) in *The Structure of Scientific Revolutions* where it is used to model major changes in the way we think about and understand the world in which we live. It should not be applied to the latest notion or new concept.

Kuhn's approach to the history of science was based around the idea that scientific thinking develops within an intellectual space or envelope. He called this envelope a 'paradigm'. A paradigm has its own set rules and understandings that are accepted as true because they are consistent within themselves. Within the paradigm there is debate but there is an essential harmony because people all think in the same way with the same norms and reference points. Kuhn argued that a paradigm breaks down when it fails to answer the questions of the day. At first these are few and not seen as important, but gradually an intellectual pressure builds up as more and more contradictions are found that cannot be explained. Finally the old paradigm can no longer sustain the pressure and it collapses and the new one takes over. 'The resulting transition to a new paradigm is scientific revolution' (Kuhn, 1975).

The Greek understanding of science lasted well into the Middle Ages in Europe and was a very successful paradigm. Then scholars like Copernicus (1473–1543),

Kepler (1571–1630) and Galileo (1564–1642) began to come up with observations and ideas that challenged it. Although this has been seen by many as a challenge to the Church, it was in fact a challenge to the science of the day that quite simply failed to explain the new discoveries. The intellectual pressure for a new scientific paradigm was building up.

'More than any other, it was the Copernican insight that provoked and symbolised the drastic, fundamental break from the ancient and medieval universe to that of the modern era' (Tarnas, 1996). Although in hindsight this was a defining moment, it was by no means obvious at the time. The scientists as much as the churchmen found it difficult to accept this insight. Even Copernicus was not happy with his new theory because it made the orbits of the planets much more complicated (Koestler, 1989). It was only later when Kepler showed that the orbits of the planets were ellipses and not circles that the whole thing simplified. But it still required Isaac Newton, born in 1642, the same year that Galileo died, to put all these ideas together. He was in his twenties when he produced the mathematics that explained these discoveries and the new paradigm was finally born. Surprisingly it took the persuasion of the astronomer Halley, some twenty years later, before Newton told the world what he had done and published his now famous *Principia Mathematica*.

The nature of this scientific revolution was well expressed by the Cambridge historian Sir Herbert Butterfield when he wrote:

> It outshines everything since the rise of Christianity and reduces the Renaissance and Reformation to the rank of mere episodes, mere internal displacements, within the system of medieval Christendom. It changed the character of men's habitual mental operations. It required a different kind of thinking cap, a transposition in the mind of the scientist himself.
>
> (Butterfield, 1957)

Over time this shift in the way scientists thought became the basis for our Western culture and the way we think. In scientific, social and economic terms this paradigm has been a great success and has provided the basis for the Western world as we know it today. The emphasis on the individual that was a feature of this paradigm was also a help to the emergence of the entrepreneur. People's lives were no longer governed by fate and the gods but by man's own efforts. The Protestant work ethic was an important motivator (Weber, 1905) and drove many successful entrepreneurs. It brought economic prosperity to certain parts of Europe. Successful groups such as the Huguenots and the Mennonites were driven out as much from economic envy as for their religious beliefs (Reaman, 1963). The USA benefited from these upheavals in Europe and has become the most successful economy the world has ever seen. Waves of immigrants have continued to top up the entrepreneurial stock in the USA, as the story of the Cuban refugees in Miami described in Chapter 11 indicates.

At the beginning of the twentieth century the Newtonian paradigm was beginning to feel the pressure just as the Greek paradigm had done 400 years earlier. Experiments concerning the nature of light and moving bodies in space were giving some strange results that were not explained by the physics of the day. Then in 1905 Albert Einstein, at that time an examiner in the patent office in Switzerland, published his first paper on relativity. This proved to be the door to a new paradigm. Not only was it able to make sense of the strange results that classical physics could not explain, but it opened up a new world of relativity and quantum mechanics. It was the world of the New Physics. Without this breakthrough the modern world of electronics, semiconductors and microprocessors would not have been possible. High technology as we know it today is a product of this new paradigm.

Central to an understanding of the New Physics are two theories put forward in 1927; Heisenberg's Uncertainty Principle and Bohr's Theory of Complementarity. They represent the mindset of the new paradigm and show a complete break from the deterministic thinking of the Newtonian paradigm. It is not a matter of more complete scientific knowledge; it is about seeing things in a new way, about a 'different kind of thinking cap'.

To illustrate this new way of thinking we consider what one of these theories, the Theory of Complementarity, meant in practice. Since the time of Newton a debate had raged between scientists as to whether light was a wave, or a stream of particles, as Newton believed. Throughout the eighteenth century the particle or corpuscular theory, as Newton called it, was believed to be the right answer, which conversely meant that the wave theory had to be wrong. At the beginning of the nineteenth century this view was challenged by Thomas Young and later that century by James Clerk Maxwell who showed beyond doubt that light was indeed a wave. It was part of the electromagnetic spectrum of waves that start with gamma rays and X-rays of very small wavelength and move through to the visible range called light and on to radio waves of much longer wavelength. By the time Einstein came on the scene, light was understood as a wave and not as a stream of particles. Einstein stunned the scientific world by showing that the photoelectric effect could only be explained if light was a stream of discrete bundles of energy called photons. This put Newton's corpuscular theory back on the agenda. So was light a wave or a stream of particles?

Experiments could be performed which demonstrated beyond doubt the wave characteristics of light. Experiments could also be carried out which showed that light behaved as a stream of photons. The Classical Physics paradigm of Newton could not accept this. Only one answer could be valid. Bohr's Theory of Complementarity in the New Physics paradigm offers a completely different perception. Both answers are valid; the explanations are complementary not contradictory. This is not a scientific fudge, it is simply a different way of looking at things.

As this example illustrates a fundamental shift has taken place in the way scientists think. Science now has a new intellectual framework that can handle ideas of uncertainty and chaos found at the level of atoms and particles. The interesting thing is that this thinking did not stop with the scientists. Whilst an essay by Bohr entitled 'Causality and complementarity' shows they were still debating the issue in 1958 (Ferris, 1991), general Western culture had its watershed in the 1960s when it, too, embraced uncertainty and chaos at the human level. It was a time of great upheaval with the hippy free love movement, psychedelic drugs and protest marches. Much of this emanated from California, and the entrepreneurial culture of Silicon Valley is closely linked with the values and thinking that started at that time.

But there was more to the Valley than electronics: The free-speech movement at Berkeley, the summer of love in Haight-Ashbury, flower power, the Grateful Dead, the birth of a counterculture. Apple was a technological manifestation of its environment.

(Rose, 1989)

The Home Brew Club of the mid-1970s in Silicon Valley, described in Chapter 8, was a group of people who grew out of this culture and, because it became one of the main spin-off points in the valley, it spread a new approach to business. When Apple Computers began to be featured in *Business Week* and *Fortune* magazine the rest of American industry took note. When Apple challenged the supremacy of IBM in their famous Superbowl television commercial in 1984, it was clear that the business world would never be the same again. Uncertainty and chaos had entered this world too.

This shift in culture and then in business is described in rather robust terms by Alvin Toffler:

A new civilization is emerging in our lives, and blind men everywhere are trying to suppress it. This new civilization brings with it new family styles; changed ways of working, loving and living; a new economy; new political conflicts; and beyond all this an altered consciousness as well. The dawn of this new civilization is the single most explosive fact of our lifetime.

(Toffler, 1981)

In *Future Shock* ten years earlier Toffler had pointed to the 'Death of Permanence' and the change and turbulence that was becoming a characteristic of our society. 'Change sweeps through the highly industrialized countries with waves of ever accelerating speed and unprecedented impact' (Toffler, 1971).

Toffler's themes were picked up by business. Hammer and Champy who introduced the idea of 're-engineering the corporation' comment that, 'Suddenly the world is a different place. In today's environment nothing is constant or predictable. Adam Smith's world and its way of doing business are yesterday's paradigm' (Hammer and Champy, 1993).

Porter observed in his *Competitive Advantage of Nations* (1990) that 'there is a growing consensus that the dominant paradigm used to date to explain international success in particular industries is inadequate'. He found that classical economic theory could not explain the emergence of the newly industrialized countries such as Taiwan and Korea.

It is as if the physicists were first on the scene and broke through into their new paradigm in the early part of the twentieth century to be followed by general culture in the Western world in the 1960s and by business and industry in the 1970s and 1980s. What is remarkable is that they all have change, uncertainty and turbulence as key characteristics. In some ways it is one huge paradigm shift encompassing science, society and business.

Many writers have picked up these themes. Some have done this under the heading of postmodernism (Lyon, 1994) and others have applied it to their special area of interest such as business (Handy, 1993). Lyon uses the film *Blade Runner* to pick out three elements of postmodernism: the debate about reality, an industrial order based on 'new organizing principles structured around knowledge' and a consumer society 'where everything is a show and the public image is all'. In his *Age of Unreason* Handy (1993) argues that we need 'creative upside-down thinking in today's world of discontinuous change' and uses shamrocks, doughnuts and portfolios as models to help us think differently.

Toffler has put these themes in a historical perspective with a three wave model which has parallels with our use of paradigms:

> The First Wave – the agricultural revolution – took thousands of years to play itself out. The Second Wave – the rise of industrial civilization – took a mere three hundred years. Today history is even more accelerative, and it is likely that the Third Wave will sweep across history and complete itself in a few decades.
>
> (Toffler, 1981)

Whilst Toffler's waves relate to society as a whole there is a correspondence between his 'Second Wave' and the deterministic world of the Newtonian paradigm and his 'Third Wave' and the world of the New Physics paradigm of Einstein. John Sculley (1987) applied Toffler's wave model to business and used it to compare his very different experiences at Pepsi Cola and Apple Computers. Under the heading 'Contrasting Management Paradigms' he compared 'Second Wave' Pepsi Cola with 'Third Wave' Apple. Table 10.1, taken in part from this analysis and similar listings by Kawasaki (1992), compares some of the characteristics of Second and Third Wave companies. Kawasaki was a 'software evangelist at Apple Computer Inc. from 1983 to 1987'.

The Third Wave company is the entrepreneurial business with its flat and flexible management structures and its ability not only to embrace change but to stimulate it. People in Third Wave companies are valued as persons and are not seen simply as a human resource. It is the new that is important and not the institution, so that for the potential entrepreneur the Third Wave company is a natural habitat.

Table 10.1   *Two management paradigms*

Parameter	Second Wave	Third Wave
Structure	Hierarchy	Flat and flexible
Ability	To organize	To embrace change
Output	Market share	Market creation
Personnel	Human resource	The person
Focus	The institution	The new
Motivation	To make money	To make history
Status	Title and rank	Building the new
Working environment	Formal, regulated	Informal, chaotic
Culture	Tradition	Genetic code
Philosophy	Fit into roles	Build on strengths
Mission	Goals/strategic plans	Identity/direction/values
Where	Clubhouse	Anywhere
When	9.00 a.m. to 5.30 p.m.	Anytime

The main motivation is to make history. As reported earlier, John Sculley's decision to leave the security of Pepsi Cola for the roller coaster that was Apple was based around the one question from Steve Jobs: 'Do you want to spend the rest of your life selling sugared water or do you want a chance to change the world?' Status and rank are not important. The big office and access to the managers' dining room do not matter anymore. Third Wave companies, like entrepreneurs, want to build something, to do things that have not been done before. They are not interested in the status quo.

The working environment is completely different in Second Wave and Third Wave companies. Rules, regulations and tradition are important to the former but have no place in the latter. The board meetings at Second Wave Pepsi Cola and Third Wave Apple Computers could not have been more different. Sculley (1987) tells us that at Pepsi Cola:

> Everyone wore the unofficial corporate uniform: a blue pin-striped suit, white shirt, and a sincere red tie. None of us would ever remove his jacket. At Apple all of us dressed casually, sans ties and jackets. Steve Jobs sat on the floor lotus style, in blue jeans, absent-mindedly playing with the toes of his bare feet.

Table 10.1 gives the options for culture as tradition or genetic code from Sculley's list. Tradition is derived from the past. Companies like Pepsi Cola have their legends and heroes. They have their own way of doing things. Almost their only business indicator was their market share compared with Coca-Cola's. Apple by contrast was a living dynamic organization driven by elements deep in its culture that, like the genetic code, are always present but express themselves 'differently in different organisms'. Sculley believed that the company's vision and direction derived from this.

In Chapter 1 the role of talent and temperament was discussed and related directly to what a person did best. Sculley's genetic code analogy makes the same point. Third Wave companies allow people to discover what they are good at and then help them to do it. They build upon the strengths of their staff. Second Wave companies put people into predetermined roles and if they do not fit then they have to adapt or leave. Personal development is focused on strengthening weaknesses rather than building on strengths.

The relevance of all this to entrepreneurs is that they suddenly find themselves in a world that is far more in tune with their approach to life than was the old deterministic paradigm. The turbulence of the new paradigm throws up many more opportunities than the previously slow-moving and fairly predictable world. Risk and uncertainty is now inherent in the system, so entrepreneurs have less to lose. Today in the USA if you fail in business it is seen as a qualification and not a handicap. Creativity and doing things in new and innovative ways are now seen as positive and are encouraged. Those who say something cannot be done because it has never been done before are living in the old paradigm. Networking, market creation, values, making a difference and building, are all things that warm the entrepreneur's heart. They are central to his or her view of the world so that, for perhaps the first time in history, we have a match between the entrepreneur's world and the world around him or her.

How true is it? A critique

Some important assertions have been made above and it is important to evaluate with some care the basis on which they are made. So how true is all this?

Whether or not we are moving into a new paradigm there is little doubt that times are changing and changing very rapidly. The pace of technology alone brings a momentum that seems unstoppable. Computers, telecommunications and the World Wide Web are changing the world in which we live. But this was also true of railways, sanitation, telephones, motorcars, tarmac roads, mass production, electrical power, aeroplanes, plastics, the jet engine, television and supermarkets. These innovations only produce a discontinuity when people cannot cope with the rate at which they come along. It is certainly true that new technology is being adopted more rapidly than in the past. Mobile phones and PCs took thirteen and fifteen years respectively to reach 25 per cent of the US population compared with the telephone that took thirty-five years. But thirteen years is still quite a long time and hardly worthy of the word 'revolution'. Even were these technology 'adoption times' to reduce further as seems to be the case with the World Wide Web there is no evidence that society will not be able to cope with such changes.

The key question is not whether times are changing but whether the Western world is experiencing a major intellectual and social transition. This is the real issue. Is society moving from the deterministic paradigm brought in by Newton into a new one where change and turbulence are the way it is? If so, then it is good news for the entrepreneur; if not, it will be just as much a struggle for him or her as it has always been. Is Toffler right when he describes the three waves that have swept over humanity, or is the division between Second and Third Wave companies just a convenient way of explaining a few differences? Is it yet another management fad that will soon be replaced?

There has certainly been no shortage of new approaches to management over recent years. Management book titles tell their own story. Examples are *In Search of Excellence* (Peters and Waterman, 1982), *When Giants Learn to Dance* (Kanter, 1990), *Thriving on Chaos* (Peters, 1989), *The Innovation Marathon* (Jelinek and Schoonhoven, 1990) and *Reengineering the Corporation* (Hammer and Champy, 1993). Other books offering a new approach include *Competitive Advantage* (Porter, 1985), *The 80/20 Principle* (Koch, 1997), *The Fifth Discipline* (Senge, 1990) and *Principle-Centred Leadership* (Covey, 1990). Books on successful individuals and their way of doing things have also been common: *Making It Happen* (Harvey-Jones, 1988), *Talking Straight* (Iacocca, 1989), *Business the Bill Gates Way* (Dearlove, 1999), *Direct from Dell* (Dell and Fredman, 1999) and *In Sam We Trust* (Ortega, 1999). Is this plethora of such books a sign that things really are different now or is it simply that we are 'dedicated followers of fashion'?

Certainly there are signs that some have had too much of these fashions and want to get back to basics. Titles like *Managing without Management: A Post-Management Manifesto for Business Simplicity* (Koch and Godden, 1998) and *The Power of Simplicity: A Management Guide to Cutting through Nonsense and Doing Things Right* (Trout and Rivkin, 1998) show this trend.

Whilst this view is understandable it is surely a sign of turbulent times when so many new solutions appear to the old problems. Thanks to mass communication the world is a much smaller place and, conversely, the marketplace is suddenly much bigger. Combine this with the advances of technology and one has a major shift in the economic and social environment. Even the large multinationals cannot assume a 'business as usual' approach. In the 1960s, it took twenty years to displace the top 35 per cent of the top 500 American companies; now it takes four or five years' (Bygrave, 1998).

There is little doubt that the world is entering a new paradigm as profound as that identified by Thomas Kuhn (1975) for the scientific world. What is less sure is the model proposed by Toffler that sees the old replaced by the new as a third wave sweeps in. This just does not accord with the facts. As every secondary school student of mathematics and physics knows the Scientific Revolution of the sixteenth and seventeenth centuries did not throw out Euclid's geometry, the Pythagoras theorem or Archimedes' principle. The Newtonian paradigm certainly did embody a major shift in the way scientists approached their science but not all of the findings of Greek science were rejected.

The same thing is seen with the present shift to the world of Einstein and his colleagues. Although the way of thinking has changed profoundly Newton's Laws of Motion are still taught and engineers still design things using these principles. The difference is that it is now known that Newton's laws and similar findings of deterministic science have their limits.

This carry-over from one paradigm to the next is important to recognize. A paradigm shift idea is a new envelope of thinking but not everything in the envelope is new. As Butterfield (1985) put it 'there is a new kind of thinking cap' but the content of the paradigm is a mixture of the completely new and some of the old that has been carried over. It is rather like moving into a new house when most of the furniture is new but there is also furniture from the old house. Both sets of furniture are arranged to fit in with the new setting.

Applying this to the analysis of the Second and Third Wave company in Table 10.1 the modern company has to take on board the new and yet keep some of the old, and see both in a new light. Whilst 'management by objectives' may have had its day, the goals and targets of the Second Wave are just as important as the direction and vision of the Third Wave. The difference is that the goals and targets can no longer be set in stone. They must be flexible and serve the direction and vision of the organization. Management structures that are strongly hierarchical are not likely to survive and will need to be replaced by flexible networks, but at the same time responsibility, authority and accountability must be retained.

Any company that has only the Third Wave elements will have serious problems, as Apple Computers discovered to its cost. Their experience was the result of focusing on market creation and ignoring market share, considering only direction and not targets (Carlton, 1998). But acceptance of the contradictions of the Second and Third Wave characteristics of Table 10.1 is not easy and there is generally a polarization of view around the boardroom table. It is market share *versus* market creation rather than market share *and* market creation. Under the old way of thinking they are a contradiction as much as was the description of light as both a wave and a particle, but if the scientist's Theory of Complementarity is applied then both can be accepted.

This understanding has been articulated by Charles Handy (1995). In *The Empty Raincoat* he argues that with all the old certainties gone, and change and turbulence about us, we must accept the 'paradoxes of our time' and learn to live with them both in society and in business. Jelinek and Schoonhoven (1990), in the *Innovation Marathon*, report on how the best US electronics companies are able to survive and grow in a fast-moving industry. They have learnt how to achieve stability and change at the same time with the stability of the Second Wave company and the change of the Third Wave business held in balance. This same point is found in *In Search of Excellence* by Peters and Waterman (1982). Among the characteristics of top-performing companies they identified the ability to manage both tight and loose structures at the same time. Successful companies are able to manage this paradox.

From this critique it is concluded that the developed world and its way of doing business is indeed entering a new paradigm but it is one which includes elements of the old set in the context of the new. It does require a new way of thinking and specifically calls for the ability to hold opposites in balance and to manage paradox. Kuhn (1985) has called this 'the essential tension'. Handled in the right way it can be highly positive and creative, but handled badly and it can be destructive.

The key ingredient in managing paradox is the level of trust between those who hold opposing views. All organizations, whatever the corporate approach, are a combination of Second and Third Wave people and this produces tensions. Within an organization the level of trust will decide whether this inherent tension works for good or ill. If a sufficient level of trust is achieved then the paradox of stability and change and of tight and loose structures can be handled. This is where the network organization is so important because it has a much greater potential to generate and build trust than does a hierarchy. 'The ability of companies to move from large hierarchies to flexible networks of smaller firms will depend on the degree of trust and social capital present in the broader society' (Fukuyama, 1995).

Entrepreneurs can now be set in this context for they have this same dichotomy within themselves. Their opportunity-spotting talents are at home in the Third Wave business and their ability to get things done line up with some of the elements of the Second Wave. As in the case of a company there is a tension within entrepreneurs between these two sets of characteristics and in order to be successful they must be able to hold this tension creatively.

Temperament is the element that controls this tension. It can moderate it or increase it. A person with a strong ego drive pushes his or her talent to the limit. The tension snaps when this limit is exceeded and the individual may slip into depression and a deep sense of failure. But if the tension is held then a person can perform with excellence, stretching and developing his or her talent.

Equally a person may possess outstanding talent and not have the temperament in terms of drive and motivation to develop it to the full. Roger Black, the athlete, found winning races so easy at school that he was not interested in athletics. There was no challenge in it. His temperament and talent were out of step. Instead his desire was to play the guitar and sing in a band. This he did achieve but not having real talent in this area he made little progress. At Southampton University he got into serious athletics and with his temperament and talent then in step with each other he reached the national team without difficulty. Despite injury he persevered and achieved an Olympic Silver medal and was a key member of the 1991 World Champion 4 × 400 men's relay team.

Talent and temperament are both required and must work together and stimulate each other if real excellence is to be achieved. The link between the two builds up a kind of internal trust that we generally describe as self-confidence. Upbringing and life's experiences can build or destroy a person's internal trust.

The key question for entrepreneurs is whether they can trust themselves to turn the opportunity that they perceive into a reality. For a few the answer is so self-evident that the question is not even considered, but for most people it does have to be thought through. For some, business training courses can make the difference. Those who have a talent for business are quick to pick up on the ideas that they learn about and are eager for more. This process generates confidence and internal trust. They begin to believe that they can actually build a business. Others benefit from a one-to-one approach and, like the athlete, have a coach or mentor that builds their confidence and helps them to believe in themselves. Whichever methods are used, the internal trust is built up as a three-way connection between talent, temperament and technique. It is the glue that binds the three elements together.

The entrepreneur's opportunity

Today's world is a time of special opportunity for the business entrepreneur. If he or she is able to seize this opportunity then there will be a remarkable explosion of entrepreneurial activity and, thereby, a new level of prosperity for all.

Prosperity, of course, is primarily a statement about economics and the creation of wealth. It is not about contentment and happiness. People can be very prosperous and also very miserable. The role of the social and aesthetic entrepreneur will be important here, although their opportunities will be less obvious and more demanding of the entrepreneur. For this reason it will be important to encourage them so that they come forward and provide a balance against the excesses that follow from a pursuit of prosperity. This suggests that special efforts should be made to identify and promote social and aesthetic entrepreneurship in our universities and that entrepreneurship courses should not be limited to those studying business, economics, design and technology.

It is also important that as wealth is created it is distributed across the population and not held by a few. This is a difficult social and political issue but it is also an entrepreneurial issue. The old idea that entrepreneurs comprise a wealthy élite is now being challenged by the facts. *Forbes Magazine* published their 1999 list of America's 400 richest people under the heading 'A century of wealth'. In that issue an article entitled 'The billionaire next door' commented that today's billionaires 'seem fanatically determined to appear middle class'. They argue that this is because most of them were not born into wealth and want to stay with their middle-class values. Fifteen years ago 40 per cent of the *Forbes* 400 made their wealth and 60 per cent inherited it. In 1999, 63 per cent of them had made their own wealth;

a figure that seems set to increase in the future. Below billionaire level the picture is even more remarkable. In 1989 there were 1.3 million dollar-millionaires. Just ten years on there are 5 million and it is estimated that in the next ten years there will be 20 million. The article concludes that:

> In the past 200 years, the great achievement of the modern West was to create a mass middle class, allowing the common man to escape poverty and live in relative comfort. Now the United States is ready to perform an even greater feat. This country is well on its way to creating the first mass affluent class in world history.

In the USA the terms 'the rich', 'the middle class' and 'the poor' no longer mean what they used to.

For some of these 'overclass' as the *Forbes* article calls them their sudden wealth makes them uncomfortable. 'They know they are doing well, but they also want to feel like they're doing good'. Wealth is being seen as something to be shared rather than indulged in. A British television programme in October 1999 featured a wealthy trader in the City of London who decided on what he and his wife regarded as a reasonable standard of living and then gave away the rest of his earnings. When interviewed he suggested that a millionaire should be someone who has given away a million pounds rather than one who has acquired a million.

With these caveats about the social and aesthetic entrepreneur and the distribution of wealth, we now consider the opportunities that make today's world so special for the entrepreneur. In some parts of the world the time of the entrepreneur has already arrived. A decade and a half ago it was commented that:

> What has emerged here, [the USA] primarily in only the past two decades, is a community of a few hundred professional investors with entrepreneurial management and advanced technology to create new products, new companies and new wealth. This has sparked the greatest burst of entrepreneurial activity the world has ever seen.
>
> (Wilson, 1986)

The same 'burst of entrepreneurial activity' has been experienced in Cambridge, England with the 'Cambridge Phenomenon' (Segal, Quince and Wicksteed, 1985) and in Bangalore, India (Singhal and Rogers, 1989). These are the first signs of a phenomenon that could encompass the whole world. This belief is based on two things. The theme that underlies this book – 'that entrepreneurial talent is to be found in people everywhere, whether they are rich or poor or in an advanced or a developing society' – and the new enterprise paradigm that is spreading around the globe creating the right conditions. The match between the entrepreneur's world and the real world has never been closer. 'In the 21st century, the winners will be those who stay ahead of the change curve, constantly defining their industries, creating new markets, blazing new trails, reinventing the competitive rules, challenging the status quo' (Gibson, 1998).

The three characteristics of today's world that make this a time of special opportunity are:

- new and converging technologies that create and disturb markets
- products and services with low market entry costs
- more entrepreneurs.

Technology and markets

Entrepreneurs thrive on change, but only within certain boundaries. In the past change, both economic and social, has come about by wars and conflict and by politics and colonization. This has been the time of the leader rather than the entrepreneur. The only entrepreneur to appear consistently throughout history has been the merchant entrepreneur. For many centuries the Great Silk Road was an entrepreneur's highway linking different worlds driven by the Romans' demand for silk and China's interest in wools, gold and silver – it was a market-driven highway. Then there were those who plied the oceans of the world bringing back exotic products to a curious Western world. The cost of mounting such expeditions was perhaps the world's first example of venture capital.

When a period of peace has been achieved, the entrepreneur has taken the opportunity to be more than just a merchant trader. As cited in the Introduction, Jardine (1997) sees the Renaissance as being as much an entrepreneurial opportunity as a period of great artistic flowering. Great wealth was accumulated by the entrepreneurs of the day whilst the kings were living off credit and, in reality, had huge debts. Entrepreneurs were beginning to build something of recognized and substantial value.

Entrepreneurs have never really been accepted as a factor in economic growth. Economists have virtually ignored their existence. 'Until the mid-nineteenth century most economists held a relative indifference to the entrepreneur, focusing instead on the dynamics of capitalism and industrial development' (Buckingham, 1987). 'As recently as 1985, very few economists paid any attention whatsoever to entrepreneurship' (Bygrave, 1998). Whilst a few voices were raised amongst the economists in support of the entrepreneur they were rare. Jean Baptiste Say (1767–1832) the influential French economist was one. With his business background he was able to appreciate their importance. He commented that 'the man who conceives or takes charge of an enterprise, sees and exploits opportunity is the motive force for economic change and improvement' (Galbraith, 1991). The subsequent experience of the US economy was to prove this point. By 1890 America had more than 4000 millionaires and the number was growing fast (Pendergrast, 1994). Industrial giants like Andrew Carnegie and Cornelius Vanderbilt were the champions of this new world of wealth.

In the early decades of the twentieth century the link between economic growth and invention and technology was being made. The evidence for this was there for all to see. In his *Theory of Economic Development* published in 1911 Joseph Schumpeter (1883–1950) put the entrepreneur centre stage seeing him or her as the one who introduces new ideas and 'challenges the established equilibrium with a new product, a new process or a new type of productive organization' (Galbraith, 1991). Asa Candler (1851–1929) was such a man who became a self-made millionaire thanks to a new product called Coca-Cola. There were many entrepreneurs around like Candler for people like Schumpeter to observe. Candler was not the inventor but he made it happen. John Pemberton, its inventor died in 1888 penniless but 'if the Pembertons had not sold the formula it would have stayed an old drink somewhere and been lost in time' (Pendergrast, 1994). It was Asa Candler, the entrepreneur, who made it all happen.

Despite Schumpeter making the connection between the entrepreneur and innovation, others chose to focus only on the innovation. They saw science and technology as the driver of economic progress and gave the entrepreneur a back seat. In 1919 Kondratieff proposed his 'long wave' theory of economic growth and technological innovation. Working from the 1700s he identified cycles of growth and decline of approximately fifty years. Growth arose from a cluster of innovations that led to the creation of new industries giving prosperity to certain regions. Other groups would pick up the next wave of innovations and using this competitive advantage would overtake the rest that would then go into relative decline. Thus the invention of the power loom created the cotton industry and steam power made possible the iron industry. These made Britain the 'workshop of the world' (Malecki, 1997) in the first of Kondratieff's waves from 1787 to 1845. The Bessemer steel process, the steamship and the railways were the innovations that led to new industries now on a large scale in the period 1846 to 1895. Despite Mr Bessemer inventing his process in Britain and entrepreneur engineers like Brunel building steam ships and railways this period saw Germany and the USA challenging Britain's supremacy.

The third period from 1896 to 1947 was under way when Kondratieff put his idea of 'long waves' forward. This was picked up by others (Ayres, 1990; Hall and Preston, 1988), who have brought the analysis up to date. The exciting new sciences of chemistry and electricity, and the technology of the internal combustion engine, all gave rise to huge industries to the benefit of the economies of Germany and the USA. The fourth period from 1948 to 2000 saw science and technology merge as the transistor and microprocessor led to the electronics, computer and telecommunications industries.

This model not only gives some interesting historical insights but also shows that science and technology are important drivers and sustainers of the economy. It is clearly a necessary condition for the present world's economy as we know it. As Malecki (1997) puts it: 'Technology is central to regional change, positive and negative, and to economic change, job-creating and job-destroying. It is the most obvious cause and effect of the cumulative wealth of rich nations.'

In introducing a government White Paper in 1999 on the knowledge-driven economy the UK's Prime Minister, Tony Blair, commented that: 'The modern world is swept by change. New technologies emerge constantly, new markets are opened up. There are new competitors but also great new opportunities' (UK government, 1998). This link between technology and markets is a key point. Technology alone cannot create a viable opportunity, only the market can do that. It is the response of the customer to the technology that creates the market. Internet service providers (ISPs) like Compuserve and America On-Line (AOL) had been around for a few years but it was when the retailer Dixon's launched its free ISP, Freeserve, in 1998 and scooped a million subscribers in just nine months that the market really took off. With the imagination of the entrepreneur, technology becomes a great disturber of markets and even more opportunities are created.

Opportunities are also coming from the convergence of different technologies. Computers and telecommunications have come together to produce a huge wave of opportunities linked with the World Wide Web. With digital television and the Internet linked up, the face of retailing could change forever as on-line shopping establishes itself. The technology of the mobile phone is picking up a number of different technologies to offer the customer more and more services, from e-mail to knowing your exact location in an emergency.

All these trends result in ever more opportunities for the entrepreneur so that we are on the threshold of a period that could perhaps one day be truly the age of the entrepreneur. For the first time an age will be described not by a science or a technology as was the atomic age and the computer age but by the exploiter of that technology, the entrepreneur.

Low market entry costs

The science and technology that led to the major industries identified in Kondratieff's 'long waves' had increasingly high entry costs. The power loom and steam power of the late eighteenth century was too expensive for the cottage industry to take up so the first factories were formed and people began to 'go to work'. The price that had to be paid for capital equipment continued to increase and the small factory was replaced by larger and larger ones as economy of scale was pursued. By the end of the Second World War the scientific and technical talent of the UK was being absorbed by large sectors such as the chemical and aircraft industries and the potentially large nuclear power industry. These sectors had huge entry costs so that for graduates and others at that time the idea of setting up one's own technology-based business was simply not an option. Even when the computer industry began to take shape, it was dominated by large mainframe manufacturers like IBM. Everything was big and appeared to offer secure jobs with promotion guaranteed for the career-minded graduate.

In the 1960s and 1970s the inventions of the semiconductor, the integrated circuit and the microprocessor came together and changed everything. With the personal computer and its software an unprecedented period with low market entry costs had begun. Individual entrepreneurs could actually think of starting their own business without a family fortune behind them. This is why the majority of millionaires in the world today have made their money in their own lifetime.

Of course, as these industries have grown some big players have emerged and have created their own market entry problems for the new business. Microsoft represents the large company that has maximized its hold on the marketplace. Yet even as they were being charged with taking unfair advantage of their monopoly position, a young man from Finland, Linus Torvald, was offering a new operating system, Linux, free of charge on the World Wide Web. Linux is fast becoming a serious competitor to Microsoft's Windows operating system yet it had no venture capital backing and was not supported by a large company. Torvald wrote the operating system at home and sent it around on the web, only asking that users sent him a postcard. Torvald's secret was to offer software developers low-cost entry to a new and powerful operating system.

Biotechnology is another new industry that has opened up over the past twenty years. Although entry costs are not high there is a requirement for laboratories and the time to market is significantly longer than other technology sectors because of the regulatory nature of the drug industry. This means that the start-up company often spots the opportunity and takes it through to the proof of principal and even working prototype stage but goes no further. By this time it can have created sufficient intellectual property for the company to have real value. Some have been able to achieve huge stock valuations on this basis or have been bought out by one of the big pharmaceutical companies.

Although some of the early start-up companies such as Microsoft and Intel have risen to dominate their sectors and biotechnology start-ups have a longer road to travel than in other sectors, the opportunities for technology-based start-ups just go on increasing and the low-cost market entry situation still prevails. This was recognized in the UK government White Paper on the knowledge-driven economy in December 1998 (UK government, 1998) which concluded that it:

- gives small firms new opportunities to access international markets without the need for a global marketing network
- permits more contracting out of activities, particularly those based on codified knowledge, and creates possibilities for new forms of organization such as 'virtual' companies.

Information technology, the knowledge-driven economy, the Internet age and the e-commerce era are all terms used to describe this new world of opportunity but it only works to the benefit of the entrepreneur if he or she can enter that world at low cost with limited resources. It is this fact that that is central to the present opportunity. The current Internet boom has come about because of this. As Steve Bennett of Jungle.com has commented: 'The beauty of the internet is that the cost of entry is really low. Someone can sit in their bedroom and look like a massive company' (*e-business*, 1999). They no longer need a strong profitability record to succeed. Some of the major players like Amazon.com and Yahoo! have billion dollar valuations and have not yet made a profit. This is a new world for the financial community who are having to invent new ways of valuing a business. Loss-making ISP Freeserve was valued at £1.5 billion when it was launched on the Stock Exchange in July 1999 because its one million customers who paid no fee were each valued at £1500. Many think that the Internet bubble has burst. It is certainly a very volatile market. The announcement of a deal with the mobile phone operator Cellnet saw Freeserve's shares rise from a starting point of 150p to break the 500p barrier six months later, dropping back to 400p via a 900p peak.

More entrepreneurs

Science and technology with its turbulent markets and low entry costs is, however, only part of the story. As Schumpeter observed, the entrepreneur is needed to turn the opportunities that science and technology bring into an economic reality. Malecki

(1997) comments that 'the process of entrepreneurship may be more important to regional and local economies than the process of technological change'. In many ways new technology and the entrepreneur are made for each other, both are about change in the marketplace. It is science and technology that makes possible this turbulence but it is the actions of the entrepreneur and the entrepreneurial business that actually creates the turbulence, upsets established markets and opens up new ones. Often these changes can be enormous and produce completely new markets.

The personal computer market came out of nowhere in the 1980s the result of clever science and a host of entrepreneurs. The mobile phone market was a variant of the existing telephone market but now has a life of its own. Its driver was the miniaturization made possible by modern electronics, the microprocessor and the entrepreneurial companies of the early days, notably Vodafone and Nokia.

There is no diminution of today's turbulence in the marketplace as science and technology continue to bring us new opportunities at an ever increasing rate. The entrepreneur has 'never had it so good'. The real question is whether there are enough experienced entrepreneurs to make the most of this abundance of opportunity. This is a key factor in international competitiveness. As Porter (1990) has put it: 'Invention and entrepreneurship are at the heart of national advantage.' The country that encourages and stimulates its entrepreneurial talent will be the winner. We already have the technology and the low cost of entry but do we have the entrepreneurs?

Though entrepreneurs are emerging in increasing numbers it is taking some time for their role in economic development to be really accepted. Much effort and a great deal of money is spent trying to get hold of promising technology with commercial potential but a similar effort is not made on the entrepreneur side of the equation. As long ago as 1982 the *Investors Chronicle* presented a version of this equation on its front cover:

Academic + Entrepreneur = Profit

It then commented: 'Dragging commercial products out of ivory towers is the latest twist to the venture capital boom.' Whilst an understandable comment, it does show that the old attitudes were still there. The academics were seen as living in ivory towers remote from reality and the venture capitalists were the entrepreneurs who extracted and exploited for profit the commercial products that were there for the taking. This polarized view is one reason why it has taken so long to forge an effective partnership between those who generate the technology and those who can take it on to commercial reality. There was also the erroneous assumption that venture capitalists were entrepreneurs.

The UK situation has improved since 1982 and an effective liaison is developing between the academic world and the venture capitalist, but the entrepreneur's position is still not recognized. In the USA there is a better picture. The Gallup Organization polled sixteen- to eighteen-year-old high school students and found that 70 per cent would like to have their own business. Bill Bygrave, Professor of Entrepreneurship at Babson College in the USA believes that: 'Most young Americans want to be entrepreneurs: entrepreneurs are highly rated in their society and being an entrepreneur is a very respectable career and an honourable profession'

(Bygrave, 1998). In the UK the recognition of the entrepreneur achieved in the USA has yet to arrive. In a MORI poll conducted in 1989 after the Thatcher government's promotion of enterprise and wealth creation had had time to make an impact, only 32 per cent of people thought that the entrepreneur contributed a great deal to society. A similar percentage thought that the plumber made an equal level of contribution (*The Economist*, 1994).

Despite this there are grounds to hope that the role of the entrepreneur will gradually achieve its rightful recognition. One key reason is that the career aspirations of young people are changing. In 1973 Schumacher's influential *Small is Beautiful* (Schumacher, 1973) was published and young people particularly began to develop attitudes that were against big business. The idea of a job for life was also being challenged as companies began to lay off workers. Staff with qualifications were at first spared but then cuts were made across a company at all levels including the board. In the 1980s the Thatcher government began a massive privatization policy which soon spread around the world as other governments took on the idea. Then in the 1990s came the notion of downsizing and concentration upon the core business. These changes have all contributed to a distrust of the large enterprise and a feeling that 'I might as well be in control of my own destiny as be dictated to by others'.

This enthusiasm for the small and the arrival of low-cost entry opportunities should mean that starting one's own business is now an option being considered by ever more people as they begin their careers. Whilst the logic is there, society attitudes still need to change before this happens on a large enough scale. In 1994 *The Economist* featured on its front cover a picture of the television character Arthur Daley with the heading 'How Britain sees its entrepreneurs'. The editorial commented that Daley was a 'symbol of a country where "trade" is a bit disreputable, where starting a firm that fails is worse than not starting one at all'.

This caricature is the image that many have of the entrepreneur and it is in serious need of correction. The entrepreneur should hold a position of respect and value in our society. To do this the word 'entrepreneur' needs to not only be given its rightful place, it needs to be redeemed. Its image needs to be cleaned up and brought back from its 'dodgy' past. Entrepreneurs like Richard Branson, Anita Roddick and others, whom we have described in earlier chapters, are helping to change the public perspective. The fact that the *Sunday Times* continues to run its regular series of articles on how entrepreneurs got started is a sign of the increasing interest in the entrepreneur.

The entrepreneur is the third of the factors with technology and low entry costs that give us today's special opportunity. It is difficult to say which of the three factors is the most important because they interlink. It is technology that makes the low entry costs possible and it is the entrepreneur who takes up the opportunity that this combination presents. But it should be understood that technology does not have to be leading edge. The computer and the Internet should now be regarded as tools that can be applied in many sectors to create competitive businesses. The sectors themselves do not need to be high technology. The tourist industry, for example, is the biggest industry that there is and is set to become even bigger. 'It employs one out of nine people in the world. But apart from a few big players like the airlines, who provide the infrastructure, tourism is made up of millions and millions of entrepreneurs' (Naisbitt, 1998). Technology has given us all the tools that entrepreneurs need to operate in the world market, whatever their business; they simply have to learn how to use them.

References

Ayres, R. U. (1990). Technology transformations and long waves. *Technological Forecasting and Social Change*, **36**.
Bolton, J. E. (1971). Report of the Committee of Enquiry on Small Firms. Cm 4811. HMSO.
Buckingham, M. W. (1987). Entrepreneurship. Dissertation, Faculty of Social and Political Science, Cambridge University.
Butterfield, H. (1957). *The Origins of Modern Science*. 2nd edn. Bell and Hyman.
Bygrave, B. (1998). Building an entrepreneurial economy: lessons from the United States. *Business Strategy Review*, **9** (2), 11–18.
Carlton, J. (1998). *Apple*. HarperCollins.
Covey, F. (1990). *Principle-Centred Leadership*. Simon and Schuster.
Dearlove, D. (1999). *Business the Bill Gates Way*. Capstone.
Dell, M. and Fredman, C. (1999). *Direct from Dell*. HarperCollins Business.
e-business (1999). Jungle fever. December, 71–73.
Ferris, T. (ed.) (1991). *The World Treasury of Physics, Astronomy and Mathematics*. Little, Brown.
Fukuyama, F. (1995). *Trust*. Hamish Hamilton.
Galbraith, J. K. (1991). *A History of Economics*. Penguin Books.
Gibson, R. (1998). Rethinking business. In *Rethinking the Future* (R. Gibson, ed.), Nicholas Brealey.
Hall, P. and Preston, P. (1988). *The Carrier Wave: New Information Technology and the Geography of Innovation 1846–2003*. Unwin Hyman.
Hammer, M. and Champy, J. (1993). *Reengineering the Corporation*. Nicholas Brealey.
Handy, C. (1989). *The Age of Unreason*. 2nd edn. Century Business.
Handy, C. (1995). *The Empty Raincoat*. Arrow Books.
Harvey-Jones, J. (1988). *Making It Happen*. HarperCollins.
Iacocca, L. (1989). *Talking Straight*. Bantam Books.
Investors Chronicle (1982) Academic + entrepreneur = profit?, 23 April, 190–191.
Jardine, L. (1997). *Worldly Goods*. Papermac.
Jelinek, M. and Schoonhoven, C. B. (1990). *The Innovation Marathon*. Blackwell.
Kanter, R. M. (1990). *When Giants Learn to Dance*. Unwin Paperbacks.
Kawasaki, G. (1992). *Selling the Dream*. HarperBusiness.
Koch, R. (1997). *The 80/20 Principle*. Nicholas Brealey.
Koch, R. and Godden, I. (1998). *Managing without Management*. Nicholas Brealey.
Koestler, A. (1989). *The Sleepwalkers*. Arkana Penguin.
Kuhn, T. (1975). *The Structure of Scientific Revolutions*. 2nd edn. University of Chicago Press.
Kuhn, T. (1985). *The Essential Tension*. University of Chicago Press.
Lyon, D. (1994). *Postmodernity*. Open University Press.
Malecki, E. J. (1997). *Technology and Economic Development*. 2nd edn. Longman.
Naisbitt, J. (1998). From nation states to networks. In *Rethinking the Future* (R. Gibson, ed.), Nicholas Brealey.
Ortega, R. (1999). *In Sam We Trust*. Kogan Page.
Pendergrast, M. (1994). *For God, Country and Coca-Cola*. Phoenix Paperback.
Peters, T. J. (1989). *Thriving on Chaos*. Pan Books.
Peters, T. J. and Waterman, R. H. (1982). *In Search of Excellence*. Harper and Row.
Porter, M. E. (1985). *Competitive Advantage: Creating and Sustaining Superior Performance*. The Free Press.

Porter, M. E. (1990). *The Competitive Advantage of Nations*. Macmillan.

Reaman, G. E. (1963). *The Trail of the Huguenots*. Frederick Muller.

Rose, F. (1989). *West of Eden*. Business Books.

Schumacher, E. F. (1973). *Small is Beautiful*. Blond & Briggs.

Sculley, J. (1987). *Odyssey: Pepsi to Apple*. Collins.

Segal, N., Quince R. E. and Wicksteed, W. (1985). *The Cambridge Phenomenon*. Segal Quince Wicksteed and Brand Brothers.

Senge, P. M. (1990). *The Fifth Discipline*. Century Business.

Singhal, A. and Rogers, E. M. (1989). *India's Information Revolution*. Sage.

Tarnas, R. (1996). *The Passion of the Western Mind*. Pimlico.

The Economist (1994). The unloved entrepreneur, 28 May, 105.

Toffler, A. (1971). *Future Shock*. Pan Books.

Toffler, A. (1981). *The Third Wave*. Pan Books.

Trout, J. and Rivkin, S. (1998). *The Power of Simplicity*. McGraw-Hill.

UK government (1998). *Our Competitive Future: Building the Knowledge Driven Economy*, White Paper cm 4176. HMSO.

Weber, M. (1905). *The Protestant Ethic and the Spirit of Capitalism*. Unwin Counterpoint.

Wilson, J. W. (1986). *The New Venturers*. Addison-Wesley.

11   How the entrepreneur operates

Entrepreneurs operate within a process. It starts with the entrepreneur and a perceived opportunity and its output is something of recognized value. Within the process the entrepreneur creates, innovates and builds. In this chapter we present our model of the enterprise process and describe the key elements involved. Its focus is the enterprise that is being built in which the entrepreneur and the opportunity are the key players. It is a practical model against which the progress of the enterprise can be measured and any remedial action that may be required can be identified.

The enterprise process model

Entrepreneurs are individuals with very different ways of doing things but the things that they do are similar. They all identify an opportunity, put together the necessary resources and build something of recognized value; but how do they do it? What stages do they go through in the process? Figure 11.1 is a model of the enterprise process that seeks to answer these questions (Bolton, 1993; 1997).

The model identifies the inputs, the process itself and the output. People and ideas are the raw material that feed the process. In this chapter the people side is considered first as the roles of the *entrepreneur*, the *manager* and the *leader* are examined. This distinction is important because all three are often involved with starting enterprises when it is really the province of the entrepreneur. On the ideas side, the *sources of ideas* available to the entrepreneur are outlined.

The enterprise process is often set off by some form of trigger event. As Larson and Rogers (1986) put it when describing entrepreneurship in Silicon Valley: 'Setting off the initial spark is the key.' This chiefly affects the *people* input and examples of the important triggers are discussed. Most *idea*-based triggers link directly with the people input as when the entrepreneur suddenly has a bright idea. An important exception, when the idea side is not linked directly with the people side, is the trigger associated with a particular sector of technology. The Silicon Valley story in Chapter 8 shows how a series of technology triggers came along and fuelled the

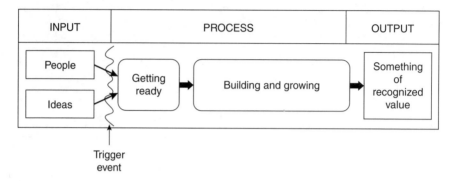

Figure 11.1   *The enterprise process model*

entrepreneurial process. The Internet linked to the World Wide Web is the latest of these triggers and its effect is being felt across the world. It has given birth to its own type of entrepreneur, the *Netpreneur*, for whom the key issue is not profitability but branding and customer service. Thirty-three-year-old Steve Bennett believes that the Internet will come down to two or three brands and he intends his company Jungle.com to be one of them (*e.business*, 1999).

The enterpise process is considered as two stages. A *getting ready* stage and a *building and growing* stage. Each is broken down into a series of elements or substages through which the process passes. The real entrepreneurs are often unaware that they travel this road, but its features and milestones are described so that they can recognize the road and be encouraged. Its true value is in guiding inexperienced and less confident travellers so that they can chart their progress and understand what to expect on their entrepreneurial journey. It provides a useful framework for those who would encourage and support the potential entrepreneur. It enables an intervention strategy to be developed for the promotion of indigenous businesses whereby specific stages of the process are targeted.

The output from the enterprise process is something of recognized value. For the economic entrepreneur part of that recognition is achieved by the creation of a viable business and sustainable jobs. For the social and aesthetic entrepreneur the recognition comes from the group they serve and ultimately the general public.

The inputs

People: the entrepreneur, the manager and the leader

The characteristics and personality of the entrepreneur have already been discussed in Chapter 1. Here the entrepreneur is considered in relation to managers and leaders since all can be involved in starting up and running enterprises whether for business, social or aesthetic reasons. It is, of course, the entrepreneur whose talents suit this process best.

The manager can be involved; he or she can be a team member but must not be the driving force. In a business-start programme run in the UK one of the teams that was put together consisted of three well-qualified professional managers. This combination proved to be a mistake. The team talked and debated a great deal and produced many excellent plans but they never started a business. By contrast a team of four which included an entrepreneur started their business before the programme was finished. In fact they did not really need the programme, other than to help them form into a team and give them basic advice.

Using the earlier point that a project manager is an entrepreneur but without the ability to see opportunities, it could be argued that managers can be entrepreneurs as long as somebody else provides the opportunity. It is certainly true that managers can set up businesses if someone else gives them the idea but they will be managed businesses and not entrepreneurial ones. This is because issues such as creativity and opportunity-spotting are something that characterizes an entrepreneurial business all through its life and not just at start up.

Leaders are a different group to the manager and are much more in tune with the entrepreneur. This is because a number of their life themes overlap. As discussed in Chapter 1 the Gallup Organization has studied both groups in great detail and identified twenty life themes for the leader and twelve for the entrepreneur, with seven common to both. In comparing these life themes in Figure 11.2 some simplifications have been made. The performance orientation of the leader and the profit orientation of the entrepreneur have been taken to be the same, although they are slightly different. There are also some differences when the same life themes have a slightly different meaning for the entrepreneur and the leader. Thus 'focus' for the entrepreneur has only a two months horizon whereas for the leader it has three years. Accepting these small differences, Figure 11.2 indicates that there is a clear overlap between the entrepreneur and the leader, and that depending upon the life theme mix there are entrepreneurial leaders and leader entrepreneurs.

Fifty-eight per cent of the entrepreneur's life themes are shared with the leader but only 35 per cent of the leader's are shared with the entrepreneur. Whilst more life themes could be added for the entrepreneur, as discussed in Chapter 1, it is probably true to say that the entrepreneur has more in common with the leader

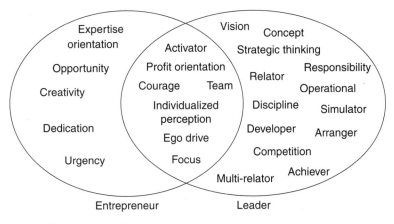

Figure 11.2 *Entrepreneur and leader envelopes*

than the other way round. The entrepreneur is not a subset of the leader because the points of difference are extremely important. What makes the entrepreneur different are the life themes of opportunity, creativity, dedication, urgency and expertise orientation. These are key talents unique to the entrepreneur. The opportunity and creativity life themes are particularly important and explain why an entrepreneur rather than a leader is the best person to start an enterprise in the turbulent market conditions of today.

Another way to see the difference between the entrepreneur and the leader is to compare definitions: an entrepreneur is 'a person who habitually creates and innovates to build something of recognized value based on perceived opportunities.'

Howard Gardner's (1995) definition gives a leader as 'a person who, by word and/or personal example, markedly influences the behaviours, thoughts, and/or feelings of a significant number of their fellow human beings'.

Thus the entrepreneur is concerned with building something whilst the leader influences people. Leaders appear in the same domains as the entrepreneur. There can be leaders in business, in society and in the arts but they are the influencers, they affect the way people behave, think and feel. The entrepreneur may do this but he or she is essentially a builder of something that is tangible and real. Entrepreneurs who successfully start a trend or a new approach to a product have this leadership ability to influence people. Anita Roddick changed the approach to selling cosmetics. In the process she embraced a cause and changed the way people think about her product. Guy Kawasaki (1992) of Apple Computers was not selling a product, he was 'selling the dream'. He put into words what Steve Jobs was really trying to do with Apple. He influenced the way people thought about computers. This is seen when an Apple computer is switched on. The first screen has a computer icon with a smiling face. Its competitor, the PC, has a screen full of incomprehensible listings. One is a dream, the other is a piece of equipment.

The distinction made between an entrepreneur, a manager and a leader is often seen as convenient shorthand for roles that people play. Some fit the role well; others find it more difficult. This idea needs to be turned around so that, like the definitions quoted above, the words describe 'a person who . . .' rather than 'a role that . . .'. Thus the enterprise process starts with a person who is an entrepreneur rather than with someone who merely fulfils that role to the best of their abilities. Most leaders and all managers who try to take on the role of the entrepreneur are almost certain to fail.

Hickman (1990) has studied managers and leaders and used the Myers Briggs Indicator to describe their personality characteristics. He assigns eight of the possible sixteen personality types to the manager and eight to the leader. The difference rests on whether a person is an S-type, a Sensing person, or an N-type an iNtuition person; with the S-type being the manager and the N-type the leader. Whilst this does not tell us anything about the entrepreneur Hickman presents a number of lists of what managers and leaders do, and some of these things entrepreneurs also do. Table 11.1 has been drawn up to show how these activities compare.

These lists shows that there are similarities as well as differences. Thus the entrepreneur and leader both innovate whilst the manager administers. The entrepreneur and manager both act short term when the leader thinks long term. In other respects

Table 11.1 *What entrepreneurs, managers and leaders do*

The entrepreneur	The manager	The leader
has fun	manages	leads
innovates	administers	innovates
creates	maintains	develops
focuses on the business	focuses on systems	focuses on people
builds his or her team	relies on control	inspires trust
sees opportunities	sees problems	sees the future
asks how and when	asks how and when	asks what and why
acts short term	acts short term	thinks long term
does the right things	does things right	uses his or her influence

the entrepreneur, manager and leader are not the same. The entrepreneur sees opportunities, the manager sees problems and the leader sees the future. The entrepreneur builds something based on a perceived opportunity, the manager runs an organization and the leader influences people to follow his or her dream. Finally the entrepreneur is effective – he or she does the right things.

Ideas: where they can come from

The true entrepreneur has ideas all the time. As Victor Kiam puts it: 'Entrepreneurs are simply those who understand that there is little difference between obstacle and opportunity and are able to turn both to their advantage.' He bought the Remington company after it had turned in losses of $30 million over five years with the simple maxim: 'I liked the shaver so much, I bought the company.' Soon Remington became a leader in the shaver market.

The entrepreneur sees opportunities all around and knows which are the best to go for. It is not a matter of analysis but of instinct. Bernie Ecclestone believes 'You have an instinct. You can't learn business' (Steiner, 1998). His first business move came at nine when he exploited wartime food shortages. He sold Chelsea buns to his school friends in the lunch break. He saw the opportunity and it was obvious to him to take it.

Ideas come from many sources. In this section a number of common ones are considered.

Our own needs Because we understand them well, needs that we have found for ourselves often provide the business opportunity. In 1984 Tom Hunter was an unemployed graduate in marketing and economics living in Ayrshire, Scotland. He liked to wear training shoes and found that there was no shop around where he could see a good selection. 'I noticed a growing demand for training shoes. I thought maybe I could do something in this area of business.' He borrowed money from his father and the bank to buy stock and rented space from a retail group that had stores in Aberdeen, Leeds and Sunderland. Soon he had fifty such outlets. He then set up his own shops and by 1995 he had forty-five with annual sales of £36 million.

The acquisition of a competitor moved his company, Sports Division, to top spot in the UK with annual sales of £260 million. Some fifteen years on Tom Hunter sold the business and became a millionaire. Showing signs of the habitual entrepreneur Hunter is now involved with Toyzone, the on-line retailer that plans a stock market listing in 2000, hopefully in the order of £250 million.

New inventions are often spurred by this recognition of a need. As reported in Chapter 3, James Dyson's invention of the dual cyclone cleaner came out of a problem he had with his old reconditioned Hoover Junior vacuum cleaner. It was not working very well because the bag was full. When he found that there were no new bags in the cupboard he began to improvise. His inventive talent finally led him to a complete redesign of the vacuum cleaner.

Niche-spotting   is a major provider of opportunity. Two examples first reported in the *Sunday Times* and then summarized in a book (Steiner, 1989) illustrate the point. 'It set me thinking there was a niche, Indian restaurants being so popular.' This niche was to provide Indian beer for Indian restaurants. Karan Bilimoria set up Cobra Beer and became the largest bottler of Indian beer in Britain. Laura Tenison found a niche in the clothing market with the obvious thought that 'Just because women become pregnant it doesn't mean they suddenly do not want to look good'. She set up Jojo Maman Bébé Ltd selling mainly by mail order. In 1993 she won the British Telecom Retailer of the Year award.

Not all niches can sustain viable businesses. Indeed a niche can become a tomb. Niches are by their nature small and self-limiting in terms of company growth but they are a good place for the entrepreneur to gain experience before moving up to something larger. Often niche markets can suddenly expand to be quite big ones. Ink jet printing on irregular surfaces was a niche market until government regulations required sell-by dates to be printed on all food products. Domino Printing Sciences in Cambridge was ready when this opportunity came and grew rapidly. Oxford Instruments had a similar experience when the body scanner was invented and their niche market in small high-powered magnets suddenly opened up.

Niche markets can also provide access to a customer base that has niche opportunities in addition to the one identified. An entrepreneur who provided music and lighting for discos was asked by the manager of a hotel if he did security lighting. When he finally said 'Yes', he soon found he had the security lighting contract for a major hotel group. His business grew so rapidly that he abandoned his disco work. One niche had led to a much larger one via the customer.

Hobbies   It was computer hobbyists in the USA that created the personal computer industry. Bill Gates's hobby was writing software! Most hobbies are not in this league though they can be the basis of a successful business. Hobbyists, however, have some of the characteristics of the inventor – they are in love with their hobby. This often makes it difficult for them to approach things in a commercial way because it takes the joy out of their hobby. It is no longer such fun.

Artists have a similar difficulty. They often feel that to produce things commercially devalues their art and kills their creativity. Titian, one of the great Renaissance painters and an entrepreneur, had no problem with this. He employed assistants to do most of his painting for him, filling in the sky, the landscape and the drapery. El Greco who was apprenticed to Titian was at first appalled by this because Titian always signed the finished canvas – but he 'learnt from the Master' as we saw in Chapter 6. By 'the end of the year he saw how impossible it would be for one man to produce the number of paintings that Titian sold; and he conceded that what Titian did contribute transformed a routine canvas into a masterpiece' (Braider, 1967).

Inventions and the application of technology This is an area full of opportunities that seem to be never-ending. Inventions and research discoveries can open up huge markets, but spotting the application is the secret. This is one of the entrepreneur's real talents.

The world would not be what it is today if the microprocessor had not been invented. It has created many new markets moving from calculators to personal computers to telecommunications and the Internet. But it was when a pair of Apple fanatics at MIT invented the Visicalc spreadsheet programme and gave it a real-life application that the personal computer entered the American office (Rose, 1989) and a billion dollar market was born. It was when Tim Berners-Lee in 1989 proposed the World Wide Web as a means of sharing physics research information that the Internet gold rush began. Communications between computers had found their application.

Laser Scan plc came out of nuclear research at the Cavendish Laboratory of Cambridge University. The commercial application was spotted when somebody made the connection between a research apparatus that could digitize irregular lines and the opportunity to digitize the contour lines on maps. Twenty years later the company has a full Stock Exchange listing and is the largest quoted Geographic Information Systems Company (*Cambridge Science Park Newsletter*, 1996).

Vertical integration offers the opportunity to expand from one activity in the production and supply chain to others.

'It was in 1883 the Essex farmer, Arthur Charles Wilkin, was driving a consignment of his strawberries to the London-bound train. Returning home with groceries and jam for his wife, he mused that quite possibly the jam contained his own fruit . . .' Wilkin had seen the opportunity of making the jam himself and the now famous Tiptree range of jams, preserves and jellies came into being in June 1885. His great-grandson Peter Wilkin is chairman of this privately owned company which now has annual sales in excess of £10 million and exports to more than sixty countries.

Downsizing is the opposite of vertical integration and is more popular today as companies concentrate on their core business. This can mean the closure of whole departments but with it comes the opportunity for teams with experience to spin-off almost intact from the parent. This is similar in principle to the management buy-out (MBO) when an existing team is able to buy out the whole company and run it for themselves. Downsizing however carries less risk because it usually has its previous owner as the first customer.

The UK manufacturing plant of an international tractor company was closing down its apprentice training shop and its component manufacturing activities to concentrate on its core business of tractor assembly. With support from the local Training and Enterprise Council the apprentice training shop was able to spin off as a separate business and provide a service to several companies in the area, including its parent.

Demerging   is a variant of downsizing in which a whole activity is spun off from the parent. In 1999 Hewlett-Packard demerged its test and measurement division as a company called Agilent. In 1997 IBM demerged its printer division as Lexmark. The chief justification for demergers is to reduce costs and increase competitiveness but part of the reason can also be to bring the entrepreneurial advantages of the smaller business. It is surprising in such situations how previously frustrated managers suddenly discover that they have entrepreneurial talent, and they and the spin-off enterprise find that they have a new lease of life.

Subcontracting   Large companies usually have thousands of suppliers and the advent of just in time (JIT) procedures has made them seek out local suppliers to reduce delivery uncertainties. In a study conducted by a company in north-east England it was found that 70 per cent of their suppliers were located outside the region. This company then set about helping potential entrepreneurs to create local businesses to which they could subcontract the manufacture of the components they required.

The Ford Motor Company recognized the same need at their Dagenham plant. Their £500 million investment plan announced in May 1999 included a purpose-built 'supplier park' to house component manufacturers (*Financial Times*, 1999).

Franchising   For many would-be entrepreneurs franchising is an obvious opportunity. It provides a ready-made business and offers them and their staff appropriate training. This may be a good starting point to gain valuable experience but the real entrepreneurs are those who start the franchise in the first place.

One of the earliest into this field was Coca-Cola and its bottlers. In 1899 Asa Candler missed a trick when he signed away all bottling rights to two entrepreneur lawyers, Thomas and Whitehead. He agreed to sell them syrup at $1 a gallon and provide all the advertising. This simple contract was to revolutionize the Coca-Cola business, giving birth to one of the most innovative, dynamic franchising systems in the world. To become a bottler franchisee required an investment of $2000 for the bottling equipment and another $2000 for a horse and wagon and working capital. The special syrup had to be bought from Thomas and Whitehead who provided an expert bottler, bottle caps and advertising. Half of the plant's profits went to Thomas and Whitehead. Although many bottlers failed, the entrepreneurs amongst them did well. By 1919 there were 1200 plants; virtually every town in the USA had a Coca-Cola bottler (Pendergrast, 1994).

Sectors   Opportunities can often be identified by focusing on sectors where the prospects look good, such as tourism, leisure, security, the Internet or something similar. These are all large and growing sectors with entrepreneurs already operating in them. This means competition but if the entrepreneur has some inside knowledge of a particular sector this need not be an obstacle.

Young Charles Forte had some inside knowledge of the catering industry from working with his father. When he saw an article in the London *Evening Standard* about a milk bar recently opened in Fleet Street he went to take a look. Instead of the ornate furnishing of the cafés of the day there was a large serving counter and a minimum of stools, chairs and tables. What Charles Forte saw in 1934 was a fast-food outlet and recognized the innovation at once. He comments in his autobiography: 'It was certainly an original approach to catering, and one which appealed to me' (Forte, 1997). It took him five years to establish five milk bars in London but they were all in prime sites and he had taken his first step to becoming a hotel and catering multimillionaire.

The trigger event

In order for the inputs of *people* and *ideas* to come together and start on the road some form of *trigger event* appears to be necessary. This is as true for the large entrepreneurial movements that have taken place throughout history as it is for the individual entrepreneur making his own decision.

Displacement trigger   Probably the most important type of trigger is the displacement trigger because of the large number of people involved and the entirely new economies that have developed. The history of the USA provides many examples of immigrant waves that became entrepreneurial waves. Gilder (1986) documents the case of the Cuban refugees who settled in Miami, Florida. In 1961 the economy of Miami was in a bad way and more than 1000 homes lay empty in the inner city area. Then 200 000 destitute immigrants arrived over a period of two years. Their tragic dislocation acted as a trigger to those with entrepreneurial talent and an economic miracle ensued. By 1980 there were 10 000 Cuban-owned businesses and at least 200 Cuban millionaires.

A similar example in the UK was the forced displacement of the Indian business and professional community from Uganda by President Amin in the 1960s. Many of this group came to the UK and brought their entrepreneurial spirit with them and built significant businesses.

Culture change   is a trigger that also affects a large number of people and can transform economies. In this case it is the change to an entrepreneurial culture that provides the trigger. It is not just a matter of removing the inhibitions of the previous culture but also of replacing them by positive stimulation. The idea of a critical mass effect that becomes self-sustaining has already been mentioned, and Silicon Valley given as the classic example. This produces an environment in which it becomes 'natural' for people to think about starting their own business.

In the 1980s the Thatcher government in the UK endeavoured to promote the idea of an 'Enterprise Culture' (Young, 1990) but failed to trigger entrepreneurship. During this same period and without any government intervention an entrepreneurial culture was developing in the Cambridge area of East Anglia. It mirrored what had happened in Silicon Valley decades earlier. In March 1981 *Computer Weekly*, under the headline 'The Cambridge Phenomenon', commented that 'over the last decade a phenomenon with a good deal of significance for British industry has occurred in Cambridge. Forty-one computer-based high technology firms have been established there during the period and are now flourishing, (Levi, 1981). The 'Cambridge Phenomenon' (Segal, Quince and Wicksteed, 1985) gave the East Anglia region the fastest growing economy in the UK throughout the 1980s. The culture change trigger was amazingly effective in revealing the entrepreneurs within the academic community.

Opportunity trigger   Turning to individual entrepreneurs perhaps the most important trigger is the opportunity trigger. The would-be entrepreneur sees an opportunity that he or she cannot resist and decides to go for it with the feeling that if 'I don't do it soon somebody else will'. Opportunity triggers often include place and time factors that combine with the opportunity to give the necessary impetus. As the entrepreneur stories recounted earlier show, it is a matter of being in the right place at the right time with the right opportunity. The skill of the entrepreneur is to recognize that this is the true situation and then take action.

Crisis triggers   have an important role to play for those whose entrepreneurial talent has been buried or suppressed. Redundancy is a major trigger for many, particularly as redundancy payments can be quite generous and can provide the start-up money for a business. Such people often comment 'I wish had done this earlier'. For others, of course, it can be a serious mistake and they should have tried to find another job.

Dame Cicely Saunders, reported in Chapter 5, experienced a trigger that was both a crisis and an opportunity. The crisis was the death of her friend, David Tasma, and that then led her to see the opportunity of setting up the first hospice in the UK.

These trigger events are unplanned interventions as far as the entrepreneur is concerned. Castro may have planned the exit of people who did not like his regime but it was certainly not part of his plan to create millionaires and restore the economy of Miami. Similarly most people do not plan their own redundancy; it is something that happens to them to which they respond. This, of course, does not mean that people have to sit around waiting for a trigger event before they do anything. True entrepreneurs make their own trigger or at least do not need much of a push to get going. Economic development agencies are able to create business start-up opportunities for people that effectively act as a trigger, and the methodologies described in this Part Three of the book present an intervention framework to help the structuring of this process.

The enterprise process

The enterprise process model set out in Figure 11.1 has two stages within the process itself. These are the *getting ready* stage and the *building and growing* stage. These are now reviewed in turn.

Getting ready

In this first stage the people and the idea come together and the necessary prepa-rations are made to launch the enterprise. The inputs of people and ideas have important backgrounds that they bring with them. The individual brings the effect of family background, education and age and work experience discussed in Chapter 1. It has been assessed that 70 per cent of entrepreneurs can identify some signif-icant shaping event in their childhood (Cooper, quoted in Steiner, 1998). Richard Branson (1998), one of the legendary entrepreneurs in Chapter 3, recalls that his mother kept giving him challenges to develop his independence. When four years old she left him on a roadside and told him to walk home across the fields. When he was under twelve she sent him on a fifty-mile cycle ride to Bournemouth, leaving home in the dark one January morning. A sense of independence and self-confi-dence meant that he was in the right frame of mind to do something about the opportunities that he later saw around him.

For the idea there may have been some earlier development or the gradual opening of a market opportunity. The emergence of e-commerce has taken time but the oppor-tunity is now upon us. With the current rapid rate of technological progress and mar-ket change the preparation time for the idea will be less than that for the individual.

Sometimes it is during this preparation that the people and the ideas gradually come together. This is often the case with the social entrepreneur where the final vision takes time to mature. William and Catherine Booth started their work in the East End of London some thirteen years before the Salvation Army was formed. Their experience of working amongst the very poor shaped their thinking and the development of their vision.

Figure 11.3 shows the steps of the getting ready stage and indicates its precur-sors of a preparation period and a trigger event discussed earlier.

The activities of 'training and assessing' and 'research and evaluation' are areas of expertise in their own right represented respectively by the 'education and training sector' and the 'research and development sector'. As these fit more appro-priately into the support infrastructure they are discussed in Chapter 12, but some comment is required at this stage on the more difficult *training and assessing* of

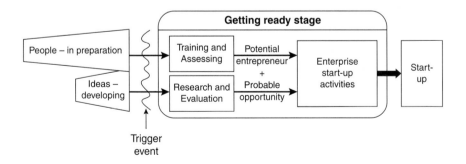

Figure 11.3   *The elements of the* getting ready *stage*

potential entrepreneurs. This is the weakest link in the entire enterprise process with no agreed methodology for identifying and assessing the entrepreneur. By contrast *researching and evaluating* the idea, although not an exact science, is relatively straightforward.

Training and assessing   Training is the first formal step in developing the entrepreneur's technique and know-how. It involves learning the basics of business. Most entrepreneurs prefer learning by doing and do not respond well to formal training sessions. This poses its own problems but the real difficulty is finding and assessing the entrepreneur. Here we identify three possible approaches, though they need to be used with caution and understanding. There will always be exceptions with any entrepreneur assessment procedure because the nature of the entrepreneur is to be different. The only real test is direct practical experience. Spotting the entrepreneur after the event is easy, spotting him or her in advance is difficult, if not impossible, although the following may help.

The questionnaire approach   Most personality tests use this approach and the methodology involved is fairly well proven. The difficulty in applying it to the entrepreneur is that personality tests fail to give a clear picture of the entrepreneur, as discussed in Chapter 1. Gallup's life themes approach is better because it considers talents and sees these as inherent strengths on which to build. A life theme is defined as a 'talent that fits a role'. The question then becomes 'what talents and temperament does an entrepreneur need?' rather than 'what personality type should he or she be?' The question that then follows is 'can these attributes be measured?'

Gallup has done work in both these areas, though this has been with people who are known to be entrepreneurs or who are already running businesses. The enterprise process model calls for people to be identified as potential entrepreneurs much earlier, before they have started on the road. With further work the Gallup approach should be able to produce a questionnaire-based screening procedure that would identify potential entrepreneurs. This would be enough to start the enterprise process. Thereafter the process itself would confirm, or otherwise, the existence of entrepreneurial talent.

There will always be difficulties with a questionnaire-based approach especially with the entrepreneur who tends to be a maverick anyway. They should therefore be used with care and only applied as a first-level screening procedure. But even this would be a valuable step forward because it would permit screening of large groups of several hundred people such as arise when there is a major redundancy programme in a company or when a student year group is to be evaluated.

Interview approach   This approach is difficult because it is the most time-consuming and can be rather subjective. It depends critically upon the skills of the interviewer and there is also a limit to the number of people that can be taken through this process. To interview any more than fifty people is a very taxing experience for the interviewer.

Interviews are best used as a second-level screening procedure but its practicality depends very much upon what first-level screening procedure has been used. The more effective this is the better yield there will be from the interviews. In most business start programmes in the UK the initial screening is done by a carefully worded advertisement and an evaluation of application forms that would normally include curricula vitae (CVs). Using this procedure the real difficulty is the advertisement. If it is too enthusiastic or offers too much it will attract one kind of person and if it is dull and factual it will attract another. The answer lies somewhere in between but it is not easy to get it right.

Once there is a group of people that are genuinely interested in starting their own business then the interviewer can assess their entrepreneurial potential by talking them through a number of areas. Discussion about their early childhood noting any examples of entrepreneurship and what motivated them to do things is an important starting point. It is always relevant to see how much of this has extended into adulthood and if not, why not. Most people who apply for courses about running their own business have already thought about it and some even have gone as far as writing a business plan. This is another important area of discussion.

A person's work ethic and their approach to obstacles that they have met in life are key indicators of their entrepreneurial potential and need to be probed at length. The lazy person who panics at the first sign of trouble clearly has little potential. Failure is also an area to explore as it gives a good indication of ego drive and how people see themselves.

Creativity should be explored in the interview and examples from the applicant's own experience discussed. Finally, it is important to find out what they enjoy doing most. This is another way of asking what are they best at doing.

Interviewers need training before they embark on this kind of interview because the right prompts and knowing when to speak and when to listen are so important.

Discovery approach   The alternative to searching for the potential entrepreneurs by external screening methods is to set up mechanisms that will reveal them. These internal screening methods by which the entrepreneur identifies him or herself can be cultural, enabling or educational mechanisms.

When a region or organization develops an entrepreneurial culture it acts as a mechanism for revealing entrepreneurs. They simply emerge as if from the woodwork. The 'Cambridge phenomenon' that began in the 1980s brought with it an entrepreneurial culture and there were examples of successful entrepreneurs for all to see. When an entrepreneurial professor arrived at the department in a bright red Porsche others noticed it! This kind of cultural peer group influence developed a feeling particularly in the university: 'If he can do it then so can I!'

Enabling mechanisms tend to be situation and organization specific. The company 3M is the classic case of the mechanism to promote innovation but there is no equivalent for the promotion of entrepreneurship, although there are some positive signs. Fairchild Semiconductor described in Chapter 8 was itself a mechanism for revealing entrepreneurs and generating spin-off businesses. In the UK, Cambridge University has introduced a scheme whereby academics can take leave of absence for five years. This allows them to get involved in start-ups on a full-time basis with the knowledge that they still have a job back at the university if things go wrong.

Educational mechanisms for revealing entrepreneurs are discussed more fully in Chapter 12. The ideal situation is that students with entrepreneur potential are revealed within the context of the normal courses across all disciplines. Those revealed in this way can then enrol on specific entrepreneur programmes. It is of course not easy to embed entrepreneur issues within already overcrowded curricula and there often are not the staff available to communicate entrepreneurship effectively. These difficulties aside, mechanisms built into the teaching programmes can be extremely effective and provide high-quality candidates for more specialist entrepreneur programmes.

The people plus ideas combination

The two activity blocks of *training and assessing* for the people input and *research and evaluation* for the ideas input are an important part of any intervention strategy to promote the generation of new enterprises. Whatever the influence of the earlier events the unproven inputs of people and ideas need to be processed to assess and improve their quality. If this is not done then the odds are heavily stacked against success as the following arithmetic shows.

Assuming that among the general population 10 per cent to 15 per cent of people have the potential to be entrepreneurs and that 1 per cent to 2 per cent of unscreened opportunities appear to be viable, then the chance of combining a potential entrepreneur with a probable opportunity is between 0.1 per cent and 0.3 per cent.

If some sorting is done beforehand then the situation is improved but the odds are still not high. By starting with people who say they want to have their own business rather than with the general public, the percentage of potential entrepreneurs could be higher at 20 per cent to 25 per cent. If a panel of experts screens the ideas first then the percentage of probable opportunities could rise to 20 per cent or even 40 per cent depending on the ability of the panel and the information they have available. With these figures the chance of a successful combination rises to between 4 per cent and 10 per cent which is still a low figure.

A more helpful approach is to evelute the person/idea combination on a case-by-case basis and plot the results on the diagram shown in Figure 11.4. Whilst the percentages discussed above put most *people plus idea* combinations in the bottom left quadrant the diagram shows the advantage of working on either the people or the ideas side to increase the yield.

A typical example of a project in the upper left quadrant would be where there is an individual or team with some entrepreneurial experience but the idea is not proven. This could be a group that has spun out of an existing business and has a good track record but their idea needs working on. The lower right quadrant has a well-developed low-risk opportunity but the individual or team is new and the entrepreneurial skills have not been tested. A franchise opportunity could be in this quadrant. The upper right quadrant carries the best chance of success with a

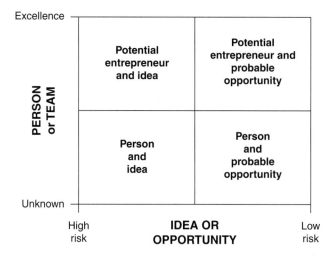

Figure 11.4   *People/idea combination[1]*

potential entrepreneur and a probable opportunity. The management buy-out would fit here as would the team that spins out from an existing company as a result of downsizing.

This methodology can also be used to decide which of a number of different projects to support. This is a problem often faced by economic development agencies with their limited resources. In one study in the rural areas of western Scotland some twenty projects were identified and plotted on Figure 11.4. Most were in the lower left quadrant but there were three in the upper right quadrant on which priority was then placed. Steps were also suggested to improve the position of some of the weaker projects in the upper left and lower right quadrants by working on the people and the ideas to improve their chances of success and so move them into the upper right quadrant.

Another aspect of the relation between the person and the idea that the model highlights is the assumption that people with the ideas are the right ones to run the enterprise. Many schemes, often promoted by the public sector, make this assumption when they offer training programmes to help people who have good ideas, to get into business. One of the important points from the model in Figures 11.1 and 11.3 is that the people and the ideas are separate inputs. They come together in the true entrepreneur but for everybody else they are distinct. The inventor with the great idea and the academic whose research has shown up an opportunity are almost certainly not the right people to translate the opportunity into a business. Roberts (1991) who studied high-technology entrepreneurs in the USA has termed this problem the 'Founder's Disease, the diagnosed inability of the founding CEO to grow in managerial and leadership capacity as rapidly as the firm's size'. Some people recognize their limitations right from the start. They prefer

1 From an idea by Martijn Mugge

to remain as inventors or academics and are happy to be advisers to the business and not get further involved. Others either find it very difficult to hand their 'baby' on to somebody else or never quite feel their idea is ready. They continue to add 'bells and whistles' when the product is already marketable.

The people and the ideas are more than inputs to the process. As entrepreneur and opportunity they are two intertwined strands, rather like a double helix, which together create and build something of recognized value. Other resources such as money help the process forward but they are the basic constituents. The entrepreneur is not just the director or manager of a process, he or she is part of the process itself.

The enterprise model applies to the social and the aesthetic entrepreneur and not only the business entrepreneur. The difference lies in the nature of the link between the entrepreneur and the opportunity. Business entrepreneurs often start with an opportunity that they originated and, so, have an emotional attachment to it. With experience they learn that any viable opportunity is as good as any other and will respond to their entrepreneurial talent. Social entrepreneurs are different. One opportunity is not as good as another. Social entrepreneurs are driven by a cause or a need. It may be the need to help the marginalized in our society into jobs or to lift the poor out of poverty in the Third World. Whatever it is, social entrepreneurs have a strong calling to meet a need that they have perceived and they cannot be moved from it. This helps them to focus well and gives them exceptional courage. Temperament plays a key role in the make-up of social entrepreneurs, who feel a real burden for the task they have committed to. This often means they are misunderstood by their contemporaries who cannot see why they are wasting their life in such a cause. Florence Nightingale, William Booth and others described in Chapter 5 illustrate this point.

Aesthetic entrepreneurs are driven by their own talent, which means that they have to express themselves through their art or music. For them their talent represents their opportunity. Artists often express the fear that their talent may desert them. For many this can be a cause of real depression. They see the ideas that come to them as external, from somewhere outside themselves that they cannot control. There are similarities with business entrepreneurs who can spot opportunities. They do not know when they will see their next opportunity and, as with artistic inspiration, it can just 'come out of nowhere'.

Enterprise start-up activities

With the quality of the inputs now improved the process moves forward to engage directly in the enterprise start-up activities. For the true entrepreneur who has spotted an opportunity this is the time to make the necessary preparations to start his or her enterprise. He or she decides to go for it and prepares some form of business plan, decides the company name, talks to the bank, finds premises, buys any equipment needed and so on. Many do this in a frenzy of activity. They cannot wait to get started, in fact they often start before they have the formalities in place, such is their enthusiasm.

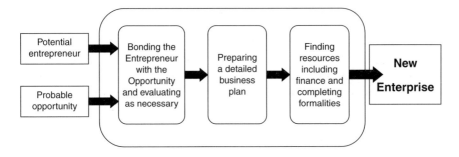

Figure 11.5   *Enterprise start-up activities*

Figure 11.5 present as formal version of this stage, breaking it down into three elements.

The entrepreneur and the opportunity

In the first element the entrepreneur accepts a specific opportunity as the basis for the enterprise. The true entrepreneur is not always conscious of this, for it is self-evident. Sometimes the trigger event can happen at this point rather than earlier, when the potential entrepreneur suddenly realizes that the opportunity is now ready to run with. It has moved from an idea to a probable opportunity in the perception of the entrepreneur. In January 1975 Bill Gates and Paul Allen stood in Harvard Square eagerly reading the description of a kit computer in the magazine *Popular Electronics*. Bill Gates (1995) comments: 'As we read excitedly about the first truly personal computer, Paul and I didn't know exactly how it would be used, but we were sure it would change us and the world of computing. We were right.' Immediately they set about writing a basic language for this computer and Microsoft was born.

This first element is often the point at which many would-be entrepreneurs come to a halt. They may have been on a business training programme or completed an entrepreneur course of some kind but they now have to take steps to make something happen. Perhaps they have difficulty in being sure of the opportunity or they have too many to choose from. Some people enjoy lingering at this early stage and never make a commitment to go forward. Others can do the same thing at the business plan stage and produce endless variations of their plan.

Often a level of planned intervention is helpful at this point so that people can focus on a decision or complete a specific task within an agreed timetable. The planned intervention helps to move people along so that they feel that this is the best opportunity they are ever likely to get to start their own business. Intervention can be in the form of a business start programme or of an assigned mentor or adviser. Most regions of the UK have business start programmes of one kind or another provided by both the public and private sectors, and some of these also involve the assignment of a mentor. For young people the Prince's Youth Business Trust in the UK has done an excellent job over the years in providing those who want to start their own business with grant money in the context of a business plan and an experienced business adviser.

The team-based business start programme is an important example of the planned intervention. It takes people who have an interest in being part of a business team and puts them together around a business opportunity. The results have been mixed but encouraging. Three or four small businesses are generated per programme and now and again one hits the jackpot. Within four years of start up one business was employing 700 people (*Financial Times*, 1995). The main lesson learned from these experiences is that the intervention has to be clear and decisive so that people are put into teams and have a limited choice of carefully researched business opportunities. In line with Figure 11.4 the aim is to reduce the risk as far as possible on both the people and the idea sides.

Most programmes now employ some form of psychometric testing and put the teams together on the basis of people's personality and skill set to give a good mix and balance in the team. It is helpful to include elements in the programme that will build the commitment and focus in the team. One route that has been used is to get the team members to discuss and agree at the outset how much money each would be able to put into the venture. This can then link in with the equally important discussion about share ownership. A team that comes out positively from these discussions will have been well bonded together.

Some business start programmes have offered the availability of a business idea as a major feature of the programme. This kind of offer attracts the type of candidate who naïvely thinks that 'get rich quick ideas' actually exist and then is very critical when the ideas do not meet his or her unrealistic expectations. Generating a sufficient number of quality opportunities for such a programme is extremely difficult because good ideas do not remain open long enough to bridge the time between their selection for the 'ideas bank' and their take up by one of the business start teams.

In this first element of the 'getting ready' stage in Figure 11.5 the individual or team takes on board the opportunity and begins to *own* it both intellectually and emotionally. For the entrepreneur who sees the opportunity and makes it happen this is not a difficulty, but with the intervention approach to a business start-up it is one of the problem areas. If it is difficult to put a business team together then getting it to adopt a business opportunity adds another level of difficulty. The earlier analysis of the probability of finding an entrepreneur and an opportunity needs to include an additional factor to cover the probability of the entrepreneur accepting the opportunity. This further reduces the chance of a successful intervention in the process.

An important part of this first stage is for the entrepreneur or team to conduct a formal evaluation of the opportunity before moving to the business plan stage. This is a rerun of the original evaluation that took the *idea* on to become a *probable opportunity* but now it is carried out by those who hope to make it happen. This sharpens the evaluation and as it proceeds it should build confidence that it really is a viable opportunity for them. If this does not happen then the process can be repeated with another probable opportunity or changes can be made to the original idea so that it is viable. It is far better to drop the opportunity at this early stage, as the further through the process it is done the more difficult and expensive it becomes.

Market research is an important part of the evaluation. It needs to be practical and relevant to the business. When Charles Forte was thinking of starting his milk-bar project his research involved standing outside the milk bar of his competitor in Fleet Street, London, and counting the number of people going by and the number who went in. When he had identified a possible site for himself near Regent Street Polytechnic he carried out the same counts and compared the two. On this basis he rented the shop and started his first milk bar.

The business plan stage

Once the individual or team is comfortable with the enterprise opportunity the process moves forward to the second element in Figure 11.5, the preparation of a detailed business plan. The business plan has two purposes: for the potential entre-preneur or team it is to confirm that the enterprise has a good chance of success, and for the financial backers it is to convince them that the proposal is worthy of their investment. These are not quite the same things. The first priority must be for the team to be quite sure that the project is viable. If the business plan throws up doubts or seriously questions viability of the project, the matter should be dealt with there and then and not left till later. Also it is the belief and commitment of the entrepre-neur that convinces the backers as much as the business plan itself. They are expert at exposing doubts and watch for the integrity of the answer. The business plan for the backers will need to be amended and probably expanded so that it may be under-stood by people who are less familiar with the details of the technology or the appli-cation. An outline for a business plan is provided in Chapter 14.

Mentors and advisers can play an important role at this stage and they can be a useful bridge to the third element in Figure 11.5 where resources and finance are put together. Rather like the athletics or football coach, the mentor can use these early stages to bring on the talent and develop technique and know-how. He or she can also watch for signs of temperament problems. Some will want to run before they can walk, others will not meet deadlines or simply treat the whole exercise as a game.

The identifying and training of mentors is just as important an issue as identi-fying and training entrepreneurs. People who take on this role often have a banking or big company background, usually because they have taken early retirement. Whilst there are obviously exceptions this is not an ideal experience-base from which to draw mentors. They will need to have been through the process of starting up and growing an enterprise for themselves, and probably to have failed a few times. As in football, it is those who understand the game rather than those who played it well that make the best coaches.

Finding resources

The final stage is in two parts: finding resources, including finance, and completing the formalities. Both require contact with the outside world, so from this stage on others know what is being planned. At this point the decision to make a start has been made whether the entrepreneur is aware of it or not although the exact date will not be known. It is important to tie this down in order to avoid drifting into a level of commitment without realizing it. The resource side is another reason why setting a start date is important. There will never be a time when the potential entrepreneur has sufficient resources to start the business. It is a chicken and egg situation in which risk and judgement are involved. The resource issue, more than any other, is what separates the entrepreneur from the rest. The ability to handle this stage well is one of the clearest indicators of entrepreneurial talent. The spotting of opportunities gives some indication but the resources issue shows whether the potential entrepreneur can link opportunity with implementation. If he or she can, then the enterprising person and the project champion are present in the same person and there is a true entrepreneur.

The resources issue is even more of a challenge for social and aesthetic entrepreneurs than it is for business entrepreneurs because their focus is on their vision or their art and resources like finance comes some way behind. Entrepreneurs working in these areas need to have the resource-finding talent in abundance. Social entrepreneur Elliot Tepper, discussed in Chapter 5, is one such. He always has visions well beyond his current financial resources but seems to be able to find the money from somewhere. When we visited him in Madrid he drove us around the large building he planned to buy. With his MBA and economics training he quickly went through the financial advantages of owning rather than renting property and he needed the extra space anyway. His confidence in finding the money was remarkable. As Tepper would put it: 'The Lord will provide the money if he means me to have the building.' When that is combined with his entrepreneurial talent the combination is unbeatable!

If the social or aesthetic entrepreneur is weak on this resources side or is simply not an entrepreneur then there is a role for the agent entrepreneur to come alongside. This is already an established mechanism in sport and music. The Beatles were certainly a very talented band that brought in a new era of pop music but it was the partnership with the entrepreneur Brian Epstein, their agent, that really made them so successful (Geller, 1999). There are signs that this agent idea is beginning to be applied to social projects. The first step has been to use professional money-raisers but amongst them have been some entrepreneurs who have really driven the project rather than simply helped with the funding.

Completing formalities in this final stage covers all the things that have to be done to set up and run a company. It involves contact with banks, solicitors, property agents, government offices, and suppliers like printers and stationers. Many forms have to be completed and signed as the entrepreneur enters the world of bureaucracy. These things take a great deal of time and become quite complicated but they are tangible and real. For this reason some people prefer to sort these areas out before they have completed the business plan and made a real commitment to go forward. This, of course, is a mistake and is often a sign that a manager rather than an entrepreneur is at work. Managers enjoy this involvement with practical things whereas most entrepreneurs find them a chore and only do them when they have to.

The above has set out the getting ready stage as a series of activities through which the entrepreneur has to pass. In practice it is unlikely that he or she will do so in such a structured and linear way but each activity will need to take place in some form. If they are not done before the enterprise is launched then they will have to take place afterwards, which is likely to be less efficient and could even seriously hinder the early progress of the business.

Comments have been made throughout about the difficulties with business start programmes that try to replicate the start-up process. Despite these factors interventions that follow through the stages of the model are being run successfully and at a cost per job created which compares well with other job creation schemes. The proviso is that businesses created in this way will not necessarily be entrepreneurial and, therefore, are most likely to remain as small businesses. The entrepreneur business will only emerge consistently when entrepreneur selection procedures become more reliable. This is the only element in the methodology that is currently unproven though, of course, it is a crucial one.

Building and growing

The *getting ready* stage leads on to the *building and growing* stage. This is where the enterprise really happens and entrepreneurial talent comes into its own. It is characterized by a number of phases or stages that the enterprise passes through as it grows and builds to something of recognized value. Various models based on research studies define the process as a series of stages (Churchill and Lewis (1983), Greiner (1972), Jolly (1997) and Scott and Bruce (1987)). The model (Bolton, 1987; 1989; 1993; 1997) presented in Figure 11.6 uses a similar approach but is based on practical experience. The growth stages follow those found in the natural world, from the embryo through to take off and full independence. The output is a viable and growing enterprise that has recognized value.

Before describing the stages of the building process a major objection to this kind of linear sequential model needs to be considered. It has been common in recent years to dismiss such models as too simplistic (McKinsey report, 1991) because of the considerable overlap and feedback between any stages of the process. The argument is not so much with the stages themselves as with how they relate to each other. The concern is that a linear model does not allow for feedback or for activities

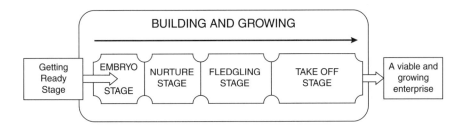

Figure 11.6 *Building and growing*

to run in parallel with each other and interact. Whilst these points have some validity the essential feature that a linear model tries to capture is that the process has a beginning and operates in real time. The purpose of the model in Figure 11.6 is to help the entrepreneur understand the stages that his or her enterprise can expect to pass through. Without this understanding the enterprise is likely to drift from one stage to the other unaware of what is happening, with a consequent loss of focus. The transfer from one stage to another offers a time to stop, reflect and plan the next stage. Next to finance, the handling of time is the most critical issue facing the growing enterprise so that a model based on time as its axis is clearly of value.

In setting out stages on a time base it is easy to imply that there is a pattern to how long each stage will take. Whilst the stages would be expected to increase in length as the process goes forward, from perhaps a few months to three or four years, there are so many exceptions that it is difficult to generalize. The problem is that it is easy to get stuck in one of the stages because things have not gone according to plan. In this case it is often necessary to go back to the start of the stage or even to the one before.

The stages described

The description of the stages is taken from the natural world. The bird makes a good analogy because it finally takes off and becomes independent.

Embryo stage   The embryo stage is the starting point in Figure 11.6. It begins with conception and ends when the egg hatches and the chick appears. This is a very formative stage and determines what the enterprise will look like and its direction. It is its potential that is being developed. The embryo stage is crucial for any enterprise whether it is a commercial business, or a social or aesthetic undertaking. The arrow from the 'Getting ready' stage is shown running into this stage because the founders and the opportunity may have already come together and, as happens in conception, the characteristics of both will now be in the embryo. The point at which a legal entity, such as a company, is set up will depend upon the local circumstances. In principle it is best to do this as soon as possible because it ties the founders into the project and makes for a sharper focus by all concerned. It also helps to resolve any questions of commitment before they become a problem.

Nurture stage   The nurture stage was a later addition to the model (Bolton, 1993) but came out of the experience of working with start-ups. Many enterprises find it difficult to take the step that finally gets a reliable product out of the door to a real customer. Like the chick that has to be fed and nurtured by its parent, the enterprise needs to be helped along through this stage. This is the point at which the business incubator described in Chapter 12 can be so important in providing a supportive and nurturing environment. It is a very formative time for the entrepreneur and the team as the business becomes a reality. Their learning curve is probably at its steepest in this stage.

Fledgling stage   In the fledgling stage the chick loses its down and grows real feathers as the enterprise begins to look like a serious business. The dependency on outside help is steadily reduced as the baby bird learns to fend for itself. It is able to fly greater and greater distances and find more and more of its own food. Here there are less new tricks to learn but the enterprise has to become proficient at doing them. Speed of response and finding resources become second nature. Staying alive becomes much easier and the enterprise is less vulnerable to predators or accident.

Take-off stage   The final stage to becoming a viable and growing business is what we have previously called the 'maturing stage' (Bolton, 1997) but now prefer to call the 'take-off stage'. This is because it is in this stage that the enterprise either takes off or else remains as a small business. The difference between the real entrepreneur and the lifestyle entrepreneur is now revealed. The lifestyle person is quite happy to settle down maybe in a niche market and the enterprise matures and settles down. The true entrepreneur is stimulated by what he or she has already achieved and is now ready to race ahead. Once Charles Forte had grown his chain of milk bars he went for hotels and never stopped. As explained further in Chapter 13 it is in this stage that the product/service offered by the enterprise is taken up or adopted by the marketplace. It is here that a market share is achieved that puts the new business among the leaders, if not in the lead.

A critique

Flamholtz (1990) and others see the entrepreneurial process as the first stage in a company's progression to being a professional business. He defines seven growth stages. The first two, the 'new venture' and the 'expansion' stages correspond with those covered by the model in Figure 11.6 and take the business to a sales level of $1 million to $10 million. The take-off stage extends into what Flamholtz calls the 'professionalization' stage with a limit of $100 million annual sales. He sees this as the final stage to organizational maturity with the remaining three, 'diversification', 'integration and decline' and 'revitalization' as simply stages in a company's life cycle.

There are two issues that Flamholtz's model raises for the entrepreneurial enterprise. The first is the transition from the entrepreneurial enterprise to the professional business. Does this really have to happen? Experience certainly shows that some company founders are often not the right people to take the company through to maturity but then these founders were probably not true entrepreneurs. If they had been they would have grown and developed their business just as many of the entrepreneurs described in this book have done. These true entrepreneurs have been able to keep their businesses entrepreneurial and yet at the same time have very professional operations. The question is not whether a company has to stop being entrepreneurial and become professional but how it can be both at the same time. Handling this paradox is the key.

The second issue that this transition model raises takes us back to the discussion about Second and Third Wave companies in Chapter 10. Flamholtz describes the need 'for a fundamental transition from the spontaneous, ad hoc, free-spirited enterprise to a more formally planned, organized and disciplined entity'. That is, the organization has to change from a Third Wave to a Second Wave company. This conventional wisdom is not supported by the facts. Second Wave companies can only survive in well-structured non-changing markets so that professionalizing a business and dropping the entrepreneurial culture will be the kiss of death for most companies in today's changing business world. Apple Computers Inc. replaced Steve Jobs, the entrepreneur, with John Sculley, the corporate man, and failed to compete in the turbulent computer market. Professionalizing an entrepreneurial company did not work.

The real issue is not whether the transition to professionalism should be engineered but how one can stop it happening. In reality there is a kind of bureaucratic gravity that pulls companies into structure and system. The fun and excitement that was there in the company's early days is lost and is replaced by its exact opposite: routine and boredom. The entrepreneurs cannot survive in such a business and leave to be replaced by administrators. In today's world, Third Wave companies that have gravitated to the Second Wave find it very difficult to survive, let alone grow and develop. Far from engineering this transition we should seek ways of keeping the entrepreneurial spirit alive. Certainly systems and discipline are required as a company grows but this should serve the business and not strangle it.

The stages defined

The enterprise growth model of Figure 11.6 describes what is in reality a natural progression. The entrepreneur moves steadily through these stages as he or she builds the enterprise. The value in structuring the growth is that it provides an understanding for less experienced entrepreneurs and tells them what to expect. Those who work with entrepreneurs can use it to plan how they will support and promote the process.

To be of real value the growth stages need definitions that can be used in practice with a minimum of ambiguity. Figure 11.7 gives criteria for the break point between

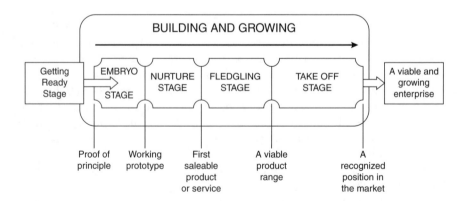

Figure 11.7 *Growth stage criteria*

the stages. They are based on the development stage that the product/service offered by the enterprise has reached. The benefit when compared with other possible criteria is that they can be quantified. There is either a prototype of the product or service that can be demonstrated or there is not. There is either a saleable product or there is not.

One problem with this approach is that it can be confused with the ongoing development of new products that often run in parallel as the company itself develops. This model is about the growth of the business and uses the development of its first product line as an indicator of the stage the business has reached. The terms for each stage refer to the embryo, nurture, fledgling and take-off of the enterprise itself and not the product/service. Using the development of the first product as the indicator has the advantage of focusing the team on which product that actually is. Often it is not clear in the early days exactly the product or market to really go for, and focus can be achieved by linking this with consideration of what stage the company has reached. Another advantage of these criteria is that they are easily understood by inventors, engineers and technologists, and the link with business development makes sense to them.

The stage criteria begin with 'proof of principle'. This means that the idea upon which the business opportunity is based does actually work and that there are no unknowns that would kill the opportunity. The term arises in the context of technology where the science behind it has first to be proved before it can be applied. This is done in the research and development stage that precedes the embryo stage. Because science and technology has an increasingly stronger commercial focus it may become appropriate to include a 'pre-embryo' stage in the model. For opportunities that do not involve technology the proof of principle would involve proof that a market does really exist and that the product or service that will be offered to that market can actually be delivered. Proof of principle is the entry point to the process and requires the opportunity to be researched and evaluated as described in the getting ready stage. Ideally there will be some form of demonstration of the proposed product or service. Something tangible is far more telling than any document or verbal presentation, though a business plan should be available to back up the commercial claims of the opportunity.

In the embryo stage the enterprise gives the opportunity life by developing it to the point where it can be shown to potential customers and users. Several prototypes might be required during this stage as the opportunity takes on its final form. It may not be like the finished article but its potential should be clear to the customer and not just the enthusiastic team behind it. When the opportunity is technology based this stage is a good one in which to hand the technology over from the originator to a commercial team. An inventor could hand over in a similar way. The exit from this stage is a good point for the opportunity and the team to be spun out from their existing organization if there is one.

The nurture stage moves the opportunity into the real world, from a working prototype to a product or service that can be sold to real customers. It is likely that some trials will have been carried out with tame customers and the market tested. The formalities for trading will have been put in place with billing and financial systems and some expansion of the team. This will be a time when the cash flow has to be carefully watched as there will be little or no income but expenditure will have begun to rise. It is possible that in this stage the enterprise moves into its own premises and sets its stall out to begin trading operations. This is a testing time for the entrepreneur but if he or she is good enough he or she will rise to the challenge and the whole thing will be great fun. The dynamic of the enterprise will begin to be created.

The fledgling stage sees the enterprise operating as a business and moving into profit. The business plan for entry to this stage will be more specific than previous ones, with a clear statement of the cash flow and working capital requirements of the business on a monthly basis. It will also provide the growth strategy for the enterprise over the next three years showing how it will capture the market it has targeted. As the team grows, personnel matters will become increasingly important. Growth from ten to twenty people, and then to fifty, mark transitions in management that need to be recognized. This may require the recruitment of managers from outside and this is always a disturbing experience for those who have been involved from the start.

The output of this stage is a range of products that broadens the business base and may now be serving a number of different markets. The transition to the take-off stage is probably the most difficult of all and many never make it. Instead they stay in a kind of permanent fledgling state catering for a specific group of customers, many of whom become good friends. This is the 'stay small and stay happy' syndrome. There is nothing inherently wrong with this approach but it is the domain of the lifestyle entrepreneur and not the real entrepreneur who wants to go onward and upward and cannot stop him or herself. Others do move from the fledgling stage and mature but see no real growth. This is the manager's domain and the founding entrepreneur has often left by this time to pursue other interests.

The take-off stage is where the entrepreneur builds something of recognized value. Its output is an established position in the marketplace, preferably as market leader. One reason that this is difficult to achieve is that there has to be a fundamental shift in the view of the market. Up to this point the market is seen as something you supply to but now it becomes something you take over and seek to control. Intel and Microsoft made this transition some years ago, and in view of the monopoly ruling against Microsoft they have done it too well! Cisco is in the process of effecting this transition to dominance in the Internet market (Business Week, 1999).

The stages applied

Using these definitions of the growth stages the move from one to the other can be used as an evaluation and decision point. Progress can be assessed by a formal evaluation of the stage just completed and a business plan for the next stage. Most business plans are somewhat unrealistic because they have to make too many assumptions about a future that is unknown. By breaking the future down into four stages it is possible to have business plans that become closer and closer to reality as the enterprise passes from one stage to the other. This business plan can then be used by the entrepreneur and others who have a stake in the business to decide what to do next.

A formal appraisal of this kind between each stage allows the following options to be considered:

1 *Continue in business.* This will mean that there is a good continuity between the business plan for the stage just ended with that for the one ahead. There may be some personnel changes required and perhaps a renegotiation of the bank overdraft, but basically it is a matter of continuing on with things according to the plan.

2 *Close the business down.* Here things will have gone wrong. The earlier business plan will have failed to materialize and the best thing for all concerned is to close the operation down before things get worse. This is a difficult decision to face and most people put it off until it is unavoidable. By considering this option at the start of each stage it minimizes losses and provides a framework in which those involved can withdraw from the situation 'with honour'. As people often have their egos heavily involved in this kind of decision, it is extremely helpful to have a basis upon which the decision can be made objectively and honourably.

3 *Seek additional funding.* Some of the most successful enterprises can require significant funding as they move from one stage to another. A typical high-tech business might require one or even two major funding rounds during its nurture stage. This always takes time and can be a difficult and vulnerable period for the enterprise. It is important to realize the need for cash well in advance so that raising the necessary funds can be planned in plenty of time rather than being a panic measure when it is really too late.

4 *Sell off the business or part of it.* This option can be attractive to an entrepreneur who has other interests or wants to concentrate on one of the many opportunities he or she has opened up. It may also be part of the original strategy. Technology-based companies often have technology that is of interest to the large corporation, particularly in biotechnology and the Internet sectors. It is better to plan be taken over than simply have it happen. This option can also arise when the product or service does not provide an adequate base for a business. A company that has developed a product with a limited market size may be of interest to an existing business to supplement its product range.

5 *Seek a joint venture partner.* The main attraction of this option is when partnership with another business can bring benefits to both parties. It is not easy to make joint ventures work and in reality they are often a take-over by one of the parties. However when they do work they can strengthen the management team, improve productivity and efficiency, and speed up entry into new markets.

6 *Change direction.* It is often quite difficult at the embryo stage to know which of several directions an opportunity should be developed. There can be as many as five applications, all with potential but not the resources to follow them all up. In this case one or two of the applications could be taken through to the embryo stage with the option that if they hit problems then there can be a change in direction and another route followed.

7   *Licensing.* This option applies mainly to technology-based businesses. It may be that a research team takes an opportunity through to the end of the embryo or even the nurture stage and then decides they really want to go back to being researchers. This can happen when an individual has taken sabbatical leave for a year and then has to decide between the new business and his or her research post. Licensing can also be an option when a number of applications with significant potential have emerged from the embryo stage. One of them may be a licensing candidate that can bring in much needed cash and allow the team to focus on the other applications. In this case one has to be careful that the application that has been licensed out does not at a later stage impact on the other markets that you are likely to work in.

These options can help to focus the entrepreneur and the team, and ensure that some system and rigour is applied to the start-up process. It is better to face up to issues ahead of time rather than wait until there is little room to manoeuvre. Personal egos often get in the way of making clear and objective decisions at the critical points in the growth of a business. The growth stages and the above list of options to be considered as the business moves on to the next stage provide a decision framework that can minimize the influence of egos and allow people to withdraw from a situation that they might otherwise cling to.

Conclusion

We have presented a process model that covers the start-up and early stage growth of a business. The elements that have been described form the building blocks of the process. These need to link together to form as far as is possible a smooth and continuous activity with milestones to assess progress and possibly to regroup resources.

In principle the model and the sequential growth methodology it employs is not limited to an enterprise or business. The social and the aesthetic entrepreneur pass through a similar process as they build something of recognized value. Experience with social entrepreneurs shows that the getting ready stages are almost exactly the same as for a business but with the resource element, particularly finance, playing a more dominant role. The building and growing stages are similar but may need to be defined differently. The business stage definitions used work well if the social entrepreneur is providing a service that is tangible and can be measured, but if there are only soft measures this is more difficult. Even so social entrepreneurs generally recognize the stages and find them useful in discussing their progress.

The enterprise process does not stand alone. It is set in the context of a support infrastructure and an operational environment which determine the strength and development of the process in a region. To reach a point where the process is self-sustaining, attention has to be paid to the internal elements of the process already described and the external infrastructure and environment factors we describe in the next two chapters. We believe that some level of critical mass can be achieved in most situations but it takes time and requires long-term commitment and co-operation from a wide range of institutions and individuals. Entrepreneurs play a key role in all this but they cannot do it without the help and support of the other stakeholders in the local economy.

References

Bolton, W. K. (1987). Securing the start-up company. 2nd International Symposium on Technical Innovation and Entrepreneurship, Birmingham, England, September.

Bolton, W. K. (1989). Growing an economic infrastructure from the university sector. 16th International Small Business Congress, Sao Paulo, October.

Bolton, W. K. (1993). The enterprise paradigm. Latin American Seminar on the Development of Technology-Based Enterprises, Rio de Janeiro, May.

Bolton, W. K. (1997). *The University Handbook on Enterprise Development*. Columbus.

Braider, D. (1967). *The Master Painter*. Bodley Head.

Branson, R. (1998). *Richard Branson: Losing my Virginity*. Virgin Publishing.

Business Week (1999). Meet Cisco's Mr Internet. 13 September.

Cambridge Science Park Newsletter (1996) Laser-scan moves from USM to Stock Exchange listing. Autumn, **32.**

Churchill, N. C. and Lewis, V. L (1983). The five stages of small business growth. *Harvard Business Review*, May–June.

Levi, P. (1981). The Cambridge phenomenon. *Computer Weekly*, 19 March, 21.

e-business (1999). Jungle fever. December, 71–73.

Financial Times (1995). Business Links set sights on winners. 30 May.

Financial Times (1999). Ford set to invest £500m in revamp at Dagenham. 6 May.

Flamholtz, E. G. (1990). *Growing Pains*. Jossey-Bass.

Forte, C. (1997). *Forte*. Pan Books.

Gardner, H. (1995). *Leading Minds*. Basic Books.

Gates, W. H. (1995). *The Road Ahead*. Viking.

Geller, D. (1999). *The Brian Epstein Story*. Faber and Faber.

Gilder, G. (1986). *The Spirit of Enterprise*. Penguin.

Greiner, L. E. (1972). Evolution and revolution as organisations grow. *Harvard Business Review*, July–August.

Hickman, C. R. (1990). *Mind of a Manager, Soul of a Leader*. John Wiley.

Jolly, V. K. (1997) *Commercialising New Technologies*. Harvard Business School Press.

Kawasaki, G. (1992). *Selling the Dream*. HarperBusiness.

Larson, J. K. and Rogers, E. M. (1986). *Silicon Valley Fever*. Unwin Counterpoint.

McKinsey Report (1991). *Partners in Innovation*. McKinsey and Co.

Pendergrast, M. (1994). *For God, Country and Coca-Cola*. Phoenix Paperback.

Roberts, E. B. (1991). *Entrepreneurs in High-technology*, Oxford University Press.

Rose, F. (1989). *West of Eden*. Business Books.

Scott, M. and Bruce, R. (1987). Five stages of growth in small business. *Long Range Planning*, **20** (3).

Segal, N., Quince R. E. and Wicksteed, W. (1985). *The Cambridge Phenomenon*. Segal, Quince, Wicksteed and Brand Brothers.

Steiner, R. (1998). *My First Break*. News International.

Young, D. (1990). *The Enterprise Years*. Headline.

12 How the entrepreneur can be helped and supported

Entrepreneurs, like dormant seeds, will emerge and grow if the right help and support is available. The ground has to be tilled and the soil watered. Weeds have to be kept under control and harmful insects destroyed. The support infrastructure that we describe in this chapter has this cultivation role. Entrepreneurs are a species. Its more hardy members grow whatever the soil condition but the rest require more friendly conditions if they are to flourish. Here we explain how those conditions can be created and a successful garden developed.

Introduction

Most of the entrepreneurs described earlier in this book simply 'got on with it'. They were very self-sufficient people and liked to do things their way. *Some entrepreneurs are like this but not all.* We see around us only those entrepreneurs who have had enough courage and ego drive to go it alone. These are the ones who do not need much help but they are the small percentage at one end of an axis of potential entrepreneurs. The rest have not surfaced.

The notion of an axis along which the potential entrepreneur can be positioned is an important one. Those that come forward first are at the right-hand end of the axis in Figure 12.1 and those who have to be encouraged and pushed into it are at the other end.

The initial position on the axis in Figure 12.1 depends mainly upon the strength of the entrepreneur's temperament life themes, specifically ego drive, urgency and mission, as discussed in Chapter 1. Life experiences, opportunity and education move people along the axis in one direction or the other making them more or less likely to emerge as entrepreneurs. The help and support discussed in this chapter can move the potential entrepreneur along the axis to the right in Figure 12.1, to the point where he or she launches out as an entrepreneur.

The idea of the axis of entrepreneurship is developed further in Figure 12.2 to illustrate how barriers in the system influence the emergence of the entrepreneur.

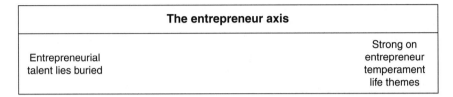

| Entrepreneurs that have to be pushed | Entrepreneurs that respond to support and help | Entrepreneurs that just 'get on with it' |

| **The entrepreneur axis** |
| Entrepreneurial talent lies buried | Strong on entrepreneur temperament life themes |

Figure 12.1   *The entrepreneur axis*

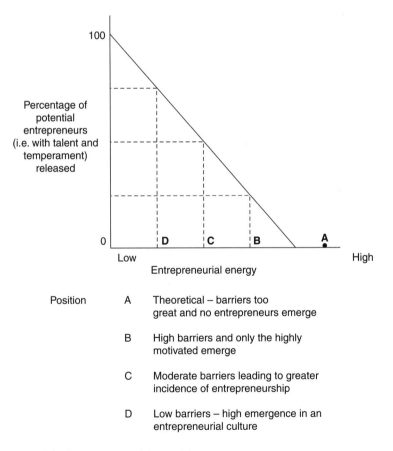

Position	A	Theoretical – barriers too great and no entrepreneurs emerge
	B	High barriers and only the highly motivated emerge
	C	Moderate barriers leading to greater incidence of entrepreneurship
	D	Low barriers – high emergence in an entrepreneurial culture

Figure 12.2   *Releasing entrepreneurial potential*

The entrepreneur is positioned along the horizontal axis in Figure 12.2 according to what might be called his or her 'entrepreneurial energy'. As in Figure 12.1 the entrepreneur who is positioned to the right along the axis will be more likely to emerge as an entrepreneur. He or she is the one with the highest 'entrepreneurial energy'. The one to the left is low on 'entrepreneurial energy'. Within a particular situation the percentage of potential entrepreneurs who will actually emerge and become real entrepreneurs depends upon the barriers that exist. As Figure 12.2 illustrates if there are high barriers then only those with sufficient 'entrepreneurial energy' will emerge. If the barriers are lower then more entrepreneurs will come forward and an entrepreneurial culture can develop which will reduce the barriers still further releasing more entrepreneurs.

The two factors that control the release of entrepreneurial potential are the level of 'entrepreneurial energy' within an individual and the energy required to overcome the barriers. In Chapter 1 we considered the entrepreneur and the talent, temperament and technique that together provide the 'entrepreneurial energy'. In this chapter we are concerned both with how this energy can be developed further and how the barriers can be replaced by positive factors. The outcome being that the barriers in Figure 12.2 drop to position D and more entrepreneurial talent is released.

The purpose of the support infrastructure is not simply to support the enterprise process but to enable the continued release of entrepreneurial potential. It is the extent to which this is achieved that should be the measure of success. One of the great dangers of infrastructure projects is that they become an end in themselves and develop their own set of norms that do not serve the release of entrepreneurial potential. Business incubators can lose their original vision of being a seedbed for start-ups and become merely a property venture from which the owners collect a rent. Seed capital firms can move away from providing seed money to become second-stage funders. These pressures are similar to the gravity effect noted in Chapter 10 whereby the Third Wave business degrades to a Second Wave business over time. The innovative and the dynamic are replaced by the traditional and the routine. These are the pressures that all entrepreneurial activity has to face at some time but they can be overcome by creativity and courage. Those who help and support entrepreneurs need the characteristics of the entrepreneur as much as the entrepreneur does if they are to stay the course.

The support infrastructure

The support elements

Economic geographers have presented lists of factors related to 'The role of the local environment in entrepreneurship and entrepreneurial success' (Malecki, 1997). One by Bruno and Tyebjee (1982) has the following twelve factors: venture capital availability; presence of experienced entrepreneurs; technically skilled workforce; accessibility of suppliers; accessibility of customers or new markets; favourable government policies; proximity of universities; availability of land or facilities;

accessibility to transport; receptive population; availability of supporting services; attractive living conditions.

These factors correspond well with the support infrastructure elements (Bolton, 1993) given in Table 12.1 where they are presented in three groups indicating their role in the enterprise process:

- support related to people and potential entrepreneurs
- support related to ideas and business opportunities
- support related to the enterprise and its growth.

The first two groups are important in the early start-up period and relate to the getting ready stage discussed in Chapter 11. They provide the mechanisms that are needed to begin the enterprise process, though they also have an ongoing role that links in with the third group that promotes the process and ensures its strength and vitality.

The 'presence of experienced entrepreneurs' on Bruno and Tyebjee's list falls within the 'business support' sector because it is in the 'clubs and associations' that the entrepreneurs meet each other and from where a peer grouping develops. The Cambridge Computer Club fulfilled this role in the early 1980s when the 'Cambridge phenomenon' was getting under way. As the entrepreneurial culture developed, more and more groupings formed, both formal and informal, and the collective experience was openly shared.

'Accessibility of customers or new markets' and 'favourable government policies' are part of the operational environment discussed in Chapter 13, because they are not factors that can be easily influenced by either economic developers or the enterprise itself. If a start-up business is a long way from its market then it has to either move closer to it or accept the consequent difficulties that this presents. Accessibility to the customer or the market, like government policies, is something that the new enterprise has to learn to live with.

Inward investment

The customer question does require some further comment at this stage because it raises the important issue of inward investment, which could be seen as a support infrastructure element. This is the policy whereby large companies are attracted into an area or region to create jobs and develop the local economy. Since the infrastructure in Table 12.1 is made up of elements that support the generation and growth of new businesses, should the large company be included amongst them? The answer to this question is generally 'No', because there is little evidence that the presence of a large company in a region enhances the entrepreneurial culture or results in more entrepreneurs coming forward to start businesses. The best that can be achieved is that a network of subcontractors is developed but these will be, almost certainly, small businesses run by managers and not entrepreneurs.

In the early 1960s IBM was refused planning permission to establish a research facility in Cambridge, UK. 'This indirectly triggered a chain of events that led to the establishment of the Cambridge Science Park' (Segal, Quince and Wicksteed, 1985).

Table 12.1 *The support infrastructure*

	People	*Ideas*	*The enterprise*				
			Property	*Finance*	*Supply*	*Business support*	*Community development*
Sector	Education and training	Research and development					
Facility	School, college, university; training facility; entrepreneur school	Industry, university and garage	Business incubator; innovation centre; science, technology and business parks	Seed and venture capital	Subcontractors; labour pool	Government agencies; clubs and associations; consultants and business advisers	Housing; schools; hospitals; recreation; transport; telecommunications
Activity	Courses and programmes	Technology transfer	Premises and support	Equity and loans	Staff and suppliers	Training, advice and networking	Amenity provision

Whilst cause and effect is difficult to prove, there was a view in the early 1980s, as the 'Cambridge Phenomenon' got under way, that had IBM been allowed to set up in Cambridge they would have absorbed local talent and the 'phenomenon' might not have happened. As it was, entrepreneurial and innovative talent was able to flourish resulting in a remarkable growth of indigenous businesses with a formation rate, sustained over a number of years, of around two technology-based companies per week.

Although the larger company is not included as a factor in the support infrastructure there are two situations where their presence can be beneficial to the enterprise process and the entrepreneur. The first is when a large indigenous business is itself the result of the local entrepreneurial culture. When this happens the company often becomes a spin-off point for new businesses. For example Nokia, the mobile phone company, has played a key role in stimulating the entrepreneurial activity that has seen Oulu in Finland become a major high-technology centre with many new businesses and more than 8000 technology-based jobs.

The second situation is when inward investment is part of an economic development strategy to develop an entrepreneurial culture around a key sector. This policy has been pursued by Highlands and Islands Enterprise (HIE) in the north of Scotland. Because of the region's relative remoteness it required a proactive and focused policy that was achievable. It targeted health care as a sector because the local hospital in Inverness was already a centre of expertise. In 1996 HIE attracted a major health care company as an inward investor to a site adjacent to the hospital. In 1999 a business incubator and business support centre was opened on the same site with a focus on the health care sector. It is hoped that this strategy will result in a clustering of health care start-ups in the incubator and the surrounding district.

Application

Malecki (1997) has made the important point that entrepreneurship is a local issue. The elements listed in Table 12.1 need to be available locally and readily accessible to the enterprise. An urban area is more likely to have these resources but it does not mean that smaller urban areas and even rural areas cannot become involved in entrepreneurship, as the examples above indicate. Indeed there is some evidence that rural areas can have an advantage in the high-technology sector where quality of life is an important factor. There has been entrepreneurial success among the orchards of Silicon Valley, in the farming district around Cambridge, England, in Oulu, Finland close to the Arctic Circle and in the hillsides north of the French Riviera at Sophia Antipolis.

The infrastructure elements listed in Table 12.1 are placed in seven main sectors, from education and training to community development. These sectors have very little in common and operate with their own agendas, timescales and decision-making processes. Most crucial of all, they have quite different cultures. Herein lies one of the major difficulties faced by economic developers and those who seek to promote entrepreneurship within a region. It is not easy for these sectors to work together and align priorities even when the project is to the benefit of the majority.

In an area like entrepreneurship that is not well understood it is particularly diffi-cult to develop a strategy across the sectors.

The sector leaders play an important role in all this and if they are able to share a common vision then things can really happen. In one region in Wales the college principal, the head of the local authority and the head of the regional hospital came together with a shared vision and the result was an excellent technology park adjacent to the hospital. It housed hospital spin-offs, a business incubator and a number of start-up companies and succeeded in creating an entrepreneurial culture in the area.

Table 12.1 can be useful when developing a strategy for the promotion of entrepreneurship within a region. An audit of the main elements of the support infrastructure that are already in place is a good starting point. They can be evaluated against their actual and potential contribution to the enterprise process and their impact on the local entrepreneurs. From this audit, barriers to entrepre-neurship in the form of gaps in provision and inadequacies in performance can be identified.

An entrepreneurship strategy for a region needs to focus on what is required to promote and stimulate the enterprise process. It is not necessary to have all the infrastructure elements listed in Table 12.1 in place. Some are more important than others and there is also some interdependency. Thus there is little point in setting up a business incubator if there is not a supply of start-up businesses to be its tenants. There is no point in targeting a particular technology sector if the region has no research expertise in that sector. The aim is to put the infrastructure ele-ments in place that will ensure that the enterprise process can flow without major blockages.

The infrastructure elements listed in Table 12.1 are now discussed by sector. The first two, the 'education and training' sector and the 'research and development' sector correspond respectively to the activities of 'training and assessing' and 'research and evaluation' of Figure 11.3 in the previous chapter. The remainder concern the enterprise as it grows and develops.

People: educational and training sector

Universities in the USA lead the world in the area of entrepreneurship. Their expe-rience goes back to the early 1970s, with the University of Southern California in Los Angeles starting the first course in 1971. By the mid-1980s there were over 250 universities offering courses and by the mid-1990s this had risen to more than 500. (Kuratko and Hodgetts, 1998; Vesper, 1986; 1993).

Some of these universities now have excellent entrepreneurial programmes that link in with technology transfer mechanisms, funding provision, a business incu-bator and a technology park. Rensselaer Polytechnic Institute 'has developed since 1981 a comprehensive infrastructure for technological entrepreneurship' (Abetti and Savoy, 1991). This total package approach is important because it allows students to move easily into starting their own enterprise with appropriate support as they develop it into a growing business. It recognizes that students of entrepreneurship require a different kind of support when they leave college to those who are simply looking for a job. It is rather simplistic to say that because they are entrepreneurs they will sort themselves out. This may be true in the long run but in the early days unless they are quite exceptional they will need help to get started and make progress. One of the main purposes of support at this point is to stop unnecessary business mistakes being made.

For the entrepreneur the educational and training activities are the beginning of the journey and should be seen as such. They are not an end in themselves. Courses in entrepreneurship can be placed in one of the following three categories:

- entrepreneurship as a subject
- entrepreneurship as an activity
- entrepreneur enabling.

Entrepreneurship as a subject

The majority of courses are in this category. At worst they are courses on small business or other traditional business school courses with an entrepreneurial spin. At best they cover all the key areas from economic development to business plan preparation with a major focus on the entrepreneur. The American *Success* magazine provides an annual review of entrepreneur programmes in the USA and lists the '25 Best Business Schools for Entrepreneurs'. Most offer masters and doctoral programmes.

These courses have two main difficulties as far as the potential entrepreneur is concerned. First, they are *about* entrepreneurship and approach the subject as if, like most other academic subjects, it were based around a body of knowledge. The educational process is then about imparting that body of knowledge. Whilst there is certainly much that the would-be entrepreneur has to know, entrepreneurship, like medicine and engineering, has a strong 'learning by doing' element. Many courses involve local entrepreneurs and run projects in their companies, and this should be encouraged. They are, however, curriculum driven which means they are topic focused and are examined in traditional ways. There is no reason to believe that this approach will identify or develop entrepreneurs but there is a clear possibility that it might put off and constrain the potential entrepreneur and bury his or her talent still deeper.

The second difficulty with this approach is inherent in any new subject. Whilst it is relatively well established in the USA it is new to the UK and suffers accordingly. The problem is that either the subject is ignored by the academic mainstream or else it is highjacked by one department that interprets entrepreneurship within the perceptions of its specialisms. There is a similarity here with the new subject of Contemporary Cultural Studies which Richard Hoggart (1996) tells us is an area of study that can 'draw fruitfully from several disciplines: the social sciences, history, psychology, anthropology, literary study and other. Each discipline can make its case for pre-eminence'. Others simply ignore it. Hoggart quotes a professor of English who said: 'All very interesting but I don't see how to fit it in. The syllabus is already crammed.' Entrepreneurship meets similar responses. Cultural Studies found its place because the students voted with their feet. 'In 1995 Media Studies, a branch of Cultural Studies, was the subject most sought by all applicants to Higher Education courses in the UK.' It is to be hoped that the same thing will happen with entrepreneurship.

Entrepreneurship as an activity

These courses have a different approach. They do talk *about* entrepreneurship but they are also *for* entrepreneurs. They teach a range of topics in entrepreneurship but the main focus is the preparation of a viable business plan. Students can take part on a competitive basis within their university and across other universities. Some universities base their whole programme around a business plan competition and/or an Entrepreneur of the Year award. The major business plan competition in the USA is the MOOT CORP® award, at the University of Texas, Austin, which started in 1984 and went international in 1990. It has been referred to as 'The Super-Bowl of World Business-Plan Competitions' (*Business Week*, 1993) and 'The Mother of all Business-Plan Competitions' (*Success*, 1997).

The MIT Enterprise Forum has a similar business plan focus but the participants are seeking funding for real businesses. Participants make a presentation to a large audience and then are *grilled* in public by a team of assessors. It is backed by an educational programme that seeks to promote 'the formation and growth of innovative and technologically-oriented companies'. Plans are in hand to replicate the MIT Enterprise Forum in Cambridge, England.

These courses are a good way of revealing the entrepreneurs, although there can be an air of unreality about them depending on whether the business plans are 'for real'. In the early years the MOOT CORP® competition was internal to the university and was an academic assessment. As things developed some participants used the business plan as a basis for their own business and this brought a real dynamic to the programme.

The main disadvantage of this competition-based approach is that it produces a few winners and many losers, based on somewhat artificial criteria. The ability to prepare a good business plan or to stand up to a grilling from potential investors, is in itself no proof that those involved will be able to run a successful business or that the idea will turn out to be commercially viable. It can be a useful indicator but it is not a sufficiently effective instrument to do anything more than pick potential winners, and it can seriously demotivate the losers.

Entrepreneur enabling

The two approaches discussed above are important and each meets different needs. The first produces people who know about entrepreneurship and the second will challenge the potential entrepreneur. Both will develop technique and understanding, and the *activity*-type course will also test temperament and identify talent, though not in a structured manner.

This third type of course is concerned with the potential entrepreneur and how talent can be identified, temperament managed and technique developed. Its participants have already decided that they want to be entrepreneurs. They bring a dedication and focus to the course that is motivated by their desire to run their own business. The downside is that they may discover that they are not entrepreneurs or that the opportunity they have selected is not viable, and the course needs to be structured to cope with such eventualities.

These *enabling* courses can be found in the university sector and the employment sector, both public and private, though certainly not as extensively as are 'subject-based' courses. We profile two that have worked well, one in Holland and the other in Ireland.

In 1984 the University of Twente in Holland set up its TOP programme. It runs for one year and provides a part-time university appointment for the potential entrepreneur. This gives the person some income and the opportunity to use the resources of the university in developing the product, assessing the market and preparing the business plan. A start-up loan is available on favourable terms. Participants attend a course on 'How to become an entrepreneur' by the Twente Centre for Entrepreneurship. This centre is run by the university's department of graduate studies in management in close collaboration with a Business and Development Centre, a major Dutch bank and a firm of innovation consultants. The programme has been very successful with more than 84 per cent of participants going on to run their own businesses.

The University Industry Programme at University College, Dublin runs a similar enabling programme in conjunction with the Dublin Business Innovation Centre. Termed the 'Campus Company Development Programme' it addresses the needs of potential entrepreneurs to develop their innovative ideas, to build multidisciplinary teams and to prepare a detailed business plan. The programme runs annually for a period of nine months and accepts a maximum of fifteen projects. In terms of the enterprise process model described in Chapter 11 they see themselves as taking the idea through the embryo stage from proof of principle to working prototype. Mentors are assigned to each project team and there is a half-day interactive workshop each month with seminars on selected topics. One of the main benefits of the programme is the supportive relationship that develops between the entrepreneurs themselves. Prizes are awarded to the top three projects in each programme.

The employment sector normally see its enabling courses in terms of training for self-employment. As an indication of the level of this activity, one of the leading private training providers in the north of England and Scotland helps around 2000 people to start their own businesses each year. Programmes are also available that will build business teams and assist the growing business by advice and mentoring. Most of them are based on the framework and elements of the start-up stage outlined in Chapter 11. They tend to produce well-managed businesses but not necessarily entrepreneurial ones. This is because the focus is on 'training' rather than 'enabling' the participants. This is an important distinction for those seeking to promote entrepreneurship but for the employment sector the main concern is job creation, and a well-managed business is a satisfactory outcome.

Ideas: research and development sector

Ideas always involve some form of research and development either to generate them in the first place or to turn them into practical use. Archimedes generated one of his many ideas in a bath. It was an ideal laboratory for research into hydrostatic weighing though he probably did not think of it in that way. King Hiero, ruler of Syracuse, Sicily, had posed Archimedes the problem of checking if he had been cheated by the goldsmith who had made him a new crown. The suspicion was that the gold had been alloyed with silver though the weight of the crown was correct. The story goes that Archimedes hit on the idea of hydrostatic weighing when in the public bath and was so excited by his idea that he ran home through the streets naked, shouting 'Heureka! Heureka!' (I have found it! I have found it!).

These days we think of research and development (R&D) in more formal terms though there is still a role for the informal laboratory, especially where the entrepreneur is concerned. Hewlett and Packard in the 1930s and Jobs and Wozniak in 1970s carried out their early R&D in the family garage. Even outside of technology, R&D and ideas go hand in hand. Though the R&D stage is the domain of the inventor and researcher, many entrepreneurs pick up their ideas at this point. The entrepreneur's support infrastructure needs R&D facilities in some shape or form if there is to be a steady flow of new ideas.

Ideas that are as clever yet as obvious as Archimedes' raise serious problems for the entrepreneur who wants to exploit the idea commercially. If the idea comes from the entrepreneur he or she wants to make sure that no one takes or steals it. If the idea belongs to somebody else then the entrepreneur wants access to it as cheaply as possible. We once met a would-be entrepreneur who said he had a great idea and wanted some marketing advice but he would not tell us what the idea was because someone might steal it. We got as far as finding out that it was used in the home and asked if it was a fixed item or a consumable one. To illustrate the point we asked him if it was the toilet roll holder or the toilet roll. It turned out it was a consumable item and we gave him marketing advice along that line. The inventor or entrepreneur who is obsessive about secrecy is not uncommon.

The generation and development of ideas in an R&D facility, whether bath, garage or formal laboratory, and their commercial exploitation are covered by the term 'technology transfer'. It has become an industry in itself and books, reports and conferences on the subject appear regularly. For the entrepreneur it is the transfer that is important rather than the technology. He or she is really concerned with any business opportunity whether or not it has technical content. Even if there is some technical content it may be incidental to the opportunity itself. For this reason we prefer the term 'business idea transfer' even if it lacks literation. It makes the point that it is a business idea that is being transferred and not simply technology, and implies a commercial focus. In respect of the input to the enterprise model it is the activity where the idea is assessed as a business opportunity and then passed on to the potential entrepreneur as discussed in Chapter 11.

The main aspects of 'technology transfer' that are of interest to the entrepreneur are:

- the role of the R&D laboratory
- intellectual property rights
- supporting the opportunity.

The role of the R&D laboratory

Whether in the university or in industry the R&D laboratory is an important part of the support infrastructure because of its formal role in the generation of new ideas. Where these ideas are easily released they become important spin-off points for new businesses. The 'Cambridge phenomenon' was serviced by six spin-off points. Three were the university laboratories of physics, engineering and computing, two were private contract research organizations and one was a government research centre.

The problem with most R&D laboratories is that they exist for themselves or the organizations they serve. They are not there to provide ideas for start-ups. Behind this is the long-standing debate between pure and applied research which over the years the UK government has used to decide funding priorities. This is a very simplistic approach not shared by many researchers who see the division as arbitrary and contrary to good research (Medawar, 1984).

The situation is compounded by the funding mechanisms employed. Funding is related to academic performance, which in the UK university system is measured by the number of published papers in refereed journals. This is a peer group assessment so that the focus is on academic rigour and not commercial application. With this approach it is quite easy for the researcher to miss a commercial opportunity and publish his or her paper, putting the idea into the public domain for all to read and exploit. In some university departments this has become a big issue. The question is 'do we publish in order to score validation points and secure future grants' or 'do we work on to the stage where the idea can be patented and forget about publishing papers and the grant money'. A system that produces such tensions is clearly not sustainable. The danger from the entrepreneur's point of view is that the 'publish or perish' approach will prevail and ideas will remain locked in the research laboratories.

Apart from these difficulties, which can be serious, the R&D laboratory is a valuable resource for a region and can be an important component in an entrepreneur strategy. In the 1980s Finland selected certain cities to promote as 'mini-Silicon Valleys' and the selection criteria included the presence of a university with R&D capability.

Intellectual property rights

Intellectual property rights (IPR) are a major subset of technology transfer. Large companies and many universities employ people to 'capture' the intellectual property that they generate. This is usually in the form of a patent that provides legal protection against their idea being exploited by somebody else. Although this appears to be an important safeguard it is by no means a straightforward issue. Patenting can be very expensive when worldwide protection is required.

Industry tends to use IPR in a much more aggressive way than the university sector. Many large companies have technology watchers who scan scientific publications and new patents to enhance their own products and to fight the competition. In one case a scientific discovery, with huge commercial potential, was carefully patented by the university before a paper was published. This activity was spotted by a major company that then wrote its own patent close to the original and used it to negotiate access to the ongoing research in the university. In another case an American company sued a British competitor for patent infringement knowing that they would lose the case and it would cost them several million dollars. Their objective was to delay the entry of the competitor's product on to the American market by two years and challenging the patent became the means of doing this.

The university approach to IPR is generally rather an ambivalent one. They want to hold on to what they consider is their IPR and yet do not have the wherewithal in terms of money to pay for patents, nor do they have the human resources to follow them up and realize their full potential. This means that their claim to have IPR is something of an illusion. IPR only exists if there is a patent that defines it. The procedures for this in most universities in the UK are significantly under-resourced.

Many universities have tightened their control over IPR in recent years in the mistaken belief that if they do not do this others, especially their employees, will steal what is rightly theirs. This is a notion taken from industry and the UK 1977 Patent Act where any ideas or discoveries made and developed in company time belong to the company. The difference is that in a company the employee has to work on projects that he or she is assigned to and it is the employee's job to make money for the company. The university researcher is in quite a different position. His or her research does not have to make money for anybody, so he or she is not obliged to pursue a commercial application. When the university adds IPR pressures to career advancement pressures it is small wonder that this immense idea resource remains largely untapped.

The challenge is to find a way to release the ideas potential in the university sector. This requires at least three steps. First, give equal merit to patents and published papers in assessments of research excellence. Second, open up the IPR situation in the university so that staff and students are motivated to exploit their ideas. The third step, discussed in the next section, is to support commercial exploitation by encouraging spin-offs.

From the entrepreneur's point of view the ideas generated within an R&D facility are only as good as the access he or she has to them. Intellectual property rights should be used as a tool to provide that access and ensure a fair deal for all concerned.

Supporting the opportunity

The general approach to the commercialization of IPR generated within an R&D facility is to license it to the highest bidder. In recent years many large industrial groups have actually set up within or adjacent to university departments to have access to the research. Most universities have a technology transfer unit (TTU) that controls all the contracts with industry and handles the licensing of technology. To have a sufficient flow of licensing opportunities a TTU needs to be able to draw on a research base of at least £60 million. The university has to ensure that this kind of commercial activity does not adversely affect its charitable status. Cambridge and Oxford universities and Imperial College, London, all have separate companies through which this commercial activity is channelled.

Some UK universities have achieved licensing income in excess of £1 million. Whilst this is obviously welcome, the main benefactors are those who take the research and exploit it. In commercial terms it makes little sense to receive a £1 licence fee for every £100 spent on research. The universities, of course, see this as bonus money because their research has already been paid for mainly by grant money.

Our interest is not in licensing, although some entrepreneurs have licensed research successfully. We see licensing as the easy option that returns less money to the R&D laboratory and the researcher than is their due. Stanford University's technology licensing office has been the most successful in the world. Its cumulative licence income since it opened in 1970 is 'more than $300 million'. This seems an excellent figure until it is realized that 'the annual revenues of companies born at the university total more than $100 billion' (Fisher, 1998). Although the job of a university is not to run commercial enterprises, it does have an opportunity to enable the start-up of new businesses and take an equity position in return for the transfer of technology. In due time the equity holding can be realized and the capital gain passed to the university. Stanford University has done the former very well and enabled many companies to get started. Surprisingly they have not done the latter. Until 1981 they were not permitted to take an equity position. When one considers the current valuation of the many Silicon Valley companies that owe their origins to that university they certainly missed a huge opportunity.

The enterprise

The support elements described above are primarily, though not exclusively, concerned with the start-up stage of the enterprise. We now consider the elements that directly support the enterprise itself. The property and the financial sector are the most important. If there is plenty of good-quality property available at reasonable cost and if seed and venture capital is readily available, then enterprises should grow and prosper.

Finally in this chapter we consider briefly the other three sectors listed in Table 12.1 namely supply, business support and community development.

Enterprise: the property sector

The economic development imperative

Commercial and business property is nothing new, but specialist property for business start-ups is. It began in 1950 when Stanford University set up its park for technology- and science-based businesses as reported in Chapter 8. At that time it was a property development initiative to raise money for the university. The idea that it might be an economic development tool and be part of a range of facilities to support a new business through its early stages of growth was not yet born. This realization came in the USA in the early 1980s due to three factors:

- the experience of industrial restructuring in the Boston area
- the recognition of the important economic role of small businesses
- the role of the business incubator and innovation centre.

Industrial restructuring   In the period 1968 to 1975 the Greater Boston area was in serious decline with the loss of more than 250 000 manufacturing jobs. Recovery required a miracle, and it happened. Between 1975 and 1980 the area had its own Silicon Valley experience. The jobs lost in traditional industries, mainly in textiles, were replaced by gains in technology-based businesses with MIT playing the same role as Stanford University had done in Silicon Valley. By 1980 there were more than 1600 firms in the area either in the manufacture of high-tech products or in services and consultancy (Castells and Hall, 1994).

Small businesses   There was a recognition at senior levels in government that small businesses played an important part in the economy as a creator of new jobs. A study by MIT in 1981 showed that between 1969 and 1976 nearly two-thirds of all jobs in the USA were created by firms with twenty employees or less. A report for the President by the US Small Business Administration in 1984 found that 'small enterprises with less than twenty employees generated all of the net new jobs in the economy between 1980 and 1982'.

The business incubator and innovation centre   The business incubator linked in with the importance of small firms because it was seen as one way of reducing their mortality rate. Typically 80 per cent of start-ups in incubators survive for five years or more compared with the normal figure of only 20 per cent. The innovation centre, with its focus on technology, linked in with the first factor to promote the emergence and growth of technology-based businesses. In the 1970s the National Science Foundation funded nine innovation centres and started this particular ball rolling (Smilor and Gill, 1986).

In the 1980s all these drivers came together and the role of the research park and the business incubator in economic development was realized and promoted. In a visit to Stanford in 1989 we were told by the university office that 'if we did the Stanford Research Park again we would begin with a business incubator'.

The UK situation

This progression from property-based research and technology parks in the 1970s to business promotion initiatives in the 1980s was mirrored in the UK ten to fifteen years later.

The UK's first science parks appeared in the early 1970s in Cambridge and Edinburgh, and like Stanford were property driven, although there was an acknowledgement of their role in technology transfer. In those days the board at the entrance to the Cambridge Science Park simply said that it was a low-density, landscaped site for science-based industrial development. The real surge for science parks came in the 1980s. Although the UK Science Park Association tried to promote the business start aspects the majority of the science parks set up during this period were property development initiatives.

In the mid-1980s business incubators began to appear based on the American model. The St John's Innovation Centre in Cambridge, proposed in 1984 and opened in 1987, was the result of visits by key people to the University of Utah Innovation Centre set up in 1978. The St John's Innovation Centre was seen, right from the start, as a means of supporting early start technology-based businesses. It was set in the context of an innovation park that would offer longer-term accommodation to companies graduating from the innovation centre.

Several other incubators were established in the UK at that time but promotion of business incubators at a national level had to wait until 1996 when the government-initiated report, *Growing Success, Helping Companies to Generate Wealth and Create Jobs through Business Incubation* (The Enterprise Panel, 1986), was published. A national centre for the promotion of business incubators has now been set up.

Business growth stages

The response of the property sector to the needs of the start-up and growing business is now complete. Each of the growth stages of the start-up business are provided for as indicated in Figure 12.3.

Ideally the embryo stage should take place in the R&D laboratory. Whether this is a formal laboratory or a small garage the emphasis is on keeping the costs down

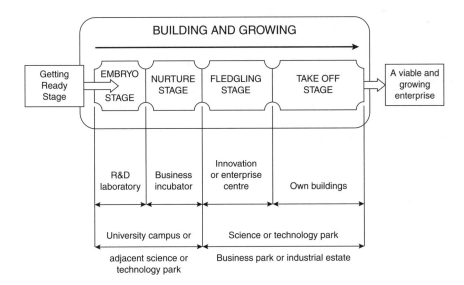

Figure 12.3 *Premises requirement*

and using equipment that can be borrowed. Once there is a greater certainty that the project will go forward then it can move into a supportive environment that is commercially oriented. The business incubator provides the ideal setting for this nurture stage. It offers a range of office and unit sizes in a single building with central services and business support. Because of its importance to the start-up venture the business incubator is discussed further in a later section.

Once the enterprise has a product or service that it can sell and it begins to trade it enters the fledgling stage. The property needs are similar to the previous stage but with less hands-on support. Many businesses want to present a professional image to their clients and the building that they occupy can provide this. They also need flexibility because their space requirements can fluctuate as orders come and go. Two types of centre have developed to meet this need. These are the 'business hotel' and the 'business home'. The Regus Business Centres that now operate around the world are an excellent example of the business 'hotel' approach. Very professional reception and telephone services are provided with fully fitted offices. The business 'home' approach has a different feel about it. Tenants provide their own furniture and equipment but there are central services and the centre provides business support and help to the tenants as and when needed. These centres have names such as Innovation or Enterprise Centre. Some carry proprietary names such as the Magdalen Centre on the Oxford Science Park.

As the company grows and reaches the take-off stage it will require larger premises and want its own 'front door'. At this stage it can locate anywhere but companies generally stay close to their origins and join the business community in the area. Parks and estates of various kinds offer a wide range of building sizes that meet most requirements.

The embryo and nurture stages benefit from close proximity to the source of the idea particularly if it is technology based. By the time the fledgling and take off stages are reached the enterprise has a life of its own and needs to be free to develop its products and services in its own way. Even in those cases where some links with the research behind the technology are still needed it is best if there is some separation so that a commercial rather than a research focus is achieved. The Cambridge Science Park is about three miles from the university laboratories, and that provides the necessary separation.

The range of property that is now available covers the growth stages of start-up business well but the enterprise process will not flourish unless each element interrelates and the right mechanisms are in place. Table 12.2 lists the growth stages and the support facility, and indicates the corresponding mechanisms that are needed. This table extends the boundaries at either end of the growth stage model discussed earlier in order to cover the entry from the R&D stage to the exit into the corporate sector when the enterprise is an international operation. The mechanisms listed are fairly straightforward and most have been discussed earlier in this chapter. A steady flow of enterprises through these stages produces, in due time, a critical mass of indigenous businesses in a region and the process becomes self-sustaining.

The important thing is to be able to identify gaps or inefficiencies in the process and rectify them as soon as possible. Because the support facility side is property

Table 12.2 *Mechanisms and support facilities*

Process stage	Mechanism	Support facility
Research and development	R&D programmes with a commercial focus	University or other research laboratory
Embryo stage	Technology transfer programmes; enterprise generation programmes	Entrepreneur school; business centre
Nurture stage	Enterprise support programmes including mentoring	Business incubators
Fledgling stage	Mentoring with specialist programmes, e.g. marketing	Innovation or enterprise centre
Take-off stage	Specialist programmes, e.g. exporting	Science or technology park
Corporate stage	General consultancy support	International offices

driven this often attracts undue and piecemeal attention. The rush by the university sector in the UK to build science parks in the 1980s was done in isolation and there was little thought given to the idea of them being one component within a process. The original proposal put to St John's College, Cambridge, in 1984 to build an innovation centre and park also included the idea of an entrepreneur school that would act as a feeder to the centre and the park. This idea was not accepted by the college and only the centre and the park were built. Now more than fifteen years later there are active discussions taking place in Cambridge about the establishment of an entrepreneur school and the first Cambridge Summer School for Entrepreneurs was held in July 1999.

A property model for enterprise

Figure 12.4 is a model of how the various property elements interrelate to make a synergistic whole. The heart of the model is the business incubator and innovation centre. People and ideas enter the incubator from outside perhaps fed from an entrepreneur programme and research activities in the local university. They may also come from the research laboratories on the park itself shown in the outer circle.

These are companies at the nurture stage. As they grow they move to the fledgling stage and enter the innovation centre. This may be the same building but the incubator and innovation centre roles are different as explained above. When companies leave the innovation centre they move to their own building but on the same site. They are now self-sufficient and interact with the institutions and larger businesses shown in the outer circle of the model. Some may even grow to the size

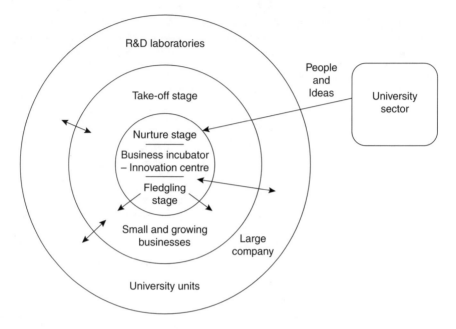

Figure 12.4 *Science or technology park model*

where they can join this outer circle. The technopolis in Oulu, Finland has used this model with considerable success.

The business incubator and the innovation centre

Because of the importance of these specialist support facilities to the start-up business we consider here:

- their role
- their advantages
- operational issues.

Their role These types of support centres were developed in the USA in the 1970s and are now common around the world. Those addressing the early needs of the start-up company – the business incubators – go by a number of different names. Other terms are 'nursery unit', 'seed-bed centre' and 'greenhouse'. The French use the word *pépinière* meaning nursery or garden centre. Support is provided through training courses, the provision of advisers and mentors, help with business plan preparation and so on.

As the names imply, they incubate, nurse and tend the business until it is ready to survive on its own. This can have a negative connotation for a potential customer who is unlikely to work with a company that has health problems! The terms 'innovation centre' or 'enterprise centre' gets around this and is often used even though the companies might not yet be trading. Because of this confusion of terminology we define the business incubator and innovation centre in respect of their function. As illustrated in Figure 12.3 the business incubator supports the nurture stage business and the innovation centre supports at the fledgling stage. Both are very similar in property terms. They provide a range of room sizes from 15 to 100 square metres with central facilities such as reception. Though they vary in total size experience shows that anything less than 3500 square metres is not likely to be viable either in economic or social terms.

The incubator offers organized direct support to the businesses in their care whereas the innovation or enterprise centre provides support when it is requested. Because the physical facilities are very similar there can be some businesses at the nurture stage and others at the fledgling stage in the same building. This is not a problem and can have some advantages as long as the nurture stage companies are encouraged to move through the process and do not develop a dependency upon the support provided. It is also important that the management of the incubator and innovation centre understand what their support role is and what stage their tenants have reached.

Their advantages   From the entrepreneur's point of view these specialist facilities reduce the cost of start up because the centre provides the reception, the telephone service and so on. A service charge is normally levied for these services but the costs are shared among the tenants which reduces costs overall. A high-speed photocopier with collating facilities and laser printers are normally available and charged on an as-used basis but, again, the start-up avoids the high capital cost of these items.

The 'organized' support of the incubator or the 'as required' support of the innovation centre shorten the entrepreneur's learning curve. Specialist advice is often available free of charge. The St John's Innovation Centre, Cambridge, offered free consultation one afternoon a week with a solicitor, an accountant, a patent agent and a business adviser on successive weeks.

These type of centres attract a great deal of interest from the local business community and the media. This means that the tenant companies are soon networking with potential suppliers and customers, and have the opportunity of free publicity that they can use to their advantage. Another benefit to the entrepreneur is that his or her credibility in the eyes of the customer is enhanced. We know of one tenant company whose customer was very impressed because they thought that it owned the whole building! In another case the large company was only prepared to place a contract with the start-up company if and when it was accepted by the incubator.

These are real benefits that can be easily demonstrated but in practice they are perhaps not the most important. The St John's Innovation Centre in Cambridge was successful because it built up a community of entrepreneurs that provided mutual support and help. This was due to the 'tender loving care' (TLC) approach of the centre management and the coffee shop at the centre of the building. This feature provided a social focal point in the building and was a far more successful way of getting people to interact and meet each other than any of the seminars or social events that were organized. Almost without realizing it a community spirit developed that gave the place a special feel that visitors often commented upon. It was a fun place to work.

These benefits for the entrepreneur show themselves in the survival rates of their businesses. Data from the US National Business Incubator Association and from assessments by the United Nations around the world show that 80 per cent survival rates over five years are normal. The figure for the St John's Centre given in the 1996 government-initiated *Growing Success* report mentioned above was that 88 per cent of tenant companies survived over a five-year period.

Operational issues   There are many issues with this type of centre that need to be understood if they are to be operated effectively (Bolton, 1997). One issue that entrepreneurs are always interested in is how much rent they have to pay and what rental liability they are taking on.

Property agents always act in their own interest and try to impose as long as lease on the tenant as they can. Because entrepreneurs are enthusiastic and often overconfident they can easily be persuaded to sign up for premises which are much bigger than they need to start with. One entrepreneur of our acquaintance took a twenty-five year lease on five large bays of a new factory unit when he only needed two. He succeeded in expanding into four within two years and then things went wrong and he contracted down to one bay leaving the others empty. When he tried to sell the business the sticking point was always the twenty-two years still outstanding on the lease on premises that were too big for the business.

Business incubators and innovation centres are a very effective way around this kind of problem. Leasing terms have improved over the years so that most centres now operate an 'easy-in, easy-out' policy. This allows tenants to leave at one or three months' notice so that they are not tied into the financial liability of a long lease. Length of tenure is a more difficult matter and it is now normal for tenants to operate under a one-year renewable licence. The aim in both the business incubators and the innovation centres is that the entrepreneurs grow their businesses and then move on. Ideally no company should stay more than three years in this kind of centre. In most cases this is not a problem but when the company is run by a lifestyle entrepreneur he or she can settle down in the centre blocking off a place for the next potential entrepreneur.

These facilities provide entrepreneurs with the flexibility they require, but there is always the issue of cost. Commercial premises are the cheapest option but they do not offer the leasing terms, facilities, location, image or support of these specialist start-up centres. Some centres charge a premium rent that can be double or treble those charged for commercial premises. Other centres, particularly business incubators, are part of an economic development strategy so that the rent is subsidized to reduce costs for the start-up business.

Rent subsidy is a contentious issue. The argument in favour is that it helps to reduce the cost of start-up for the young business especially if it is at the nurture stage and is not yet trading. The argument against this is that entrepreneurs need to understand the cost of running their business and any form of subsidy is bad for financial discipline. Rent subsidy also has a direct effect on the financial viability of the incubator as its costs have to be covered. Grants given generously in the first few years have a habit of disappearing over time. Many incubators that were set up on the basis of subsidies are now simply premises rented to the highest bidder on the longest lease possible; they have had to abandon the idea of incubating new businesses.

A business incubator in Los Angeles has a novel approach to this problem. Its aim is to promote the formation of new business in the area and the rent is subsidized accordingly. Each tenant company knows the cost of this support in their case. If on leaving the incubator the company locates in the local area then the accumulated rental charges are waived but if they move outside the area then they have to pay back the amount of the subsidy in full.

Enterprise: the financial sector

There are many issues for the entrepreneur in the area of finance. In Chapter 14 we review the items with which he or she should be most concerned, noting the difference between working capital and investment capital and between loan and equity financing. In this section we are concerned with where the entrepreneur gets his or her money from in the first place and what sources of finance are available. At the heart of this question lies a major difference of experience between the entrepreneur who needs the money and those who provide it. Most start-ups struggle along finding money where they can and are grossly underfunded. Yet bankers and venture capitalists say again and again that they are awash with money and that there is no shortage of funds for the right project. Both statements are true and both sides carry a share of the blame. The attitudes and structural differences that are responsible for this perversity lie in the operational environment part of our model discussed in Chapter 13 rather than the support infrastructure being discussed here. This is because the entrepreneur cannot influence the differences in the short term. They are built into the system.

In this section we discuss the financial support elements that can be put in place to provide the potential entrepreneur with the fuel he or she needs to launch the enterprise. The structure of the enterprise, its people and its product are the body of the rocket but the fuel is what gets it off the launch pad and into orbit. To do this it needs the right combination of propellants that will combine together to generate enough thrust, not only to achieve lift-off, but also to reach terminal velocity so that it can escape the earth's gravitational pull and reach the required orbit position. Money is a vital fuel for the start-up business and many never have enough to really achieve lift-off let alone reach their planned orbit.

Most start-ups begin with what money the entrepreneur and other founders can scrape together from their own resources. They start on a shoestring. Data from the early 1990s of 500 successful 'star' small businesses in the USA showed that a quarter of these winners started with less than $5000, half had less than $25 000 and three-quarters had less than $100 000 – and these were growth winners.

We now consider the funding sources for the potential entrepreneur ranked in order of practical value (perhaps surprisingly, venture capital sources come last!):

- own resources
- high street banks
- business angels
- credit cards
- venture capital.

Own resources

Looked at in one way entrepreneurs are their own best sources of start-up money. In 1971 the Bolton Report on small firms found that self-financing was the main source of funding for small businesses (Bolton, 1971). In 1982 a study showed that personal savings were the main source of funding for 56 per cent of new independent firms in the north-east of England (Storey, 1982). In 1986 a KPMG study of 280 new technology-based businesses in the UK produced a similar figure of 55 per cent (Monck et al., 1988). The USA study in the early 1990s of 500 'star' start-ups quoted above showed that personal savings including redundancy money was the source of funding for 78.5 per cent of them.

If one adds to these figures 10 per cent to 20 per cent for funding from family and friends then the financial community's contribution is remarkably small. Entrepreneurs are the best providers of money because they have to be; they simply cannot get it from anywhere else. We believe that many more entrepreneurs would 'surface' if the financial supports were better structured and more readily available for start-ups.

The high street banks

The financial sector generally thinks that it is doing a good job in this area and argues that it is taking the risk and that start-ups take it a disproportionate amount of time to evaluate and control. There is clearly some truth in this but the financial sector is basically risk averse and does not understand the start-up business. Figure 12.5 shows the growth stages in the enterprise model in terms of risk and investment requirement.

Though only qualitative the graph in Figure 12.5 shows that risks are highest when investment needs are lowest and risks are lowest when investment needs are highest. This surely means that there ought to be the basis for a deal with the financial sector. The difficulty is that there is not the data to take this graph to the next level of detail. The curves would obviously be different for a business that manufactured a product and a software company. The new Internet businesses would also have their own risk/investment curves. Another difficulty is that average figures only help if the investor has a sufficiently large portfolio for averages to apply, though it could be adopted by the high street banks that have a wide range of clients at different growth stages. They also know the local conditions well and can keep close to a business at critical stages.

In the UK the high street bank is the second most common source of start-up finance. The study in the north-east of England, reported above, found that 27 per cent of start-ups had bank loans and overdrafts as their most important source of

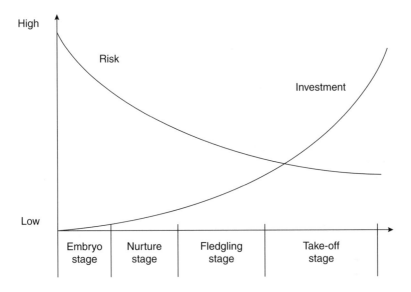

Figure 12.5 *Risk and investment curves*

funding. The equivalent figure for the KPMG study of high-technology firms was only 17 per cent suggesting that the high street banks are wary of technology-based start-ups. Once these technology-based start-ups had a trading record then this figure rose to 25 per cent. This is clearly a matter of perception by the banks because the main funding source for 26 per cent of these technology-based start-ups with a trading record was retained earnings; they did not need the bank! By this point personal savings, as the main source of funding, had dropped from 55 per cent down to 20 per cent.

Business angels

Since the above figures came out in the 1980s two new sources of funding have become important for the start-up company in the UK, though both were present earlier in the USA: the business angel and the credit card. Business angels are individuals who want to use their wealth to invest in early stage businesses. For some the motive is to make money but for many it is simply to help the potential entrepreneur to get started. Often they are entrepreneurs themselves who feel that life has been kind to them and they want to put something back.

In the USA a number of business incubators operate business angel 'dating' agencies in which the business angel and the business start-up are introduced to each other. In the UK most accounting firms have a list of wealthy individuals who are always pleased to talk about a new business opportunity. The growing interest in this area in the UK is indicated by a study published under the title *Business Angels: Securing Start-Up Finance* (Coveney and Moore, 1998).

Credit cards

'The fastest growing source of capital for small businesses is credit cards. One-third of all companies with less than nineteen people used credit cards to fund themselves. These figures have doubled in the last five years' (data from Arthur Andersen). The credit card is an easy way to raise the money and no bank guarantees are necessary. If four people get together to start a business and each has a £10 000 limit on their card then the team has £40 000 immediately available. If each person has two credit cards then they have £80 000 between them. It is that easy! This approach to start-up funding is now quite common in the USA where credit cards are readily available, and we know of one interesting case in the UK in the 1980s. A business adviser used his own credit card to provide funding at a very critical time in the early life of the business. In return he received a minority shareholding. In due course he changed career direction and was ordained as a parish priest in the Church of England. In the meantime his investment grew significantly and the company achieved a Stock Exchange listing. He then sold his shares and with the money bought an old country house as a holiday home for disadvantaged children in the English Lake District. The business adviser became a social entrepreneur.

Venture capital

Historically venture capital came out of the investment banking sector in the 1960s in the USA. 'Born in New York, nurtured in Boston, and almost smothered in Washington, venture capital did not really come of age until it moved to California and joined forces with the brash young technologists of Silicon Valley' (Wilson, 1986). It was the combination of talent, technology and capital that gave venture capital its early successes and put it on the world scene. Venture capitalists get their money from pension funds, major institutions, universities and wealthy individuals, and invest it on their behalf. Throughout the 1980s and early 1990s the USA venture capital industry committed between $1 billion and $5 billion every year. From 1994 onwards there has been a steady increase in this figure, which reached more than $22 billion in 1998 and could climb to $30 billion in 1999. Sadly for the start-up business most of this money is spent on management buy-outs and major deals.

Davis and Rock were one of the first venture capital teams in Silicon Valley. In the 1960s they invested $257 000 in a small computer company, Scientific Data Systems. It grew rapidly reaching sales of $100 million in 1968. It was then bought by the Xerox Corporation for almost $1 billion with Davis and Rock's investment worth $60 million. They had achieved a 233-fold return.

The venture capital industry is full of stories like this but the real question is do they actually help the entrepreneur. The answer is 'No' and 'Yes'. On the 'No' side there is the fact that very few start-ups ever get any venture fund money. The KPMG survey found that it was the main source of start-up finance for only 3 per cent of the high-technology companies they surveyed. The figure for the next stage of funding was only slightly higher at 8 per cent. This data was collected in 1986 but there is no reason to think that the situation has improved. The conclusion is that the venture capital industry is not a major source of finance for the start-up company.

Of course they are all looking for winners and given a choice between a start-up with no track record and a company that is already doing well in the market place they back the latter. In the late 1980s a small high-technology venture capital company saw 340 business plans a year, made eight investments and only one of them was a start-up. They were not interested in investing less than £200 000 and the investment decision took six months. None of this is good news for the start-up company and, although these figures are from more than a decade ago, the present situation is not a great deal better, though it is improving as we shall see.

On the 'Yes' side the industry has had some remarkable success stories and the amount of money available has increased enormously. Today there is more venture fund money available than there has ever been and the amount going to start-ups has increased accordingly. Table 12.3 gives the level of funding in order of magnitude terms for the growth stages we defined in Chapter 11.

Most venture funds operate at the fledgling and take-off stages but a few are now specializing in the embryo and nurture stages. From 1987 to 1996 early stage investment by the venture capital community in Europe was between $200 and $400 million annually. In 1997 this rose to $700 million and in 1998 it reached $1600 million. These are encouraging signs that this early stage sector is now being serviced more effectively, and the European Union has a number of schemes for supporting seed capital funds.

Table 12.3 indicates the classification used by the venture capital industry in relation to the growth stages. Seed capital and start-up funding generally mean the same thing though sometimes seed funding is linked in with R&D funding when the business is not yet at the start-up stage. In the biotechnology sector, for example, the idea may need to be tested before a start-up can be considered. The second classification is more recent and has come about as a result of the emerging Internet sector. Little or no funding is required at the embryo stage. The introduction of the term 'incubator funding' for the nurture stage is very significant. It shows recognition of the need for the kind of support discussed earlier. The incubator aspects can include office space, administration and IT support. Hewlett-Packard has an incubator-funding programme for the year 2000 that plans to fund thirty to fifty

Table 12.3 *Venture capital categories*

Growth stage	Embryo	Nurture	Fledgling	Take-off
Funding order of magnitude	£10 000s	£100 000s	£1 millions	£10 millions upward
Venture capital industry classification	R&D/seed	Start-up/seed	Early stage	Development
Internet funding classification	Not applicable	Incubator funding	Second stage funding	Expansion funding

new Internet businesses up to $600 000 each. Second stage funding and expansion funding follow at the fledgling and take-off stages respectively.

One of the main difficulties facing venture funds is how best to exit from a funding situation. Companies always need more and more money and finding buyers is never easy. Figures from the USA show that for 10 per cent of the investments made by venture capitalists the success is obvious and there are plenty of buyers. Fifteen per cent of the companies fail and the investment is written off. For the remaining 75 per cent it is hard work to find a profitable exit route (Wilson, 1986) though this does depend on what is meant by profitable. For a venture capitalist an annual rate of return of 40 per cent is expected and so it is no wonder that entrepreneurs often call them 'vulture capitalists'!

There are, of course, venture capitalists and venture capitalists. The better ones cover all stages of funding and avoid the serious discontinuities that arise by specializing in growth stages. Seed funds find it very difficult to exit from an investment because the follow-on funder wants them to keep their money in. The USA venture capitalists in Silicon Valley seem to have the best approach. When we asked how they structured their funding we were told that they only invest if they can see that a multibillion-dollar business will result, but that they then invest all that is necessary to achieve that end and do not bother with piecemeal funding. 'We do not just invest, we build companies. Our primary object is to grow a successful business. Capital gains are a reward, not a goal' (Wilson, 1986). These are great sentiments but experience of funding in the UK suggests that this world has still to arrive here. The main difference seems to be that in the USA there is an entrepreneurial approach to venture funding, whereas in the UK it is a banker's approach of caution and control.

Enterprise: the supply, business support and community development sectors

The remaining three sectors of the support infrastructure listed in Table 12.1 will normally be present within a region or district, to a greater or lesser extent. Only in specific cases of deficiency would efforts need to be made to strengthen them. As the prosperity of a region increases these sectors develop anyway but it is helpful if they can be planned.

The supply sector

Businesses that intend to grow need access to a range of subcontractors and to a pool of suitably skilled labour. For this reason urban areas are generally more attractive to the potential entrepreneur than rural and remote areas, but there can be disadvantages as well. Old industries can leave a legacy of inappropriate skills and an inflexible work ethic.

Cambridge, England, is a rural area but the university science and engineering departments have been producing technicians for generations so that there is an excellent network of small subcontractors who can turn out high-quality work with a minimum of instructions. Graduate and postgraduate students provide a well-educated workforce ideal for the technology-based companies in the area.

It is possible to measure the level and range of subcontractors available within a region and to determine the age and skill profile of the labour pool. This is generally done when regions seek to promote inward investment but it is rarely part of a strategy to promote indigenous businesses and encourage entrepreneurship.

These issues of subcontractors and labour availability become paramount when the start-up company begins to grow. They can actually determine the growth rate that can be achieved. A Cambridge start-up that achieved a stock valuation of around £500 million in about five years hit limits when it had absorbed a significant proportion of the software skills available in the area. When it crashed it gave the poor performance of its major subcontractor in the West Country as an important factor. In this case not using a local supplier had resulted in a loss of control.

Business support sector

Over the past decade this sector has expanded considerably in the UK. When the Government Training Agency was replaced by Training and Enterprise Councils across the country and then Business Links were set up, there was a proliferation of provision for business, particularly for the small and medium-sized enterprises (SMEs). This proliferation led to confusion and so a 'one-stop shop' approach was adopted where SMEs could get help and support from a single information point.

In principle these organizations are there to provide the help and support that young growing business need. They fund a wide range of training programmes, provide business counsellors, help people to set up new businesses and many other good things. Their main drawback is that they bring bureaucracy to a support process that needs to be simple, easy to access and has real flexibility. Although there are some outstanding exceptions, in the main the personnel involved are administrators and there is an attitude and culture clash with the entrepreneur.

Business clubs both formal and informal are an essential part of any business infrastructure. They provide the networking opportunities that have been referred to earlier and are an important source of role models for up and coming entrepreneurs. The most effective clubs or associations are those that occur naturally as the entrepreneurial culture develops. There are generally many of them and they come and go, but the net effect is very beneficial.

Behind the growth of a business sector there is always an infrastructure of consultants and specialist advisers. Often there can be more advisers than there are companies to advise but they do provide an important service for the company in a hurry. Marketing and recruitment services are the most in demand and the local networks help the start-up company to know which are the best ones to use. One of the entrepreneur's talents is to know when he or she needs an expert and how to find a good one. Without that talent large amounts of time and money can be wasted, as all consultants can tell a good tale but most deliver very indifferent services.

Community development

This includes all the amenities that most of us take for granted: housing, schools, hospitals, recreation, transport and telecommunications. They serve the community as well as the business. One of the major problems when economic success comes to a region is that it gets 'overheated' with high house prices and living costs, congested roads, crowded shops and overstretched educational, medical and recreational facilities. Good planning can avoid most of these problems but, in reality, the supply is several years behind the demand. Like the lack of subcontractors and a labour pool, these factors can seriously impact the growth rate of a business.

When an area is developing a strategy to promote local businesses it can often influence many of these issues, but it must do so to a well thought through plan. When Milton Keynes was set up in the 1970s there was a serious mismatch between homes and jobs. People had somewhere to live but nowhere to work. When the Docklands in London was developed most of the jobs created were for outsiders and not local people and the transport provision was so poor that the outsider could not get to work. Even today City Airport has no direct rail or underground link.

Conclusion

This review of infrastructure provision shows that many different sectors are involved. Co-ordination between them is a major problem and so most infrastructures are a mixture of good and bad. In describing the main elements we have tried to show how they can and should work together. If a region is seriously interested in developing a strong indigenous business base then all parties have to co-operate. When this happens the results can be beyond people's expectations. The opportunities for creating an entrepreneurial culture and thereby a prosperous region are too important for local rivalries or the attitudes of a few people to be allowed to prevent them. There can be no change without a vision but it must be a vision that everybody can feel part of and own. There is enough evidence from around the world to show that an entrepreneurial culture can become a reality and that disadvantaged regions can be turned round, but their needs to be a vision and a will to make it happen. As with the individual entrepreneur the region has to see the opportunity and then implement it.

References

Abetti, P. A. and Savoy, R. (1991). Management training of technological entrepreneurs. *International Journal of Continuing Engineering Education*, **1** (4).
Bolton, J. E. (1971). *Report of the Committee of Enquiry on Small Firms*. Cm 4811. HMSO.
Bolton, W. K. (1993). The enterprise paradigm. Latin American Seminar on the Development of Technology-Based Enterprises, Rio de Janeiro, May.
Bolton, W. K. (1997). *The University Handbook on Enterprise Development*. Columbus.
Bruno, A. V. and Tyebjee, T. T. (1982). The environment for entrepreneurship. In *Encyclopaedia of Entrepreneurship* (C. Kent, D. L. Sexton and K. H. Vesper, eds), Prentice-Hall.

Business Week (1993). Special bonus issue on enterprise.

Castells, M. and Hall, P. (1994). *Technopoles of the World*. Routledge.

Coveney, P. and Moore, K. (1998). *Business Angels: Securing Start-up Finance*. John Wiley.

Enterprise Panel, The (1996). *Growing Success*. MCP 2288. HM Treasury.

Fisher, L. M. (1998). Technology transfer at Stanford University, *Policy*, **13**, 76–84.

Hoggart, R. (1996). *The Way We Live Now*. Pimlico.

Kuratko, D. F. and Hodgetts, R. M. (1998). *Entrepreneurship: A Contemporary Approach*. 4th edn. The Dryden Press.

Malecki, E. J. (1997). *Technology and Economic Development*. 2nd edn. Longman.

Medawar, P. (1984). *Pluto's Republic*. Oxford University Press.

Monck, C. S. P., Porter, R. B., Quintas, P. R. and Storey, D. J. (1988). *Science Parks and the Growth of High Technology Firms*. Croom Helm.

Segal, N., Quince R. E. and Wicksteed, W. (1985). *The Cambridge Phenomenon*. Segal, Quince, Wicksteed and Brand Brothers.

Smilor, R. W. and Gill, M. D. (1986). *The New Business Incubator*. Lexington Books.

Storey, D. J. (1982). *Entrepreneurship and the New Firm*. Croom Helm.

Success (1997). A golden future. May.

Vesper, K. H. (1986) New directions in entrepreneurship education. In *The Art and Science of Entrepreneurship* (D. Sexton and R. W. Smilor, eds), Ballinger.

Vesper, K. H. (1993). *Entrepreneurship Education*. The Anderson School, University of California, Los Angeles.

Wilson, J. W. (1986). *The New Venturers*. Addison-Wesley.

13 How the entrepreneur survives and wins

By now we understand entrepreneurs a little better and the process whereby they build something of recognized value. We have identified some of the support elements that help them along the way but it is still a journey fraught with difficulty. It is mostly an uphill fight demanding strength as well as courage. The operational environment we consider in this chapter is the background to this aspect of the journey. By giving it structure and form we hope that it will make it easier for entrepreneurs to understand their situation and deal with it. The market is the main element in an environment where entrepreneurs have to survive and win, and is therefore considered in some detail. The other elements they have to learn to handle in a positive and creative way. Most entrepreneurs seem to enjoy these challenges and, if anything, run harder and faster because of them.

The operational environment

The operational environment is the weather through which the good ship 'Enterprise' has to sail. The ship may have been well prepared and stocked with provisions but a severe storm and all is lost. Hidden rocks, dangerous headlands, fog are all hazards. Navigation and sailing skills, good communications and weather forecasting help, but it is essentially a battle with the elements. Growing a business often feels like this. There is the sudden headline in the press aimed directly at your market. A recent one proclaimed: 'Tapeless TV recorders set to make videos obsolete.' How should those in the video market respond? Is the journalist being sensationalist or has he a point? What happens when the customers read the same headline? Will they delay their purchase for a while? Is there a need to change course or does the industry just keep going?

What happens when the government suddenly changes the rules? In 1969 the US Congress raised the tax level on long-term capital gains from 28 per cent to 49 per cent and overnight halted the growing venture capital industry in its tracks. Annual private investment dropped from $171 million to $10 million. When the tax rate was returned to the 1969 level of 28 per cent nine years later, and then reduced further to 20 per cent in 1981, investment rose dramatically reaching $1425 million in 1982. As Larson and Rogers (1986) comment: 'That's enough money to start 2,800 small high-tech companies or 350 good-sized ones.' There was now a fair wind and the ship sailed on but the early 1970s had been very difficult years for those start-ups looking for money.

Entrepreneurs will succeed and win to the extent that they are able to cope with these vicissitudes. Just like the true sailor, the true entrepreneur relishes these challenges and gets real satisfaction from winning through. It is often when the ship has ridden the early storms and is set on a steady course that the entrepreneur loses interest and gets bored. He or she looks back to the excitement and challenge of it all and wants to return to those days. This is one reason why entrepreneurs develop a habit of growing new enterprises. It becomes an addiction; it is what stimulates them.

Table 13.1 shows the activities that make up the operational environment. They determine the weather conditions. They are the things that the entrepreneur cannot change or influence easily. We identify five sectors: the market, the economy, the legal system, politics and culture. They all impact in their own way upon the start-up enterprise, but there is one issue that cuts across all sectors and that is risk. It is inherent in everything that we do in life but the entrepreneur sees and handles risk in his or her own special way.

At first sight these lists are somewhat daunting and can deter the faint-hearted, but for the entrepreneur they are issues that he or she must face up to and learn to deal with. Many start-ups fail because entrepreneurs have not paid sufficient attention to them at the operational level. The entrepreneur has to learn which are important and which can be left. Thus when cash flow is under pressure and

Table 13.1 *The operational environment*

Sector	The enterprise				
	Market	*Economic*	*Legislative*	*Political*	*Cultural*
Activity	Risk				
	Limits to trade, e.g. tax duties, cartels	Inflation and interest rates	Company law, e.g. share ownership	Degree of stability	Attitudes towards entrepreneurs
	Market access and entry problems	Access to working capital and banking rules	Labour and factory law, e.g. union and employment rules	Short-termism	Press and the media
	The market situation at a local, regional, national and global levels	Government policy on zoning and taxation	Patent law and IPR rulings	National and regional policies which are politically driven	Business and job culture; work ethic
					University culture

cheques begin to 'bounce' the entrepreneur must make sure that those sent to the tax man will be honoured by the bank, otherwise the entrepreneur will be in serious trouble. Value added tax (VAT) and Companies House returns have to be made on time or penalties will be incurred. These might seem details but they can become major irritants for the entrepreneur if they are not watched and can take his or her eye off the really important task of growing the business.

Before considering the sectors we look at the general issues of risk. We are not concerned to provide a detailed discussion of the subject but, rather, to consider how the entrepreneur perceives and deals with risk.

Risk

The ordinary rate of profit rises ... with risk.

(Adam Smith)

Sir, it's not a gamble, it's an investment.

(Punter at the Cheltenham Gold Cup)

These are the words of the 'risk aware' economist and the 'opportunity aware' gambler. The financial investor and the gambler operate in uncertain worlds. Past experience, inside knowledge and 'form' all help them understand this uncertainty but the future is essentially unknown. Both are also people of action who need to make a decision. One makes the decision on the basis of risk–reward considerations as Adam Smith would have done. He demands a rate of return commensurate with the risk he is taking. The other is seized by the opportunity and the size of the reward. Failure and loss is not an option considered by the punter, even though it may be the reality half an hour later. A bet is an investment and not a gamble as a punter once told a BBC interviewer.

Entrepreneurs who have attended a business school or are financially oriented will have the Adam Smith approach. They will find this restricts their natural inclinations to go for an opportunity and they may well miss some that they would have been able to take had they not spent so much time in analysis. Other entrepreneurs are more like the gambler. They are seized and sometimes mesmerized by the opportunity. This gives them great focus and they storm through obstacles. They can also be foolhardy and live in a fantasy world. Even so the gambler entrepreneur is more likely to win 'big' than is the risk-analysis entrepreneur, but then perhaps he or she will not win very often.

True entrepreneurs are neither investment bankers nor gamblers. They are mountain climbers with a unique talent, temperament, technique set that they apply to what others would regard as a high-risk activity. Like climbing mountains it is a risk that they do not have to take but somehow it is in the blood. Mountaineers know the risks because they have had friends who have died climbing. None of this deters them. Mountains are there to be climbed. Perceived opportunities are the entrepreneur's mountains. Observing them is not enough; they have to be climbed. Risk is inherent. It is the way things are. Just like the mountaineer, entrepreneurs reduce risk by learning proven techniques and building experience. They take a calculated risk, weighing the options carefully. Like the experienced mountaineer, they know their limitations but delight in testing themselves, always pushing the boundary so as to improve.

Most entrepreneurs see themselves as not taking undue risks, some even claim to be risk averse. They say this because they do not perceive risks in the way that most of us do. It is not that they are not risk averse or that they are prone to take risks. They are simply not *risk aware*. Some children take to swimming very easily. Others who are risk aware realize that it is possible to drown in water and are much more cautious. Entrepreneurs often appear to be naïve about business risk but the truth is that they do not see it. This is one reason why they have such difficulties with bankers and financiers. They have a completely different perception of risk. This lack of risk awareness can be a serious weakness for the entrepreneur but it can also be a major strength. 'If I had realized what was involved I would probably never have started' is a sentiment often expressed by entrepreneurs but they are always glad they did. This lack of risk awareness goes hand in hand with the entrepreneur life theme of 'courage'. Without courage he or she would not be able to face up to the consequence of the risk-taking when things went wrong. Maybe courageous people take more risks because they know they can deal with the consequences.

There is clearly no point in entrepreneurs taking unwarranted and unnecessary risks. The basic rules of business and of profit and loss are things that entrepreneurs forget at their peril. But there is always risk in doing something that has not been done before or doing something in a new and different way. It is this category of risk that entrepreneurs takes in their stride because they are not really aware of how great a risk they are taking.

When Richard Branson launched Mike Oldfield's record *Tubular Bells* he was doing something that had not been done before. An analysis would have shown that the greatest risk was in its promotion. Oldfield was an unknown and he had produced a forty-five minute long play record, not a three-minute single. Endorsement by a well-known disc jockey (DJ) on the radio was essential but would not be easy. Branson was turned down by BBC Radios 1 and 3 because the performance was too long. Finally he persuaded the well-known DJ, John Peel, a contact from his student days, to play it on his late night show. 'Tonight I'm not going to play a whole lot of records. I'm just going to play one by a young composer called Mike Oldfield. It's his first record and it's called *Tubular Bells*. I've never heard anything like it in my life.' In his autobiography Branson recalls his anxiety as he listened to the broadcast. It was an all or nothing situation. 'I was too aware that Virgin had to sell a lot of copies to make money for next month's tax repayment.' The record was a great success and gave Virgin Records the start it so badly needed. Branson's risk in taking on Mike Oldfield had been justified but a major problem was just around the corner – one that a careful risk analysis would probably not have spotted. Branson hired the Queen Elizabeth Hall in London for a *Tubular Bells* concert. On the morning of the concert Oldfield called Branson and told him he could not go through with the concert that evening. Tickets were sold, television coverage organized and now the main artist was pulling out. 'I felt a wave of despair,' recalls Branson 'I knew that Mike could be as stubborn as me when he wanted to be.' By a combination of courage and creativity Branson solved the problem. He gave Oldfield his beloved Bentley in return for that performance (Branson, 1998).

Branson's first risk would have come out of an analysis of the market and the difficulty of market entry would have been identified. Branson knew the market well enough to take that risk. His second risk was less easy to predict and had it been, then its solution would have been in terms of a formal binding contract on Oldfield. Branson's solution was completely different. It retained the commitment of the artist and solved Branson's problem.

Risk for entrepreneurs is not a major consideration. This approach fascinates the commentators who find it difficult to believe that they can live with such huge risks. They wonder how entrepreneurs sleep at night. As the example shows, Branson was anxious and nervous, he was in despair but he kept going and he won through. Entrepreneurs do not see risk in the normal business sense, they simply take things as they come. They are not risk aware and this makes them vulnerable, but this is counteracted by their courage and creativity when things go wrong.

There is much that can be said about risk at the level of technique, and the risk assessment methodologies that are around can be extremely helpful. Most business plans require a section on the risk aspects of the investment and it is certainly a topic with which the entrepreneur has to engage but it is lack of risk awareness that is both the entrepreneur's strength and weakness. Most things that people worry about never happen, but some do and it is better to be prepared. Entrepreneurs think differently and just get on with things dealing with problems as they arise as Branson did.

The market sector

The market and the growth stages

The understanding of the marketplace is probably the most critical success factor for the entrepreneur. Without it he or she is unlikely to survive let alone win. It is an understanding that has to change and develop as the business grows. Table 13.2 shows how the market and the growth stages discussed in Chapter 11 interrelate. Concepts and visions are necessary at the embryo stage. Here the different possibilities are picked out and evaluated. The good entrepreneur involves his or her team at this early stage so that they begin to 'buy into' the enterprise. This is usually a time of dreaming dreams and seeing great possibilities but it is important not to get stuck here but to move on to the nurture stage to focus and target the opportunities. The 'possible' and 'probable' opportunities have to be differentiated and priorities set within a market strategy. This is necessary preparation for market entry at the fledgling stage. Without it market entry will be confused and fragmented. This is a critical stage for the business because all the market assumptions will be tested. It is much easier to generate an interest in the product or service you plan to offer than it is to land an order. Getting close to the customer is important at this stage but there must be a spread of customers to avoid bias and narrowing of the marketplace.

Table 13.2 *The market and the business*

	Embryo stage	*Nurture stage*	*Fledgling stage*	*Take-off stage*
Market stage	Concept	Focus and target	Entry	Capture and dominance
Market focus	Vision	Opportunities	Product/service	Solutions
Activity	See possibilities and evaluate	Prioritize and formulate strategy	Get close to the customer	Manage the market
Adoption	Internal adoption		Innovators	Early adopters	Early majority

The take-off stage moves the business into a different world. This is a crucial transition for the business and the entrepreneur. It is the point at which he or she moves from being the owner manager of a small business to the builder of something of recognized value. It is the watershed between a lifestyle entrepreneur and the true entrepreneur. The aim is to capture the market and dominate it, as we shall see later.

The diffusion of innovation

Before discussing market entry further we need to understand the key ideas behind what has been termed 'the diffusion of innovation' (Rogers, 1995). These ideas were applied to marketing in 1969 when Frank Bass used them to describe how markets adopted new products. Since then the methodology has been developed to monitor early sales campaigns and predict the likely take up of a new product (Mahajan, Muller and Bass, 1990).

The word 'adoption' is used to describe the extent to which an innovation is taken up by the end user and an 'innovation' is anything that is perceived as new by the user. The adoption of an innovation follows the 'diffusion' S-curve shown in Figure 13.1 (Rogers, 1995).

The steeper the S-curve the faster the adoption and the flatter the S-curve the slower the adoption. Fifty per cent adoption is achieved when the S-curve has reached its inflection or halfway point. It is made up of 'innovators' who are the first to adopt the innovation, followed by the 'early adopters' and then the 'early majority' up to the halfway point. Beyond that come the 'late majority' and finally 'the laggards'. Figure 13.1 suggests that around 10 per cent never adopt the innovation.

The area of real interest is the start of the S-curve. The *innovators* are the first 2.5 per cent of the users according to Rogers (1995). *Early adopters* are the next 13.5 per cent so that together the innovators and the early adopters make up 16 per cent of the customer base. The *early majority* are the next 34 per cent of customers and take the total adoption to the halfway point. These figures correspond approximately to the standard deviation multiples of the 'normal' probability distribution curve from which the S-curve is derived.

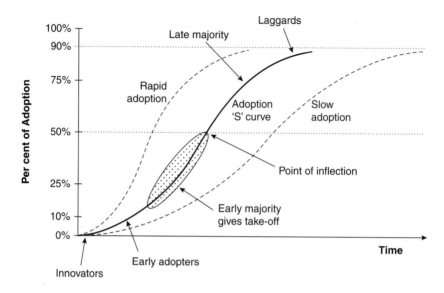

Figure 13.1   *Adoption S-curve*

Adoption stages

Following this brief outline we now return to Table 13.2 and set these adoption stages on to the growth stage model. For convenience this is illustrated in Figure 13.2. In the early stages of the business the market has to be 'adopted' and taken on board internally within the company. It is important for the entrepreneur to manage this internal adoption process and not to assume that it will just happen. The whole team must catch the vision and believe in the market focus and strategy.

In Figure 13.2 the external adoption follows the adopter categories proposed by Rogers (1995). The innovators are the potential customers that the start-up company has identified during the nurture stage and is doing business with at the start of

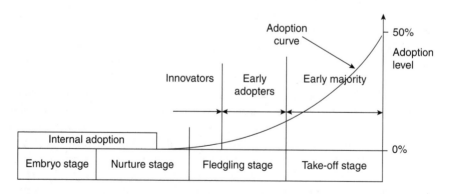

Figure 13.2   *Adoption profile*

the fledgling stage. Innovators will try the product out as soon as they can get their hands on it. They are the people who will respond to any publicity that is launched as long as it emphasizes newness. Price is not the criterion by which these people make a purchase decision, so margins can be higher at this stage.

Care should be taken with the 2.5 per cent adoption figure by the innovators because it depends on the market being targeted. For the start-up company it really means 2.5 per cent of the market that can be realistically reached in the short term. We have seen business plans that have assumed that the new business will capture a few per cent of a world market. This has predicted a huge sales level in the first year which is quite unrealistic. The error in this kind of calculation is that there is no way the company can ever reach that market until it is a well-established international business. The only exception to this, and it is an important one, is an Internet company, which can reach the world market very easily and at low cost. But that exception apart, the start-up company must focus at this stage on the market that can be captured in the short term.

Whilst the innovators are prepared to take risks on the product or service the next target group, the early adopters, think more carefully about it and their opinion is valued by others. The product therefore has to function well and do what it is claimed it will do. These are the people that the fledgling company has to capture. It is possible for businesses to fail because they are not able to win over these early adopters. The innovators are much more tolerant than the early adopter who requires products that are delivered on time and that work first time.

The innovators and the early adopters together make up 16 per cent of a customer base. These customers can be in a particular geographical region or market niche and the start-up company can achieve further expansion simply by moving into new regions or applications. This can be a viable strategy in the short term and will certainly produce increased sales but there is an important caution. The start-up company must move through the fledgling stage and not get stuck there. It must continue to the take-off stage where the primary marketing task is to attract more and more of the early majority of adopters. These represent the next 34 per cent of a customer base. When this is done the company is a mainstream supplier in a mainstream market with a real opportunity to establish a leadership position.

Though this approach is about the adoption of innovations it applies as much to old products in old markets as it does to new products in new markets. Innovation means anything perceived as new and this can be a new pricing or delivery approach in an old market. Shopping on the Internet is a new purchase and delivery mechanism but the products and services have not changed. The book, video or airline ticket is still the same item. They may be old products in old markets but there is purchasing novelty and the laws of innovation diffusion apply. On-line shopping is at the early adopter stage and the big test will be whether or not it can cross the divide to become mainstream.

The take-off stage

The move from the fledgling stage to the take-off stage requires a fundamental shift in the market focus. As indicated in Table 13.2, the market focus changes as the company passes through its different stages of growth. The focus moves from the vision at the embryo stage to opportunities at the nurture stage and to product/service at the fledgling stage. This is a fairly natural progression that generally goes smoothly. With a real product and real customers it is easy for the entrepreneur to think that he or she now has a viable and maturing business. In reality the business has reached a critical stage. It can either grow to be a force in the industry or it can stay small with the likelihood of a slow decline. The business can either pass through to take-off or else stay as a fledgling business. It is possible to disguise this reality by believing that the business has reached a steady state and is now mature. For some companies this 'comfort zone' can last for a number of years but sooner or later it will turn into a 'crisis zone' and the company will find it difficult to survive. To build real value the entrepreneur has no option but to go for take-off.

Moore (1991; 1998) has applied these diffusion-of-innovation ideas to marketing strategies for high-technology businesses. He sees the transition from fledgling stage to take-off stage as the move from the early stage market to the mainstream market. He describes the transition as a chasm that the start-up company has to cross if it is to succeed. The analogy of a chasm suggests that the gap is both deep and wide, and that most who try to cross it fall to their death. Certainly the high-technology sector has a large graveyard!

Two quite different markets stand either side of this divide. Up to this stage the start-up business has been concerned with the early market and the early adopters but now it has to enter the mainstream market and go for the early majority (Moore, 1998). This would simply mean more of the same with increased efficiency if it were not for the fact that these markets have quite different characteristics. What sells in one will not sell in the other. The early market is prepared to shop around and has a DIY approach to solving its problems but the mainstream market does not have the time or the interest. This is the reason why it is so difficult to break into a market once it has become mainstream. The market has adopted a particular approach and will stay with it often when there are better products around. This shows the magnitude of Dyson's achievement in breaking into the vacuum cleaner market, which he did on the basis of functional excellence and not price. New products into old markets have a huge hill to climb but, as Dyson showed, 'it can be done'.

This transition period has particular dangers for sales-oriented entrepreneurs. They have been very successful to date and feel they know and understand their market. They recognize that the early majority market is twice as big as the early adopter market and are ready to go for it. But it is not more of the same. They need to recognize that a different approach is needed and that without it they will fail. The shift to a focus on application rather than product may mean new business alliances, or even acquisitions, in order that the company can offer the customer a complete solution. This calls for new talents and skills from entrepreneurs but their creativity and courage will still serve them well. Entrepreneurs like Charles Forte and Richard Branson excelled in this take-off stage. Both demonstrated real talent for negotiating the deal and building the right alliances. They survived and won because they were not intimidated by a market environment dominated by 'big players'. The take-off stage was where they excelled.

The market limits

There are limits to growth built into most markets, due to competition. Market share is the main indicator of market performance. The Boston Consulting Group uses the idea of 'relative market share' in their well-known Growth-Share Matrix (Thompson, 1997). This is the ratio of a company's market share to that of its nearest competitor so that a ratio greater than 1 means that that company is the market leader. For the static or declining market the matrix has a ratio of 1 as the dividing line between the cash cow product that you milk and the dog that you should kick out. Similarly for a growing market this dividing line is between the stars and the problem children. This means that only the market leader benefits from having a cash cow and star products, the rest have dogs and problem children.

This presents the start-up business with a serious problem. How can it hope to penetrate a market and achieve dominance? Part of the answer has been given above in terms of market adoption and the transition to the take-off stage. Another part is for the entrepreneur to be aware of how players in the market behave. If there is one dominant player with say 40 per cent market share and the rest have around 10 per cent, then a newcomer would probably go unnoticed up to about 3 per cent or 4 per cent. Thereafter pressure will come from all except the dominant player who will simply watch the fight. This may be open and honest competition in the marketplace but it can also be underhand and illegal. We know of one entrepreneur whose business expansion was effectively capped by the competition who 'persuaded' his supplier to limit deliveries of vital components.

In some markets the business is shared out among a group of companies so that an informal cartel operates that keeps out newcomers. In others as soon as a business reaches a certain size there is a telephone call that offers to safeguard markets and ensure delivery for a 'consideration'. These are all problems that the entrepreneur has to be able to cope with, and there is never an easy answer. Ricardo Semler, the Brazilian entrepreneur, has quoted the maxim 'You can either run a successful business or be ethical. Take your pick.' He then goes on to give examples that show this maxim need not be true (Semler, 1993).

As we comment later, corruption affects other areas of the operational environment but the marketplace is perhaps the most difficult to deal with. The first big order may carry a 'commission' payment to the person placing the order which from that point on becomes the accepted way of doing business. The entrepreneur needs to decide his or her position on these issues before they arise. There can be some advantage in talking things over with other entrepreneurs in the same region or area of activity so that a common stand is taken. A group of almost fifty entrepreneurs in Romania have come together in this way to develop what they term 'islands of integrity in a sea of corruption' (Murray, 1997).

The economic, legislative, political and cultural sectors

Here we present our views of how these sectors affect entrepreneurs. In general they are not particularly friendly to entrepreneurs or at least they present them with problems that they could well do without. This section has something of a lobbying tone and we present opinions rather than facts, but we do so at the end of a book that has tried to champion entrepreneurs and the release of their valuable talent amongst us.

The economic sector

Next to the market this is the sector that the entrepreneur has to pay the closest attention to. The economic situation in a country has a direct bearing on the success or otherwise of the business. Most governments are trying to create the conditions that will keep the business sector in good shape and produce a healthy expanding economy. They do this against an international economy that is driven by the large trading nations such as the USA and Japan so that recession in one soon becomes a global issue. Entrepreneurs come and go in these economic cycles and investors become more and more cautious. The net result is to suppress entrepreneurial endeavour in favour of low-risk prudent strategies.

Inflation and interest rates are economic indictors that affect the bottom line of a business, its net profit, but they are outside the control of the entrepreneur. Inflation affects both the costs of raw material and the prices that can be charged in the marketplace. If the raw material is imported or exports are a major part of the business then changes in exchange rates can almost kill a business overnight. These are serious problems but the amazing thing is that entrepreneurs still succeed and win. Ricardo Semler describes the Brazilian economy in his first eleven years running Semco: 'Inflation averaged more than 400 per cent, swinging from yearly highs of 1,600 per cent to lows of a mere 100 per cent. From 1986 to 1990, the country endured five economic shock plans, knocked three zeros off its currency twice and on two occasions changed it altogether.' If this was not bad enough in 1990 a new finance minister seized 80 per cent of the cash in the country. 'Chaos does not begin to describe the reaction. Companies didn't have money to meet their payrolls, much less to conduct business. At Semco we struggled through several months of zero sales.' Despite all this Semco under Semler's leadership rode the storm and came out a fitter and leaner company (Semler, 1993).

Access to working capital to run the business is a constant source of difficulty for the entrepreneur. Because of the rules that the lending banks apply, most start-up businesses simply do not have enough cash to grow and become strong. In many countries the entrepreneur has to provide a financial guarantee well in excess of the overdraft limit allowed or the loan taken out. If he or she is unable to do this then access to money is denied.

In the UK it is common for the directors of the business to each give personal guarantees to the bank. This generally involves signing the entire business over to the bank and sometimes the family home as a security in case things go wrong. Surprisingly most entrepreneurs simply accept this and the risk does not seem to bother them.

Banks can assume powers to conduct financial audits of companies to which they have lent money. The cost of the audit has to be borne by the company. In one case the auditors put in by the bank concluded that the company did need an increased overdraft but recommended that it not be given. This perversity is not untypical and represents the kind of unnecessary pressures that some banks put on the entrepreneur.

Taxation is another area of difficulty because it is usually imposed arbitrarily by government without consultation. There is always a public outcry when personal taxation is increased but taxes on business often go unnoticed. Some countries find it necessary to have tax police to ensure that taxes get paid. They are empowered to come into the company at any time and see any records they wish. In some cases they confiscate everything and leave the business to carry on while they continue their investigation. This power is absolute and so can be abused. Ricardo Semler became a national hero in Brazil when he exposed corruption in a government tax department and the officials concerned received a prison sentence. He comments:

> There was no reason to rejoice. The inspector's superiors were not even brought in for questioning. A little while later one of our clerks went to a government department for a document and was told 'Tell your boss he doesn't just have one inspector to worry about, he's got 100,000 against him now'.
>
> (Semler, 1993)

Businesses, of course, are not always the innocent party and many are expert in exploiting loopholes and avoiding the payment of tax for as long as possible. Some also exploit well-meaning government policy for their own ends. The more deprived and underdeveloped regions in a country are often designated to receive grant aid of one form or another. We know of one case in the UK where the entrepreneur moved to a new building in a development area. The building was rent and rate free for three years and he received a grant for every job he created. When the three-year period was up he closed the operation down. It appeared that he had never had the intention of setting up a permanent business in the area.

The legislative sector

There are a great many laws and regulations that the start-up business has to comply with and the entrepreneur will need legal advice right from the start. The three most critical areas are Company Law, Employment Law and Patent Law although Property Law can sometimes be an issue. The social entrepreneur will need to comply with Charity Law if he or she decides to operate as a charity. This is where the entrepreneurs' talent of 'expertise orientation' is important. They know their own limits and when to call in the experts. They are also good at identifying the right experts who will not waste their time and money and will give sound advice.

Company Law is concerned with the legal entity of the business. The entrepreneur will need to decide whether he or she will be a sole trader, a partnership or some form of limited company. For the entrepreneur who intends to build something of recognized value this will almost certainly mean a limited company. The social entrepreneur may need to explore the possibility of setting up as a charity. If the entrepreneur does both then in the UK he or she would be required to send annual accounts to Companies House as a limited company and the Charity Commissioners as a charity. Couple this with the complexities of setting up as a company and/or a charity and it is clear that professional advice is necessary.

Whilst legal safeguards obviously are required, they appear to be unnecessarily complex and in practice legal formalities can go back and forth for months delaying the start-up of the business, or else the business starts without them in place and runs into trouble later on. With all these legal company matters to sort out it is easy for the entrepreneur to forget the obvious ones like 'terms and conditions of sale' or what is legally required to be on the letterheads of the new business.

Company law in respect of shareholders is a very important area. What happens to the shareholding of a founder director who is dismissed or leaves? Can the director retain it or can he or she be forced to surrender it, and if so at what value? Most start-ups face this problem within their first year or two.

These days it is not only directors who own shares in the business. It is increasingly common for employees to be given share options. Microsoft is said to have created more millionaires among its employees than any other company. What are their rights? All these issues need to be addressed and legal advice is essential. In a litigious society like the USA most companies will go to court at some time, even in their early years. The most common areas concern employees and patents. Key people leave and set up in competition, or out of the blue there is a challenge to the patent upon which the product and the business is based. These are nightmare scenarios but they do happen and the entrepreneur has to be able to cope. The successful entrepreneur builds a team around him or her and has experts so that he or she is well prepared.

In the UK, employment and labour law is becoming increasingly demanding on the business. Whilst it is there to safeguard the rights of employees it has reduced the willingness of businesses to take on permanent employees. Start-up companies are often run below strength so that those who are employed have to work harder and longer. In some sectors such as computing there is now a large army of contractors who are self-employed and move from contract to contract. The entrepreneur needs flexibility and, good though the intentions of labour law might be, it is a constraint on the start-up business.

Patent law as we discussed in Chapter 12 is very important for the technology-based business and venture capitalists are unlikely to invest unless the patent situation is strong. This can increase the start-up costs significantly as cover in the USA, Europe and Japan is almost the minimum required. Professional patent agents will be needed. It is certainly not an area where the entrepreneur should adopt a DIY approach, though some do.

Once all these matters are sorted out and the business is up and running then a whole host of regulations have to be complied with. One entrepreneur who had started a successful business in her garden shed went to the local council to see if larger premises might be available. Their first response was to say that as she did not have planning permission to operate a business from her garden shed she would have to close down. Health and safety and environmental issues are now highly regulated and whilst this is obviously a good thing overall it is another area that the entrepreneur and his or her team have to familiarize themselves with.

These kind of regulations enforced by administrators can be a source of great frustration to the entrepreneur. In some countries they are a source of serious corruption. Semler had a similar experience with factory inspectors before the one with tax inspectors reported above.

The political sector

The main impact of the political situation for the entrepreneur is the degree of stability it brings to the country. The rise of entrepreneurial activity in the Renaissance period was linked with a period of relative peace and a power balance between kings, as we reported in the Introduction. War may give some entrepreneurs a fresh opportunity but it prevents the build-up of an entrepreneurial culture and entrepreneurs can find a life's work in ruins.

The politicians' job is to create an environment that is conducive to the entrepreneur; one that encourages and rewards personal endeavour and hard work and that does not penalize the entrepreneur who has tried and failed. The assumption behind British law seems to have been that anybody declared bankrupt is a bad person who deserves all he or she gets. In truth many have just made bad business decisions or were simply unlucky. Recent efforts by the British government to amend the law of bankruptcy are to be commended.

Because of the electoral system in many countries the economic and legislation cycle is between three and five years. This leads to start-stop policies and short-termism which make life very difficult for the entrepreneur and particularly for those who are trying to put in place the kind of support infrastructure discussed in Chapter 12. We know of a case in Brazil where the construction of a business incubator was halted because the mayor who was behind the scheme was not re-elected and the new mayor stopped all building projects. Similar start-stop effects occur in universities when the principal or vice-chancellor is an elected post and the new appointee is not interested in the plans of his or her predecessor. Academic issues have a way of being resolved but peripheral things such as business incubators or special entrepreneurial initiatives always seem to suffer.

National and regional policies that are politically driven can seriously impact the entrepreneur. There may be a drive to promote employment in a difficult area and create jobs. The easy fix is to encourage a large company to move into the area, as we discussed in Chapter 12 when we commented on inward investment. Little or no thought is given to creating an indigenous business base driven by entrepreneurs. This was certainly the case a few years ago but now the role of the local company is more clearly recognized by the politicians who devise these schemes. Even so most government schemes are not user friendly and it is normal for private sector companies working in the field of job creation to have to adjust their plans to meet the latest idea from government. We know of one group that has decided it is was not worth the effort and it has used its entrepreneurial skills so that its work among young entrepreneurs is funded by a separate commercial venture and grants are no longer needed.

Perhaps the biggest complaint against the government sector's involvement in entrepreneurial activity is that they seem to think only in terms of job creation.

Their contracts are set up on the basis of the cost per job created. This is done because of the political sensitivity to employment levels, when in fact what is needed are sustainable jobs in viable businesses and not just any jobs. There is no virtue in a company employing more people than it needs simply to qualify for a grant, but that is how most schemes are structured.

The cultural sector

Culture is the most deeply rooted of these environmental parameters and the most difficult to change. It varies from country to country and region to region. The USA has the most entrepreneurial culture in the world, which no doubt owes much to its pioneering origins, but places like Hong Kong and Singapore have developed their own brand of entrepreneurship. The role of the small start-up has never had to be argued in these places. It is self-evident, a product of the Chinese culture and the dominant role of the family unit (Fukuyama, 1995). Japan, though it does not see itself as particularly inventive, has proved to be an excellent innovator. They may not be natural entrepreneurs but they are certainly outstanding project champions with remarkable focus and a strong work ethic. In Europe we see an interesting mixture but with no entrepreneur culture other than in a few places. Cambridge, England, and Oulu, Finland, have already been mentioned but there is also northern Italy (Porter, 1990) and the Basque region of Spain around Mondragon (Whyte and Whyte, 1991). Both have seen real entrepreneurial activity over the years.

The former communist countries have an anti-entrepreneurial culture at present due to their long history of centralist government. There are signs that this is now beginning to change, though this is more likely to be to a capitalist culture rather than an entrepreneurial one. The Indian subcontinent, Latin America, Africa and China have huge populations and for historic and religious reasons each has its own approach to entrepreneurship. Though it is allowed and even encouraged, it is only within certain boundaries, so it has not become the major influence that it could be. The surprise amongst these groups is that Latin America has not been more successful since its origins are not dissimilar to those of the USA. No doubt their experience with military dictatorships and union solidarity has worked against individualism and the emergence of the entrepreneur. There are welcome signs that things are changing and entrepreneurship is now an increasingly important topic in their universities.

These observations present a mixed picture of how the cultures across the world relate to the entrepreneur. Though there is certainly some way to go before our comments in Chapter 10 about a world in tune with the entrepreneur are a reality we do believe the opportunity is there and that things are moving in the right direction. The entrepreneur is central to this culture change and the challenge is to release his or her potential in a positive and constructive manner to the economic and social benefit of us all.

Conclusion

We have made a number of assertions in this chapter as we have sought to present the entrepreneur's point of view. Most entrepreneurs are too busy running their enterprises to engage in this debate, but it is a serious one. Just as the sectors in the support infrastructure need to understand each other, so do those in the operational environment. The structural divisions in our society and the way career routes are organized make this difficult but unless it happens the development of an entrepreneurial culture and the release of entrepreneur talent will be seriously delayed and we will all be the losers.

References

Branson, R. (1998). *Richard Branson: Losing my Virginity*. Virgin Publishing.

Fukuyama, F. (1995). *Trust*. Hamish Hamilton.

Larson, J. K. and Rogers, E. M. (1986). *Silicon Valley Fever*. Unwin Counterpoint.

Mahajan, V., Muller, E. and Bass, F. M. (1990). New product diffusion models in marketing. *Journal of Marketing*, **54**, 1–26.

Moore, G. A. (1991). *Crossing the Chasm*. HarperBusiness.

Moore, G. A. (1998). *Inside the Tornado*. Capstone.

Murray, D. (1997). *Ethics in Organisations*. Kogan Page.

Porter, M. E. (1990). *The Competitive Advantage of Nations*. Macmillan.

Rogers, E. M. (1995). *Diffusion of Innovation*. 4th edn. Free Press.

Semler. R. (1993). *Maverick*. Century.

Thompson, J. L. (1997). *Strategic Management*. 3rd edn. International Thomson Business Press.

Whyte, W. F. and Whyte, K. G. (1991). *Making Mondragon*. 2nd edn. Cornell University ILR Press.

14 Techniques for the entrepreneur

Techniques need to be applied in the right way. Techniques that are proven and linked with a recognized body of knowledge can make most people reasonably competent in the field to which they relate. But they are not sufficient to achieve excellence. Talent and temperament must be added into the equation. When talent and technique clash then talent should be the winner. Without that condition innovation and new ideas will be stifled. We therefore present this brief discussion of technique with that proviso. For entrepreneurs nothing is set in stone and they must remain free to do things their way – they probably will anyway!

Understanding the business

Business textbooks present a series of models that purport to describe the early years of a business. These are helpful in general terms but their greater value is in understanding why, how and where many companies deviate from a so-called normality. Here we discuss three common models and one that is perhaps less well-known. Their links to the business adoption model (Figures 13.1 and 13.2) will be readily appreciated.

Business or product life cycle

Revenue and profit increase in the early years of the business as shown in Figure 14.1 and then level off as things stabilize. After a period of maturity the business or product declines and dies.

For some businesses the start-up phase can last a very long time. Using our earlier terminology businesses can get stuck at the embryo stage. Most of the reasons for this are linked with shortcomings of the market, the product or the people involved, so undue delay here is an important warning sign. But there can be cases when this delay is legitimate. Oxford Instruments mentioned in connection with niche markets in Chapter 11 is a case in point. It ran along the time axis of Figure

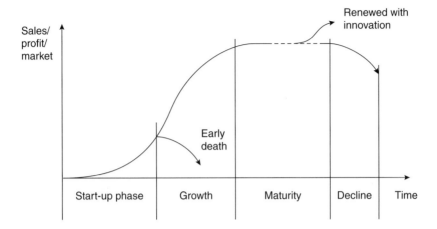

Figure 14.1 *The life-cycle curve*

14.1 for ten years, until the arrival of the NMR body-scanner opened a market for its product. From then on it moved up the life-cycle curve and is now a major international company.

Movement up the curve cannot be guaranteed and many fall to an early death as indicated. The mature period can be short or long. Most often it is assumed that the life expectancy of a product is short and certainly in technology a two-year life cycle is all there may be. But some products do seem to go on for ever, renewed with innovation. When the computer came on the scene the demise of paper was widely predicted but this has not happened. If anything, computers have increased the demand for paper rather than reduced it.

Although the precise time of movement along the life-cycle track can rarely be forecast, this technique is useful for understanding the stage a product or business has reached. One final comment about the life-cycle curve is that it is rarely smooth. Instead it can be a seesaw of ups and downs as the business goes from crisis to crisis with an average line that hopefully follows the curve upwards. Jolly (1997) reports seeing a 'Business Enthusiasm Curve' framed on a wall at the offices of Raychem in Silicon Valley. It was a version of the life-cycle curve ranging from 'despair' to 'ecstasy' along a time axis that zigzagged its way upwards.

Cash flow models

There are two important cash flow models. The 'breakeven model' and the 'cash demand model'. Both have the idea that there is a 'breakeven' point in the sales level where the costs and the income match. Before this point there is a loss situation and after it a profit. Figure 14.2 depicts the breakeven model.

The 'fixed costs' are costs incurred whether or not anything is sold and are represented by a horizontal line in Figure 14.2. They cover the costs of the premises, the administrative staff, telephones, electricity, cars and so on. Next there is the cost of making the products, termed the 'variable costs' that increase with the number

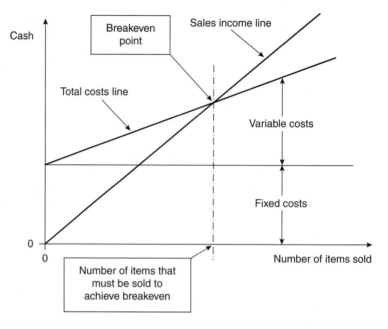

Figure 14.2   *The breakeven model*

of units made. Assuming the cost of each unit to be the same, then the 'variable costs' can be represented by a diagonal straight line as shown.

Income is the sales or turnover level. This increases as more items or units are sold. Again assuming that each item is sold for the same amount, this is also a diagonal straight line but starting from the origin. Breakeven is achieved when the sales income equals the total costs made up of the fixed and variable costs. The number of items that have to be sold in order to break even can be read from the graph.

This model helps to show that fixed costs or overheads have to be paid for and that if sales are insufficient then there will be a loss. It helps to assess breakeven quantities. For example, a simple calculation might show that thousands of items need to be sold every month to achieve breakeven when a market analysis has indicated that the market is only likely to require hundreds a month. In this case the business would not be viable. It can also help in assessing the potential to link some costs more closely with sales so that apparently 'fixed costs' become 'variable'.

The model is difficult to apply if there is more than one product or if the business offers a service where fixed and variable costs are hard to determine or distinguish. It is best to make a few assumptions and keep things as simple as possible. With a little juggling between the price and the fixed and variable costs it is possible to see whether or not the proposed business could be made profitable.

The cash demand model is shown in Figure 14.3.

The vertical axis can be actual cash or the accumulated cash – here it is the latter. The cash demand is measured over time. The curve starts off in the 'Valley of Death' in a loss situation and moves into profit in the 'Land of Plenty'. The

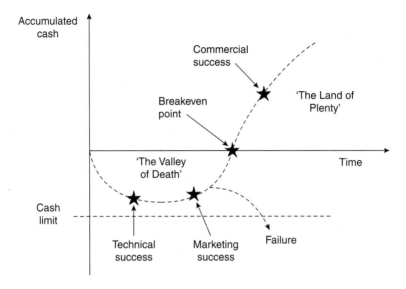

Figure 14.3 *The cash demand curve*

cross-over or breakeven point is when total income to date equals total expenditure to date.

Success can be achieved in the 'Valley of Death'. 'Technical success' is reached when development costs have stopped and the product is ready for sale. In practice these costs are often difficult to control and it can be useful to set a limit on this expenditure, as indicated in Figure 14.3. The next point is 'marketing success' when the innovators buy the product and the feedback from them suggests that the early adopters will not be far behind. After breakeven 'commercial success' is achieved in the 'Land of Plenty'. Profit is being generated and the market is increasing steadily.

This model is a useful control device, though in practice the 'Valley of Death' can continue for some time with technical success but few sales so that income generation is low and the business never comes out of the valley and may even die there.

The soft–hard model

This is a model that conserves cash for the start-up company and enables it 'to pull itself up by its own bootstraps'. The company starts 'soft' offering a consultancy service with low overheads. The margins are high for this kind of business so that it should be possible to put money in the bank and build up cash reserves. When it has done this for two or three years the company should be in a position to fund the development of its own products and make the transition into a 'hard' product-based business. This company then follows the cash demand curve of Figure 14.3 but the cash accumulated in the 'soft' years should enable it to pay its own way through the 'Valley of Death'.

This model was developed by Matthew Bullock of Barclays Bank based on his experience with high-technology companies in Cambridge, England, and a study

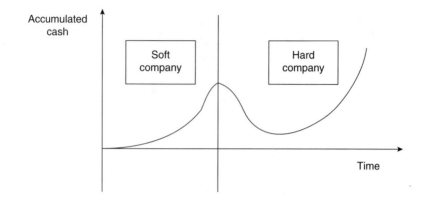

Figure 14.4   *The soft–hard model*

tour of US high-technology businesses. Whilst we accept that this model describes what does happen with some start-ups, it does so because they have no other option. Were the funding available from the banks and venture capital sector in the first place then there would be no need to waste time in consultancy when the window of opportunity may be missed. The model also presents a major personnel problem because the staff that are needed to run a successful consultancy are not the ones required for a successful product-based company. We know of companies that have successfully followed this strategy but we also know of one company that failed because it was not able to make the transition from a 'soft' contract research company to a 'hard' product-based manufacturing company.

Evaluating the opportunity

Figure 14.5 presents a very simple assessment model, based on the extent to which a market need can be demonstrated, and the ability and potential of the business and its product or service to satisfy that need and thus generate profits. However, an enterprise opportunity can be evaluated at a number of levels. Entrepreneurs who are carried along by their enthusiasm tend to do a very superficial evaluation. Others, prompted usually by their bank manager or business adviser, embark on a detailed and complex business plan and assume that when it has been completed they will have evaluated the opportunity. The truth lies between the two, and here we present a short but effective way of evaluating an opportunity in greater detail. The evaluation makes the assumption that the business is up and running on the grounds that there is little point in working out a start-up strategy if the business is not going to be viable anyway.

For this evaluation the entrepreneur needs three numbers with £ signs in front of them. The first is the *money in*, the second is the *money out* and the third is the *margin*. Simple subtraction of the first two will give the margin. This indicates whether or not the business will be financially viable.

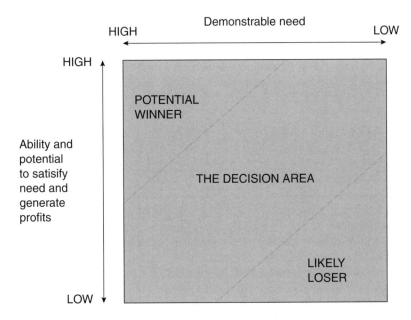

Figure 14.5 *Evaluating the opportunity*

Money in

To arrive at this number the entrepreneur needs information about the market and price levels. The key questions that need to be answered for the market are:

- How big is the market that can be reasonably reached and serviced?
- What are the main market characteristics? Are there niches and if so what size are they?
- What competitors are out there and how is the market shared out between them?
- What percentage of the market can be captured within a year? Anything more than 5 per cent is probably unrealistic.

The aim is to focus down on to a target market of a known size and to arrive at a realistic figure of the number of items that can be sold annually.

The key questions that need to be answered for pricing are:

- What price can be charged for each item sold?
- Will the product be sold by a third party? If so, it is reasonable to assume that the producer's price will be halved each time the product changes hands. Thus an item selling to the end user for £10 will be bought by the retailer for £5 from a warehouse that will pay the producer £2.50.

Unless the product or service is completely new there will be information about the existing price structure operating in the marketplace. New products may be able to set their own prices but competition will soon arrive if the opportunity is that good. In general the market decides the price not the producer.

The 'money in' is the multiple of the number of items that can be sold and the price of each item. Depending on the nature of the business this calculation can be done for a three-month period or a full year. If sales are likely to be seasonal then it should be done for the four quarters to cover a full year.

It is possible to do these calculations on a worst case, average and best case basis but that can come later. The point now is to see if the opportunity will 'stand up'.

Money out

Money goes out of the business in two ways. As discussed when we were considering the breakeven graph in Figure 14.2, there are the 'fixed' costs' and the 'variable costs'. In this quick evaluation it is sufficient to concentrate on the 'variable costs' to start with rather than spend a long time working out details of the 'fixed costs' and their allocation.

The 'variable costs' are all the costs associated with an order. Normally this has two elements, a people cost and a material cost. The people costs are the costs of those people directly associated with the product or service. In a factory it would be the machine operatives but not the quality department. The people cost per item comes from the multiple of the total time spent making the item and the hourly rate cost (including social charges) of the people making it. The material cost per item is the cost of all materials used for that item.

The 'variable' money out is the multiple of the cost per item by the number of items to be manufactured in a given period. At this stage it is sufficient to assume that the number manufactured is equal to the number sold, so the item quantities from the money in calculations can be used. Making for stock is a later consideration and only relevant if this assessment shows viability.

Sometimes this 'variable' money out is termed the 'cost of goods sold' (CoGS).

Gross margin

Accountants have a number of margins by which they measure a business. Here we are concerned with the 'gross margin' which is the difference between the money in and the 'variable' money out. It is normally expressed as a percentage of the money in.

A viable 'gross margin' depends upon the industry or market sector so that retailing is quite different from manufacturing and many new Internet businesses seem happy to operate on a negative 'gross margin'. The 'gross margins' given in Table 14.1 are for product-based businesses with some degree of manufacturing or assembly but the principle applies to all sectors. Tighter margins need better entrepreneurs and better businesses.

Technology-based businesses often have 'gross margins' of 70 per cent and 80 per cent in their early years but as competition arrives prices come under pressure and margins are reduced. The entrepreneur, hopefully, will have learnt the techniques of running an efficient business during the 70 per cent 'gross margin' days so that he or she can still run a profitable business when the margin falls to 50 per cent. In practice, early success with high margins can often make entrepreneurs think that

Table 14.1 *Gross margin*

Gross margin (%)	Comment
70	Anybody can run this business
50	Moderate competence required
30	Good entrepreneur required
10	Don't even try

running a business is easy and ego stops them from learning as much as they should. This is one reason for the 'Founder's Disease' mentioned in Chapter 11, whereby the founder has to be replaced after a couple of years when losses begin to appear. Entrepreneurs need to see these early days as good learning opportunities.

Profit margin

This 'money in', 'money out' and 'margin' evaluation can be taken to the next level of detail by including the 'fixed costs' in the money out calculation. The difference between the 'money in' and the total 'money out' (i.e. fixed costs plus variable costs) is the 'profit margin' which, like the 'gross margin', is expressed as a percentage of the 'money in'. Unless the profit margin comes out at around 10 per cent the opportunity is rarely worth pursuing. Another way to approach this evaluation is to set the 'profit margin' at, say, 10 per cent and deduct this from the 'gross margin' figure calculated. The difference will be the percentage of the money in that is available to cover the fixed overheads.

These overheads can be broken down into a number of areas, depending on the type of business. The running costs of the business are generally in two or three parts, normally related to the 'fixed costs' attributable to production, administration and sales. When these are added together they must be less than the money available to cover the fixed overheads, otherwise the business will not be viable. Hopefully, cash will be left over because it may be needed to fund the 'fixed costs' of research and development and an advertising campaign. If there is still money left after these costs, then there is probably a viable business.

Evaluation and critique

The difficulty with all financial evaluations for the start-up company is that the numbers are forecasts and estimations. The 'profit margin' is arrived at by the difference of two large numbers. If the 'money in' figure is wrong by –5 per cent and the 'money out' figure is wrong by +5 per cent then the 'profit margin' will be nearer zero rather than the 10 per cent hoped for. This is why entrepreneurs need to keep a close eye on the finances of their business even if there is a financial specialist to do all the calculations.

The business plan

The business plan, rather like the CV, has been professionalized and to some extent sanitized. Most banks provide information guides and CDs about business plans, and there are many books that guide the reader through the process. Bankers and investors expect a certain standard of business plan and without it the start-up company is unlikely to get a hearing. The business plan is basically a selling document to obtain financial backing. It must be realistic and not overconfident. It should adopt the language of its audience. There is no point in a lengthy description of the product, which is full of jargon, but there will need to be plenty of numbers and facts. The layout should be clear and easy to understand with no spelling or arithmetic mistakes.

Table 14.2 provides a typical list of topics that have to be addressed.

Table 14.2   *The business plan*

Components of the business plan

- *Description of what the business is about.* This can include the background and information about the product or service that is to be offered.
- *Description of the marketplace.* This will tell the reader how well the entrepreneur understands the market and how he sees his place in it. Unless this is convincing the rest of the business plan may not be read! This section needs some hard data, generalizations will not do. It should identify the competitive advantage.
- *Explanation and reasoning behind the proposed business strategy.* This will need to include the market entry and the growth strategy.
- *Delivering the product or service.* This covers the stage that the product or service has reached at the moment and what else is needed to get it to market. What strategy will be adopted to put the product or service together and how will it get to the customer?
- *The financials.* This covers costs, pricing strategy, margins and so on.
- *The legals.* The shareholding position and the legal status of the start-up business need to be explained.
- *The people.* For investors the people are as important as the product and its market and they will want to know the background of the key individuals. For a start-up this can be difficult as these people may still be in their previous job waiting for the investment money to arrive before they join the new venture.
- *Risks.* A realistic appraisal of the risks of the venture is generally required.
- *What is being asked for.* The business plan needs a focus and should lead to a request for investment funding, a loan or an overdraft facility.

Assessing the risks

Entrepreneurs take and, in their own way, manage risks. We have already seen that real entrepreneurs have a particular perspective on the risks involved in a venture. They take risks that many others would avoid. They believe they can manage the risk, partly because they think they understand its magnitude and partly because they believe they can manage any unexpected setbacks and challenges. Tennis player

David Lloyd, who has become a millionaire businessman with a group of leisure centres, believes in taking a series of 50:50 bets – over a period, he contends, he is likely to come out on top. The most successful entrepreneurs are correct in their beliefs and assumptions; they find opportunities in crises and 'come out fighting'. Others are – or become – overoptimistic and overconfident and underestimate the risks involved. Their risk can be metaphorically compared to climbing a tree. As the climber gets further up the tree, the branches he or she meets become increasingly fragile and less likely to carry his or her weight. Whilst it is never going to be possibly to quantify every risk involved in a venture, that is no excuse for not assessing the risks. Table 14.3 provides a framework for this. It will be realized from this comprehensive list that the topic of risk is more complex than many first imagine. Every business decision really relates to a risk of some form.

Once they understand the risk, entrepreneurs are faced with a number of options. First, they can opt to retain the risk, logically preparing for any downside event. Second, they can transfer it by, for example, insurance. This, of course, can prove

Table 14.3 *Assessing business risks*

Type of risk	Example
External environmental risks	
Supply risks	Over-dependency on a supplier
	Outsourcing something which is strategically critical
Market/demand risks	Customer preference changes
Stakeholder risks	Misjudged priorities
Social responsibility and ethical issues	Failure to deal effectively with a chemical spill or a major incident
Politico-economic risks	Turbulence in an overseas market
Innovation risks	Misjudging market acceptance for a new idea
Competitive risks	Existing competitors 'out-innovate' the business
	Price competition
	Powerful new rivals enter the industry
Resource-based risks	
Materials risks	Need to handle/transport dangerous materials
Process risks	'Corner-cutting' to save time and money
Managerial risks	People's ability to cope with the dynamics of change in the organization
People risks	Inadequate or inappropriate training
Commitment risks	Individuals do not 'pull their weight', especially in a crisis
Structural risks	Inappropriate balance between centralization (for control) and decentralization (for flexibility)
	Internal barriers to co-operation
Complexity	The spread of activities is too complex and leads to fragmentation and internal conflict
Financial risks	Under-capitalization
	Cash flow problems
Technology risks	Inadequate information systems

costly, which explains why some businesses turn out to be inadequately insured. Third, they can reduce the risk by investing in better controls and systems. Again this requires investment.

Getting it right

There are many aspects to 'getting it right'. Figure 14.6 gives eight steps to a successful start-up. The good idea, the defined market opportunity, the founding team, a sound business plan and start-up capital are what puts the show on the road. That gets 25 per cent of the way; the rest is about customers and orders.

These issues need to be supported by putting the right financial structures in place and by careful control of the business against selected parameters.

The right structure

This refers to the shareholding and financial structure of the business. The entrepreneur needs to decide if he or she wants to own all the business or is prepared to allow others, even the employees, to own part of the business. Most entrepreneurs already have a view on this. They either want total control or are prepared to share it and the question of which might be the best option does not come into it. The only real point to make is that if the business requires significant funding, and most do if they want to grow, then the founders will have to be prepared to make some of the equity available to the investors. Typically 30 per cent is the starting point which means that the entrepreneur is passing over a third of his or her company in return for funding.

The financial structure of a business will comprise borrowings of various kinds and these need to be kept in balance. Debt is something most companies carry all the time and the level of the debt will be related to the equity or value of the business. The ratio of debt to equity is termed the 'gearing'. If it is 1/1 then the company can pay off all its debts if it sold up. In practice this is rather theoretical in the case of the start-up business because it has debts but little real value. Therefore, it is perhaps not surprising that bankers get nervous about start-ups.

Equity funding comes from investors who take a shareholding in the business. Equity funding stays with the company and the only cost involved is the payment of an annual dividend if that is appropriate. When shares are issued and traded in some way, their price at any time helps determine the value of a business. Loan funding also comes from investors but can come from the bank. Loans carry interest and the capital sum has to be paid off over a set period of time. The banks also provide an *overdraft facility* that enables the business to run 'in the red' as long as it does not exceed an agreed overdraft limit. Banks have their own policies for the mix of loans and overdrafts but both will cost the entrepreneur money. A loan is slightly more secure because banks can call in an overdraft at any time.

A business needs to structure the equity, loan and overdraft funding in the best way for its present and future growth. There is a difference between funding for capital equipment and funding for the day-to-day operations of the business. The

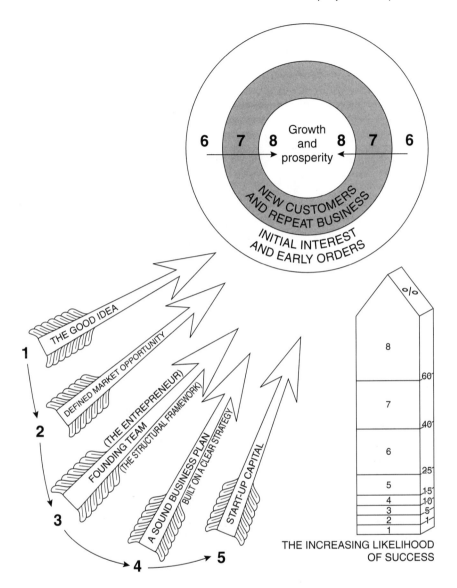

Figure 14.6 *Hitting the bull's-eye*

former is referred to as *fixed or investment capital* and the latter as *working capital*, though for most start-ups this distinction is rather blurred. The overdraft is meant to provide the working capital.

These are all issues that should be discussed with specialist advisers as it is very easy for a business to be underfunded, but the entrepreneur needs to be sure he or she understands what is going on and should not simply accept the advice of the experts. We know of one entrepreneur whose investors suggested he would be better advised to have a loan from them rather than sell them equity in his

Table 14.4   *The banker likes CAMPARI*

C	Character of the borrower
A	Ability to borrow and repay
M	Margin of profit
P	Purpose of the loan – funding what?
A	Amount of the loan
R	Repayment terms
I	Insurance against non-payment

business. This seemed good advice at the time but when the first year's loan was spent the venture fund called it in and the entrepreneur was given the choice of leaving or being declared bankrupt. He chose the former and the venture fund got all of the company for the price of their loan.

Table 14.4 provides a list of the factors that the banker is looking for under the acronym CAMPARI.

The right controls

Running a successful business is like a three-dimensional jigsaw puzzle. All the pieces need to be in the right place but there is a time dimension that keeps changing the size and shape of each piece. Table 14.5 lists the ten most important pieces of this living jigsaw. The questions asked apply to the start-up company as it sets out but similar questions need to be considered as it continues along the road.

In any business there are a number of parameters that the entrepreneur must keep an eye on. The main ones are borrowing, cash, sales, market share and profit margin

Borrowing   On the financial side the entrepreneur needs to watch his or her level of borrowing and to know where costs are coming from. If they are one-off costs that show the right rate of return, that is one thing, but if they are day-to-day costs then the company could be 'bleeding to death'. We know of one company in the 1970s where borrowing increased at the rate of £1 million per month and went on at that rate for eighteen months before the multinational parent took action.

Cash   The control of working capital, or rather lack of it, is the main reason most start-ups fail. The cash position is made up of four parts that all need to be controlled, namely:

- the weekly or monthly payroll
- the money owed to others (the creditors)
- the money others owe to the business (the debtors)
- the money tied up in stock.

These regular calls on cash can be thrown by special expenditure such as an advertising campaign or a special development project.

Table 14.5 *The pieces of the jigsaw*

1.	Customers	Who may have to be persuaded to try or switch
		How long does it take to close a sale?
		Who are they?
		Where are they?
		How are they reached (selling and advertising)?
		Are your customers your consumers?
		Paradoxically eventual take-off can be rapid and exponential, bringing different problems
2.	Suppliers	You are likely to be relatively insignificant, not in line for favours – yet you are very dependent on them
3.	Distributors	Do they have to get rid of someone else to take you on?
		Credit arrangements with suppliers and distributors; suppliers may want instant cash at first.
		Logistics issues – do you need (expensive) third parties to handle your deliveries?
4.	Premises	Where?
		Cost?
		Lease/purchase arrangements
5.	Regulations	Anything that affects your area of activity, e.g. food, chemicals
		Do not forget your products could end up in another country
6.	Team development	Where do you need help? (You may, for example, not fancy the actual selling role)
		Partners? Friends? Employees?
		Skills, trust and cost
		Why are they working for you?
7.	Equipment (including IT)	What do you need?
		New or used?
		Can you beg or borrow?
		Expertise to handle it and get the best out of it
8.	Money	Start-up finance
		Cash flow – getting paid
9.	Time, energy and commitment	Can you/should you do it full time?
		Strategy time and 'doing' time
		Are you a seventy hours a week person?
		Given all the people you have to meet, have you got time to produce anything?
		Can you take the disappointments?
		Who else has to make a sacrifice?
		Time out of the business
10.	Credibility	You have got things to improve
		You have to keep all your stakeholders 'sweet'

Various ratios are used to monitor these four factors but in broad terms the following approach is recommended:

- The payroll costs should be kept to a minimum.
- The money owed to others should be stretched out as long as possible consistent with good supplier relations.

- The money others owe should be collected as promptly as possible.
- Stock levels are always difficult to control and need to be watched carefully. They should be kept as low as possible consistent with meeting customer needs.

In practice because everybody is trying to do the same thing and there is a lag between when the raw materials are bought and when the finished product is sold with its added value, the business will always be owed more than it owes to others. In some industries this can mean a company is owed one-quarter or even one-third of its annual turnover.

Numbers can be put to all these factors, and it is a good idea to find out the ratios that work best and compare them with their general levels for the industry. This idea of benchmarking is now being developed extensively and can provide a useful yardstick.

Sales   The entrepreneur will probably develop his or her own indicators to assess the sales position but three parameters that are useful are:

- the ratio of orders to quotations
- the size of the order book as a proportion of the annual sales
- the percentage of late deliveries.

These are industry sector specific, so the entrepreneur may not need to be too discouraged if he or she only lands one order for every seven quotations if that is the industry average.

The entrepreneur needs to know what factors control sales. The traditional sales-person will invariably say it is price, but it is usually more subtle than that. As we discussed in Chapter 13, when a company is in the mainstream its customers buy on service and convenience so that delivery, quality and a reputation for service are more important than price.

Market share and profit margin   These two parameters work against each other and need to be held in balance. The entrepreneur who buys market share by selling at low prices will lose his or her profit margin. The entrepreneur who goes only for profit can lose market share because of his or her higher prices. This might seem rather obvious but it does happen to the best of businesses. Apple Computers kept their profit margin high and lost the market to the IBM PC. This happened because Sculley, head of Apple and ex-Pepsi Cola, confused the computer industry with the drinks industry. 'My theory was to price the product at a premium and then plow some of that back into advertising and build our market share. What I missed was that the key number in the business is gross margin' (Sculley, 1987). Sculley then went for gross margin and lost market share! Both must be watched and managed.

Figure 14.7 indicates these competing parameters and shows how it is possible to lose market share and make a greater cash profit. This is the trick used by the 'new broom' managing director who suddenly turns an ailing company into profit. In practice any company that drops its market share from 33 per cent to 20 per cent is likely to be in serious trouble in the long run.

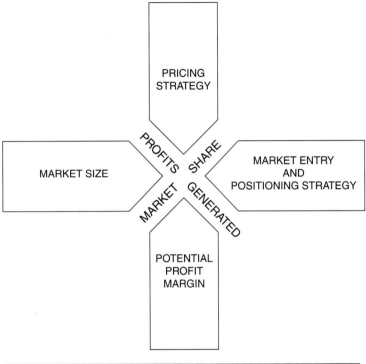

Figure 14.7 *Market share and margin*

In the past, the Boston Consulting Group has argued that market share is the single most important variable in the life of a business. The British motorcycle industry died off because it lost market share without knowing it. Their steady sales level in the USA became a smaller and smaller percentage of a rapidly growing market being stimulated by motorcycles from Japan. Sales and profitability were monitored but not market share and so they did not realize they were losing their grip on the market. When the Japanese turned their attention to the UK market, British manufacturers had no answer. They were already beaten.

Conclusion

This final chapter has given a brief look at the techniques that are important for the entrepreneur to master. An increasing number of university programmes are available that cover this material but most have come from the traditional business school background and draw their experience from the small to medium-sized enterprise. They therefore generally fail to provide the input that the entrepreneur who wants to builds something of recognized value is actually looking for. In practice business technique is learnt by doing and by making mistakes. Sculley's own admission of the mistakes he made at Apple Computers show that despite his MBA from a prestigious US business school he still learnt in this way. 'I had mistakenly thought . . . What I hadn't realised was . . . I should have understood . . . I discovered . . .' (Sculley, 1987).

Sport uses the same 'learning by doing' approach and has developed the idea of 'the coach' to promote this learning process. Some businesses encourage a coaching style of management (see Fortgang, 1999), which many others could do well to emulate.

Entrepreneurs certainly need this kind of coaching. At present entrepreneurship is at the amateur level, as sport was some years ago when training and coaching was rather *ad hoc*. Things need to change, but along the line of the sports model rather than the academic business model. Simply, the training needs to be 'hands on' rather than 'talk about' – and the entrepreneur must be prepared to accept that he or she needs the coaching. Perhaps this is the most difficult task of all!

Further reading

Many of the ideas and techniques introduced in this chapter are to be found explained in greater detail in a number of good books on business planning. Readers interested in more information could usefully refer to:

Barrow, C., Barrow, P. and Brown, R. (1998). *The Business Plan Workbook*. 3rd edn. Kogan Page.
Butler, D. (2000). *Business Planning: a guide to business start-up*. Butterworth-Heinemann.
Stutely, R., (1999). *The Definitive Business Plan*. Financial Times Management.

References

Fortgang, L. B. (1999). *Take Yourself to the Top*. Thorsons.
Jolly, V. K. (1997). *Commercialising New Technologies*. Harvard Business School Press.
Sculley, J. (1987). *Odyssey: Pepsi to Apple*. Collins.

Concluding comment

The central theme of this book has been talent, temperament and technique. With a mixture of argument and storytelling we have put forward this framework as an opportunity for identifying potential entrepreneurs and then focusing attention on developing them. This way we believe is the best way to exploit the well of talent, and help build important values in various walks of life with financial, social and aesthetic entrepreneurs.

We have isolated a series of life themes (Chapter 1) and argued that these are the ones we will find in abundance in successful entrepreneurs and in those with the potential to become successful entrepreneurs. An appropriate mixture of talent, temperament and technique life themes is a potent force. We accept and believe that the techniques provide a spearhead for the entrepreneur (see figure below[1]) but without the essential talent and temperament to underpin them, these skills would be a blunt instrument.

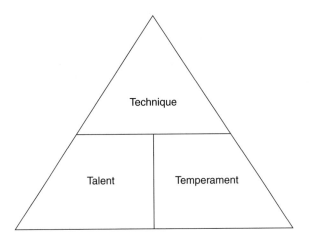

Talent, Temperament, Technique revisited

1 From an idea by Tapani Väänänen and Kari Voutila.

We have been careful to point out, though, that while we need to look for the existence of particular life themes, their relative priority is not necessarily an issue. The balance between the strongest and the weakest in the cluster simply determines the type and style of the individual entrepreneur. However, we do need to find people with an appropriate balance *across* talent, temperament and technique. In just the same way that technique without underpinning talent and temperament is a weakness, an overabundance of either talent or temperament is also a potential weakness.

Where the temperament element of our triangle is too big – as we saw with many of our shadow entrepreneurs in Chapter 7 – the natural talent can be overwhelmed and important techniques and controls ignored or overlooked. Where the talent element is too strong, in relation to temperament and technique, we are likely to find people who are temperamentally unsuited to be an entrepreneur or who possess too much self-belief and are too arrogant to seek and utilize the help and support that is available to them.

With these provisos we hope that this book will encourage a much wider consideration of the entrepreneur option for individuals and communities and provide a framework for a better understanding of this important subject.

We also hope that it will lead to a new drive to release the entrepreneurial talent that lies dormant in our midst. We believe this to be one of the greatest challenges facing our society at this time. Our future as a prosperous and democratic society will rest upon our response to this challenge.

Index